Sinful Self, Saintly Self

Sinful Self, Saintly Self

The Puritan Experience of Poetry

Jeffrey A. Hammond

The University of Georgia Press   *Athens and London*

© 1993 by the University of Georgia Press
Athens, Georgia 30602
All rights reserved
Designed by Mary Mendell
Set in 10/13 Janson Text by Tseng Information Systems, Inc.
Printed and bound by Braun-Brumfield, Inc.
The paper in this book meets the guidelines for permanence and
durability of the Committee on Production Guidelines
for Book Longevity of the Council on Library Resources.
Printed in the United States of America
97 96 95 94 93 C 5 4 3 2 1

Library of Congress Cataloging in Publication Data
Hammond, Jeffrey.
Sinful self, saintly self : the Puritan experience of poetry / Jeffrey A. Hammond.
p. cm.
Includes bibliographical references and index.
ISBN 0-8203-1500-1 (alk. paper)
1. American poetry—Colonial period, ca. 1600–1775—History and criticism.
2. Wigglesworth, Michael, 1631–1705—Criticism and interpretation.
3. Bradstreet, Anne, 1612?–1672—Criticism and interpretation.   4. Taylor, Edward, 1642–1729—Criticism and interpretation.   5. American poetry—Puritan authors—History and criticism.   6. American poetry—New England—History and criticism.   7. Christian poetry, American—History and criticism.
8. Puritans—New England—Intellectual life.   9. Puritans in literature.
10. Self in literature.   I. Title.
PS312.H36 1993
811'.109—dc20   92-18709
British Library Cataloging in Publication Data available

For Tom and Gina

Contents

Preface ix

Acknowledgments xiii

PART ONE The Forgotten Pilgrim: "As Weary Pilgrim" and Puritan Poetics

One. The Forgotten Pilgrim: Biblical Reading and the Puritan Experience of Poetry 3

PART TWO The Pilgrimage Preached: Michael Wigglesworth

Two. "By Ladders of Your Own": Eschatology and the Selflessness of Reading 39

Three. "A Sinful Self . . . Remaining in My Heart": Riddles of Comfort for the Saintly Self 60

PART THREE The Pilgrimage Lived: Anne Bradstreet

Four. "Setting Up My Ebenezer": Anne Bradstreet and the Examined Self 83

Five. "Hidden Manna That the World Knows Not": The Pilgrim's Inner Life 103

Six. "Make Use of What I Leave in Love": The Saintly Self on Trial … 123

PART FOUR   The Pilgrimage Absorbed: Edward Taylor

Seven. Apostle to a Naked Christ: *Gods Determinations* for Pilgrim Readers … 145

Eight. "Both Wayes Born": Edward Taylor as Weary Pilgrim … 164

Nine. "This Crumb of Dust": Pilgrim Voice and Christic Reader in the *Preparatory Meditations* … 186

Ten. "In Sacred Text I Write": The Taylorian Self as the Word … 213

Notes … 239

Works Cited … 281

Index … 297

Preface

The purpose of this study is to reconstruct the American Puritan experience of poetry. The importance of role-playing in the act of reading is central to this aim. I argue that in order to make Puritan poetry come alive in a manner that conventional ways of reading simply do not permit, the modern reader must make an effort to recover a sense of how Puritans felt when they wrote and read verse. I base this reconstructed experience of texts on clues offered in Bible commentaries, sermons, spiritual journals, theological treatises, and, of course, the poems themselves. Rather than addressing issues raised by traditional literary history—distinguishing "good" texts from "bad," classifying schools of poets, or demonstrating lines of influence connecting Puritan with other kinds of verse—I have tried to take a more anthropological approach. This study does not emphasize what *we* should appreciate in these texts, but how they seem to have been written and read by participants in the culture that produced them.[1]

The "Puritan reader" is defined here simply as anyone who participated—or wished to—in the Bible-centered Protestantism that prevailed in early New England. Puritan reading and writing are similarly construed within a "spiritual" rather than a traditionally "literary" context. Because the desire to be saved was central to the Puritan use of texts, I describe the codes governing literary praxis in seventeenth-century New England in terms of the religious experience defined and fostered by Puritan theology. What circumscribed this writing/reading community—what made Puritan poets and readers "Puritan"—was their adherence to theological, psychological, and aesthetic beliefs that translated into artistic choices and responses every time its members wrote or read a poem. Because a great deal of Puritan poetry was written to help poets monitor their own responses to the faith, I focus as much on speakers as on readers. Often, as we shall see, these two categories merge into a single paradigm reflecting Puritan models of true belief.

Much that has been written on Puritan poetry explicates the verse in terms of aesthetic frameworks alien to these artistic purposes. Anne Bradstreet's "Contemplations," for example, is sometimes seen as a prototype of the Romantic sensitivity to natural beauty, and Edward Taylor's *Preparatory Meditations* are often praised for their conflicted, modern-sounding expressiveness. But while such assessments make the Puritan poem more accessible to modern readers, they keep us from seeing the text in terms of its own reading dynamic and standards of performance. There was a Puritan way of reading and it was not like ours. Moreover, it governed the experience of texts as diverse as Wigglesworth's verse jeremiads and Taylor's private colloquies with Christ. Although the Puritan community was hardly monolithic in matters of church polity and specific doctrine, it exhibited fundamental agreement regarding the nature of religious verse. The role of pious reading in sustaining the collective mentality of seventeenth-century New England is nowhere more evident than in poetry and the strategies governing its use. Moreover, these strategies were inseparable from Puritan conceptions of the self and of spiritual experience. It is widely recognized that verbal formulations of the redemptive process, oral as well as written, were decisive in structuring individual self-experience: paradigms of religious psychology given in Puritan sermons and treatises were repeatedly enacted in private accounts recorded in diaries, journals, and conversion narratives. Cultural definitions of salvific experience, as this study tries to show, were equally decisive to the Puritan way of writing and reading poetry.[2]

This experience of poetry embodied features of Reformed thought central to the New England way: the pervasive and complex influence of doctrine and exegesis, the assumption of a constant interaction of sin and grace within the believer's soul, and the vital role of the Bible, whether read, preached, or incorporated into edifying poems, in meeting the spiritual needs of readers anxious about the great question of the Reformation: "What must I do to be saved?" (Acts 16:30). Precisely because of the culture's obsession with this question, Puritans were not merely content with their poetry but seem to have delighted in its didacticism and conventionality—the very qualities that distance the texts from us. By probing the sources and nature of their delight, we find that Puritan poetry often provoked responses that contradict the modern assumption that the verse of early New England was grim and dehortative. For most of us it would be; for most Puritans, it was not.

Seeking an aesthetic empathy with seventeenth-century New Englanders does not require a modern reader to become a Puritan, only to try *reading* like one, and in so doing to confront the radical "otherness" of the Puritan poem and its demands. The underlying value of criticism that is both historical and experiential lies, I think, in helping us to understand and appreciate this difference. Such understanding can help minimize the distortions arising from a naive historicism that valorizes modern-seeming traits in older texts but falls silent at features that are more difficult to justify. Paradoxically, perhaps, a clear sense of this otherness makes possible a deeper understanding of what Puritan poetry shares with the poetry of all eras. Despite their alien cultural and aesthetic structures, Puritans experienced their art as an embodiment of the fundamentals of verbal discourse: the reliance on conventional codes and strategies intelligible within a community of writers and readers; the power of language to form and deform perceptions of the self and the world; the tension, stimulated by the act of reading, between the self that one is and the self that one wants to be; and the emotional response embedded in any act of self-recognition or self-discovery. Behind the readings offered here is the conviction that the real value of Puritan poetry, as with all verse, resides in its articulation of this deepest human dimension. Beneath the explicit formulations of Puritan culture—the desire for salvation, the abhorrence of sin, and the search for signs of grace—the Puritan poem was designed, like all poetry, to move readers in the most profound way imaginable: by shaping their experience of the self.

Acknowledgments

I am grateful to the National Endowment for the Humanities and to the George Mason University Research Office for grants supporting this project in its initial phases. The staff of the Library of Congress extended many courtesies during the research. The following journals have graciously granted permission to incorporate, in altered form, material that first appeared in their pages: *Early American Literature* and the University of North Carolina Press for portions of chapters 1, 2, and 10; *Religion and Literature* and the English Department of the University of Notre Dame for a portion of chapter 6; *Texas Studies in Literature and Language* and the University of Texas Press for a portion of chapter 9; *American Poetry* and the University of New Mexico English Department for portions of chapters 9 and 10. I also wish to thank Nancy Grayson Holmes of the University of Georgia Press for her encouragement, and Madelaine Cooke and Debbie Winter for their thoughtful and efficient help as the book made its way through the publishing process.

This study would not exist if it were not for my students in early American literature at George Mason University and St. Mary's College of Maryland, who have never hesitated to remind me of the "otherness" of the Puritan poem. It is also a pleasure to record my gratitude to friends and colleagues who have helped and encouraged me not only with this book in its various stages but in more general ways: Joseph L. Baird, Raymond A. Craig, Thomas M. Davis, Virginia L.

Davis, Everett Emerson, Rosemary Fithian Guruswamy, Andrea Hammer, C. L. Jentoft, David Kuebrich, Michelle Massé, Charles W. Mignon, John O'Connor, William J. Scheick, Michael Schuldiner, Norma J. Tilden, and Peter White. I am especially grateful to Professors Scheick, Davis, and White for their perceptive and helpful critiques of this study; that they are not responsible for its flaws will be obvious. Finally, for many years of personal and professional support I cannot begin to repay Professor Davis, who introduced me to early American writing and who remains not merely my ideal of what a scholar-teacher should be, but someone whose friendship I cherish.

Part One

The Forgotten Pilgrim: "As Weary Pilgrim" and Puritan Poetics

A pilgrim I, on earth perplexed
    With sins, with cares and sorrows vext,
By age and pains brought to decay,
    And my clay house mold'ring away.
Oh, how I long to be at rest
    And soar on high among the blest.

—Anne Bradstreet, "As Weary Pilgrim"

CHAPTER ONE

THE FORGOTTEN PILGRIM: BIBLICAL READING AND

THE PURITAN EXPERIENCE OF POETRY

It would be difficult to find a more typical Puritan poem than "As Weary Pilgrim," the only poem to survive in Anne Bradstreet's own hand. Thoroughly doctrinal in theme and didactic in intent, "Pilgrim" exploits a contrast between the "erring paths" of earth and the "lasting joys" of heaven that could scarcely be more orthodox. The imagery invokes doctrinal cliché: the weary but steadfast pilgrim, the difficult journey through life, the "hungry" wolves of this world, the bedlike grave, the sleep of death, and the joys of heaven are all commonplaces of Christian writing. Moreover, the speaker defines herself almost entirely in theological terms, with nothing of the inner conflict that modern critics value most in Bradstreet's work. We hardly know what to say about "As Weary Pilgrim" except to read it as evidence that the poet finally overcame her earlier struggles with the faith, that "she finally accepts," as Ann Stanford observes, "even embraces, the everlasting state she had never seemed quite sure of."[1] In light of events recorded in other texts — illnesses, the deaths of grandchildren, episodes of spiritual doubt, the fire that destroyed her home — the poem is interesting chiefly because of what it does *not* say. In its suppression of conflict the text seems to witness the triumph of faith over art. In finally becoming a good Puritan, Bradstreet seems to have turned herself into a second-rate poet.

Puritan attacks on verbal art, including early tirades against the theater and other frivolities common in Old England, suggest that Bradstreet had good reason to choose piety over poetry. Stephen Gosson, among others, insisted that a Reformed England was no place for such entertainments as those offered at Bankside or the amorous sonnet sequences so popular among lovers of verse. The young scholar working through Gosson's "Schoole of Abuse" begins, ominously enough, with "poetry" in a descent that finally leads "from death to the Devil, if you take your learning apace and pass through every form without revolting." Such aesthetic rigidity seemed to transfer easily to the New World. In the first book of verse published in New England, the Bay Psalm translators somewhat defensively claimed to be seeking "Conscience rather then Elegance, fidelity rather then poetry" in their renderings. Two decades later Michael Wigglesworth introduced *The Day of Doom* by attacking the conventional invocation of the Muses, "Which is th' Unchristian use, and trade, / Of some that Christians would be thought." Nearly twenty years after that, Urian Oakes scorned "Poetick Raptures" and "Daring *Hyperboles*" in his famous elegy on Thomas Shepard II. And some fifty years after Oakes, nearly a century after the Bay Psalm preface, Cotton Mather conceded that while candidates for the ministry could "make a little recreation of poetry in the midst of your more painful studies," they should not be "so set upon poetry as to be always pouring on the passionate and measured pages." Lamenting "a boundless and sickly appetite for the reading of the poems, which now the rickety nation swarms withal," Mather advised his young charges to "preserve the chastity of your soul from the dangers you may incur by a conversation with muses that are no better than harlots."[2]

Despite such warnings, a great deal of poetry got written and read in early New England. Bradstreet persisted, after all, in this supposedly subversive art throughout her life, making no attempt to conceal emotional struggle in her verse. However "obnoxious" she may have been to male censure, "vulnerable" to it in the sense that Milton's Samson was "obnoxious more / To all the miseries of life," she was accorded lavish if patronizing praise by the males who wrote prefatory poems for *The Tenth Muse*. Indeed, the second, expanded edition published in Boston six years after the poet's death suggests that Bradstreet provoked not scandal but genuine pride among New Englanders. The phenomenal popularity of Wigglesworth's *The Day of Doom* and *Meat Out of the Eater* is also hardly indicative of a culture indifferent to poetry. The nearly two thousand first-edition copies of the doomsday epic sold out within a year, and it has been estimated that at its publication one copy of the poem existed for every twenty-five to thirty-five New Englanders. Edward Johnson, recording New England's glory for the ages, interspersed his history with numerous verse celebrations of the places and heroes of his narrative, as did Mather nearly fifty years later when he recorded the wonders of Christ in America. The Puritan regard for public and commemorative verse is also clear from the numerous elegies and other occasional poems written and circulated in early New England. And in frontier Westfield, isolated from literary society and steeped in "clonian rusticity," Edward Taylor chose poetry as the vehicle for over forty years of meditative self-scrutiny—the most important task imaginable for a Puritan and thus scarcely to be entrusted to a suspect genre.[3]

New England's chief bearers of culture, at least, were well acquainted with classical poetry. Even if acquiring language skills and pulpit eloquence was the main reason for studying the Greek and Latin poets, their inclusion in the curriculum at Cambridge and Harvard and the common practice of delivering verse declamations at graduations indicate a healthy respect for poetry's ability to move the affections. By allegedly quoting Euripides in his first letter to the Corinthians (1 Cor. 15:33), Paul had anticipated the standard Puritan attitude toward the classics: to draw from the Ancients what was of value while condemning their benighted spiritual state. Although Ovid, Horace, and Virgil lived under a pagan shadow, they could teach much regarding the power of language to delight and edify. Wigglesworth owned a copy of Horace, and if few modern readers see the Horatian mix of *utile et dulce* in *The Day of Doom*, Jonathan Mitchell had no trouble finding it in his former pupil's ability to roll "Truth in Sugar" that it "may taste the sweeter." That seventeenth-century New Englanders also read poetry in the vernacular is attested by the library and bookseller inventories of the day, in which the number of poets, modern as well as classical, is substantial. Sidney and the French Calvinist DuBartas were admired, as Bradstreet's commemorative poems make clear, as were Donne, Herbert, Quarles, Spenser, and later, Milton.[4]

Most of all, perhaps, New Englanders were avid readers of each other's poetry. Wigglesworth and John Wilson were immensely popular, the latter achieving fame not only as the author of *A Song of Deliverance* but also, as Nathaniel Ward's poetic joke attested, as "the great Epigrammatist" who could "let out an Anagram / even as he list." Cotton Mather, who praised Wigglesworth's ability to convey doctrine "dressed up in a *Plaine Meeter*," quoted one of Wigglesworth's poems while extolling Urian Oakes's "Maro-like" skill as an elegist; Thomas Hinckley in turn borrowed from Oakes's elegy in his own poem on Thomas Walley. Edward Taylor owned a copy of Bradstreet's poems and attested that his wife memorized at least some of *The Day of Doom*; Mather published two stanzas from a Taylor poem in a sermon on handling grief.[5]

For all their complaints against the dangers of verse, Puritans wrote and read prodigious amounts of it. Indeed, they could almost be called verse-obsessed. With the exception of Gosson's and Mather's statements, every aesthetic warning cited above occurs either in verse or in a preface to verse—and even Mather recommended "a little recreation" in the genre. It is also important to remember that Mather issued his pronouncement in 1726, when the "rickety nation" was beginning to turn toward secular verse written in newer, neoclassical modes. Moreover, what Puritans *said* about poetry was, as several critics have noted, at odds with how they actually wrote it. Commenting on a radical split between Puritan literary theory and practice, Norman S. Grabo observed thirty years ago that while nothing in Taylor's "comments on poetic theory" reveals "any profound notions of art," "his poems simultaneously betray another, quite sophisticated symbolic sense that might be said to be built into Puritan thought through its theology." The possibility of finding a sophisticated aesthetic at work in poems like "As Weary Pilgrim" has been subverted by the unyielding absolutes in Puritan statements about art. The Puritan as literary theorist has all but shouted down the Puritan as practicing poet.[6]

But there is a deeper reason for our difficulty in responding to Puritan poetry: because poems like "As Weary Pilgrim" so clearly disappoint modern artistic expectations, we usually assume too quickly that there is no art in them at all. This assumption has long characterized the standard critical reaction to the verse. With the notable exceptions of Edward Taylor's *Preparatory Meditations* and *Gods Determinations* (about one-fourth of his poetry) and Bradstreet's more personal lyrics (about one-third of hers), Puritan verse has been treated as little more than a metrical supplement to the historical record ever since the late nineteenth century, when Moses Coit Tyler found "an unappeasable feud between religion and art" in poetry devoted to the Puritan's "master-purpose of promoting religion."[7]

The conflict between religion and art that still underlies many critical discussions has always contained a concealed question: whose definition of art? The real conflict is between Puritan religion and the sort of art that literary critics and historians generally value. Poetry valorized by nineteenth- and twentieth-century aesthetics presents vivid images that can be "perceived" in the imagination. The good poem often features tension, paradox, or some other clearly defined mental activity on the part of a speaker who articulates a unique and identifiable human voice. The poem's originality demands that it be considered as a self-sufficient artistic product that creates an effect rather than teaches a lesson. Post-

Romantic demands for uniqueness and originality often translate into the assumption that serious literary art in some sense subverts the culture in which it is produced. Poems that promote the dominant values of their culture are usually dismissed as propaganda, useful as historical documents or reflections of mass taste but not worthy of rigorous analysis. The power of these preferences has always made it difficult to avoid discussing the Puritan poem in terms of what *we* want from poetry rather than what seventeenth-century readers may have wanted. As Kathleen Blake once summed up the problem, the poetry is usually seen as either "too Puritan to be good or too good to be Puritan." The Puritan poem satisfies us only if it seems exceptional within its culture, if it seems to violate Puritan definitions of literary art.[8]

This modernist bias has centered critical attention on Taylor and Bradstreet to the nearly total exclusion of their contemporaries.[9] It has also determined which Bradstreet and Taylor texts receive the most commentary. Bradstreet, for instance, has always been most admired not as a Puritan poet but for her rebellion against religion and society and her sensitive response to the natural world, features highly valued within later aesthetic frameworks. We prefer those poems that seem to strike a modern chord — "The Flesh and the Spirit," "Contemplations," "The Prologue," the elegies on her grandchildren, and the poem on the burning of her house — in part because they project a conflicted voice to which modern readers easily respond. But poems unambiguously affirmative of her faith — "As Weary Pilgrim," "The Vanity of All Worldly Things," the verse Meditations on affliction and deliverance — push her back into a disappointingly remote seventeenth-century milieu. These two sets of poems have even produced two Bradstreets, one who frustrates our artistic expectations and another who fulfills them. The fit between the Puritan "dogmatist" and the modern-sounding "rebel," to use Stanford's terms, is an uneasy one. How could the poet who voiced such vivid struggle in the elegy on grandson Simon have settled for such flat expressions of dogma as "Pilgrim" or "Vanity"?[10]

Taylor, of course, is the other Puritan poet who simultaneously fulfills and frustrates post-Romantic aesthetic expectations. Earlier discussions in particular praised his work not so much for what it actually did as for how closely it approximated other, non-Puritan literary traditions. His *Preparatory Meditations*, widely admired for their emotional expressiveness and vivid imagery, traits highly valued in the modern poem, have received far more attention than his other, seemingly more conventional works. But when read as a proto-modern poet, Taylor has serious lapses. The Meditations, with their sudden tonal shifts and seemingly mixed metaphors, often subvert the unity of effect, logical development, and textual coherence that we have come to expect from a close reading of poetry. Like Bradstreet, he fails to play by our rules, and the charge that his images are grotesque, inconsistent, and randomly constructed has been a major feature of the criticism ever since his work was rediscovered in the 1930s.[11]

Of the three major Puritan poets, Michael Wigglesworth fails us the most. Although occasionally praised for its accessibility and dramatic appeal, his work is usually seen as hopelessly marred by overt didacticism and a rigid adherence to theology. Like Bradstreet's "Pilgrim," Wigglesworth's poetry seems far too transparent: such qualities as tension, ambiguity, and imagistic concreteness seem difficult to identify, let alone appreciate, in poems that seem so bluntly to mean exactly what they say. Because Wigglesworth seems *not* to have struggled against a theological system that we dislike, he remains sealed in his seventeenth-century world. While Taylor and Bradstreet have assumed uneasy niches in the story of literary progress, Wigglesworth has not, largely because his poems are perceived as being more inescapably "Puritan," more alien to the aesthetic categories that normally inform historical criticism.[12]

Instead of applying aesthetic expectations external to the poetry itself and thereby stressing what it fails to do, we might profitably read it on its own terms, accepting its frankly didactic aims and discussing it in light of those aims. Behind such a reading lie two fundamental assumptions. First, Puritan poetry cannot be understood apart from the aesthetic expectations of Puritan writers and readers. And second, Puritan literary experience cannot be divorced from Puritan religious experience. Would readers who did not distinguish between aesthetic and spiritual response have been disappointed by the trite imagery of "As Weary Pilgrim" or the generic nature of its speaker? Would its relentlessly biblical message and diction have suggested to them, as it might to us, a failure of poetic invention, a substituting of formula for art? And how would such readers reconcile the resigned speaker of "Pilgrim" with the darker, more troubled voice of the family elegies and the house-fire poem? Would they have even perceived a split between these two speakers?

Answering these questions in terms of the larger question that Puritan poems were written to answer—whether or not one was saved—permits our recovery of an experiential dimension in these texts that stems ultimately from biblical definitions of literary art and personal identity. From the Bible, especially the Psalms and the Song of Songs, Puritans derived their notions of poetry in its right use and generic models appropriate to that use. Biblical exegesis, based on the conviction that the entire Word bore a single Christological message, encouraged a poetic in which the conflation of seemingly disparate images produced new and deeper resonances of meaning. Far from pulling a poem apart, such conflations aligned the experience of reading with redemptive patterns embodied in Scripture. Finally, homiletic theory and practice exerted a profound influence on poetic voice. Whether the poet issued legal warnings to backsliders or gospel balms to humbled souls determined the dominant tone of a poem. Such traditions shaped the literary situation of the poem: how the text was meant to be read, the speaker's role as transmitter of the biblical message, the reader's relationship to speaker and text, and the reader's expected religio-aesthetic response.

This experience of poetry, which encompassed texts as diverse as Taylor's *Preparatory Meditations* and Wigglesworth's *Meat Out of the Eater*, defines an artistic framework in which "As Weary Pilgrim" becomes not a failure but an exemplum. It was within this framework that the Puritan poet found a voice—and his or her most immediate model was not secular poetry but hortatory and didactic texts comprising a vital literature of salvific experience: the extemporaneous prayer, the meditation, the spiritual journal or autobiography, the saint's life, the redemptive history, the catechism, the theological treatise, the sermon, and of course, the Bible itself.

As heirs of the Renaissance, Puritans had no need to be reminded of the power of verse. George Puttenham's popular handbook for versifiers confirmed that poetry, "a maner of utterance more eloquent and rethoricall then the ordinarie prose," even "sooner invegleth the judgement of man, and carieth his opinion this way and that, whither soever the heart by impression of the eare shalbe most affectionately bent and directed." Puritans needed to look no further than the faith for proof of the necessity and force of what we would call a "poetic" imagination. The three cornerstones of Puritanism—Christ, the Bible, and the Lord's Supper—emphasized the mediating role of divinely sanctioned figuralism in any earthly expression of sacred truth. Since God-written metaphor offered the fullest revelation of that truth available on this side of the grave, Puritan faith in the Word constituted a near-deification of the symbolic and the verbal. As a written text, the Bible revealed God's condescension in addressing fallen humanity in figures and similitudes necessitated by the sin that separated humanity from God but also capable of reuniting them. The Fall also made necessary another metaphoric bridge between the human and the divine, the Christic *Logos* or Word Incarnate as a "verbal" expression of divine mercy. Finally, metaphorical discourse defined Puritan sacramentalism in the Protestant insistence that the Lord's Supper was symbolic rather than literal. A "poetic" dimension lay at the very core of the Feast as a seal, a sign whose distinct separation from the Thing Signified—a *spiritual* feeding on Christ—was ignored only at the believer's peril. Such metaphors—including the very fact that they *were* metaphors—underscored the inexpressible nature of divine glory. Any "knowing" of God, Puritans insisted, was necessarily indirect, a result of the expedient medium of "human Language," as Richard Steere attested, by which "Heav'n conveys to us, / High Apprehensions of Eternal Bliss." To cling to the Word on all of its interrelated levels was to act out Paul's definition of faith as belief in the "evidence of things not seen" (Heb. 11:1) but warmly felt, grasped by means of a complex network of metaphorical expressions by which the fallen self could at once reconfirm and transcend the limitations of merely human sense and thought.[13]

By modern definitions, all of this certainly constitutes image-making and image-using. But Puritans construed the images that they attacked in far more limited terms. Underlying the harshness of their aesthetic formulations was the Second Commandment, which forbade the worship of "any graven image, or any likeness of anything that is in heaven above, or that is in the earth beneath, or that is in the water under the earth." It is easy to misread the Puritan interpretation of the commandment, especially in light of how vehemently the Bay Psalm translators, Mather, and others denounced those who broke it. It has been argued, for instance, that Taylor "reconstituted in his poetry the images his theology abhorred"; his innate drive toward visualization "was apparently forceful enough to exact a compromise with the prohibitions against making 'similitudes' of things religious in Exodus 20.4–5." But as Robert Daly summarizes typologist Samuel Mather's influential reading of the commandment, "only images used as objects of worship and religious images devised by man are anathema."[14] If, like Scripture and like Christ as *Logos*, metaphorical language led the imagination beyond the sensory surface to the evidence of things not seen, its use was not only legitimate but mandated as the sole means by which fallen sensibilities could be edified. Puritans attacked metaphor only when it became, in their view, dangerously self-referential—when it separated itself from biblical parameters designed to curb the natural tendency toward sinful autonomy that they believed language shared with all things human.

That such cherished texts as the Psalms and the Song of Solomon had been written in poetic form virtually forced Word-centered Protestants to see verse not as an inherently debased mode of discourse, but as one that had been debased, like everything else under the sun, by human sin and corruption. Poets, Puttenham insisted, were not only "the first Priests and ministers of the holy mysteries" but were also, by virtue of their "visions, both waking and sleeping," the first "Prophets or seears." Luke Milbourne later defended Psalm singing on similar grounds. Early priests, he maintained, "were generally *Poets;* and *Poets,* and the *Writers* of *such Hymns,* were their principal Divines." Bible commentator Matthew Henry similarly argued that secular verse represented the corruption of a discourse invented by God: the ultimate shame was that God's "*Corn, and Wine, and Oil,* should be *prepar'd for Baal.*" "It is therefore much to be lamented," Henry complained, "that so powerful an Art which was at first consecrated to the Honour of God, and hath been so often employ'd in his Service, should be debauch'd as it has been, and is at this Day, into the Service of his Enemies." It was commonly asserted that pagan poets held such charm because of what they had stolen from the poetry of the Old Testament. Nathaniel Holmes insisted that "*Philosophers, Poets, Mythogists*" had "rather apishly in natural and moral things imitated the Scriptures in this way, expressing divine things." Cotton Mather leveled the charge in more specific terms by claiming a pervasive influence of the Psalms, especially Psalm 18, on Homer. It was thus with good reason that most Protestants refused to condemn poetry out of hand. To do so would be to repudiate a form of expression stemming from no less an authority than the Holy Spirit. In a prefatory poem to *The Pilgrim's Progress,* Bunyan issued the standard argument that the use of "Metaphors" need not undermine the "solidness" of the matter: "Were not God's Laws, / His Gospel-Laws, in olden time held forth / By Types, Shadows, and Metaphors?" Robert Fleming, author of popular verse paraphrases of Old Testament poetry, stated the case even more directly: "Those then who contemn *Poets and Poetry* in the general, without distinction, ought to take heed lest they Contemn the *Holy Scriptures,* yea, *God Himselfe* . . . who hath both *sanctified and honoured this Art,* by setting down thus the most excellent and useful part of the Old Testament." [15]

For Puritans, a vast gulf separated this "sanctified" art from its subsequent perversion. Whether poetic language fed the sheep or titillated the goats involved the highest of stakes, since the songs one sang in this life anticipated those that one would probably sing in the next. As William Tans'ur put it,

> Our *Songs* on *Earth* shall *praise* GOD's Name,
> That we in *Heav'n* may do the same;
> To sinful *Songs* we'll bid farewell,
> From which we learn the Speech of *Hell*.

Acknowledging that the "Speech of Hell" had made vast inroads into popular literary taste, Protestant poets were determined to oppose infernal language in an all-out battle for the aesthetic preferences, and consequently the souls, of readers. After chiding "wanton Lads" addicted to pagan verse, poet James Day urged them to "stay: / I may subvert your rude conceit; / And every verse may proove a heavenly baite: / O that ye were such Captives!" In their attempts to lure such readers, poet-reformers used "baite" that was as much aesthetic as religious by trumpeting the pleasures that readers of secular verse were missing. John Collinges, extolling the verbal beauty of Canticles, conceded the charms of secular poetry even as he urged readers to abandon it: "If a wanton Love-Song, which discourseth the vertues, and beauty of Creatures, can lay such an hold upon our Ears, and Hearts; what should this Song do!"[16]

The worst consequence of an obsession with secular verse, in the view of aesthetic reformers, was its preoccupation with tired old themes that they denounced as pap for childish minds, fit only for those whose tastes had been stunted by an addiction to what Jude Smith called "metamorphorall toyes" and "olde bables, as I may terme them, or stale tales of Chauser." A frivolous eagerness "to learne howe Acteon came by his horned head" was hardly worthy of a mature Christian sensibility; readers with a taste for verse could surely learn to relish poems that dealt with real things. Wigglesworth, who sounded this theme more explicitly than any other American Puritan, complained that many so-called "Christian Poets" commit "Blasphemy, / And Heathenish Impiety" by making

> ... *Jehovah* to stand by,
> Till *Juno, Venus, Mercury,*
> With frowning *Mars*, and thundering *Jove*
> Rule Earth below, and Heaven above.

Such vehemence was certainly not limited to the more radical New Englanders. Aesthetic reform also moved George Herbert to ask the divine Muse whether poetry can only "Wear *Venus* Livery? only serve her turn? / Why are not *Sonnets* made of thee?" Michael Drayton similarly distinguished the fictive from the real in his *Harmonie of the Church*: "I speak not of *Mars*, the God of Wars, nor of *Venus*, the goddesse of love, but of the Lord of Hostes, that made heaven and earth: Not of Toyes in Mount *Ida*, but of triumphes in Mount *Sion:* Not of Vanitie, but of Veritie: not of Tales, but of Truethes." As Drayton's dichotomies suggest, the Christian poet had the loftiest of missions: to redeem verse from the fictions and false hair that had been permitted to spoil it.[17]

Would-be purifiers of verse agreed that while no form of language had been so badly abused, none held such rich possibilities for moving readers to piety. Only by returning to the aims for which the Holy Spirit had originally intended the sacred art could the reformed poet provide, as William Baldwin called his verse paraphrase of Canticles, songs that "myght once drive out of office the baudy balades of lecherous love" popular among "idle courtyers in princes and noble mens houses." What higher artistic goal than to praise not earthly princes but the Prince of Peace, not mere nobles and kings but the King of Kings? In the dedication to his hymnbook Joseph Stennett, like Milton, invoked this ultimate Muse while reclaiming the original and glorious calling of a poet: "O Thou to whom all Love and Praise belongs! / To Thee I give my Heart, to Thee my Songs." In New England Wigglesworth agreed that the true poet's allegiance was to the "Dearest Dread, most glorious King" as his inspiration "To Sing aright, as I desire." Although Wigglesworth replaced classical with Christian content, the invocation formula remained intact, reclaimed for a use consistent with his desired role as a "Christian Poet," a title that Jonathan Mitchell gave him for his example of what a maker of verse should be.[18]

Although few tasks seemed more daunting than reforming literary tastes that, like every other carnal trait, had lapsed so badly, the Puritan poet was convinced that the Lord had provided ample direction in the sacred Canon. Harvard president Charles Chauncy, in a defense of the Bible as the primary text for virtually all branches of "humane learning," underscored its verbal beauty: "And where are there such high strains of all sorts of *Rhetoricall Tropes, & figures*, to be found in any Author, as there are in the writings of the *Prophets & Apostles?*" Cotton Mather similarly called the Bible "the Sacred *Grammar*, where / The *Rules of speaking well*, contained are." Determined to write poetry in accordance with biblical rule and precedent, Puritans believed that they were following a practice sanctioned by Christ himself in his frequent citations from the Law and the Prophets as well as his use of parables reminiscent of Old Testament wisdom literature. While on the Cross, as Henry Hammond and others pointed out, Christ chose "at last to breath out his soule in this *Psalmist's* forme of words rather than in his own" — a reference to the Psalmic source of

"My God, my God, why hast thou forsaken me?" (Ps. 22:1), and "Into thine hand I commit my spirit" (Ps. 31:5).[19] For Puritans, this striking vignette offered the ultimate fusion of human and divine language: the Incarnate Word became the Revealed Word even as he cited it, completing a sacred circle of elevated piety and eloquent speech. It was within this circle that Puritan writers and readers constantly struggled to enter, straining to find not just their themes and images but their very identities.

The most immediate models for the sacred poet were God's own poems: the Psalms, Job, Canticles, Proverbs, and Ecclesiastes. Most Protestants agreed with Arthur Jackson that these texts were "the choicest pieces of the Old Testament," in which "the discoveries that are made of divine truths are set forth with the intricacies and elegancies of many florid figurative expressions, purposely to render them the more delightfull to us." Commentator James Durham went even further, suggesting that the Holy Spirit had dictated the Song of Songs in poetic form in order to ensure that it "ought especially to be learned and taken notice of." "It is recorded of the *Hebrews*," he explained, "that whatever Scripture was delivered in a poetical frame, they accounted themselves specially bound to take notice of that, and to get it by heart."[20] If believers living under the shadowy Old Dispensation so cherished godly poetry, those under the New could certainly do no less.

The Puritan, like Jerome struggling against his love for Cicero, could admit to the attractions of "pagan" poetry as yet one more confirmation of the pervasive and insidious pull of the world. But while lewd "balades" appealed to an Old Creature destined to be slain under the Law, God's rhetoric was sweet to the New Creature destined for eternal life. By shifting allegiance from the classical to the divine Muse, believers could exchange mere verbal charm for verbal power suggestive of true faith. Even though the Ancients were, as Henry Hammond admitted in his commentary on the Psalms, "famous for their *Odes* or *Poetic* Songs," yet "*David* to us supplies abundantly the place of all of them." The Westminster divines agreed. In contrast to secular verse, "much more vertue is there in a pure coelestial Poem, which is filled with the raptures of divine love, and prompted, not by a fabulous or wanton Muse, but by the Spirit of grace, and love, and joy. If any thing be able to warm and fire the soul, this will." Whoever moved from Orpheus to Christ could attest to aesthetic sensibilities transformed by a sincere desire to be saved. For such readers, Matthew Henry insisted, biblical poems offer "Poetick force and Flame, without Poetick Fury and Fiction, and strangely command and move the Affections, without corrupting the Imagination, or putting a Cheat upon that; and while they gratify the Ear, edify the Mind, and profit the more by *pleasing*."²¹

David and Solomon achieved poetic and prophetic "force and Flame" by transcending their personal limitations as fallen individuals and assuming the voice of any elect soul set aflame by the Spirit. David's flirtations with idolatry and with Bathsheba did not keep the Holy Ghost from conferring upon him the role of Israel's Sweet Singer. Solomon, famous for the licentiousness of his youth, offered an equally accessible model of spiritual perseverance despite sin and weakness. "The Lord did not cast off *Solomon* for his stains and blemishes," Thomas Ager assured perfectionist believers, "but had an Eye still to that good which was in him, whereby he would make him a worthy Instrument to set forth his Praise." Singing his way from this world to the next in a progression from Proverbs through Ecclesiastes to the Song of Songs, Solomon offered special comfort to the contrite soul: as John Dove urged, "let them which have fallen with Salomon, rise with Salomon." Read as prototypes of the saint's colloquy with the Lord, the Psalms and Canticles offered sublime models for all who wished to intensify their experience of the faith. Commentator Edward Leigh held that David's varied moods as supplicant, celebrant, and penitent gave the Psalms special status not only as "an Epitome of the whole Bible" but as "the very Anatomy of the soul, the Characters and representations of the thoughts, meditations, affections, and workings of it, towards God, towards her self, throughout all the changes of her pilgrimage in this world." By delineating the shifting moods of the Bride of Christ, Solomon similarly provided "A Gracious Record," as John Owen termed it, "of the Divine Communications of Christ in Love and Grace unto his Church, with their returns of love unto him, and delight in him." Francis Roberts agreed that Canticles offered "a lively Representation of the spirituall State of Christs spouse in this world, sometimes inclining to carnall *security*, sometimes lamenting under *spirituall desertions*, and sometimes conflicting with sharp temptations." What made the biblical poem so "lively" was the poet's inspired ability to speak extrapersonally, to voice a sanctity that encompassed not just the pen-man but all who had ears to hear.²²

The paradigmatic speakers of Bible poetry virtually demanded the reader's active response. To read the Psalms or Canticles passively was to abuse their purpose as stimulants to holy love. As commentator Samuel Clark explained, such texts as the Psalms were "not only written by holy Men, but by holy Men in holy flames (as one saith) who were not only moved by the Holy Spirit to write 'em, but were in the Spirit when they penn'd 'em," fired by "inward Affection, warmth of Zeal, and sensible Experience." Readers of Scripture were urged to recover something of this "sensible Experience" for themselves. "Be not at rest," Cotton Mather advised, "until you find your *Heart-strings quaver* at the *Touch* upon the Writer, as being brought into a *Unison* with it, and the *Two Souls* go up in a *Flame* together."[23]

Whether or not the reader could achieve inward "unison" with the biblical poem provided a telling index of his or her spiritual condition. As Herbert proclaimed, Scripture served as "the thankfull glasse, / That mends the lookers eyes"; its "words do finde me out, & parallels bring, / And in another make me understood." In addition to confirming that the prophecies of Christic intimacy set forth in the Bible were fulfilled in the experience of all true believers, a warm congruence of reading self with biblical text suggested the true saint's "delight" in "the law of the Lord" (Ps. 1:2). Poetry had been enshrined within "the shadowy Old Testament," Holmes argued, because "God did not intend" for believers to be "melancholy, of a sad spirit, but that they should be of a rejoycing spirit in the Lord." The "style and composition" of such poetry as Canticles was so "Divine and excellent," Durham claimed, that the text could scarcely fail to delight truly pious readers by "captivating them in the very reading; so that few can read this Song, but they must fall in love with it." Those who cherished the biblical poem internalized the engaged response to the Word that Paul transferred from the Legal to the Evangelical framework in his affirmation that "I delight in the law of God after the inward man" (Rom. 7:22). Because Paul's "inward man" underwent, among other changes, a species of aesthetic transformation, readers who delighted in God's language could feel that they too had escaped, however temporarily, the limitations of the fallen self. Secular wit, after all, was "the soules worst carver," claimed John Collinges, "and pieces of wit, are no better than pieces of selfe." Believers who overcame carnal obsessions would simply lose interest in the damning celebrations of human vanity that existed, as George Wither maintained, merely "for *Wittie men* to shew Tricks to one another."[24]

Literary taste thereby became an accurate index of one's spiritual state. Taking delight in God's art—the antithesis of those "pieces of selfe" that had so corrupted profane letters—signaled a sincere desire to achieve the selflessness of true belief. No higher approval could be bestowed upon a text than Ager's assertion that an understanding of Canticles "wil raise us up beyond our selves." Sidney had praised the Psalms for this otherworldly power; although they were wonderful examples of "an art of imitation," theirs was a *mimesis* of another realm because they "did imitate the inconceivable excellences of God." The sacred text considered most capable of inducing a meditative link with the next world, however, was Solomon's Song. When Collinges affirmed that "certainly the hearing of these discourses must ravish every spiritual heart," his qualifier was crucial: it was the *spiritual* and not the carnal heart that would be moved, even though the means for generating the believer's response—the language of love and sexual desire—derived from the experience of this world. Through Solomon's Song, Richard Sibbes maintained, God took "advantage of the sweetest passage of our life (*Mariage*) and the most delightfull affection (*Love*) in the sweetest manner of Expression (*by a Song*)" in order to "carrie up the Soule to things of an Heavenly Nature." An engaged response to such a text indicated that the reader was seeing and thinking with the renewed faculties of a graced soul.[25]

To internalize the Word this fully was to rewrite the text within one's heart—to experience the self as an inner expression of biblical pattern. Whenever readers appropriated the text as an expression of felt belief, the result was not a mere aping of biblical language, but heartfelt empathy with the biblical speaker as representative saint. Henry Hammond warned that David's efficacy as a meditative model depended on the believer's efforts to ensure "that the *Psalmist's* effusions have the *Psalmist's* spirit and affection to accompany them, that we borrow his hand & breath, as well as his instrument and ditties." And John Reeve opened his verse paraphrase of Canticles by proclaiming his interior conformity with the text:

> 'Twas *Solomon*'s Song, but now 'tis mine:
> 'Tis yours, you blessed Saints on high:
> You Mil'tants come and make your claim;
> All you that are athirst, draw nigh.

For the inspired reader, Reeve insisted, Solomon did not "singly sing his part in this." Each saint had a full share not only in the promise of Canticles but in the very identity of its allegorical speaker, the true Bride. Thomas Draxe urged "every man" to "trie by the touch-stone of Gods word, whether he feele the spirit of God in lightning and renuing him, and faith purging his heart, and firmely apprehending and applying Christ with-all his benefits unto himselfe." Such response to the poetry of the Bible suggested a match of text with reader that was profoundly reassuring. Commentator Edward Pearse affirmed that an engaged reaction to the ardent language of Canticles indicated the existence of "but an hair's breadth, as it were, between Christ and the Soul."[26]

Conversely, a spiritually flat reading of the Bible poem suggested the reader's need for correction. Cotton Mather argued that while nothing brought stronger assurance than an affectionate identification with such saintly voices as the Psalmist's, an ineffectual reading of the Psalms clearly exposed one's spiritual incapacities. An *"Unregenerate Mind,"* Mather explained, "is poorly qualified for such an Exercise as this." For such failure of response the text itself offered the best antidote; persistence in seeking inner harmony with the biblical singer could rekindle the reader's faith. Commending David as a model for the assured soul, especially in Psalm 119 ("Blessed are the undefiled in the way, who walk in the law of the Lord"), Mather encouraged readers to "Endeavour to get the like pious Frame Excited and Exercised in you. Do this, till you find your souls *Mount up* as with the Wings of Eagles, and get up to the World of Rest, and Peace, and Joy, and you shall do nothing but with a Joyful Heart Sing the Praises of your GOD."[27] As Mather suggests, biblical poetry embodied an aesthetic model based not on detached artistic appreciation but on vital spiritual response—a poetic that was deeply experiential in its emphasis on the text's capacity to engage the reader's entire being. This goal was not lost on Puritan poets, who wrote to facilitate a similarly heartfelt reconstruction of the salvific themes of Scripture within their readers. Urging readers to become "writers" of the redemptive message within their own hearts, poets helped them feel capable of replicating, in some measure, those colloquies with God enjoyed by the Sweet Singer of Israel and Solomon in all his glory.

The key to such an experience of poetry was not the letter of the text but the spirit of the reader. It was for this reason that Mather, determined not to take liberties with his texts "meerly for the sake of preserving the *Clink* of the *Rhime:* Which, after all, is of small consequence unto a Generous *Poem,*" chose blank verse for his translation of the Psalms. What, for Mather, *was* of consequence to such "Generous" poetry as the Psalms? "The *Sublime Thought,* and the *Divine Flame,* alone is enough: to challenge the Character of *Poetry* for these Holy Composures." True poetry, Mather and his contemporaries believed, was defined by affect rather than form. Like the effective sermon, the good poem would include no formal device that did not convey the speaker's response to grace or provoke the reader's desire to share in such response. As a Harvard thesis put it, "Eloquentia naturalis excellit artificialem." Natural eloquence was measured not by figures of speech, but by the power of a text to stir its readers to piety. "And there is no where to be found any such *Rhetoric,*" Mather insisted, "as there is in our *Sacred Scriptures.*"[28]

David and Solomon set sublime if intimidating artistic examples by writing poems capable of being absorbed into the reader's consciousness as felt belief. In their use of figures and similitudes to provoke a fervent religio-aesthetic reaction to the Christocentric message of the entire Bible, their poetry offered an affective link to other biblical texts, a verbal bridge between the redemptive message and the true believer's response to it. Following God's artistic precedent, Puritan poets set out to emulate the biblical pen-men in drawing readers toward the redemptive message of the Word through a poetry of experience, a poetry similarly designed to encourage the reader's assimilation of biblical pattern and response.

In their pursuit of this aim, poets exploited the Bible as a "metatext" underlying their own poems, a God-written Text in which all human texts of pious intent were embedded and to which they all referred. As bridges to the sacred metatext that delineated and sustained them, poems mediated between Scripture and the reading self. By constructing these bridges, poets pursued an artistic ideal voiced by Joseph Stennett, who pronounced himself "Happy! if these my Songs successful prove / To make one Sinner look on Thee, and love." In keeping with their neobiblical role, poets assumed a variety of biblical personas ranging from sinful wretch to commiserating saint to thundering prophet, each capable of provoking a spectrum of responses echoing those stimulated by Scripture itself. In addition, exegetical traditions inseparable from the biblical metatext provided an interpretive framework that poets could invoke through a kind of associative shorthand. The mere mention of particular images or passages from Scripture could be counted on to set in motion a chain of standard associations in the minds of readers who had been exposed to hours of painstaking biblical explication in sermons. For these readers nearly every poem "meant" much more than it literally said. The poem's meaning was completed only in terms of its essential and underlying relation with the metatext of Scripture and with the religious experience of the reader. Only when the poem had stimulated such biblical resonances could readers feel that they had read it properly. As a porch to Scripture, Puritan poetry invoked a reading experience meaningful only in relation to the House itself.[29]

Such dependence on the biblical metatext did not preclude the poet's imaginative use of its contents. If God's altar could not be polished, it could certainly be modified to convey the scriptural message more forcefully. It could be broken down into more digestible form for the young or spiritually uninitiated; it could be repeated as a virtual incantation until the reader felt its verbal force echoing within; it could, through expansion and elaboration, be linked more directly with the reader's spiritual situation; and it could be deconstructed and reassembled in new forms and combinations as a means of emphasizing or personalizing doctrine—all techniques exploited by Puritan poets. The Puritan version of "literary competence" derived ultimately from the proper way of reading Scripture. Like the biblical poem, the Puritan poem demanded not just a literary response but a spiritual transformation. Designed first and last to mediate between the Word and the reader, the Puritan poem was written and read as a text based on yet another Text authored by no less than the Holy Spirit. Consequently, while it was certainly possible to reject the perspective offered by a poem like "As Weary Pilgrim," to do so was to reject the Bible itself. For Puritans, right reading signaled a receptivity to the decision to accept Christ—to achieve the pure "yes" of an assenting will that was the goal of all Puritan rhetoric. As one text in a system of texts pointing toward the ultimate Text of Scripture, the Puritan poem ensured that biblical structures of belief were activated and intensified within the reader. Within the dynamics of Puritan reading, the deepest "meaning" of a poem lay not so much in the text as in the interaction of the reader with the text and with the Bible as the underlying Text to which the poem pointed. Through reading, readers discovered their relation to the Word and to the gracious self depicted in its pages.[30]

Puritan poetry, like all Puritan writing, fostered a particular experience of self consistent with the psychology of the redeemed soul. Just as the Bible served as a thematic and rhetorical metatext for the poem, the paradigm of the saved soul served as a "metaself" underlying the experience of the poem. This metaself, an embodiment of traits derived from Puritan psychology, homiletic theory and practice, and exegetical tradition, was thought to be essentially identical in all true believers. As William Ames insisted, "Inasmuch as faith is in each believer individually it is in the form of those that are called." Edward Taylor agreed that the redemptive process was "the Same in one and in all, and the Same in all as in thee." All elect souls manifested traits clearly lined out in the Bible, which provided a "form and pattern" that was reenacted, Ames maintained, in each saved soul.[31]

Treatises on conversion, devotional manuals, and sermons offered a remarkably consistent story of how this identity developed through an ongoing struggle between opposing forces within: a carnal self born in sin and a gracious self born at conversion. This struggle toward sanctification was never completed in this life; if it were, Thomas Shepard confirmed, "we should war and wrestle no more." This inner wrestling produced an experience of self defined by what Ames called a "double form—that of sin and that of grace." As Ames attested, "a spiritual war is continually waged between these parts" in "a daily renewal of repentance." Meditative life became an inner oscillation between these dimensions of selfhood as the post-conversion saint attempted to recover the intensity of initial conversion in moments of religious assurance. The double form of earthly belief—the duality formed from sinful tendencies and a saintly opposition to them—recurs in nearly all Puritan life-narratives, English as well as American. Bunyan wondered whether his faith in Christ and Scripture could be, like the beliefs of "Jews and Moors, and Pagans," nothing "but a think-so too," while Shepard confessed in his *Journal* to feeling "a wonderful cloud of darkness and atheism over my head, and unbelief, and my weakness to see or believe God." Wigglesworth began his *Diary* with a self-damning lesson prompted by his experience as a Harvard tutor: "If the unloving carriages of my pupils can goe so to my heart as they doe; how then doe my vain thoughts, my detestable pride, my *unnatural filthy lust that are so oft and even at this day in some measure stirring in me* how do these griev my Lord Jesus that loves me infinitely more then I doe them?" Cotton Mather similarly confessed that the contemplation of his sins "would have my *Soul*, in as much *Pain*, as a *Bone out of Joint*." Even Edward Taylor's "Personal Relation," generally restrained in tone, attests to struggles against "deadness, dulness, unspiritualness." Far from implying spiritual perfection, the paradigm of sainthood in fact demanded a keen recognition of its antithesis.[32]

Suffering and doubt initiated the other half of redemptive experience. The Puritan autobiographical formula demanded confirmation that, as Mather summarized his recovery from an efficacious humbling, "this *Repentance* has Restored me." Because assurance was expected to bring a renewed ability to endure worldly suffering, it was necessary to record the relief—or at least the desire for relief—that witnessed Christ's power to make all things right again. Taylor enacted this gracious rewriting of weakness into strength by affirming "that by howmuch I grew the more offended with myselfe by So much the more lovely, & longed-after did Christ appear in my eye." Shepard's "cloud of darkness and atheism" offered a similar spur toward "the spirit of light" by forcing him to heal more completely "this wound, which was but skinned over before, of secret atheism and unbelief." Even the acutely sensitive Wigglesworth transformed his "want of dear affection" to Christ into evidence that God "dist give me a heart (though vile) to lay hold of the desiring all from thee. and this gives me hope. blessed be thy name."[33]

Rigorous self-scrutiny mandated by Puritan devotional practice was rewarded with the believer's confirmation of these two "selves" and their ongoing struggle within: the waxing and waning of each in his or her meditative life, their relative proportions at any given time, hopeful signs of a gradual transformation from sinful to saintly self, and the comfort generated by the assurance that the redemptive process was at work. Because this ongoing psychomachia defined the saved identity that believers sought, the very desire to resist the carnal self was itself evidence that the salvific struggle was probably taking place. Only grace could give believers the will and the strength to resist their carnal dimension, to conceive of themselves in terms of two distinct inner dimensions, each the antithesis of the other but both indispensable to the dynamics of true belief.

In "Riddles Unriddled" Wigglesworth extolled pious self-division as the chief experiential benefit of harsh dehortations from the Word:

> Well, let it humble thee
> To feel a treacherous part:
> A sinful Self; a wicked Flesh
> Remaining in my heart.
> Yet for thy comfort know,
> Thou hast not lost the field,
> So long as thou do'st sin resist,
> And striveth not to yield.

Bunyan invoked this dichotomy more subtly in Christian's response to hearing a dream of the Judgment. When the Interpreter asks "Hast thou considered all these things?" Christian replies, "Yes, and they put me in hope and fear." Hope and fear intersect in the holy yearning at the center of Puritan interiority. As John Weemse attested, if believers "cry out with *Paul, O wretched man that I am, who shall deliver me*. It is a sure note, that they shall not dye but live." Milton's Satan exemplifies the antithesis of saintly doubleness. Incapable of opposing depravity through redemptive self-splitting, Satan embraces sin as his defining essence, thereby denying Christ's ability to conquer sin within the self: "Which way I flie is Hell; my self am Hell." The true believer, by contrast, clung doggedly to the hope that sin comprised only one part of the self's story. In current terminology, the Puritan self was radically decentered. Although it could be "read" at any given moment, its ultimate identity was unknowable because of the imperfect nature of assurance. However clearly the sinful and saintly selves could be delineated, believers could not be absolutely certain which one would finally prevail. The theology thus encouraged a fundamental instability of identity. To see oneself as hopelessly carnal was to lapse into despair, but to see oneself as securely redeemed was presumptuous.³⁴

In their constant reenactment of Paul's promise that "with the mouth confession is made unto salvation" (Rom. 10:10), Puritan expressions of unworth cannot be read as strictly "personal" in a modern sense. Bradstreet and her contemporaries diligently sought inner confirmation that, as Shepard put it, "the greatest part of a Christian's grace lies in mourning for the want of it." Shepard insisted that "the Lord when he shows mercy to any of his, it is in withholding much spiritual life and letting them feel much corruption."³⁵ Puritans never tired of pointing out that Christ came into the world to save sinners, a lesson that Bradstreet exemplifies in "Pilgrim" through a speaker who recognizes herself as a feeble, sin-worn soul in desperate need of Christic deliverance. Nor were Puritan autobiographical statements, with their consistent blending of the personal and the paradigmatic, self-deluding or insincere. Rather than consciously imposing extrapersonal pattern upon personal experience as a means of cynically replacing one self with another, Puritans accepted as real the patterns that they found within, however conventional those patterns may appear to us. Texts of self-examination repeatedly enacted a pious suppression of the "real" self (as we might call it) in the mandated search for redeemed identity.

In their ongoing search for a God-shaped self, Puritans experienced personal identity more as a process than a fixed entity, more as a nexus of spiritual goals and devotional acts than an isolated, unique "I" at the center of the physical world. The similar speakers of most Puritan poems—their embodiment, in varying degrees, of stylized responses acted out by Bradstreet in "As Weary Pilgrim"—suggest that even the most private verse manifests an unconscious persona shaped by spiritual paradigms that served to deemphasize what we would normally call "confessional" features in the verse. Although all poetry is in some sense "expressive" of the poet's mind, to approach the Puritan poem chiefly as a personal utterance of the writer's "actual" self is to impose upon it a literally autobiographical function that was relatively insignificant in Puritan art. Poetry offered one of many opportunities for Puritan writers and readers to create themselves through language— and the selves that they created were consistent with the psychology of redemption as taught by their theology. Self-expression in a modern sense was minimized because the mere self—one's private identity as a fallen individual—was precisely what Puritans wished to overcome. This unconscious aligning of private voice with saintly paradigm, a rhetorical response to the biblical command to lose the self in order to find it, recurs in nearly all Puritan autobiographical texts. Thomas Hooker admonished believers to "loose your selves, and all ordinances, and creatures, and all that you have, and do, in the Lord Christ," a goal encapsulated in a couplet appended to Mather's introduction to the *Magnalia Christi Americana*: "Quid sum? Nil. — Quis sum? Nullus. — Sed gratia CHRISTI, / Quod sum, quod vivo, quodque laboro, facit" ("What am I? Nothing. Who am I? No one. But the grace of Christ makes what I am, how I live, and what I do").³⁶

Placed within this experiential framework, Bradstreet's two voices can be reconciled as embodiments of the two inescapable facets of the redeemed personality. Taylor's mood swings similarly emerge not as reflections of reluctant belief but as vivid and appropriate articulations of a deep and vigorous faith. Puritan poems were shaped by—and helped shape—such inner activity for writers and readers who approached them not as literary productions but as practical aids to their pilgrimage through the world. Poetry helped Puritans undertake this spiritual work by stimulating their liminal identity as living embodiments of salvific struggle. Read in light of this struggle, these poems begin to emerge not as mere documents of propaganda or pathology but as poems— that is, as texts vividly reflective of culturally grounded psychological and hermeneutic processes active in reader as well as writer. The relatively impersonal and interchangeable speaker of many Puritan poems does not reveal a failure of art or imagination, but was a vehicle designed to enhance the legibility and accessibility of the inner paradigm articulated in the text. The reader's personal assimilation of that paradigm hinged in part on this impersonality within a text that invoked its own effacement as an entity. American Puritan poems were written and read as spiritual workbooks, catalysts of inner experience designed to be used up in an identification with a redeemed view of the self and the world. By undermining its own integrity as object, the Puritan poem was consumed in its own redemptive use, absorbed into the writing and reading self at the moment of assent to its redemptive message. Puritan poetry offered a ritual that was fully "performative"—and the performance it demanded was the reader's selfless alignment with the perspective afforded by saving grace, an alignment that depended on the willing participation of those who had ears to hear. For Puritans, poems provided scripts that were enacted through a ritual absorption of redeemed selflessness by the writing and reading soul.³⁷

Puritan poets wrote in the belief that pious reading—both in the Bible and in devotional texts that mediated between self and Scripture—offered a vital help to salvation. Like the preacher, who repeatedly lined out the inner signs of redemptive experience as a goad to the hearer's self-examination, the poet sought to destabilize the reader's tranquil place in a fallen world and to instill a consequent desire for saving grace. In this sense—and in this sense only—Puritan poetry enacted the unsettling function of art valorized by modern aesthetic theory. By reinforcing an instability of carnal selfhood, the text called into question not the theological system but the reader's position within it. For Puritans, the proper interpretation of any text centered on an interpretation of the self in light of the redemptive experience that the text both stimulated and embodied.

Bradstreet encouraged such a reading of "As Weary Pilgrim" by recapitulating the role of those Old Testament singers who turned God-sent trials into rich praise and edifying lessons, the same role that Jonathan Mitchell extolled in Wigglesworth. Like David, whose "affliction bred us many a Psalm," Wigglesworth is an *ecce homo* of the afflicted saint able to "send thee Counsels from the mouth o' th' Grave." For Mitchell, Wigglesworth's efficacy as a "Christian Poet" is inseparable from his dichotomized identity as part Old Creature and part New, a condition underscored by his sickly state, with "One foot i' th' other world" even though "His heart is all therein."[38] The speaker of "As Weary Pilgrim" similarly hovers between earth and heaven, the interior stance of all who labored to transfer their affections from this world to the next.

Bradstreet's appropriation of a neobiblical identity capable of anticipating a time when "soul and body shall unite / And of their Maker have the sight" required the projection of a self that was conceivable only within scriptural conventions of belief and art. Writing to confirm her share in the promises of the Bible, she sought to perceive herself as its subject as well as its reader. In reading the Bible, elect souls were reading a God-written song of the self, a verbal celebration of an identity that faith was nurturing daily within them. It was the repeated rediscovery of this neobiblical identity that Bradstreet described in her autobiographical letter to her children. "The consideration" of suffering and religious doubt, she wrote in a concise summary of Puritan self-experience, "would soon turn me to my own religion again." In "Pilgrim" this duality of experience anticipated in Scripture emerges in the contrast between the speaker's present weariness and her anticipation of future rest, a contrast that pits the faithful dimension of the self against a carnal identity defined as the source of religious doubt.

Witnessing a determination not to remain mired in carnality by denying Christ's power to transform sinful half into gracious whole, Bradstreet articulates an exercising of dichotomized identity—a trying on, through language, of a saintly metaself engaged "in the skirmish," as John Weemse put it, "as *Paul* was" in Romans.[39]

Her final cry for the Christic Bridegroom dramatizes the holy yearning that lay between sin and sanctity and between fear and hope. The hopeful determination of the pilgrim, who "means in safety now to dwell," is echoed by the speaker, whose yearning ("Oh how I long to be at rest / And soar on high among the blest") moves easily into a relative certainty ("This body shall in silence sleep / Mine eyes no more shall ever weep") justified by her acknowledgment that whatever deliverance she finds will be effected "by Christ alone." A proper tempering of Christian confidence recurs at the end of the poem, where any reader who assumed that the speaker has attained a perfect preparation for death would learn otherwise from her closing plea to be made "ready for that day." As in all Puritan autobiographical texts, "Pilgrim" projects weakness as an indispensable foil to a divine strength that could assume no verbal expression without the confession of its antithesis. Paul insisted that the saint's reliance on divine power stemmed from Christ's promise that "My grace is sufficient for thee: for my strength is made perfect in weakness." Pledging to "glory in my infirmities, that the power of Christ may rest upon me," Paul took "pleasure in infirmities, in reproaches, in necessities, in persecutions, in distresses for Christ's sake: for when I am weak, then am I strong" (2 Cor. 12:9–10). In light of the salvific role of Puritan confession, "As Weary Pilgrim" celebrates rather than laments the speaker's "decay." The speaker's weariness embodies an efficacious conviction in sin that in turn suggests a sincere desire for divine help. The "lasting joys" anticipated as the poem closes would come only to those who truly wanted them.

This inner dynamic is underscored by Bradstreet's psychological and rhetorical movement from self to Christ. Since the "corrupt carcass" of her soon-to-die speaker would be "raised by Christ alone," her "sins," "cares," and "sorrows" emerge as precursors of glory rather than signs of decay and finality. The litany of earthly trials introduces the power of a Christ who reverses the senescence elaborated in the first part of the poem. By anticipating the triumph of a saintly self whose existence depended upon the simultaneous confession and suppression of a sinful self, Bradstreet rewrote worldly afflictions into emblems of "lasting joys" that could be imagined only in contrast to present suffering: "Mine eyes no more shall ever weep, / No fainting fits shall me assail, / Nor grinding pains my body frail." Enacting a meditative progression from personal "weakness and dishonour" to Christic "power," Bradstreet internalized the promise that "whosoever will save his life shall lose it: and whosoever will lose his life for my sake shall find it" (Matt. 16:25). The meditative distancing from carnal selfhood effected by her frank confession of weakness made possible her anticipation of redeemed identity.

Asserting a voice consistent with biblical demands for selflessness, Bradstreet wrote in pursuit of a rhetorical and psychological *kenosis*, a self-emptying that emulated in reverse Christ's humility in assuming "the likeness of men" (Phil. 2:7). "Pilgrim" enacted a verbal equivalent of meeting Christ halfway: just as he partially divested his divinity in order to effect the spiritual marriage as the saint's Bridegroom, she eschewed individual identity in order to imagine her voice as Christ's Bride. The speaker of "Pilgrim" is not simply Anne Bradstreet, but Anne Bradstreet rewritten as the gracious metaself that she struggled to find within. Although we can observe her projection of a voice appropriate to self-edification, Bradstreet would have considered her voice in "Pilgrim" to be the result of meditative discovery, not an artistic creation disembodied in any way from her "actual" self. She articulated an identity that she hoped to become not as literary fiction, but as God-wrought fact—an identity that reflected what she considered the deepest truth informing her existence. The discovery of this truth was far more important to her spiritual and artistic purposes than the specific details of her earthly pilgrimage. In "Pilgrim," as in most Puritan autobiographical texts, the specific had significance only if it could be made to yield biblical and salvific pattern.[40]

Bradstreet's spiritual comfort in rewriting herself into a latter-day Job as the suffering saint makes it easy to forget that "As Weary Pilgrim" communicated the redeemed perspective to external readers as well. Not only did "Pilgrim" draw upon autobiographical texts that shaped Puritan experience, but it *became* one of those texts for the poet and her readers. By generalizing her experience in order to dramatize saintly patterns applicable to others as to herself, Bradstreet encouraged readers to emulate her identification with the neobiblical metaself. Functioning as a bridge between metaself and reading self, her voice embodied a sensitivity to audience central to Puritan homiletics. Ames insisted that "one who teaches another ought before and while he teaches to teach himself," and in his handbook for preachers William Perkins attested that "what emotions a sermon doth require, such the Preacher shall stirre up privately in his own minde, that he may kindle up the same in his hearers." In its goal of sparking the reader's faith, Puritan poetry offered a textual correlative to redemption itself.

To read properly was to intensify what Ames called "Christian confidence," the hope that was "strengthened by all evidences which assure us that the good hoped for belongs to us. Rom. 5:4, *Experience produces hope*." John Davenport agreed that "what faith believes, hope expects." Puritans read poems to find salvific hope, and the goal of stimulating it dictated virtually every artistic decision that Bradstreet and her contemporaries made.[41]

"As Weary Pilgrim" consoled the class of readers addressed in Taylor's *Gods Determinations* and Wigglesworth's "Riddles Unriddled." Far from exhibiting a headstrong refusal to believe, these readers could not believe as fervently as they wished. Like Donne in his illness, they hoped that Christ would "finde both *Adams* met in me" in saintly doubleness. Urging them to see the weakness of the Old Creature descended from the first Adam as only one facet of the self, "Pilgrim" instilled hope that the new Adam would bring the fulfillment of an ideal identity. Encouraging her readers to struggle, like Milton's Samson, against a carnal self "Proudly secure, yet liable to fall / By weakest suttleties," Bradstreet offered them entry into a battle against their own worst selves. "Pilgrim" urged this divided experience of self in the many oppositions invoked in the text. Earthly "cares and sorrows" contrast with "lasting joys" in heaven, the corporeal "clay house" with the desire to "soar on high," the "corrupt carcass" with the anticipated "glorious body," the grave as a consumer of "flesh" with the grave as a bed perfumed by Christ, and human "weakness and dishonour" with Christic "power"—all fostering the dichotomous vision indicative of a consciousness split by true belief. Like most Puritan poems, "Pilgrim" prompted an experience of reading that stimulated an optimistic seizing upon the smallest signs of grace as hopeful evidence of inner doubleness. Weemse insisted that "although there be more sinne then grace" within the earthly saint, "he takes the denomination from the best part. There is much water and little wine mixed in a glasse, yet it is called a glasse of wine."[42]

Articulating the "wine" of gracious identity through a commiserating speaker who is in no way superior to the reader, Bradstreet dramatizes Paul's belief that the "thorn" of earthly afflictions existed "lest I should be exalted above measure through the abundance of the revelations" (2 Cor. 12:7). Her confessions of struggle—her "sins," "cares," "sorrows," "age," and "pains"—manifest the exemplary humility without which salvation was impossible. She does not, for instance, ask directly for admission into the "lasting joys" of heaven but seeks only to be made "ready for that day." Writing to fulfill Christ's mandate to "strengthen thy brethren" (Luke 22:32), she confesses weakness as a redemptive antidote to the reader's. As a saintly model, she is at once theologically authoritative and comfortably imitable because she makes her unworth so legible. Her act of confession shifts the burden of redemptive work from the speaking and reading self to a Savior who transforms the grave into a perfumed "bed," raises the body "in power" to join it with the glorified soul, affords the elect the "sight" of him in heaven, and provides the "lasting joys" of the saint's reward. Significantly, neither speaker nor pilgrim is rewarded for mere performance. Nothing in the pilgrim's "erring paths" suggests inherent merit, and the speaker's confession of "sins" blocks any link between her worth and the peace that she anticipates. The inescapable presence of "erring" in earthly life is underscored by the pilgrim's stumbling progress toward "his silent nest": he has not arrived so much as he has been *permitted* to arrive. The speaker seeks similar permission in her closing plea for deliverance by the Bridegroom. Because perseverance in the faith is the only "work" that is given even the slightest efficacy, readers discouraged by a lukewarm faith could take comfort from Bradstreet's reaffirmation that salvation was a matter of hope and not performance. Through such confession as "Pilgrim" voices, believers could turn weakness into strength without risking presumption.

How readers responded to "As Weary Pilgrim" offered a test of spiritual standing based on whether they sensed a consolatory identification with the weary speaker or an unsettling discontinuity with her. Like the spiritual autobiography or journal, the poem projected a speaker who could either console or warn. Readers who heard Bradstreet's voice as an echo of their inner state and thereby passed the test that "Pilgrim" set before them could, at least during the act of reading, escape the deadly stasis of an exclusively carnal self. If, on the other hand, they felt little conformity with the text and thereby failed the test that it offered, the speaker dramatized the proper attitude by which the gap between reading self and ideal self could be narrowed. By subverting worldly identity, the poem fostered the reader's desire for salvific reconstruction.

Urging the reader to internalize Paul's command to obey "from the heart that form of doctrine which was delivered you" (Rom. 6:17) by aligning reading identity with redeemed selflessness, Bradstreet offered a touchstone for the reader's faith. Nothing in her journey metaphor or its supporting imagery was so specific as to exclude any reader's appropriation of the speaker's pious resignation. Articulating a sense of sin and weariness that troubled readers would bring to the poem, "Pilgrim" encouraged them to locate their spiritual anxieties within broader redemptive structures that grounded the anticipation of celestial bliss in rigorous self-conviction. The hint of worldly dissipation in the pilgrim's "wasted" limbs, for instance, is reinforced by the "mirey steps" and "erring paths" of life in the world and by the pilgrim's tendency "to fall" over stumps and rocks. When Bradstreet shifts from the pilgrim analogy to her own spiritual state, she demonstrates exemplary conviction by confessing her "sins," "cares," and "sorrows." Having been encouraged to identify with her weakness, readers were urged to adopt her strength and hope as well. The universality of Bradstreet's generalized self-portrait pushed them to seek their own transformation from worldly weakness to Christic power, to be made "ready for that day" in precisely the manner embodied in the pious speaker.

The ease of assimilating redeemed personality is enhanced by the extremely generalized depiction of earthly trials. The "burning sun," "stormy rains," "briars and thorns," "wolves," "rugged stones," "stumps," "rocks," "dangers," and "travails" are deliberately emblematic rather than naturalistic, as is the central motif of the pilgrim, the most common biblical archetype of the saint who journeys from carnal selfhood to gracious selflessness. The figure, which derives principally from Paul's definition of faith as "the substance of things hoped for, the evidence of things not seen" (Heb. 11:1), originates in the covenant that God made with Abraham and Moses "to give them the land of Canaan, the land of their pilgrimage, wherein they were strangers" (Exod. 6:4). After naming various Old Testament figures who persevered "by faith," Paul concludes that "These all died in faith, not having received the promises, but having seen them afar off, and were persuaded of them, and embraced them, and confessed that they were strangers and pilgrims on the earth" (Heb. 11:13). The typological link between the Old Testament faithful and Bradstreet's speaker, who also seeks a celestial home, is secured in Paul's confirmation that "now they desire a better country, that is, an heavenly" (Heb. 11:16). Through the pilgrim Bradstreet promotes the reader's experience of the covenant not as a distant event in sacred history but as current psychological reality.[43]

Like the Bible itself, "As Weary Pilgrim" offered readers an opportunity for redemptive self-scrutiny. To those who felt an inner resonance with Bradstreet's resigned but hopeful speaker, "Pilgrim" extended biblical "form and pattern" not merely as a feature of pious texts but as a fact of the reading self. Biblical texts, Herbert insisted, "are not understood but with the same Spirit that writ them." Thomas Hall similarly maintained that " 'Tis the nature of the Word to be facile and comfortable to such as are of a semblable disposition to it . . . but dark, and hard to the wicked, unregenerate, unmortified men." "Such is the harmony and power of harmony betweene the spirit and the word," commentator Francis Rous agreed, "that when you hit a spirituall truth in your soule, there will often come a sound, answer and eccho from some place in the word agreeable to it."⁴⁴ A proper reading of "As Weary Pilgrim" produced just such an echo in the reader's identification with the metaself embodied in Bradstreet's voice. By contrast, a "dark, and hard" reading brought a sense of alienation from the saintly perspective set forth in the text. For such readers "Pilgrim" became a text of conviction, a legal warning for an inner reformation by which the gap between speaker and reader could be closed.

An ideal reading of a poem like "Pilgrim" produced a gracious realignment of the reader's perspective on Scripture, the world, time, Christ, and most important, the self. Consistent with its status as a test of the reader's relation to the Word itself, "Pilgrim" exploited a biblical vocabulary that invested the text, as it did most Puritan poems, with an interpretive complexity accessible to Bradstreet's readers but obscure to us. Like the Bible, the poem was designed to be opened and applied to the reader's soul in a process made possible by the biblical patterns manifested in the speaker. Readers using the text as an aid to this process would find "Pilgrim" a suggestive rather than definitive text, with an open-endedness that was enhanced by Bradstreet's deliberate conflation of disparate biblical allusions. Such a poem offered an exercise in internalized exegesis, an experiential gauge of the reader's capacity for seeing, as commentator Henoch Clapham proclaimed, that "there is no Booke in the whole Bible, that teacheth not Christ Jesus and him crucified." Biblical reading revealed the reader's capacity for feeling Christ's love both in the Word and in Word-based poetry. In Scripture, as Matthew Henry said of Canticles, "there are Depths . . . in which an *Elephant* may swim" — but such depths were accessible only to the truly pious.⁴⁵

Like a passage from the Bible, the Puritan poem offered a surface whose inner complexities could run as deep as the reader's receptiveness to its redemptive message permitted. "As Weary Pilgrim" absorbed the profundities of its biblical metatext and reissued them, in reconstituted form, for readers to complete to the best of their ability as felt experience. Such internalizing of the Word was limited only by the human inability to grasp its deepest mysteries. For all the simplicity of "Pilgrim" if read as an autonomous text, its images gained in complexity from the reader's familiarity with their exegetical import. As mere images they were perfectly clear, even transparent. But as *biblical* images, each suggested a nearly inexhaustible network of interpretive associations, strategies, and responses. Within the exegetical framework that Puritan readers brought to the poem, seemingly flat images came alive as stimuli to redemptive self-experience. The burning sun that plagues the pilgrim, for instance, linked the journey with the heat of the Law, from which the antitypical Exodus of the elect afforded the only escape. This association was reinforced by the speaker's final role as the Canticles Bride, who finds protection from Legal wrath by resting "under his shadow with great delight" (Cant. 2:3). The opposition of gracious shade and Legal heat was heightened by an implicit contrast between the rocks that block the pilgrim's path and the Christic relief adumbrated in "the shadow of a great rock in a weary land" (Isa. 32:2). Ultimately, the "rugged stones" that impede the pilgrim come from the biblical and not the natural world; they recall the "stone of stumbling, and a rock of offence, even to them which stumble at the word, being disobedient" (1 Pet. 2:8). Similarly, Puritan readers would not have seen the rain of the pilgrimage as an underdeveloped natural image, but as an invocation of the multiple significances of rain and water in the Bible. As a worldly foil to the salvific water of Baptism and its typological prefiguration in the passage through the Red Sea, the image also suggested the frequent biblical accounts of rain falling on God's enemies, most notably the Flood and the plague of hail visited upon Egypt.

These biblical associations promoted a particular view of the corporeal world in which the carnal self was trapped. The abstract description of the pilgrim's journey, with its dreamlike representation of earthly life, reinforced the ephemeral nature of a fallen realm destined to last only as long as a temporary Law prevailed. By presenting her earthly life as an extended simile ("*As* weary pilgrim"), Bradstreet voiced the otherworldly perspective that the poem fostered: life in the world, so real to carnal sensibilities, was best seen only as metaphor. In her explicit interpretation of the central figure ("A pilgrim I, on earth perplexed"), she stressed the illusory nature of earthly identity, demonstrating in the process how to read the enigmatic text that constituted a human life. Perceived through the eyes of faith, the substantiality of the seen and the unseen is reversed. The speaker at once enacts and encourages a saintly determination to see the world as a mere shadow of a more solid realm yet to come. Bradstreet encouraged a similar shift in the reader's view of earthly time. Like "Contemplations," "As Weary Pilgrim" dramatizes the speaker's present confinement within temporal cycles that will soon end. Wracked with "age and pains" and trapped within the "clay house" of a body to which time will bring only further decay, she anticipates release from time's grip as the final reward of the saved self. By encouraging readers to locate their own lives within the salvific framework of eternity, Bradstreet reinforced their identities as selves whom time could not harm. Consigning decay and suffering to the brief span remaining to the present world, she portrayed the saint's physical death as a peaceful sleep that would make even these "few years" pass by with blissful speed, an internalized echo of the eschatological promise that "Death is swallowed up in victory" (1 Cor. 15:54).

Consistent with a saint's view of time and the world, "Pilgrim" held forth a saint's cheering perception of Christ. Just as there were two inner dimensions of the saved soul, so there were two aspects of Christ appropriate to each. Wigglesworth's *The Day of Doom* offers the most famous example of the unrelenting Christ of Justice, the Christ capable of striking terror in the carnal heart. Taylor's *Gods Determinations* provides an equally vivid rendering of the Christ of Mercy, a Christ perceived by the saintly self in moments of assured belief. The fullest biblical manifestation of this latter Christ, as Taylor's late Meditations and the final lyrics of *Gods Determinations* reveal, was the Canticles Bridegroom whom Bradstreet's speaker addresses in the closing lines of "As Weary Pilgrim." By leading her readers toward a Christ perceptible only through saving faith, Bradstreet offered an image of the Savior appropriate to the identities that they sought as pilgrims strengthened by saving faith.

The poem modeled this optimistic self-reading through the speaker's faith in her participation in the marriage of the Lamb in Revelation 22 and with the Beloved in the Song of Songs. Writing herself into Scripture by answering the allegorical Bridegroom's call for the true believer to "Rise up, my love, my fair one, and come away" (Cant. 2:10), Bradstreet responds to a summons meant only for the saved soul, thereby articulating the spiritual boldness toward which she leads her reader. Christic intimacy becomes the final reward of self-renunciation, a reward vividly conveyed in the spiritually erotic transformation of the grave into a marriage bed perfumed by Christ. The image, adapted from Proverbs 7:17 ("I have perfumed my bed with myrrh, aloes, and cinnamon"), invokes an exegetical conflation of the "myrrh and aloes" used to embalm Christ's body (John 19:39–40) with the sweet odor of the Bridegroom as Christic lover: "A bundle of myrrh is my well-beloved unto me; he shall lie all night betwixt my breasts" (Cant. 1:13). The image of the perfumed grave seals the marriage of death and love, thereby healing the redemptive split between sinful and saintly dimensions of the self. Presenting Christ's Passion as an event that can also effect the reader's resurrection from "corrupt carcass" to "A glorious body," Bradstreet models the true Bride's exchange of worldly for holy desire, thereby projecting her readers into a gracious future in which human weariness would be only a memory of a world and a self that no longer mattered.

Helping her readers oppose carnality by encouraging their identification with a biblical figure representing everything that the fallen self was not, Bradstreet tested their willingness "to be absent from the body, and to be present with the Lord" (2 Cor. 5:8). Puritans agreed with Matthew Henry that the Song of Solomon enabled believers to "see as much of Christ as can be seen of him, on this side heaven."[46] Exploiting the eschatology of the Song as a foil to the physical weakness that exposes spiritual lapses, Bradstreet made it clear that the "body frail" referred to the transitory nature of all bodies, not just that of the aging poet. The "clay house mold'ring away" transcended simple autobiographical fact: no one could trust in "them that dwell in houses of clay, whose foundation is in the dust, which are crushed before the moth" (Job 4:19).

By invoking the saint's betrothal to Christ, the final lines of "Pilgrim" reiterate Peter's admonition for "strangers and pilgrims" to "abstain from fleshly lusts, which war against the soul" (1 Pet. 2:11). The speaker's movement from a frankly "perplexed" state to an anticipation of Christic union reassured readers that their own "erring paths" were part and parcel of a holy journey that replicated the tortuous and epicyclic Old Testament Exodus. If Bradstreet's personal voice seems all but silenced in her pursuit and encouragement of assurance, it is important to remember that discovering something more than mere human identity was the goal of all Puritan meditation. By exploiting such widely recognized patterns of saintly experience, Bradstreet encouraged readers to seek their own "rest" in a meditative escape from carnal selfhood by which sin and fear could seem potentially salvific. In its contemplative calm, such a poem re-created the reading self as a vehicle of its own transcendence. Readers sharing Bradstreet's spiritual goals would have found intense dramatic possibilities outside of the text itself, in the interplay between the assured speaker and their anxiety to feel their own pilgrimage to glory. The salvific hope generated by this interplay was, for Puritans, "an anchor of the soul, both sure and stedfast" (Heb. 6:19). Bradstreet instilled this hope by animating within herself and her readers experience in the gradual and difficult transition from suffering sinner to gracious saint. Readers seeking heartfelt assent to the poem's redemptive message would have cherished its generalized speaker, its extreme dependence on Scripture, and its predictable imagery. The very qualities that most alienate "Pilgrim" from modern tastes are, when seen from a Puritan perspective, its greatest strengths.

The power of verse to stimulate the self's redemptive possibilities defined the Puritan experience of poetry. The real proof of a poem, Puritans believed, resided in its capacity for provoking within readers the hope that their earthly suffering would someday be repaid with a pilgrim's reward. "Fall to," Mitchell urged Wigglesworth's readers, "and if thy taste be good, / Thou'lt praise the Cook, and say, 'Tis choicest Food."⁴⁷ How readers responded to such poetry did not reflect on its literary quality conceived as an isolated trait—such faithful presentation of the Word "dish'd up" ruled out that possibility—but on their "taste" for its message and for the biblical metatext that was its divine source. To judge such a poem "right," as Mitchell suggests, was to gauge the self's response to the spiritual test that it offered. Although the decision whether to "help thy thoughts thereby" or to ignore poems like *The Day of Doom* and "As Weary Pilgrim" forced readers to confront their artistic and therefore spiritual allegiances, such poems were so written as to ensure the reader's proper choice. While the Puritan poem confronted its readers with a life-or-death decision, it also helped them feel more capable of making it wisely.

An experiential reading of "As Weary Pilgrim" suggests a great deal about what it meant in early New England to "enjoy" poetry. The pleasure of Puritan reading did not consist of constructing new truths from blanks in an indeterminate text, but of forging stronger and more hopeful connections between a volatile reading identity and a stable truth defined by God's Word. On one level, this pleasure was rational and intellective: through reading, Puritans could sharpen their understanding of doctrine and of the complexities of the biblical narrative. But they could also respond emotionally in their belief that the poem was strengthening their faith. While it was true, as Shepard conceded, that "*Jesus Christ* is not got with a wet finger," reading helped believers gauge their reaction to Christ and to the sacred Text that rendered him knowable. In addition to locating them within a community of like-minded believers reinforced on the most immediate level by the speaker-reader bond enacted by the text, poetry helped them clarify and thus relieve religious anxiety by accepting God's correction of a sinful identity that they longed to suppress. For Puritans, the pleasure of pious writing and reading could not have been greater. Through poetry, they could conceive of a self for whom a place in heaven had been reserved.⁴⁸

"Pilgrim" remains inert to us not because Bradstreet wrote poorly, but because the experience that she wrote to generate is foreign to us. We have forgotten how to read such poems because we have forgotten how high the stakes of right reading were to the poor doubting souls for whom she wrote. Writing and reading not to solve a puzzle but to find their place within it, Puritans felt the pleasure of the text in its articulation of a self for whom there was redemptive hope. Although they experienced reading as a surrender not to the text as a verbal artifact but to God's Word as its ultimate source, this pleasure offers perhaps the best antidote to the forbidding otherness of Puritan poetry. As texts that exploited verbal codes enabling the production of meaning by readers familiar with those codes, Puritan poems bear ample witness to the capacity of language to express and shape human desire and response. One point, at least, on which the Puritan and the modern reader could agree is that poetry can make a profound difference in people's lives.

Part Two

The Pilgrimage Preached:

Michael Wigglesworth

> Well, let it humble thee
> To feel a treacherous part:
> A sinful Self; a wicked Flesh
> Remaining in my heart.
> Yet for thy comfort know,
> Thou hast not lost the field,
> So long as thou do'st sin resist,
> And striveth not to yield.

—Michael Wigglesworth, "Riddles Unriddled" (Song 7 of "Light in Darkness")

Chapter Two

"By Ladders of Your Own": Eschatology

and the Selflessness of Reading

The otherness of Puritan poetry is nowhere more apparent than in the verse of early America's most popular poet, Michael Wigglesworth. By modern standards his poetry is nearly impenetrable, virtually devoid of those features generally valued by literary critics. His work presents few vivid images and little awareness of the natural world from which such images could arise. He seems to possess almost no poetic originality, instead relying nearly totally on the Bible for his themes and often his very words. There is not much personal expressiveness in his straightforward, doctrinal poetry. Autobiographical allusions are few and far between, and there is little overt sense of psychological struggle. When Wigglesworth is discussed at all, he serves mainly as a sad contrast to Bradstreet and Taylor, the rule that proves their exceptionalism. He is the poet they might have been had they not ventured beyond the confines of Puritan art. Even his diary reveals the very stereotype of the guilt-wracked Puritan living out his theology without a trace of the modern-sounding rebellion that most interests us. As Edmund S. Morgan observes, "So closely does Michael Wigglesworth approximate the unhappy popular conception of our seventeenth-century forebears that he seems more plausible as a satirical reconstruction than he does as a human being."[1]

In our unease with his verse, we often forget that it was Wigglesworth, and not Bradstreet or Taylor, who defined poetry as most seventeenth-century New Englanders experienced it. *The Day of Doom* (1662) sold out its eighteen hundred first-run copies within a year and went through at least six British and American editions before the poet's death in 1705. The poem even outlived the theology that fueled it: five more editions, full or abridged, appeared in the eighteenth century. A second volume of verse, *Meat Out of the Eater* (1670), went through four editions during Wigglesworth's lifetime and reached a sixth just prior to the Revolution. His contemporaries considered the Malden minister to be *the* poet of New England. Jonathan Mitchell, his former tutor at Harvard, called him the exemplary "Christian Poet" singing in the "vast Woods" of the New World, and Cotton Mather, whose literary tastes were far from stunted, acknowledged his success in providing for "the Edification of such Readers, as are for Truth's dressed up in a *Plaine Meeter*."[2]

No other Puritan poet has suffered more from modern readings that stress what his poetry fails to do rather than what it actually did. As a result, while we occasionally praise Wigglesworth's dramatic and narrative strengths, we remain unable to account for his phenomenal popularity. His diary indeed reveals an unusually morose Puritan who once had a vivid dream of Judgment Day, a dream that later inspired his doomsday epic. But dismissing *The Day of Doom* as the personal expression of his morbid and hypersensitive nature does little to explain how Wigglesworth was able to translate a private nightmare into Colonial America's best-selling poem.[3]

Wigglesworth virtually demands that we accept his frank participation in a homiletic and biblical aesthetic exemplified by Bradstreet's "As Weary Pilgrim." He forces us to reconstruct an experience of poetry based on the expectation that verse could shape reading identity in accordance with spiritual processes mandated by the faith. Readers who experienced poetry in this manner were convinced that the greatest possible aesthetic pleasure lay in contemplating the pure force of the naked Word. Repeatedly asserting and promoting such "delight in the law of God after the inward man" (Rom. 7:22), Wigglesworth constantly challenged these readers to redefine their identities and artistic preferences along biblical and doctrinal lines. It was the force and clarity with which his verse mapped out Puritan interiority that they cherished. *The Day of Doom* and "God's Controversy with New-England" exposed the fatal limitations of the carnal selfhood that he urged his readers to repudiate. *Meat Out of the Eater*, by contrast, focused more directly on the affirmative side of redemptive experience. In the first part of the volume, Wigglesworth encouraged a replacing of willful objections to the salvific scheme with a clear understanding of doctrine; in the second, he led readers beyond the application of right reason to its transcendence in the extrarational paradoxes of faith. Considered as a whole, Wigglesworth's poetry offers a clear schematic not only of Puritan spiritual experience but of Puritan literary response. Consistent with his comprehensive themes and his concern with addressing the widest possible readership, the devices of the Puritan sermon pulse more strongly in his verse than in Bradstreet's family poems or Taylor's Meditations. Because he was a popular artist writing for a broad audience, he invoked even more explicitly than they the poetry of the pulpit and of Scripture itself as the unadorned source of all truth and beauty.

From a modern critical standpoint early America's most popular poem is a real disappointment. Instead of offering vivid descriptions of the world's final destruction, *The Day of Doom* applies nearly literal scriptural paraphrase to an extended theological debate. Instead of poignant portraits of individual sinners, generic categories of reprobates plead their cases collectively. And instead of presenting a loving Savior sympathetic to the human condition, the poem depicts a harsh Judge who seizes upon one last chance to split doctrinal hairs with souls whom he has utterly no interest in saving. Even the prosody seems inept. As Kenneth Murdock once observed, "Such a theme is large enough and dignified enough to demand the most spacious and solemn form, but *The Day of Doom* actually is written in ballad measure, and the trotting verses seem sadly unsuited to the subject."[4] How could anyone's spiritual life have been quickened by such a poem or such a Christ?

To answer this question we must remember that *The Day of Doom*, like "As Weary Pilgrim," was written to invoke responses consistent with Puritan definitions of gracious experience. The saintly perspective is voiced in the poem by a Christ fully appropriate to instilling a reader's remorse for sin. The harsh Judge, speaking as the Law personified, effected a separation of reading self from saintly metaself that was reinforced by the reader's extensive and convicting identification with the damned. Extending the Law/Gospel dichotomy to a broad audience of readers at every stage of religious education and experience, the text offered itself as a converting ordinance in verse by applying the narrative of doomsday events to an insistent plea for the reader's repentance in the here and now. That Wigglesworth's most immediate purposes were persuasive rather than descriptive or even prophetic embodies an aesthetic in which Moses Coit Tyler's charge that he forgot "the very existence of the beautiful" is beside the point. For Puritan readers, theological truth *was* beauty, and once we read the poem in terms of this aesthetic we can begin to understand its remarkable success as popular art designed "To set forth Truth," as Mitchell put it, "and win men's Souls to bliss." That success hinged, as it did in all Puritan poetry, on the reading experience that the text managed to generate. Although its ostensible setting was the Judgment, the real site of the debate that Wigglesworth records was the reader's conscience.[5]

Urging repentance as the only escape from the terrors of the Judgment described in the poem, Wigglesworth mounted a pervasive and systematic attack on the ultimate source of willfulness: the sinful self's confidence in natural gifts. As Thomas Hooker affirmed, a true preparation for grace consisted of a thorough "removing of all that, out of the way which might stop or stay our Saviours coming." Thomas Shepard maintained that sinners lulled themselves into damnation with a "false bastard peace begot in the conscience," a false security resulting from a misplaced confidence in natural gifts and abilities. The "understanding's arrogancy," Shepard warned, was dangerous because it kept the soul from relying on Christ for salvation. The secure "mind, having been long rooted in this opinion, that I am in a good estate, will not suffer this conceit to be plucked out of it." Working toward just such an unsettling of the reader's identity, *The Day of Doom* portrayed carnal reason as a tool with which the unbowed soul erects self-damning barriers to Christ.[6] By pitting unregenerate thinking against the reproving power of the Word Incarnate, Wigglesworth pushed his readers to define themselves in opposition to fallen reason as a means of strengthening their receptivity to grace. Through poetry designed to reshape self-experience in accordance with spiritual demands, he forced them to see that the ladders of mere human reason and invention could never reach heaven. The terrors dramatized in the text could be avoided only if the heart was truly broken and the confident assertions of the sinful self were replaced by an unquestioning faith in Christ.

This subversion of carnal identity begins immediately. Echoing Paul's exhortation for the believer to "become a fool, that he may be wise" (1 Cor. 3:18), Wigglesworth promises in the prefatory "To the Christian Reader" to emulate Paul's "foolishness of preaching" (1 Cor. 1:21): "Reader, I am a fool, / And have adventured / To play the fool this once for Christ, / The more his fame to spread."[7] The critique of worldly wisdom extends to a final scolding in "A Postscript unto the Reader" of "foolish man, who lovest to enjoy / That which will thee distress, or else destroy" (78). Throughout *The Day of Doom* Wigglesworth repeatedly confirms that "Grace transcends mens thought" (44), that God reveals true piety to "Babes" "When to the wise he it denies" (41). The attack on human wit—and hence, on the reader's self-confidence—receives perhaps its fullest expression in one of the concluding poems, "A

Short Discourse on Eternity," in which earthly conceptions of space and number are revealed as meaningless when applied to the celestial and eternal realm. "A Cockle-shell," Wigglesworth insists, "may serve as well / to lade the Ocean dry, / As finite things and Reckonings / to bound Eternity" (69). The usual fruits of worldly wisdom fare no better. Human truth collapses with Christ's affirmation "that God is true / and that most men are liars" (40). Human justice reduces to mere selfishness: sinners have "no ground of strife" simply because divine decrees fail to coincide with their notions of fairness (51). Earthly distinctions of rank and prestige are also leveled at the Judgment, where no one is "so high in dignity, / as there to be respected" (23). In "Vanity of Vanities: A Song of Emptiness," the final poem in *The Day of Doom* sequence, Wigglesworth dismisses the great attractions of the world—beauty, friends, riches, honor, and power—as mere "Trash and Toyes" in a chantlike litany in which the words themselves, the very designations by which the carnal mind loves the world, become as empty as the pleasures that they signify. All of human history similarly presents a mere parable, a "Story, / That we might after better things aspire" (86).[8]

In their extended debate with Christ, the damned transform depraved ways of experiencing the world into an implicit attack on the reader's stable identity. In keeping with this goal, Wigglesworth dismisses the most overt evildoers—apostates, idolators, profaners, scoffers, adulterers, the covetous, vicious children and parents, murderers, witches, and Sabbath-polluters—rather quickly; they do not speak for themselves in the debate (17–19). His real interest lies in those categories in which his readers would likely find themselves: hypocrites, the presumptuous, reliers on works, the spiritually lazy, the misguided, and the uninformed. The focus on such ordinary errors made it easier for readers to locate eschatological counterparts to themselves within the text. Wigglesworth subverts any smug or defensive separation from the depraved through his consistent emphasis on secret sins of the heart and mind.

The reader's conviction begins with the very fact that the damned argue their cases in the first place. A sure trait of unbowed sinners, Hooker insisted, was their tendency to "snarle at Gods dealings, and quarrell with his dispensations, and privily grudge and repine when they see others have more and better then they."[9] The doomsday sinners give sharply unflattering voice to any private resentment or resistance within the reader. "Void of tears, but fill'd with fears" (20), they show no remorse prior to their sentence; they "grudge, / and grind their teeth" in envy of the elect (23). Their arguments, which function like "objections" inserted into a sermon as a means of refuting error or clarifying doctrine, dramatize the futility of opposing Christ. As the scriptural text cited in a marginal gloss prior to the proceedings confirms, "O man, who art thou that repliest against God?" (Rom. 9:20). And as the narrator states, "each Man's self against himself, / is forced to confess" in an act of self-conviction (24). What Christ tells the "Civil honest Men" holds true for each rank of the damned:

> Your argument shews your intent,
>   in all that you have done:
> You thought to scale Heav'ns lofty Wall
>   by Ladders of your own. (36)

One by one, the "Ladders" of human invention and discourse collapse as the sinners unwittingly reveal their true natures even as they try to clear themselves. The hypocrites, for instance, demonstrate a false show of faith by boasting that "We took great care to get a share / in endless happiness" (31); their claim that "We thought our sin had pard'ned been" reveals their presumption. The "Civil honest Men" similarly articulate the very sin for which they have been damned—a worldly pride in good works—by claiming to have been "blameless livers" who "got a name, / and no small commendation" (34). Even the reprobate infants reveal a selfish attempt to deny their share in Adam's sin, crying (much like real children) "Not we, but he, ate of the Tree / whose fruit was interdicted" (52). Their complaint that Adam had been "set free" (53) exposes not only a headstrong denial of sin but the envy that marked the damned soul. Such characterizations were sufficient to show readers that the real motive of the sinners is not "true love to things above" (32) but a selfish desire, as Christ flatly accuses, "To save your skin" (42). Consistently portrayed as petty whiners devoid of heroic rebellion, the damned finally seem more stupid than wicked. They do not even seem to know what the Judge *wants* to hear, and instead of renouncing their self-reliance they actually mount an elaborate and perverse defense of it.

Inner echoes of their arguments ensured the reader's conviction, a response intensified by the image of Christ at the center of the text. Tyler claimed that the poem, "with entire unconsciousness, attributes to the Divine Being a character the most execrable and loathsome to be met with, perhaps, in any literature, Christian or pagan."[10] But Wigglesworth's portrayal was entirely appropriate to his purposes. This is a Christ depicted in a specific role as doomsday Judge, a role theologically inconsistent with divine mercy. Three times Wigglesworth cites a text commonly interpreted as an expression of divine indifference toward the damned: "I also will laugh at your calamity; I will mock when your fear cometh" (Prov. 1:26). Articulating this final response to sin, the doomsday Christ confronts carnal security with biting sarcasm:

> They have their wish whose Souls perish
> > with Torments in Hell-fire,
> Who rather chose their Souls to lose,
> > than leave a loose desire. (48)

Demonstrating no interest in sparing those whose "wish" is fulfilled in eternal suffering, this Christ is capable of verbal play (lose/loose) as he banishes souls to the flames. Elsewhere he sarcastically urges the damned to "rejoyce" at their "portion" in hell (42), dismissing their suffering as "an equal thing" (45). Christ even mocks the reprobate infants, objects of natural sympathy that they are, with an ironic reversal of their own plea. If Adam had *not* sinned, he asks,

> Would you have said, we ne'r obey'd
> > nor did thy Laws regard;
> It ill befits with benefits,
> > us, Lord, so to reward? [11] (54)

The vengeful Christ—a far cry from the gentle Bridegroom central to "As Weary Pilgrim" and pervasive in Puritan devotional verse—was indispensable to the poem's convicting themes. By emphasizing Christ's apocalyptic transformation from Advocate to Judge, Wigglesworth attacked the natural assumption that God's mercy was sufficiently vast to be abused. One rank of sinners explicitly tries to redefine divine mercy as human pathos: "can mercy have the heart / To recompence few years offence / with Everlasting smart?" (43). But the Judge points out the fatal error of imploring a Christ of mercy on the very day of Judgment, when "all [is] too late, grief's out of date" (44):

> If now at last Mercy be past
> > from you for evermore,
> And Justice come in Mercies room,
> > yet grudge you not therefore. (45)

Wigglesworth's Christ defines and embodies the intersection of eschatological doom with current sin. If the doomsday Judge seemed impenetrable, then the Christ *outside* the poem, the Christ of mercy and present opportunity, had to be entreated at once. The still, small voice would not plead forever.

Wigglesworth's saints play a similar role in the reader's conviction. From a merely human perspective the redeemed seem as cruel as their Savior, especially in their "courage bold" and "thankful wonderment" as they watch "all those that were their foes / thus sent to punishment" (65). For true believers as for Christ, all compassion for sinners "is out of fashion, / and wholly laid aside" (59). Some of the most poignant passages occur when the saints renounce all earthly attachments in fulfillment of the promise that "henceforth know we no man after the flesh" (2 Cor. 5:16). The "tender Mother" acknowledges none of "all her numerous brood" except the elect; the "pious Father" who sees his son sentenced to the fire "doth rejoyce to hear Christ's voice / adjudging him to pain"; one brother sees another "in this astonied fit, / Yet sorrows not thereat a jot, / nor pitties him a whit"; the blessed husband "Shall mourn no more" upon seeing that his wife is a "damn'd forsaken wight" (60). However inhuman the saints' attitude may seem to us, Puritan readers would have found it appropriate precisely *because* of its inhumanity. As an embodiment of the Psalmist's prophecy that "The righteous shall rejoice when he seeth the vengeance" (Ps. 58:10), the saints' vindictive glee demonstrated a will made consistent with God's. Their scorn for their unregenerate brethren dramatized the radical nature of their transformation into New Creatures. The contrast between their austere joy and the reader's natural sympathy and fear underscored the vast gulf between divine and human perspectives on love, death, and eternity.

The reader's potential resistance to the doctrine set forth in *The Day of Doom* is linked solidly with the strident arguments of the damned, whose self-reliant "Penitence" and "diligence," as the Judge tells them, "to Read, to Pray, to Hear, / Were but to drown'd the clamorous sound / of Conscience in your ear" (33). Their willful contending is finally replaced with remorse that they should have attained when they had the opportunity. Their consciences, which "had grosly been abused" while they lived (24), finally concede that Christ's "Reasons are the stronger" (56); they "have nought to say, / But that 'tis just, and equal most / they should be damn'd for ay." Once the Babel of disputation ends, the damned stand "Like stocks . . . at Christ's left-hand, / and dare no more retort" (49); "Vain hopes are cropt, all mouths are stopt" (56); "Their mouths are shut" in "silence" and "shame: / Nor have they ought within their thought, / Christ's Justice for to blame" (57). The sinners finally achieve the silence of an efficacious conviction under the Law in which "every mouth may be stopped, and all the world may become guilty before God" (Rom. 3:19). In them the reader sees the inevitable result of all self-justifying language, especially at the end of the debate, when the damned surrender the very humanity that they have exercised their reason to defend. Upon hearing their sentence they become not New Creatures but the irrational and inarticulate beasts that they have chosen to be: "They cry, they roar for anguish sore, / and gnaw their tongues for horrour" (62).

The sinners' language presented an exaggerated mirror to the convicted reader. Dramatizing Shepard's statement that the mouths of the unregenerate "are open sepulchers, which smell filthy when they are opened," the damned embody a perpetuation of the verbal corruption initiated at the Fall. As Hooker explained, when Satan "would cast a vaile over the ugly and deformed face of Vice, and graceless courses he is forced to lay some false colors of indifferency, delight, and pleasure."[12] The sinners demonstrate that if it was fatal to rely on human reason, it was equally dangerous to replace adherence to the divine Word with the assertions of mere human discourse. Wigglesworth's insistence on the scriptural basis of divine truth also emerges in Christ's relentless doomsday role not only as the Word made flesh but as the Word of Scripture forcefully articulated and defended. As preacher-exegete within the poem, the Judge repeatedly exposes the pitfalls of careless reading. Attempting to hold Christ to the promise that "he being full of compassion, forgave their iniquity, and destroyed them not" (Ps. 78:38), presumers upon divine mercy wonder if the Word has "deceiv'd" them: "cannot his mercy great, / (As hath been told to us of old) / asswage his angers heat?" (43). Christ responds by pointing out that the promise of clemency is fulfilled "by those that here / are plac'd at my right hand" (44). Elsewhere "Civil honest Men" try to justify their reliance on works by citing Samuel's promise that "to obey . . . is more than sacrifice" (34). But by overlooking the simple exhortation to obey "the voice of the Lord" rather than their own wills (1 Sam. 15:22), they have fallen into the very trap against which the text warns. As Christ explains, "th' affection / and temper of the heart" are crucial to the efficacy of all religious duties (35). Depicted as inept exegetes throughout the poem, the sinners show how carnal reason can spoil the edifying possibilities of Scripture itself.

By opposing human words with the irresistible Word of divine utterance, Wigglesworth constructs what is actually a nondebate that invests the sinners' side of the argument with no credibility whatsoever. In "A Short Discourse" he reiterates the assumption that no argument against Scripture could possibly make sense, let alone prevail, when he replies to one last objection of the willful heart: "What, have the years of sinners tears / no limits, or no bound?" (70). Positing an ironic inversion of the divine plan, he answers that the eternal sentence could be lifted only if the unassailable verities of the Word were overturned, "When Heav'n is Hell, when Ill is Well, / when Vertue turns to Vice" (70)—

when "Christ above shall cease to love" and "God shall cease to reign" (71). This upside-down cosmos, put forth as an extreme restatement of the errors of the damned, linked the assertions of depravity not with their origins in human doubt and uncertainty but with their inevitable conclusion, as Wigglesworth saw it, in a total negation of the divine schema. Readers would see that all sins led to the ultimate Sin: the various mental errors dramatized in the poem were inseparable from the great error of denying the very power and goodness of God.

The lopsided dialectic of *The Day of Doom* does not suggest a failure of Wigglesworth's imagination or empathy, but instead reflects the Puritan belief that true remorse induced a disgust toward sin that approximated how God viewed it. Hooker urged preachers to "make sin appear truly odious and fearful to the open view of all, that all may be afraid and endeavor to avoid it." Without such a horrific view of depravity, the hardhearted soul merely "sits down willingly, well apaid with his own estate and portion, [and] sees no need of any change." In his exaggerated portrayal of fallen opinion, Wigglesworth pushed his readers to hear the objections of carnal reason as they would sound in the Judge's ears. At the Judgment all sins, however small, would finally appear "in their own proper hew" (27) as hideous affronts to the divine. Although preachers usually followed William Chappell's advice not "to buzze many, especially subtile objections into the hearers Ears, which peradventure would not otherwise enter into their thought," the doomsday poem presented a greater challenge than the standard sermon.[13] The debate required Wigglesworth to voice a wide range of carnal objections without provoking the sympathy for the damned reflective of a "human"—and hence fallen—response to divine justice. By depicting sin from the divine perspective, Wigglesworth encouraged readers to view their sins *now* as they would be judged *then*, thereby leading them toward the repentance that alone could save them.

In their exaggerated self-pride, Wigglesworth's sinners embodied Hooker's statement that "there is in every mans heart naturally such corrupt carnall pleading, that it labours to defeat, and put by the worke of the word, that it may not come home to the heart." Elaborating on the prophecy that "The Lord shall cut off all flattering lips, and the tongue that speaketh proud things" (Ps. 12:3), the poem left readers little choice but to adopt a view of depravity based not on reasonable-sounding excuses but on faith in the authority and truth of Scripture. Although rational discourse provided the external structure for *The Day of Doom*, the actual "proofs" that the poem offered were tied to an unquestioning belief in the promises of the Word. The most basic opposition invoked within the reader's consciousness was not between human and divine logic but between carnal reason and gracious belief. The essential "logic" of salvation would be faith and faith alone.[14]

By whittling away at the presumptions of the sinful self until only Christ and the Word remained, *The Day of Doom* presented a verbal parallel to doomsday itself. Wigglesworth's linking of inner conviction in sin with the broader conviction of the damned at the Judgment forced readers to confront Hooker's dictum that "you cannot be in your selves and in Christ too." Considered in light of this aim, the poem exhibits a closer match of form and purpose than is usually recognized. First, it fulfills Hooker's definition of "a plain and powerful Ministry" made possible "When the Language and Words are such as those of the meanest Capacity have some acquaintance with, and may be able to conceive." Wigglesworth certainly avoids "the frothy tinkling of quaint and far fetched Phrases, which take off, and blunt as it were the edge of the blessed Truth and Word of God." On the contrary, the diction consistently tends toward the theological and abstract. Second, the relative lack of concrete imagery reflects homiletic strategy also evident in Bradstreet's "As Weary Pilgrim." Although it is true, as Robert Daly observes, that the "reader, not Wigglesworth, provides the natural imagery and the experiential drama" of the poem, this is a strength rather than a weakness in a text designed to stimulate an experience of self shaped by salvific processes. Any imagistic gaps in the sinners' arguments would be filled in by readers, pious and otherwise, who recognized chilling echoes of their own self-confidence.[15]

Wigglesworth's refusal to deal with sin in sensory terms also allowed him to treat an enormous range of unregenerate opinion within a relatively brief compass. Puritans insisted that the final dispensation of the Law would not be acted out hastily. Shepard maintained that at the Judgment "things shall not be suddenly shuffled up, as carnal thoughts imagine." Instead, "it must take up some large quantity of time, that all the world may see the secret sins of wicked men in the world." Depravity had spread too far for a short doomsday, and given the vast catalog of errors to be exposed, Wigglesworth's narrative is remarkable for its pacing and compression. As each stanza rolled into the next and as one group of sinners quickly gave way to another, the rhythmic and structural regularity made it clear that the opportunity for mercy, whether seen as one's lifetime or as time remaining for the world, was indeed running out—that carnal reason would surely be dismissed every bit as quickly and irrevocably in salvific reality as it was in the text.[16]

Nor would fear have been the Puritan reader's sole response to the poem. *The Day of Doom* separated the reading self from the saintly metaself in order to encourage their stronger and more hopeful realignment. Beneath its dehortations the poem posits an optimistic future for its readers, a time *after* reading when they could rededicate themselves to the ongoing struggle against sin within the self. The very fear that the text instilled was itself evidence that contrition was at work within those who hoped to be made "Kings and Priests to God through Christs / dear loves transcendency" (66). It is easy to overlook the consolation that such readers would have drawn from the text. Wigglesworth clearly followed Richard Bernard's suggestion that sermons aimed at "guilty parties" should emphasize the "fiercenesse of Gods anger against sinne."[17] But for as long as time and the world existed, the biblical pronouncements that damn the sinners within the poem simultaneously held forth hope to those looking on from without. "Whoever sought heav'n as he ought," asks the doomsday Christ, "and seeking perished?" (48). The scriptural text cited at this point—"Ask, and it shall be given you; seek, and ye shall find; knock, and it shall be opened unto you" (Matt. 7:7)—underscored the reader's opportunity to stop seeking spiritual truth within the fallen self. Harsh as it seems, *The Day of Doom* offered yet another chance to knock at the door of redemption. In contrast to the doomsday sinners, who admit that they never did "believe, nor credit give, / unto our faithful Preachers" (65), the living still had time to repent. As Wigglesworth reiterates in "A Postscript," "Nor speak I this, good Reader, to torment thee / Before the time, but rather to prevent thee / From running head-long to thine own decay" (77).

"What hurt will it be to know the worst of thy condition now," Shepard asked, "when there is hope hereby of coming out of it, who must else one day see all thy 'sins in order before thee' to thy eternal anguish and terrour?" While some of Wigglesworth's readers must have resisted having their sins set before them, most would have taken comfort from his reminder to rely totally on Christ's redemptive power. Hooker alludes to the "wise fool" of the true believer—the Corinthians image with which Wigglesworth opens his exhortation "To the Christian Reader"—as proof that "if any man will have succour in his miserie, he must see himself unable to relieve himself; and then the Lord will doe it for him." Painful as it was, the sweeping away of self-reliance enacted in *The Day of Doom* embodied a comforting shift of the salvific burden from works to faith, from a fallen self to a merciful Christ. Accordingly, Wigglesworth is careful to point out that the saints did not earn their election by performing impossible acts of piety; indeed, they were in their actions and inherent worth "as vile, / and bad as any be" (21). When he recounts the reward of the martyrs, he takes pains to reserve a share of bliss for those who only stand and wait, who "had not such a tryal" but "ready were the Cross to bear" in the more mundane battles of everyday life (16). And despite its final blasting of the carnal understanding, "A Short Discourse" balances fear with redemptive consolation by encouraging the reader to "Cheer up" and "moderate your mone":

> Your sufferings and evil things
>   will suddenly be past;
> Your sweet Fruitions, and blessed Visions,
>   for evermore shall last. (69)

In its characteristically Puritan balance of the fear of hell with the hope for inner change, *The Day of Doom* sounded the dual theme of castigation and reaffirmation prominent in the many jeremiads that similarly transformed reproofs from the Word into evidence that God still cared. For the true believer such suffering was merely prelude to eternal joy. "Who would not go in sackcloth a while," Hooker asked, "that he might weare silk for ever?"[18]

Wearing the sackcloth was the first step in the pilgrimage of those who leaned on saving faith and not fallen reason as their guide to the next world. By forcing readers to assess whether they would likely stand at the Judge's right or left hand, Wigglesworth's best-seller fostered the anxiety and desire that in turn generated hope and assurance. Such a reading of *The Day of Doom* is confirmed by Edward Taylor, who recorded in an elegy on his wife that although "The Doomsday Verses much perfum'de her Breath, . . . yet she fear'd not Death." Elizabeth Fitch Taylor's reaction illustrates the effect of the poem on those who calmly, even eagerly, anticipated Wigglesworth's vision of the Judgment. Readers who found that the poem swept away futile ladders to heaven erected by their own self-reliance would feel that they, like the sinners in the poem, had been humbled by a powerful application of the legal terrors of the Word. In his handbook on the proper expounding of biblical texts and figures, Thomas Hall reiterated the purpose of such warnings. When we see in the "glass" of the Law "the numberlesse number of our sins, and those Seas of wrath due unto us for them," Hall explained, "this will make us fly to Christ, as to our City of refuge, and prize a Saviour above all the Kingdomes of the world."[19] If the Christ within the poem seemed like a son of thunder relentlessly hammering home conviction under the Law, then the Christ outside the poem—the Christ of present opportunity who still beckoned to those whose pilgrimage was not yet over—loomed even larger as a gentle son of the dove. The silence of conviction induced by the sharp reproofs of Wigglesworth's Judge could only make such readers more receptive to the gentle and ongoing pleadings of the Advocate.

What *The Day of Doom* foretold concerning the next world "God's Controversy with New-England" confirmed in this one by revealing New England as the stage upon which sacred history was unfolding. By 1662, however, the gap between mythic promise and day-to-day fulfillment had become disturbingly wide, and the severe drought that occasioned the poem was for Wigglesworth only a symptom of deeper malaise. As a minister charged with maintaining the purity of the "city that is set on an hill" (Matt. 5:14), he was convinced that the Chosen were beginning to act less like "Gods Israel" (91) than "the Carnall Brood of Israelites," "Who growing like the cursed Cananites / Upon themselves . . . heavy judgements drew" (98). As in the doomsday poem, a rhetorical split between the reading self and the saintly metaself forced readers to accept responsibility for sin, this time in its communal manifestation evidenced by New England's fall.[20] Like all jeremiads, however, "God's Controversy" provided a verbal antidote for the spiritual and behavioral sickness it attacked. By the end of the poem the breach between reading self and metaself was healed, and the reader's self-experience as hopeful saint was not merely reconfirmed but intensified. The poem assured its readers that God still cared precisely because *they* still did.

In order to make them care, Wigglesworth linked the dehortative half of his message as closely as possible to the biblical metatext. The Latin quatrain at the end of "The Author's request unto the Reader" immediately presents the speaker as a witness to the Law ("Quod Deus omnipotens regali voce minatur") and to the Prophets ("Quod tibi proclamant uno simul ore prophetae"), a latter-day pen-man of the Word who forges an unbreakable chain from God to prophets to speaker to reader:

> Nor is it I that thee reproove
> Let God himself be heard
> Whose awfull providence's voice
> No man may disregard. (89)

As William Perkins affirmed in his handbook for ministers, the inspired preacher was a prophet capable of serving as "the voyce of God" and speaking "in the name and roome of Christ, whereby men are called to the state of Grace, and conserved in it." Wigglesworth appropriates this role by framing his sternest denunciations of the times as the direct speech of God, the "tender father" (97) whose patience has been terribly abused. Wigglesworth's narrator, expressing humility and concern for fellow saints, functions throughout the poem as a buffer to this divine voice. Both voices derive from the common distinction in pulpit oratory between the son of thunder, who renders strong legal correctives to the proud and headstrong, and the son of the dove, who extends consolatory gospel hope to the fainthearted or despairing. It is the reader's conscience, the pastoral narrator insists, that will determine which message he or she deserves:

> For if those faults be none of thine
> I do not thee accuse:
> But if they be, to hear thy faults
> Why shouldest thou refuse. (89)

In a scrupulous balance of fear and hope through which the terrors of the Law set off the mercy of the Gospel, Wigglesworth allots each voice the same amount of space in the poem. Like a preacher instilling repentance before applying gospel salve, the two voices join forces to stimulate the reader's full experience of the twin dimensions of earthly belief.[21]

Reprising Christ's role in *The Day of Doom*, God speaks as Justice personified, asserting the convicting force of the text as an undiluted expression of "Quod Deus . . . minatur" (89). Threatening divine Justice as a spur to seeking divine Mercy, God warns readers to "hearken and encline your ear" or else expect "at once an All-Consuming stroke; / Nor cries nor tears shall then my fierce intent revoke" (99). The distant God-reader relation created by this "Dreadful-threatening voice" reinforced Wigglesworth's convicting aims: Puritans insisted that this was how God seemed when viewed through the perceptual filter of guilt and shame. God's thundering voice repeatedly conflates inner and outer frameworks of guilt. The sequence featured in the subtitle, "New-England planted, prospered, declining, threatned, punished," echoes the individual believer's movement from worldly security to the broken heart of a true conviction in sin. Throughout the poem the private and social contexts of belief collapse into a single attack on "a sensuall Heart all void of grace, / An Iron neck, a proud presumptuous Hand; / A self-conceited, stiff, stout, stubborn Race" (97). Because the "Generation even ripe for Vengeance stroke" suffered the same affliction with which God corrected the individual soul, the "Good christian Reader" addressed in "The Author's request" could see the society's troubles in terms of overriding patterns, however frightening, that evidenced salvific turmoil in his or her own spiritual life.

By portraying New England as a collective metaself, Wigglesworth gave readers every reason to believe that the full cycle of affliction and deliverance would manifest itself in the society as a whole. These consolatory possibilities are initiated by the contrition enacted by Wigglesworth's speaker, who reenters the poem once the thundering ends as a pastoral comforter who shares "our" fate with the reader. Dramatizing Paul's warning that "all have sinned, and come short of the glory of God" (Rom. 3:23), Wigglesworth assures the reader that he blames

>   . . . not thee to spare my self:
>   But first at home begin,
>   And judge my self, before that I
>   Reproove anothers sin.   (89)

By starting "at home"—a phrase as much geographical as psychological, given New England's decline—the speaker becomes a model believer who demonstrates the only possible remedy by confessing his share in New England's sin. As we saw in Bradstreet's "Pilgrim," such empathy with troubled readers reflected the standard practice of preachers who stirred up salvific "motions" in their "owne minde," as Perkins recommended, in order to "kindle up the same" in their hearers. Richard Bernard agreed that the "gracious and zealous heart" is a "most forcible perswader" because "It speakes to another what first it feeleth in it selfe." Like Bernard's Gospel minister, who "can not but speake to others as to himselfe," Wigglesworth's speaker made it clear that the real split fostered by the text was not between the guilty and the innocent but between those who cared about their sins and those who remained indifferent.[22]

As in Bradstreet's "Pilgrim," confession reinforced the reader's bond with a community as special as it was fallen, one destined to cohere in the lapsed present just as it had in New England's glorious past, when "We, only we, enjoyd such peace / As none enjoyd before" (92). By locating New England's decline and renewal within the hearts of those who "Repent, and turn to God" (102), the text shaped its readers into the "sweet souls" whom Wigglesworth addresses at its conclusion:

>   Cheer on, sweet souls, my heart is with you all,
>   And shall be with you, maugre Sathan's might:
>   And whereso'ere this body be a Thrall,
>   Still in New-England shall be my delight.   (102)

By the end of "God's Controversy" the reader is redefined as one of those "praying saints" whom the poem both extols and models—saints "Who dayly powre out" remorseful "plaints" in both "deed and word."

The sin that has debased New England is now distanced from the reading self with the allusion, the first in the entire poem, to Satan as an external enemy to be opposed with all one's strength. As Perkins insisted, "Howsoever the curse of the law is not to be urged against the person that is righteous and holy in the sight of God, yet it is to be urged against the sinnes of the person, which are remaining."[23] Although "God's Controversy" attacked the reader's sins, it scrupulously left that reader not merely intact but reconfirmed as a self defined in opposition to the sinful security that had brought New England to such a sorry state.

As model and stimulus for the reader's potential sanctity, Wigglesworth's narrator encourages fellow saints as much by what he is as by what he says. That it is he rather than God who offers consolation made it clear that readers were to heed their ministers, whom God calls "My painfull messengers" (98), those "bright beam'd, glist'ring, sunlike starrs I placed" to spread "cheere" (95). God himself endorses the speaker's role: "Oft have I warnd you by my Messengers; / That so you might my wrathfull ire prevent: / But who among you hath this warning taken?" (98). In the end, the two voices in the text embody complementary sources of salvation, the Word read and the Word preached. As readers drew comfort from the compassionate speaker, their experience of the poem corresponded precisely to what *should* be happening, in Wigglesworth's view, in "real" life. The humble narrator of "God's Controversy" provided comfort still to be had from all "Who toile and sweat and sweale themselves away" for the mission, whether their medium was the homily or the homiletic poem.

If readers were to internalize the promise of New England's redemption as felt belief, they first had to share as well in its collective conviction — to feel that "God's Controversy" was not simply "New-England's" but inescapably and personally their own. At the opening of the poem New England is still another place: "there the Sun of righteousness / Had never made to shine" until God's armies invaded "those forrein coastes" (90). But once the light of the Gospel enters the land, New England becomes *this* place — the *here* of the reader's present moment: "Here was the hiding place, which thou, / Jehovah, didst provide / For thy redeemed ones" (92). Similarly, the pervasive "we" of the poem begins in the search for religious purity in the Old World. New England's origin as an antitypical Ark of deliverance from "th'overflowing scourge" that passed "Through Europe, like a flood" (92) initiates a series of biblical comparisons that prompt the reader's reenactment of a neobiblical Exodus through "a desart land" (94), sustained by purified Sacraments as the manna of the new Chosen.

"Are these the folk," God asks, "On whom I rained living bread from Heaven, / Withouten Errour's bane, or Superstition's leaven?" (95). Through Wigglesworth's linking of current backsliding with lapses narrated in the Word, New England fallen becomes as fully biblical as New England graced. Even the Indians, equated with "Those curst Amalekites, that first / Lift up their hand on high / To fight against Gods Israel" (91), help define more sharply the saintly "we" whom Wigglesworth addresses. The same God who parted the Red Sea wielded the "fatall broom" to sweep the Indians away "to make my people elbow-room" (94). One is almost surprised to be reminded that the literal journey recounted in the poem started "from the brittish Iles" and not from Egypt.

Wigglesworth completes the blending of biblical and contemporary realms by recasting early New England as edenic myth, complete with a Fall and a promise of recovery. The arrival of the saints and the consequent transformation of chaotic darkness into "lightsome day" (90) create a new world of opportunity equivalent to that offered to Adam and Eve, a second earthly paradise planted in a "howling wildernes" (95). Only a biblical reading of history could generate the full horror that a place of such promise had become a "sinful-Land" (101). Aware of what happened the first time a covenant with God had been broken, Wigglesworth's readers felt threatened by a second and even grimmer expulsion. This time, instead of being driven out of Eden they would find that Eden had left *them*. Wigglesworth raises the possibility that New England could become another paradise lost "To morrow" (101) by generating a sense of things rapidly getting out of hand, of believers running "with greater speed and Courage to Damnation" (98). Illnesses increase "From yeer to yeer" (99); God's wrath has been withheld "to this present houre" (96). God's speech opens with a refrain, repeated with modifications, that conveys a rapid building up of divine wrath to the breaking point: "Are these the men"; "Are these the folk"; "Are these the people" (94–95). The controlled but mounting repetition depicts God's anger as an unsettling measure of time left in the world. In "God's Controversy," as in *The Day of Doom*, there scarcely seemed enough time to read, let alone repent.

The outcome of "God's Controversy with New-England," private as well as communal, lay in the reader's hands. The paradox inherent in Wigglesworth's consolatory warning—legal thundering that revealed evangelical love—replicated oppositions that helped to redefine his readers as earthly pilgrims: famine versus plenty, sickness versus health, fallen present versus glorious past and gracious future, "sinful Land" versus earthly paradise. These dichotomies permitted the legal significance of "controversy" as a dispute or debate to reverberate on multiple levels. Most immediately, God ponders whether to save or destroy a people who have neglected the terms of the covenant. But like Taylor's *Gods Determinations*, "God's Controversy" portrays the divine debate in terms that encompass the psychological dimensions of belief as a struggle between sin and grace within the reading self. Behind the push and pull of the Law and the Gospel embodied in the poem's two voices lay the reader's recognition that society's turmoil echoed the struggle between Old Creature and New taking place within. As "God's Controversy" made clear, the mission's outer problems and the reader's inner doubts were merely different fronts in a single war between good and evil.

On the surface, the poem necessarily left unresolved the tensions and dualities that it set forth. But because the reader was also to begin "at home," Wigglesworth's ongoing conflation of personal contrition with societal renewal replaced helplessness and anxiety with a chance to *do* something—to "seriously, and soon, repent" (97) as one of those "praying saints" (102) whose devotion would see the mission through. In this sense, the text of "God's Controversy," like that of *The Day of Doom*, was completed *outside* itself, in the reader's course of action. As a goad to such action, the neobiblical reading of New England's history offered immense comfort. What was foretold in the Bible would certainly come to pass, and if a particular people relived its story, including its most heartrendingly difficult episodes, they would surely prevail if God took such trouble to "reduce" them "by stripes" "into a better way" (96).

Perkins pointed out that "this was the manner of the Prophets in their Sermons, to denounce judgements and destructions to the wicked: and to promise deliverance in the Messias to those that doe repent."[24] Wigglesworth led his readers toward "deliverance" from the fear that the text provoked by ensuring a proper response to the great choice that it posed. As he warns, "Or God, or thou, must quickly change; / Or else thou art undon" (101). And if such a clear admonition did not change readers' minds, the sympathetic pleadings of a speaker whose "heart is with you all" would surely move their hearts (102). By the time the poem ends the rod that chastens New England has been transformed into an emblem not just of divine anger but of divine "nurture" (102). The predominant echo that "God's Controversy" left in the minds of Puritan readers was not a paralyzing fear that the vineyard would be blasted beyond repair but a keen recognition that they needed simply to ask and all things would be given. Although Justice called out for destruction, the simple fact that New England still existed was evidence that divine Mercy was restraining divine wrath. Even in the midst of legal thunderings God reminds readers of his "Covenant of peace" and of the "cords of love"—an image borrowed from Hosea 13:34—by which he draws them to him (95).

Wigglesworth drew his readers into the covenant by provoking within them an engaged response to Scripture suggestive of redeemed identity. When, like a new Moses, he presents the Law from a New English Sinai where "The air became tempestuous" and "The wilderness gan quake" (94), he dramatized the gravity and immediacy of the Word as it appeared to the saintly metaself. The efficacy of "God's Controversy" hinged on Wigglesworth's ability to see and speak like a saint, to rewrite himself not merely as witness to the mission but as one of its earthly protectors. At one point in the poem God concedes that

> . . . some there be that still retain
> Their ancient vigour and sincerity;
> Whom both their own, and others sins, constrain
> To sigh, and mourn, and weep, and wail, and cry:
> And for their sakes I have forborn to powre
> My wrath upon Revolters to this present houre.   (96)

As an articulation of the true believer's compulsion to weep for New England, "God's Controversy" reconfirmed Wigglesworth's identity as one of the "praying Saints" whose "love and faithfull service" would be rewarded. Like Bradstreet in "As Weary Pilgrim," Wigglesworth used poetry to secure a place for himself and his readers within the redemptive myth.

"God's Controversy" did with language precisely what was to be done in thought and deed if the mission was to succeed. Forcing readers to judge whether they stood with the faithful or with New England's enemies, the poem offered its own solution by helping them feel that they had already made the proper choice. Thomas Hooker insisted that one cannot be "in the Kingdom of Light and Darkness together"—and given Wigglesworth's portrayal of the two realms, who would not choose light?[25] For such believers as the assenting reader God had held back his anger, and with such souls he stood ready to renew his vows:

> To praying Saints I always have respect,
> And tender love, and pittifull regard:
> Nor will I now in any wise neglect
> Their love and faithfull service to reward.   (96)

Ultimately, the poem refashioned the remorseful reader into a praying saint worthy of God's love, while unrepentant souls became the "others" who would have to answer for their "folly." If it seemed that "jolly" reprobates were not getting what they deserved, readers could turn affliction into God-given confirmations of their special status as covenanted believers, a status validated by the sincerity of their repudiation of carnal selfhood and their renewed conviction as humbled "Backsliders" (97). Such readers, transformed into "sweet souls" (102) through the act of reading, were assured that despite their culpability in New England's "Controversy," God's full rage was reserved for someone else.

CHAPTER THREE

"A SINFUL SELF . . . REMAINING IN MY HEART":

RIDDLES OF COMFORT FOR THE SAINTLY SELF

Although *The Day of Doom* and "God's Controversy with New-England" mounted sharp attacks on the reader's sinful self, particularly the reliance of that self on carnal will and reason, both poems spoke to the affirmative half of gracious duality by insisting that time for repentance still remained. Written for a broad range of readers at every stage of religious training and experience, these poems necessarily stressed the conviction in sin that began (or renewed) the redemptive struggle against carnality. In *Meat Out of the Eater*, a lengthy two-part volume that first appeared eight years after *The Day of Doom*, Wigglesworth took up where he left off, this time addressing those whom contrition had already humbled. For these readers, already well advanced in their assimilation of a pilgrim identity, Wigglesworth offered a fuller description of the consolatory dimension of Puritan interiority. These readers, hampered not by pride or willfulness but by doubts regarding the strength of their own faith, could be encouraged to seek the benefits of grace as an antidote to their spiritual timidity.

In addressing this aim, *Meat Out of the Eater*, like all Puritan poetry, spoke directly to the reader's experience of self. To read the volume properly, at least from the perspective of Wigglesworth and his contemporaries, was to replicate the renewal of the faculties thought to be instituted by grace itself. In place of the carnal reason renounced in *The Day of Doom*, the title sequence, subtitled "Meditations Concerning the

Necessity, End, and Usefulness of Afflictions Unto God's Children," offered faithful readers clear lessons in right reason as a prelude to its transcendence in the extrarational joy set forth in the second part of the collection, "Riddles Unriddled."[1] While "Meat Out of the Eater" clarified the doctrinal parameters of belief, "Riddles Unriddled" whetted the taste for a deeper faith for which the restoration of reason was only the first step. The prevalence of clear, even mechanical doctrinal statement in "Meat Out of the Eater" helped readers feel that their reason was sufficiently renewed to grasp the essentials of a saint's experience of the world. The paradoxical themes of "Riddles Unriddled" urged them to absorb this experience as felt belief. In pursuing this dynamic, Wigglesworth offered readers glimpses of an identity in whom salvific hope was strengthened. By reducing the joys of election to imitable textual form, Wigglesworth intensified his reader's sense that the experience of self and faith that the text set forth lay within reach.

The ten "Meditations" and "conclusion Hortatory" that comprise "Meat Out of the Eater" address a single theme: in taking up the Cross and following Christ, saints must accept their lot in *"this* world" as "great Sufferers" (107). As in *The Day of Doom*, the saintly path requires a repudiation of carnal identity, a demand that Wigglesworth underscores in the opening stanza of the first Meditation by insisting that those who would be saved "must renounce themselves / And their own Wills deny" in order to "Take up their Cross and follow Christ / Through Sufferings chearfully." Urging contentment "with Pilgrims fare, / Till thou to Heaven come" (119), "Meat Out of the Eater" invokes the same inner paradigm set forth in Bradstreet's "As Weary Pilgrim": life in the world presents "Changes manifold, / And Dangers perilous" through which "We travel towards Heaven / A quiet Habitation" (120). Wigglesworth's chief concern is to show that during the pilgrim's progress, divine Justice does not always coincide with human wishes. Because worldly suffering is a prelude to celestial glory, God permits the wicked to flourish on earth "like Grass" only "for their cutting down / To perpetuity" (128). Since the wicked "chuse their Bane, / And will no warning take," "God will no more take pains / To scourge them for their sin" (127). As in "God's Controversy with New-England," the wicked prosper because God has abandoned them to this world: "They have their Portion here" (124). The good suffer, Wigglesworth repeatedly assures his readers, because God cares enough to reduce them to salvific humility.

Written expressly for such sufferers, "Meat Out of the Eater" poses the most optimistic interpretation possible of human affliction—and by extension, of its reader, whom Wigglesworth comforts in the final stanza of Meditation 4 by citing the source of his title, Samson's riddle of the lion carcass that contains honey (Judges 14:14):

> Droop not faint-hearted man,
> Thou art not yet undone:
> So long as God himself survives,
> And is thy Portion.
> Out of the Eater He
> Will surely bring forth Meat:
> And Spiritual good more sweet than hony
> Out of Affliction great. (117)

The riddle serves as a pervasive emblem of the consolation that readers are urged to draw from the poem. Like "As Weary Pilgrim," "Meat Out of the Eater" rewrites earthly suffering as a sign of God's corrective mercy, as something to cherish—or at least *strive* to cherish—as a harbinger of eternal joy.

The ten Meditations of "Meat Out of the Eater" function as carefully ordered parts of a sustained exhortation to take up the Cross, from the "*Tolle Crucem*" headnote (105) to "A Conclusion Hortatory," where readers are urged "The Cross of Christ to chuse" (138). In the motto to Meditation 6 Wigglesworth asserts that bearing the Cross is equivalent to adopting Christ's sufferings as "our Copy-Book, / Whereon we often ought to look" (121). The *imitatio Christi* that informs the entire sequence is reinforced by numerous transitions written into the poems themselves and their headnotes. The couplet prefacing Meditation 3, for instance, states that "The third doth further hint at th' Ends / For which the Lord Affliction sends" (111); Meditation 9 similarly takes up where Meditation 8 leaves off by continuing an extended description of how the saint bears up under divine affliction. Additional structural and thematic unity derives from the fact that the two longest poems, Meditations 7 and 9, explore the central issues of the entire sequence: the worldly prosperity of the wicked and the patient suffering of the pious. Wigglesworth's careful structure reflects the interrelatedness of his themes. As components of a single sustained argument, the Meditations cannot be read independently of each other; transitional statements repeatedly connect one poem with the next and with the larger concerns of the sequence. This careful organization, capped by a final invocation of hope for the individual believer and for New England collectively, suggests Wigglesworth's goal of making "Meat Out of the Eater" a practical and comprehensive source of spiritual comfort for readers "that are," as the headnote to "A conclusion Hortatory" states, "or hereafter may be in Affliction" (138).

For such readers Wigglesworth invokes corrected reason as the antithesis of the willful assertions dramatized in *The Day of Doom*. Repeatedly teaching the redemptive utility of suffering, "Meat Out of the Eater" defers the speaker-reader dynamic central to Wigglesworth's earlier verse and to "Riddles Unriddled." Before the saint can feel the faith, he or she must think it through to the very limits of right reason. The result is an emphasis on a renewed understanding as prelude to a renewed will, a rhetorical postponing of gracious experience until the reader has absorbed the implications of doctrine as fully as possible. Meditation 2 typifies this concern with teaching. The poem begins by addressing the reader directly: "If in this narrow path" of life "You meet with Difficulties great; / Be not disconsolate" (109). The immediate shift, however, to a third-person description of "all God's Children dear" who must pass "Through many Sorrows" distances the saintly paradigm from the reading self. The experiential framework is further diluted in the final stanza, where the speaker addresses his own correction: "My soul be thankful then / That God thee thus corrects" (111). This mixing of persons—an "I," a "you," and a "he" of the pious soul—delays a textual simulation of saintly experience until the lessons of Cross-bearing have been fully absorbed. Stressing neither a comforting identification of the reading "you" with the redeemed "they" nor a convicting gulf that separates them, Wigglesworth keeps his lessons, for the time being, in the reader's mind rather than heart. The relative lack of drama—what Ursula Brumm calls the "sentimental and passive" spirit of these poems—most likely reflects Wigglesworth's concern that his readers avoid a premature closing with the perspective voiced in the text, that they clearly understand the doctrine before he encourages them to replicate it within themselves.[2]

Why Wigglesworth depersonalizes his lessons becomes clearer in light of the audience whose needs he addresses. Writing for troubled or afflicted believers, he is careful to place corrected knowledge before gracious experience: his readers needed to understand the full significance of their sufferings before achieving salvific relief. What is at issue in the poem is not the reader's problematic future or the direction of New England's mission, but the present comfort of those whose salvation is not seriously called into question. The even tone of the sequence is even more striking when contrasted with Taylor's *Gods Determinations*, written for a similar audience of timid, insecure believers. While Taylor generates intense drama by immediately fixing the redemptive psychomachia of the poor doubting soul within the reader's consciousness, Wigglesworth defers that struggle in order first to teach lessons preliminary to the saintly experience promoted in "Riddles Unriddled." It may well be that this difference in strategy reflects the fact that Taylor probably knew his readers personally while Wigglesworth did not. Writing for publication, Wigglesworth perhaps felt a greater need to take no short cuts in the spiritual paradigm that he articulates. While Taylor could judge from pastoral sessions the degree of his readers' understanding, Wigglesworth could make no such assumption, and accordingly led his readers through a full correction of their reason before providing the textual equivalent of a renewed will.

While "Meat Out of the Eater" places little emphasis on an affective meeting of reading self and saintly pattern, neither are they meaningfully separated—a technique well suited, as "God's Controversy" and *The Day of Doom* illustrate, for instilling pious fear. This suggests why the speaker's identity as a paradigmatic believer—as a saintly "I"—emerges only at the end of each Meditation and in "A conclusion Hortatory," where he addresses the reader as "my Christian Friend." This final voice, an echo of the sympathetic narrator of "God's Controversy," has "endeavoured" to "adorn" the Cross "That thou might'st be encouraged / To bear it patiently" (138). The speaker's credibility stems from a pious recognition of his own need to absorb the lessons that he teaches:

> Before I wrote this sentence out
> I sat down twice to weep
> Tears of remorse and sorrow
> Because I am so poore
> In these rich graces, and because
> I have attain'd no more.   (139)

Still, the speaker testifies to an experience of belief not yet fully shared with the reader. His final identity as a brokenhearted "fool" (139) remains a relatively distant model, one who encourages the reader's continued diligence in exercising right reason.[3]

Other salvific models, similarly detached from the reader, are set forth in the third-person descriptions of saintly identity that comprise the middle stanzas of each poem. At one point a "character" of the sincere believer extends over three Meditations. Distanced from the reading "you" as well as the speaking "I," the portrait provides a catalog of pious traits for the reader's understanding rather than direct assimilation:

> Plunge him into the mire,
> Or water; God is near:

> Cast him into the burning Fire:
> God will be with him there. (129)

Close biblical paraphrase enlists Scripture as the obvious source of the character: "When thou passest through the waters, I will be with thee; and through the rivers, they shall not overflow thee: when thou walkest through the fire, thou shalt not be burned; neither shall the flame kindle upon thee" (Isa. 43:2). The result is a clear picture of the neobiblical saint who illustrates the godly response to affliction. Having clarified the desired identity for the reader's understanding, Wigglesworth offers the portrait for humble emulation as the sequence draws to a close — but not before the reader clearly grasps the nature of such a self.

> I have before thine eyes,
> An humble gracious Saint,
> Bearing the Cross upon his Back,
> Endeavoured to paint.
> Now strive to immitate,
> After this Copy write:
> This is the onely end for which,
> I did the same endite. (138)

"Meat Out of the Eater" does not stress how it feels to be such a self so much as what this identity is and why the reader's attempts to write after its "Copy" must be heartfelt. Despite Wigglesworth's claim that he has "not told thee Tales, / Of things unseen, unfelt, / But speak them from Experience" (139), he does not present himself as an articulated "Copy" of the "gracious Saint" until the very last poem, when readers would presumably have absorbed the corrected rationality that "Meat Out of the Eater" encourages.

What the sequence does present is the biblical metatext as a vehicle by which readers can begin to assess their conformity to the paradigm described in the verse. Applied mainly in a didactic rather than experiential mode, the Bible functions in the sequence as a reading of the Law that must precede the appropriation of Gospel hope. Yet because Wigglesworth assumes a humbled, contrite reader, he does not root such biblical admonitions directly and accusingly within the reader's consciousness. Despite the fact, for instance, that a scriptural warning in "A conclusion Hortatory" issues directly from the mouth of God, Wigglesworth softens its dehortative force by downplaying its experiential location:

> For thus he threateneth,
> If that ye will not be,

> By all my strokes reformed yet
> But still walk cross to me.
> Then will I also walk
> Contrary unto you,
> In wrath and fury, and seven times
> More plagues will on you throw. (140)[4]

For all its apparent harshness, the prophecy is muted by a sudden shift in the next stanza back to the pastoral speaker, who addresses the reader as "Dear Brother, Christian Friend" (140). This is one poem, at least, in which Wigglesworth does not permit the sting of biblical rebuke to last very long. Positive scriptural models are similarly distanced, for the time being, from the reading self. The exemplary figures of Scripture, for instance, are invoked not as direct precedents for personal identity but as explanatory glosses on the third-person "character" of the saint. When Wigglesworth at one point introduces a brief roster of afflicted biblical heroes—Jacob, Joseph, Moses, the three children in the fire, Daniel, and Paul "When Shipwrack'd" (130)—their pious stoicism is connected not to the reading "you" or the speaking "I," but to the "he" of the exemplary believer:

> The Everlasting Arms
> Are underneath his head
> To bear him up; and hence it comes
> He is not swallowed,
> Nor suffered wickedly
> From God to turn aside:
> As by his carriage will appear
> When troubles him betide. (130)

Reprobates assume a form just as fully stylized as that of the idealized saint: they wallow "Like filthy unclean Hogs, / And to their vomit back again / They run like greedy Dogs" (127). Such cardboard sinners have little dehortative impact, so clearly "They shew you what they are" (127). The entire sequence points up the reader's need to think and reflect in light of the Word. Without a clear understanding of the biblical structures to which believers were to compare themselves, any comfort wrought by an optimistic self-reading would be premature.

With the shift from the first part of the collection to the second, the Puritan Virgil gives way to the Puritan Beatrice. In keeping with his goal of revising the reader's understanding of earthly suffering, Wigglesworth speaks in "Meat Out of the Eater" primarily as a teacher. But in "Riddles Unriddled, or Christian Paradoxes Broke open, smelling like sweet Spice New taken out of Boxes," the reader is given a more active role in the redemptive paradigm consistent with the focus on inner paradoxes of the faith as catalysts for a new way of *experiencing* earthly affliction. "Riddles Unriddled" presents nine sequences of "Songs" or "Meditations," each treating a separate paradoxical dimension of belief. These paradoxes, chained into a metrical list appearing on the verso of a separate title page, extend the dichotomy between earthly pain and celestial joy pursued in the first sequence:

>   Light in Darkness,
>   Sick mens Health,
>   Strength in Weakness,
>   Poor mens Wealth.
>   In Confinement,
>   Liberty,
>   In Sollitude,
>   Good Company.
>   Joy in Sorrow,
>   Life in Deaths,
>   Heavenly Crowns for
>   Thorny Wreaths.   (144)

That "Riddles Unriddled" was written to provoke the reader's assimilation as felt belief of the doctrines set forth in "Meat Out of the Eater" is clear from a summary of the first sequence that appears at the beginning of the second. Having spoken "Thus far in generall / About Afflictions" (146), Wigglesworth now turns to "particular Ailes / And Exercises great" in the life of the earthly pilgrim. While "Meat Out of the Eater" applies Samson's riddle to a general consideration of why saints suffer, "Riddles Unriddled" particularizes the theme, turning to what Bradstreet called the "practic part" of belief by examining specific paradoxes embodying the contrast of fear and hope central to Puritan experience.[5]

A question is posed at the beginning of "Life in Deaths": "Can such an Honey-comb, / So sweet and precious, come forth / Of Death's devouring Womb?" (251). Offering an extended answer, "Riddles Unriddled" augments the discussion of affliction and its benefits with a full demonstration of how the paradoxes of belief resolve themselves within the redeemed perspective. As Ursula Brumm observes, the "hortatory severity of the first part is softened" by the second, and while the first sequence teaches the value of suffering, the sequel charts an experiential framework through which suffering could be transcended. Having had their rationality restored by the doctrinal emphasis of the first sequence, readers of "Riddles Unriddled" were ready to feel themselves as living paradoxes, as selves in whom the Old and New Creatures were locked in struggle. As John Weemse affirmed, within the elect soul "there is not a facultie, but it hath grace in it as well as sinne."[6] In keeping with his consolatory aims, Wigglesworth invites his readers to read themselves optimistically as paradoxical identities capable of finding redemptive hope and not frustration or despair in the riddles of the faith.

Enacting a shift from doctrine to application, from general truths to "particular Ailes" and their remedies, "Riddles Unriddled" urged its readers to penetrate beyond right reason in order to perceive divine enigmas as a source not of anxiety but of comfort. The key to achieving such extrarational experience, Wigglesworth states, is to follow the example of Christ, who makes "Trouble the way to Peace, / Sickness the way to soundest Health, / And Pain the way to Ease" (182). This perceptual transformation completes the *tolle Crucem* mandate initiated in "Meat Out of the Eater." In the final poem of "Riddles" Wigglesworth urges readers "To do all Duties, bear the Cross, / And suffer every Pain" (272). The movement from suffering to reward foreshadowed in Christ's death and Resurrection is reinforced by the consolatory conclusion toward which the entire volume points. Christ's promise in the final quatrain to "turn / Thy Cross into a Crown" (275) becomes the ultimate "sweet Spice" of the Passion, now reconfirmed as the great Affliction that would end the lesser afflictions of believers with which *Meat Out of the Eater* began.

Consistent with an overall movement from head to heart, from rational correction to redemptive experience, "Riddles Unriddled" traces a progression from "Light in Darkness" through "Life in Deaths" and "Heavenly Crowns for Thorny Wreaths" that replicates the salvific stages undergone by all saints, including the death of the body, imaged as an antitypical crossing of the "Red Sea" in an escape from "*Pharoah* (the Divel) with his Host" (255). The concluding emphasis on the resurrection of the body projects not just the end of the world but an end to the reader's anxiety. The flesh, the source of suffering and doubt, is "now in weakness sown; / But shall be rais'd in power"; the body "shall be wholly freed / From all Infirmities . . . When once it doth arise" (269). As in *The Day of Doom* and "God's Controversy with New-

England," eschatological prophecy is pressed into the service of present consolation: what seems puzzling when seen through a glass darkly, Wigglesworth insists, will become clear in the fullness of time.

The explication of the other "riddles" follows the same pattern. The introductory poem of each group, which sets up the paradox at hand, encourages the reader not only to seek an edifying solution to the riddle but to bear "Thine outward Misery / With Patience, as becomes a Saint, / And to get good thereby" (177). Throughout "Riddles" Wigglesworth insists that "these things are no Tales, / But Spiritual Mysteries" (201) for the reader to internalize. The paradoxes treated in these poems were precisely what made the faith incomprehensible to the carnal understanding. By setting forth their gracious resolution so clearly, Wigglesworth used the logic of reading to generate the reader's wish to transcend mere logic in an affective embracing of grace. The experience of reading the riddles, of penetrating their secrets through the sequential clarity of a text, offered a parallel to the experience of redemption itself.[7]

The engaging portrayal of Puritan experiential paradoxes accounts for what Richard Crowder calls Wigglesworth's "profound sense of the dialogistic situation," a sense most evident in the debate format that recurs throughout the sequence.[8] "Flesh" debates "Spirit"; "Distressed Conscience" and "Troubled Conscience" debate "Rectified Judgment"; and "Unbelief" and "Fear" debate "Faith" in exchanges that root the dynamics of conversion and assurance in the experience of the text. This strategy, exploited to the same end in Bradstreet's "The Flesh and the Spirit" and Taylor's *Gods Determinations*, provided not only a spur toward the reader's redemptive struggle but also an echo of turmoil that he or she most likely already felt in private devotions. By depicting doubt and struggle as normal and expected features of the redemptive process, Wigglesworth's debates helped readers redefine their spiritual anxiety as gracious activity. At times the Puritan psychomachia into which Wigglesworth draws his reader achieves a turbulence appropriate to an interior war with carnal selfhood. More often, however, the redeemed dimension of the self pleads more gently. Far from bullying readers into accepting Christ's yoke, "Riddles Unriddled" encouraged them to adopt an optimistic self-reading that recast their darker moments as signs of spiritual progress.

Like "God's Controversy," "Riddles" transforms the stasis of doubt into an active process of belief. To suffer, Wigglesworth assured his readers, was not only to stand corrected under the Law but was also to serve God, a welcome lesson for believers troubled at their lukewarm faith. Confirming that "Passive Obedience / More hard then Active is"

(196), Wigglesworth reiterates a comforting lesson of *The Day of Doom* by assuring believers struggling through a mundane and often difficult life that

> Thou still art serving Christ,
> Though in another way:
> And he thy Service will accept
> And crown another day. (196)

At one point "Rectified Judgment" administers the ultimate salve for readers trapped in self-doubt. Far from requiring a perfected faith, Christ asks only that the believer "Do what thou canst": "For God no more expects: / Where much he gives, he looks for much: / Where less, he less accepts" (197). Wigglesworth is not, of course, excusing sin or complacency. But his readers, like the implied readers of *Gods Determinations*, had reached a spiritual impasse stemming from a lack of Christian confidence, a paralyzing perfectionism that held back the conscience-stricken soul. Like Taylor, Wigglesworth assured his charges that no one could expect a consistently warm sense of assurance in a world where "Grief and Joy take turns" (242).

The promise of future strength and vision, a promise also central to Bradstreet's "Pilgrim" and Taylor's Meditations, becomes Wigglesworth's chief salve for easing the spiritual pressures of the reader's search for assurance in the here and now. Addressing those "in mind perplext, / And with Temptations strangely vext" (145) because they cannot savor the joys of belief, he confirms that God would have them "take and use" the "Cordials" of consolation: "Nor would he have us mourn like those, / In Christ that have no part" (237). At the heart of the text is Wigglesworth's goal of making readers *feel* more like saints. Their very doubts and insecurities, he points out, suggested the workings of the "godly Sorrow" which "eateth up, / That Sorrow that's unhallow'd" (235).

As in "God's Controversy," Wigglesworth's frequent use of "we" and "us" helps link reader and speaker in a pilgrim's identity. Only one poem in the entire sequence explicitly addresses reprobates, and the shift in reference is so clear that few readers would consider themselves earmarked for its message:

> Thus far we have apply'd
> Our Speech to mournful Saints,
> To chear them under all their Griefs,
> And silence their Complaints.
> But all Men are not Saints

> Whom Sorrow doth oppress:
> Some may be in a heavy case,
> Yet far from Holiness. (249)

But even in this theologically necessary concession that not all spiritual panic constituted an efficacious conviction, Wigglesworth retains his role as pastoral comforter. If God permitted it he would extend the sweetness of consolation even to the damned. "What shall we say to these," he asks, "That may some ease impart?" (249). At this point it is clear that "these" are *other* souls: speaker and reader are united not by a fear of damnation but by their pity for the damned. In the next stanza, when Wigglesworth addresses the unregenerate directly, his plea to these "Poor Souls" has the effect of an aside that the reader-as-saint is permitted to overhear: "peace to you I may not speak, / For God himself speaks none" (249). The reader, who *does* receive peace from the speaker throughout the poem, is safely distanced from the hopeless damned in the assurance that there is still time to "turn from every sin"—to turn "To God with all thine heart, / And make thy peace with him through Christ, / In Christ, Oh get a part" (250). Wigglesworth consistently reinforces the reader's identity as a self animated by the "happiest grieving" (250) of true contrition, a self for whom gracious paradoxes provoked joy rather than doubt. No riddle was too deep for faith to resolve, especially the riddle of salvation. If the speaker extends an opportunity to repent even to those who scarcely desired it, how much more comfort would the sequence bring to troubled readers who were separated from the "Peace" of assurance, as he repeatedly tells them, not by God's anger but by self-doubt?

"Riddles Unriddled" features a speaker who models saintly assurance for timid readers. In those poems not cast as inner dialogs, Wigglesworth adopts the voice of a fellow believer who, like the speaker of "God's Controversy," has suffered along with those whom he consoles:

> And now for want of strength
> And weakness Bodily,
> I could say much; For few, I think,
> Have felt it more then I.
> I have been many years
> So impotent and weak
> As none are able to conceive
> That onely hear me speak. (193)

Wigglesworth's humility as a fellow-sufferer is inseparable from the redemptive paradigm that he embodies in the text. By generalizing his experience, he offers his ill health as dramatic witness to the salvific uses of "weakness Bodily." Like Bradstreet, who also speaks as a self "By age and pains brought to decay," he translates physical frailty into an emblem of redemptive need, thereby rewriting himself as a guide to saintly perseverance.[9]

Precedent for this identity lay, as we have seen, in the poignant and frequent pleas for divine strength voiced throughout Scripture, especially in the Psalms, in Job, and in Paul's witness to the glories of affliction. It is Paul's text, also central to Bradstreet's "Pilgrim," that Wigglesworth cites when he biblicizes his illness: "And he said unto me, My grace is sufficient for thee: for my strength is made perfect in weakness. Most gladly therefore will I rather glory in my infirmities, that the power of Christ may rest upon me" (2 Cor. 12:9). Presenting his infirmities as a meditative aid for others, Wigglesworth also echoes David's confession that "my heart panteth, my strength faileth me: as for the light of mine eyes, it also is gone from me" (Ps. 38:10). Like the biblical poet, Wigglesworth resolves to serve God "In the most publick way." But like the Psalmist as well, he admits that "Such feebleness assails me / That I am like a man half dead, / All strength and vigour fails me" (194). Wigglesworth's "half dead" speaker, an embodiment of salvific self-dichotomizing into the fleshly Old Creature and the spiritual New Creature, encourages the same meditative separation from carnality within the reader. Such trials as those shared by speaker and reader could confirm and intensify the saint's better half. "As th' outward man decayes / And is consum'd away," Wigglesworth affirms, "The inward man thus gathereth strength / And vigour every day" (185). By articulating a dependence on Christ for deliverance from physical ills, Wigglesworth, like Bradstreet, repeatedly extends human weakness as proof of divine power: "strength in me there's none: / Therefore on thee the God of strength / I will depend alone" (194).

Bradstreet-like translations of personal experience into saintly pattern occur more frequently and explicitly in "Riddles Unriddled" than anywhere else in Wigglesworth's verse. Dramatizing the humility that he encourages within the reader, he enacts the true saint's desire not to "murmure, but abase / My self unto the dust" (181). "Hence we are never stronger," he insists, "Then when we are most weak" (193). When, at the beginning of "In Solitude Good Company," the poet briefly recalls the death of his wife and "The horrour of that Lonesomness, / (And state of Widowhood)" by which he felt "estranged farre" from God (226), he cements the bond of compassion by which one saint consoles another. Bradstreet effects the same bond when she laments the deaths of grandchildren and the burning of her house, as does Taylor when he grieves for his first wife and two daughters and when he recreates, in *Gods Determinations*, the terrified helplessness of the convicted soul. In all of these poems the confession of weakness unites speaker with reader in their shared dependence on divine help. "If my Trials had been thine," Wigglesworth attests after introducing the riddles that he is about to treat, "These would Cheer thee more then Wine" (144). The affliction that unites speaker and reader in turn invokes the consolation available only within a redeemed community of compassionate believers. "Joy in Sorrow" offers particular witness to the "Comfort" available "To Saints in misery," who "sorrow not alone: / But meet with some that heartily / Their Miseries bemoan" (246). Speaking as one of the reader's "sweet Companions," Wigglesworth offers poetry as a concrete demonstration that "It yields some comfort and relief / T'have Fellow-sufferers" (244).

"Riddles Unriddled" appropriately projects the full measure of gracious comfort into the reader's probable future as glorified saint. In Song 4 of "Heavenly Crowns for Thorny Wreaths" the saints in heaven enjoy a bliss scarcely conceivable to earthly pilgrims, especially those whose spiritual flatness has been addressed throughout the sequence. But Wigglesworth softens the daunting otherness of heaven by equating the past of the celestial saint, whose "Labour's at an end" and whose "seed in tears was sown" (271), with the current reality of the reader, whose anticipation of a gracious self-to-be is strengthened by the confirmation that "tears" were once shed by those now in glory. By emphasizing a continuity of afflicted present with celestial future and of troubled earthly believers with those "happy, happy Souls" in heaven, Wigglesworth gave his readers every reason to hope for their own heavenly crowns.

Carefully placing religious anxiety within salvific psychological structures invoked through the act of reading, Wigglesworth defines the reading self as the chief "riddle" that he addresses, the final experiential locus of the paradoxes that he explicates. At once confirming that "Nature cannot reach" such mysteries (223) and clearly lining out their secrets, he offers reading as a means of transcending "Nature" itself. At the beginning of "Joy in Sorrow" he makes explicit the goal of transforming the reader from a timid Nicodemus who wonders "How can these things be?" into an experienced pilgrim, a Nathaniel brought to Christ by the poet as a latter-day Philip (236). As in *The Day of Doom*, such transformation demanded that anxiety be channeled into clearly articulated alternatives. "Which is the better choice," Wigglesworth demands, "With Christ in Bliss to dwell, / Or for to roar eternally / Amidst the flames of Hell?" (268). Leaving the reader little room to maneuver, his mock exhortation to "chuse to burn, if that be best" clarifies access to the strait gate through which the "keys" for the various riddles (143, 189) offer entry. Reading can change perception, and perception, reality. As Wigglesworth claims, "whoso reads our Lines, / If God but give him eyes" will accept these riddles as "no Tales, / But Spiritual Mysteries" (201).

Specific textual strategies by which the reader is led toward optimistic self-experience are clearest in the first and longest sequence, "Light in Darkness." Song 1 introduces two figures, spiritual parallels to the Overburian characters so popular in England early in the century. The first is a "child of Light" (146) who is "in mind perplext" (145). Although his "state is very good," he "walks in sadness, in the night, / Till this be understood" (146). In the inevitable contrast with the second character, the "child of Darkness" who "thinks his ill state very good" (146), the reader's fears are immediately cast in the most sympathetic "Light" imaginable. It is Satan, the true saint's enemy, who makes troubled readers "see no Light / Which round about them shines" (147). Frustration at *not* seeing, Wigglesworth consoles, is evidence of a soul to whom Christ will surely speak "comfort" at the "accepted time." Having defined an identity to be sought with greater confidence, "Light in Darkness" enacts the process by which this identity could be activated and confirmed. This process begins when the speaker invites "poor distressed Souls" to "hear your Grievances" and "Learn how you may with Spiritual Arms / Temptations force repress" (148). The ambiguity of "hear" is important. Readers are urged not just to "hear" their troubles recounted in the text but to voice them in a "hearing" as they assimilate the psychology dramatized there. In short, Wigglesworth introduces readers to themselves, inviting them to overhear a debate between doubt and faith presented not as theological abstractions but as conflicting halves of the reading self. Like Taylor's *Gods Determinations* and Bradstreet's "The Flesh and the Spirit," "Riddles Unriddled" redefines "Soul-sinkings" (148) as viable redemptive activity. The light/dark paradox, like the seven others, stimulates the reader's experience of the psychomachia central to this activity, hopeful evidence of the "double form" that made possible, as William Ames confirmed, the "spiritual war" that these parts waged in "a daily renewal of repentance."[10]

Songs 2 through 6 encourage the reader's sense of doubleness through a series of debates by which despair, voiced by "Flesh" and "Distressed Conscience," is distanced from the reader's identity. Flesh, accusing

Christ of raising false hopes "that all my debts / were wholly cancelled" (148), complains that God "will not hear my suit for grace, / But wounds and casts me down" (149). If salvation were really at hand, Flesh claims, God "would more gently deal: / Nor would he always use the Rod, / But sometimes help and heal" (150). "Spirit" and "Rectified Judgment" counter these naggings by pointing out that if divine anger had been truly unleashed, Flesh—the carnal self—would no longer even exist: if God had "us'd extremities / Thou hadst been now in Hell" (151). Equating religious doubt with afflictions suffered by those "most dear" to God, Spirit invokes Jacob, Moses, Joseph, the Jews in bondage, Job, David, and Heman as biblical predecessors of the anxious reader. Such "Chastisements," Wigglesworth consoles, do not create sin; they merely "shew what was / Within the heart before" (156). The reader's sadness should trigger hope. As Rectified Judgment confirms, whoever "mourns because he mourns no more, / This man repents I trust" (158).

The reader begins to see the stubbornness of resisting Gospel consolation even if Flesh does not. Songs 5 and 6 further separate the reader's essential identity from carnal doubt by once again confirming that it is Satan who "now assayes / To ruine" Spirit through Flesh's speech (161). Satan's agency connects the reader's anxiety with the "thorn in the flesh" that Paul called a "messenger of Satan to buffet me, lest I should be exalted above measure" (2 Cor. 12:7). Like Satan's "accusations" in Taylor's *Gods Determinations*, the Flesh/Satan link dramatizes the "mighty power / Of Unbelief" that "prevails / From time to time!" (161). Attacking the satanic Flesh as "a treacherous Thief, / That robs me of my Faith, and then / Condemns for Unbelief," Spirit models the internalized Fall of an efficacious conviction, with false "wisdom" issuing from Flesh as a "Serpents mouth" invading the garden of the doubting self. In this inner Eden, however, temptation is overcome when Spirit decides *not* to debate any longer and commands Flesh to "Leave off thy Reasonings." Like Bradstreet, who articulates the same shutting off of doubt when Spirit orders her "unregenerate part" to "Disturb no more my settled heart," Wigglesworth in effect rearranges the reader's interiority by splitting off the fleshly self and offering Christ to fill the resulting void.[11] The Lord, Spirit asserts, "will compleat my Faith, / Weak though it be" (162).

Once the debates end, Wigglesworth's pastoral speaker reappears in Song 7 to drive home the consolatory results of saintly doubleness:

> Well, let it humble thee
> To feel a treacherous part:

> A sinful Self; a wicked Flesh
> Remaining in my heart.
> Yet for thy comfort know,
> Thou hast not lost the field,
> So long as thou do'st sin resist,
> And striveth not to yield. (165)

Speaker and reader are united in Songs 7 through 9 as opponents of the "sinful Self" in a struggle that brings redemptive catharsis to those safely enclosed within a redeemed community. There is, Wigglesworth consoles, "some support" in knowing that "we're not alone, / But that through such a dismal way / Some have before us gone" (164). Having exposed "vile" thoughts as "the Devils sins" and "Not thine who mournest under them / And hat'st them with thy soul" (165), he seals the reader's assurance in the promise that Christ "hath the Devil fast, / And holds him in a Chain" (166). An optimistic self-reading stemming from the conviction of carnal identity enacted in the text confirms the reader's right to "Be not too much dismay'd, / Nor 'stonished with fear" (167).

In Song 9, the first of "Two Songs in other Meetre" added to "close up all the sweeter" (170), biblical language becomes the preferred expression of this assurance. Wigglesworth's speaker becomes a neo-Psalmist who waits "for the Lord" and hopes "in his Word" (170), a personal embodiment and exemplum of the inner war mapped out in the verse. The last poem of the sequence, "A Dialogue or Discourse between the *Believing Soul* and her *Savior*," takes the final step by eliminating the mediating speaker altogether. Having undergone the redemptive self-division of the debates, a reintegrated "Soul" now speaks in the first person with a rekindled assurance suggested by a direct colloquy with Christ. Christ's response to this "poor distressed Soul" (172) is as gentle as Spirit's rebuke had been harsh. This Christ, the homiletic and experiential antithesis of the harsh Judge of *The Day of Doom*, demands far less perfection than does the reader's own conscience. His promise "To save and succour thee" (172), like Christ's lullaby in *Gods Determinations* ("Peace, Peace, my Hony, do not Cry"), articulates a Savior theologically and perceptually appropriate to readers convinced that excessive self-doubt was as great a hindrance to salvation as willful unbelief.[12]

This was, in the Puritan view, precisely how Christ appeared to those whose legal fear had been conquered by gracious love. By encouraging an experience of Christ in this manifestation, "Light in Darkness" consoled readers that their inner struggles merely reflected turmoil that plagued all children of light. Readers longing to assimilate inner patterns set forth in the poetry needed to learn that the key to transforming affliction into assurance was not the self-doubting mind but the assenting heart. Puritan readers would have felt themselves to be the deepest "riddle" explicated in Wigglesworth's text. Moreover, the perception of an inner life that was part of God's plan would have brought them considerable comfort. This suggests why the popular view of Wigglesworth as a heartless thunderer of irrevocable doom is a serious misreading. While *The Day of Doom* offered a predominantly "legal" sentence designed to push readers toward an efficacious conviction, "Riddles Unriddled" offered a "gospel" sentence that encouraged the reader's textual experience as a saintly metaself. Appropriately, the pilgrimage from darkness to light ends with Soul's willingness to serve and to praise, however faintly the "light" of Christ's face penetrates the "darkness" of a still-earthly self: "Let this sweet face of thine / Upon me allways shine" (175). Insisting that the brightest source of illumination was simply the face of Christ, Wigglesworth helped troubled readers eclipse the dark glass of sin and self to imagine that the smile reserved for the elect was directed at them.

Cotton Mather's description of the Malden pastor as "a *Faithful Physician* for the *Body* as well as the *Soul*" offers a fair summary of artistic goals that the poet set for himself. In an introductory poem to *The Day of Doom*, Wigglesworth urged the "Christian Reader" to "Accept" his work "in Love" and to "read it for thy good: / There's nothing in't can do thee hurt, / If rightly understood" (7). Encouraging his readers to "make the Judge thy Friend," he forged a corresponding identity in the text as their "real Friend, and Servant" (8), promoting their spiritual healing through a voice that spoke clearly and comfortably to their condition. Like all successful physicians, the former Harvard tutor assessed that condition well and was, as a result, more widely read than any other poet in early New England. As Samuel Eliot Morison once said of his verse, "very seldom in history has an intellectual class succeeded so well in breaking through to the common consciousness."[13]

Wigglesworth wrote poems that Puritan readers experienced not as detached texts but as catalysts and echoes of their own feelings. His major strength as a popular artist lay in his skillful control of those feelings, particularly the degree of the reader's religious anxiety. Promoting a contrition that generated its own transcendence, he repeatedly sought a reading response articulated by Soul in "Riddles Unriddled":

> ... I see I have too long
> Me with my self compar'd,
> And by much poreing on my self
> Have been too much ensnar'd. (180)

By framing rhetorical escapes from self-obsession, he taught readers to scrutinize their spiritual status without becoming "ensnar'd" by the sin that they found there. For these readers his verse, far from provoking an unrelieved confrontation with guilt and sin, clarified and hence allayed religious fears. The message underlying all his work, including *The Day of Doom*, is enunciated at the end of "God's Controversy with New-England": "Cheer on, sweet souls, my heart is with you all" (102). This consolation was inseparable from his insistent focus on broad redemptive patterns voiced by a generalized speaker who combined spiritual and artistic ideals. If it is even harder to find the "real" Wigglesworth in the poetry than the "real" Bradstreet or Taylor, it is because we are looking for a particularized self that he, like all believers, labored to overcome. The preaching saint who speaks in his verse was, from his perspective, the most significant and useful identity that he could possibly offer any reader.

The same could be said for the relentless biblicism of his diction and imagery. For Wigglesworth, mere human language, even if used with the most pious intentions, could never adequately describe the divine schema. "Who can tell," he asks toward the close of *The Day of Doom*, the "torments exquisite" and "dismal state" of the damned (63)? In the "Postscript" he reaffirms that "those Torments are an hundred fold / More terrible than ever you were told" (77). The celestial bliss of saints in glory is equally "beyond what thought / can reach, or words express" (66). Paraphrasing 1 Corinthians 13:1, he acknowledges that neither "tongues of men (nor Angels pen)" can begin to convey Christ's glory: "And therefore I must pass it by," he adds, "lest speaking should transgress" (14). And toward the end of the doomsday epic, when the narrative might seem to call for some description of the saints' reward, he adopts the biblical device of depicting their joy in terms of what it is *not*, as an absence of earthly "distress and heaviness," which "are vanished like dreams" (66). In the face of the verbal corruption that for Puritans was inseparable from the postlapsarian condition, Wigglesworth's nearly exclusive use of biblical language was not just the safest course for a poet to take but the most accurate.

The sheer theological content of Wigglesworth's work—the emphasis on sound doctrine and proper scriptural interpretation—is high even for Puritan verse. The reason is not that Wigglesworth operated under a different poetic from that of Bradstreet or Taylor but that he adapted that poetic to a more public writing and reading situation. Given his broad audience, it was necessary that he set forth doctrine so clearly as to risk prosaic statement. His readership also accounts for the fact that his invocation of the Puritan metaself is more explicit, more obviously paradigmatic, than in Bradstreet's and Taylor's private verse. His concern with clearly and comprehensively lining out the traits of the saved soul prompted him to deemphasize the specific events of everyday life in favor of broad redemptive patterns. While Bradstreet and Taylor often write within daily situational and meditative contexts and thus provide glimpses of particular moments in the saint's pilgrimage, Wigglesworth paints a broader portrait of sanctity that is largely abstracted from the ongoing give-and-take of Puritan life and devotion. He is less concerned with how the saint reacts to the world than with who and what, in general terms, the saint *is* in the world.

Wigglesworth was not more solidly "Puritan" than Bradstreet and Taylor; if he seems so, it is simply because he tried to address the spiritual needs of more Puritans. Working this broader canvas, he translated the Puritan view of the self and the world into accessible and often dramatic verse. He made his readers feel, as recipients of the admonitory and consolatory power of Scripture itself, that their inner turmoil would likely find resolution in a celestial future. In so doing, he conveys an especially vivid sense of the communal dimension of Puritan experience — of how it must have felt to derive comfort from one's hoped-for identity as a member of Christ's Bride. Given his collective themes, he is even more effective than Bradstreet or Taylor in casting the myth of New England as New Israel into verbal celebrations of sacred historiography, poetic encouragements for readers to take their place within that myth. Still, he did not neglect salvation on the most personal of levels. His surgeonlike exposing of the "sinful Self" remaining in the reader's heart provided exactly what Puritan readers demanded from poetry that offered the greatest spiritual good to the greatest number.

Part Three

The Pilgrimage Lived: Anne Bradstreet

> But give me, Lord, a better heart,
>   Then better shall I be,
> To pay the vows which I do owe
>   Forever unto Thee.
>
> Unless Thou help, what can I do
>   But still my frailty show?
> If Thou assist me, Lord, I shall
>   Return Thee what I owe.

—Anne Bradstreet, "In My Solitary Hours in my Dear Husband His Absence"

CHAPTER FOUR

"SETTING UP MY EBENEZER": ANNE BRADSTREET

AND THE EXAMINED SELF

There is an assumption in much of the criticism that Anne Bradstreet wrote two distinct sets of poems, each revealing opposing sides of a conflicted personality. One group, which includes straightforward affirmations of faith like "As Weary Pilgrim," reveals a poet working well within the expected limits of Puritan art and belief. Despite its more private and meditative situation, "Pilgrim" embodies a poetic essentially similar to Wigglesworth's in its biblical themes, its accessible imagery and, perhaps especially, its generalized, pious speaker. The second group, which receives far more commentary, reveals an ambitious Renaissance poet who achieved at best an uneasy peace with her religion and society. If we concentrate on this latter set of poems—the anguished elegies on grandchildren, the conflicted poem on the burning of her house, her attacks on male literati in the "Prologue," perhaps even the cosmological and historical poems that made up the bulk of the first edition of her work—it is not difficult to find a reluctant Puritan, a rebellious spirit for whom writing a poem like "Pilgrim" must have seemed almost an act of capitulation. When we try to account for both sets of poems, we find a consciousness split along corresponding lines. What Ann Stanford called the "dogmatist" and the "rebel" become barely reconcilable poles whose interaction provides the tension that gives the poetry its interest and vitality.[1]

An emphasis on themes that transcend particular times and places—themes like gender dynamics, psychological conflict, and cultural alienation—has had considerable value in enhancing Bradstreet's significance for twentieth-century readers, releasing her once and for all from the patronizing nineteenth-century assumption that despite her genuine "poetic endowment," the "vast bulk of her writing consists not of poetry, but of metrical theology and chronology and politics and physics."[2] This new appreciation has come, however, at the cost of oversimplifying her themes and techniques and isolating her work from its seventeenth-century context. It is entirely consistent with modern aesthetic preferences that the rebel in Bradstreet interests us more than the dogmatist. But as is the case with Wigglesworth, *our* experience of Bradstreet's poetry tends to overshadow how its initial readers may have read it. Moreover, given the historical framework provided by poets like Wigglesworth, whose work seems almost to be speaking from a different world, we often assume that Bradstreet's poetry was an anomaly within Puritan literary culture. Ironically, her very strengths as a poet are partly to blame for our difficulty in defining her relation to her Puritan milieu. No other Puritan poet reads so well today, and as a result, no one else is so hard to read historically.

Although some of her poems project undeniable anger, rebellion, and poetic ambition, these emotions acquire a different significance when seen within the Puritan experience of texts and self. Reading Bradstreet in this way suggests a need to qualify the widespread view of a poet who wrote to escape restrictive forces in her culture. The real problem in assessing her relation to that culture is not whether she expresses doubt and rebellion but whether we have been too quick to see such expressions as unusual. The struggling speaker of the family elegies, "The Flesh and the Spirit," and the house-fire poem does not repudiate Puritan interiority but reconfirms it, voicing frank confessions of spiritual turmoil that were inseparable from the faith's demands for honest self-scrutiny. Biographical evidence might seem to support an unusual rebellion in the poet. Yet the well-known confession that her "heart rose" at the "new world and new manners" in Massachusetts Bay was consistent with the orthodox reading of the earthly pilgrimage, including the pilgrimage to New England, as a series of God-sent trials. Indeed, few Puritan autobiographical texts fail to record similar conflict.[3]

Further, the assumption that much of Bradstreet's poetry risked offending Puritan sensibilities does not square well with her popularity on both sides of the Atlantic. Serious danger of censure would likely have resulted in either the complete suppression of these poems or a more skillful concealing of her troubled spirit. But she made no effort to keep inner struggle out of her poetry. And despite the fact that many of her poems actually focus on it, she was honored with a second and enlarged edition only six years after her death. Finally, if we exaggerate her sense of alienation from Puritan religion or society, we unintentionally undermine the artistic and psychological integrity of her work. If we assume on the one hand that she was sincere when she wrote "As Weary Pilgrim," we are forced to read the more rebellious poems as evidence of a lack of spiritual or artistic control. If, on the other hand, we define rebellion as her deepest and most "real" trait, we are forced to see "Pilgrim" as sadly self-deluding, perhaps even insincere. By connecting her apparent vacillations between piety and doubt to post-Romantic modes of personal expression, we assume that she was unable to reconcile opposing forces within herself simply because we cannot do so.[4]

Puritan models of self-experience permit the dogmatist and the rebel to coexist within a single ideological framework and, perhaps most important, within a single coherent personality. As we have seen, confessing a fallen resistance to God's ways was necessary for confirming a pilgrim identity. Because poetry written as a catalyst for this process necessarily stressed the speaker's need for divine correction, a motive beyond individual expression, as we usually define it, informs Bradstreet's articulations of spiritual conflict. John Harvard Ellis suggested long ago that her "doubts and fears" may have been "exaggerated in number and importance by her tender conscience." "Selected" seems more accurate than "exaggerated": her ongoing concern with humility and with the redemptive uses of suffering accounts for her emphasis on the difficulties, both within and without, that beset the earthly pilgrim. The range of emotions conveyed in her work was not foreign to Puritan definitions of that pilgrimage. On the contrary, there is no mood in her verse, however dark, that was not an acceptable and even expected part of Puritan identity and of the redemptive patterns that gave it shape.[5]

What Bradstreet and Wigglesworth have in common becomes clearer in light of this self-experience. If she seems more "modern" in her expressions of conflict, it is not because he accepted easily what she could not, but because she addressed a more intimate rhetorical situation and audience. Many of her poems, especially those that record personal or family events, were probably written for private circulation among friends and loved ones. While Wigglesworth ministered through published verse to readers whom he would never meet, Bradstreet forged a voice consistent with the goal of translating private events into consolatory lessons for readers whom she knew and loved. As we have seen, Wigglesworth only rarely drew examples from his personal life — the death of his wife, his physical infirmities — to confirm and illustrate the earthly workings of redemption. Bradstreet, by contrast, placed her own life at the very center of her work, thereby transforming personal events into dramatic witnessings to a pilgrim's experience of the self and the world.

Bradstreet's continuing appeal, especially in contrast to Wigglesworth, also reflects the fact that much of her poetry is meditative as well as hortatory. Although she shared Wigglesworth's goal of writing to enlighten and edify readers, her finest poems are self- as well as other-directed, and her lessons are enhanced by the drama of watching her speaker absorb them as well. At once confessional and didactic, her poetry embodies the Puritan consciousness looking simultaneously within and without. As Stanford notes, "Poetry for her could never become merely 'self-expression' for always behind it lies the concept of utility."[6] Repeatedly giving her life utility as a spiritual parable, she advised her children in the "Meditations Divine and Moral" that whoever "glories in his gifts and adornings should look upon his corruptions, and that will damp his high thoughts" (273). Confirming that the "sincerest Christian" has "the least self-love," she commended adversity as a spur to spiritual vigilance: "a prosperous state makes a secure Christian, but adversity makes him consider." This renunciation of "self-love" consistently shapes the identity projected in the poetry. "That house which is not often swept makes the cleanly inhabitant soon loath it," she insisted, "and that heart which is not continually purifying itself is no fit temple for the spirit of God to dwell in" (275). Poetry offered one means of enacting this self-sweeping, of pursuing the ongoing assessment of spiritual standing necessary for achieving a pilgrim's humility. The snares of this world demanded nothing less. "He that walks among briars and thorns," she warned, "will be very careful where he sets his foot, and he that passes through the wilderness of this world had need ponder all his steps" (276). By pondering her steps and recording the results in autobiographical poems, she effected her search for the saintly metaself sought by all believers.

In her brief autobiography Bradstreet told her children of her diligent emulation of Samson in setting up "my Ebenezer" (243), the altar of her faith. Her poetry, essential to building and maintaining this altar, recorded acts of pious self-examination by which her earthly roles as daughter, wife, mother, teacher, and poet found integration within what she considered to be her deepest and most significant identity. Because her family readers needed to see that the pilgrimage was difficult, she not only described the pilgrim way but dramatized it through a speaker who is unquestionably conflicted but potentially redeemed in the very honesty with which she confesses that conflict. The Ebenezer was Samson's celebration that "Hitherto hath the Lord helped us" overcome the Philistines (1 Sam. 7:12). Wigglesworth literally drew this altar into his diary as an emblem of gratitude, labeling it "A pillar to the prayse of his grace" in thanksgiving for "his former mercys received in answer to prayer." For Bradstreet, poetry constituted just such a monument to a saint's persistent struggle against the world. As witnesses to faith erected for all to see, her poetic confirmations of gracious experience and identity celebrated God's help in her battle against the rising heart and sinful self that plagued all earthly pilgrims.[7]

Consistent with the Puritan search for God's work within the self, Bradstreet repeatedly connects societal and familial roles with the paradigm of the saved soul. This reading of individual lives as generalized redemptive stories is especially clear in her family elegies. To commemorate saints, Puritan elegists insisted, was to celebrate sanctity itself, a theme set forth in the biblical model for all elegies, a text that Bradstreet paraphrased as "David's Lamentation for Saul and Jonathan." Following her scriptural source closely, she points up the universal question prompted by all saintly deaths: "How did the mighty fall, and falling die?" (199). David's response, in Bradstreet's version, was to celebrate the virtue personified in the deceased, who were "Swifter than swiftest eagles" and "Stronger than lions ramping for their prey." Bradstreet applied the Davidic focus on generalized patterns of sanctity to her lament for her father as "guide" and "instructor" (201), the ideal parent who labored, as she later defined her own parental role, "till Christ be formed" in his children (241). Thomas Dudley's political calling as one of the "Founders" and a "True patriot of this little commonweal" (201) similarly embodies the saintly metaself active in the world: "Truth's friend thou wert, to errors still a foe, / Which caused apostates to malign so" (202). In death Dudley offers a paternal version of the same personality articulated in "As Weary Pilgrim": "Upon the earth he did not build his nest, / But as a pilgrim, what he had, possessed." Like the speaker of "Pilgrim," Dudley's "ambition lay above," as evidenced by his preoccupation with the heavenly "mansion" that awaited him. Facing his end "with a smiling cheer," he undergoes the easeful death of the saint whom grace has made "fully ripe" for the next world: "Death as a sickle hath him timely mown." What the poem actually celebrates is not Thomas Dudley the individual but the redeemed identity that he achieved, an identity potentially attainable by his survivors. The deepest comfort for Bradstreet and her family lay in his saintly "legacy" (202), "His pious footsteps" that "will bring us to that happy place / Where we with joy each other's face shall see, / And parted more by death shall never be" (203). As the brief "Epitaph" suggests, the passing of such a self tested the spiritual standing of all who knew him: "The good him loved, the bad did fear, / And when his time with years was spent, / If some rejoiced, more did lament." Like other Puritan elegists, Bradstreet rewrites the deceased into an affirmative touchstone of the survivors' faith.

The same dynamic informs the poem for her mother, an equally paradigmatic "matron of unspotted life, / A loving mother and obedient wife" (204). Although Dorothy Dudley, "To servants wisely awful, but yet kind," embodies the divine dichotomy of justice and mercy, she replicates the saintly paradigm most fully in her role as "A true instructor of her family, / The which she ordered with dexterity." Such outward harmony manifests the inner grace that Bradstreet presents as the reason for a life so well lived:

> Religious in all her words and ways,
> Preparing still for death, till end of days:
> Of all her children, children lived to see,
> Then dying, left a blessed memory.

Bradstreet's mother achieves "blessed memory" precisely because her legible saintly qualities transcend the merely personal. In rhetoric as in theological assumption, Dorothy Dudley exemplifies a victory over carnal selfhood. This imposition of saintly pattern—or from a Puritan perspective, its discovery—constitutes the core of a life not just well lived but accurately read and remembered.[8]

As the speaker of "As Weary Pilgrim" reveals, such structured readings of human experience were by no means limited to the dead. In the poems to her husband Bradstreet celebrates her marriage as a confirmation of the same gracious pattern, as yet another manifestation of divine influences within the human realm. In "To My Dear and Loving Husband," for example, she praises Simon in language that recalls the saint's bond with Christ:

> If ever two were one, then surely we.
> If ever man were loved by wife, then thee;
> If ever wife was happy in a man,
> Compare with me, ye women, if you can. (225)

Bradstreet reinforces the spiritual underpinnings of her marriage by echoing the challenge issued by the Daughters of Jerusalem for the Canticles Bride to justify her "beloved more than another beloved" (Cant. 5:9). The religious validation of marital love is furthered when the poet gently mocks the conventions of the Elizabethan sonnet. Like the world itself, such language as "whole mines of gold," "the riches that the East doth hold," and the love that "rivers cannot quench" exists only to be transcended. In the end plain words undercut the traditional discourse of secular love:

> Thy love is such I can no way repay,
> The heavens reward thee manifold, I pray.
> Then while we live, in love let's so persevere
> That when we live no more, we may live ever.

Like divine love, earthly love demanded an expression emptied of pride. Earthly union derives validation from the spiritual, and as the poem closes, Bradstreet gently pulls her marriage and the language describing it from this world to the next.

The other poems to Simon also extol the marriage as an "emblem" of the saint's union with Christ, through which, as Rosamond Rosenmeier observes, the poet effects a "reconciliation of divided forces" of earth and heaven made possible by the unobtrusive biblicism informing her descriptions of their love. In "A Letter to Her Husband, Absent Upon Public Employment," her separation from Simon recalls Paul's comparison of Christ as the "head" of the Church to a husband as "the head of the wife" (Eph. 5:23). Bradstreet enters this hierarchy by invoking the "neck" of faith that joins Redeemer to redeemed: "So many steps, head from the heart to sever, / If but a neck, soon should we be together" (226). Commentator James Durham offered the standard reading of the neck of the true Bride as "the vigorous exercise of the grace of faith" that unites the believer "to Christ the head." Bradstreet domesticates the image by equating faith and love in a marital reconfirmation of biblical zeal, bonding the earthly with the sacred by linking her marriage with the divinely instituted joining of Adam and Eve in Genesis 2:23: "Flesh of thy flesh, bone of thy bone, / I here, thou there, yet both but one." Even "Phoebus make haste," the most secular of the marriage poems, invokes scriptural language to describe the speaker's love-longing:

> He that can tell the stars or ocean sand,
> Or all the grass that in the meads do stand,
> The leaves in th' woods, the hail, or drops of rain,
> Or in a corn-field number every grain,
> Or every mote that in the sunshine hops,
> May count my sighs, and number all my drops. (227)

By recalling God's promise to Abraham that "I will multiply thy seed as the stars of the heaven, and as the sand which is upon the sea shore"

(Gen. 22:17), Bradstreet lends biblical resonance to the procreative dimension of her marriage. Like the other social relationships addressed in the verse, marriage confirms the continuity of earth and heaven. The husband celebrated in these poems is less Simon Bradstreet than the idealized spouse, an earthly counterpart of the Christic Bridegroom who validates the speaker's marital role as part of a larger text and a holier self authored by a merciful God.[9]

By describing her loved ones in biblical terms, Bradstreet did not think that she was glossing over their "real" personalities; rather, she was placing them within a salvific framework that superseded worldly particulars. Such a reading of lives acted out Paul's assertion that "we are saved by hope" (Rom. 8:24). As her qualifier in the elegy to daughter-in-law Mercy suggests ("I trust"), such hope reflected the poet's faith in Christ's ability to transform a human life into a pilgrimage to glory. By defining herself in relation to such idealized Others as her parents and her husband, Bradstreet helped clarify her own identity as well. Like her autobiographical letter, poetry helped her connect personal events with an experience of self that made her feel capable not only of walking the pilgrim path but of demonstrating it to others. What repeatedly marks her verse is not a desire to escape from theological structures, but a persistent attempt to reconfirm their vitalizing presence in her life. The turmoil recorded in her verse, like that confessed in the letter, signaled the saintly doubleness that brought comfort as well as distress.[10]

Accordingly, each social role addressed in the poetry—daughter, wife, mother, even poet-historian—is subsumed under the broader paradigm of the saintly metaself. Bradstreet retells her life, as Rosenmeier observes in another context, in order to ensure "the existence in her of a 'real' nature, or self, that will *be*, despite all change."[11] As a Puritan woman she concentrated on unifying the saintly with the familial as the most direct link between who she was and who she hoped to become through grace. This conflating of the salvific with the domestic runs in both directions: just as she portrays her familial ties in spiritual terms, she consistently describes her relation to God with scriptural metaphors of family intimacy appropriate to the saint's adoption by Christ. "Lord," she asks in a prose meditation, "why should I doubt any more when Thou hast given me such assured pledges of Thy love? First, Thou art my Creator, I Thy creature, Thou my master, I Thy servant. But hence arises not my comfort, Thou art my Father, I Thy child; 'Ye shall be My sons and daughters,' saith the Lord Almighty. Christ is my brother, I ascend unto my Father, and your Father, unto my God and your God; but lest this should not be enough, thy maker is thy husband. Nay more, I am a member of His body, He my head" (250).

Bradstreet's most frequent role in relation to God, as was the case with most Puritans, is as a child who receives loving correction. She admitted to her children that "I have been with God like an untoward child, that no longer than the rod has been on my back (or at least in sight) but I have been apt to forget Him and myself, too" (242). In the "Meditations Divine and Moral" she attested that while some children require "salt" to keep them from "putrefaction, some again [are] like tender fruits that are best preserved with sugar" (273–74). Seven years earlier she had applied this image to God's dealings with her: "I have not been refined in the furnace of affliction as some have been, but have rather been preserved with sugar than brine, yet will He preserve me to His heavenly kingdom" (257). Consistently defining herself in terms of a paternal Other, Bradstreet reenacts Paul's confession to speaking "as a child" in this life, with the limited spiritual capacities of all who still peer "through a glass, darkly" (1 Cor. 13:11–12). The childlike stance lends spiritual overtones, naturally enough, to the poet's self-definition relative to her parents. In the dedicatory poem to the Quaternions she playfully addresses Thomas Dudley as a God-like father "Who must reward a thief, but with his due" (14). But like God, Dudley also has a "mild aspect," and in her submissive role as dutiful daughter Bradstreet articulates a domestic version of the saintly split between pious intentions and flawed performance: "Accept my best, my worst vouchsafe a grave." The witty poem "To Her Father With Some Verses" similarly asserts earthly and heavenly continuities by addressing Thomas as a "worthy self" from whom she has derived whatever "worth" she possesses (231). Here, too, a daughter's gratitude to her father mirrors the believer's homage to God: "Such is my bond, none can discharge but I, / Yet paying is not paid until I die." In relation to Dorothy Dudley as the ideal saint-as-parent, Bradstreet likewise speaks as the dutiful saint-as-child who profits from the "blessed memory" of her mother as a holy woman "of unspotted life" (204).

A similar psychological dynamic informs the marriage poems, in which the devoted wife to Simon becomes an earthly manifestation of the faithful Bride of Christ. Reflecting "In My Solitary Hours in my Dear Husband His Absence," Bradstreet attests that

> Though children Thou has given me,
> And friends I have also,

> Yet if I see Thee not through them,
> They are no joy, but woe. (268)

Although these lines seem a straightforward statement of devotion to an absent husband, they are addressed not to Simon but to God. Transferring her deepest loyalty to the celestial Bridegroom in a union that validates her earthly marriage, Bradstreet embodies the character of the good wife by incorporating her marital role into the spiritual identity that she seeks. The other marriage poems similarly conflate self-as-spouse with self-as-saint, most notably "To My Dear and Loving Husband," which offers Simon an affectionate exhortation to "persevere" in their love that "we may live ever" (225).

Bradstreet's complementary roles of child and bride intensified her assurance by affirming points of contact between the sacred and the secular in her life. As particularized confirmations of a pilgrim self, these roles facilitated her meditative trying on of saintly personality. Although such a self-reading could be broadly delineated in non-situational poems like "The Vanity of All Worldly Things" and "As Weary Pilgrim," Bradstreet found its clearest test in the specific events of everyday life. As she attested, "Many can speak well, but few can do well. We are better scholars in the theory than in the practic part, but he is a true Christian that is a proficient in both" (272). An exercising of the "practic part" of her faith informs all of the poems occasioned by specific events. In testimonies of good fortune and deliverance, such as the celebrations of her husband's and son's safe return or her recoveries from illness, she voices the true believer's gratitude for mercies received. Poems treating darker events, such as the elegies on her grandchildren and the lament for the burning of her house, act out the pious mandate to accept tragedy as divine correction and to trust that Christ would someday put all things right. Like the letter to her children, the poetry was written not "to show my skill, but to declare the truth, not to set forth myself, but the glory of God" (240). Such artistic goals demanded that she stress those traits and events by which a pilgrim identity could be more deeply internalized and more clearly taught.

For Bradstreet, affliction and deliverance bore equal witness to redemptive experience. "There is no object that we see," she insists in her "Meditations Divine and Moral," "no action that we do, no good that we enjoy, no evil that we feel or fear, but we may make some spiritual advantage of all; and he that makes such improvement is wise as well as pious" (272). Trials held special value because they made God's blessings all the more evident. "If we had no winter," she affirms, "the spring would not be so pleasant; if we did not sometimes taste of adversity, prosperity would not be so welcome" (274). Affliction also furthered the pious search for sincere humility: "A low man can go upright under that door where a taller is glad to stoop; so a man of weak faith and mean abilities may undergo a cross more patiently than he that excels him both in gifts and graces" (274). Bradstreet's concern with writing the gracious cycles of affliction and deliverance into clearly legible form makes even her treatments of intensely private events seem, as Adrienne Rich notes, "curiously impersonal as poetry." [12] The generalized pilgrim voice is perhaps strongest in the "Meditations When my Soul hath been Refreshed with the Consolations which the World Knows Not" (250). The title suggests the extrapersonal dimension of these pieces: the self whose spiritual progress they chart links Anne Bradstreet the individual with the paradigm of a true believer passing through the world. Most of these "Meditations" in fact contain only extremely general accounts of the circumstances that inspired them. Without their descriptive titles we would be hard-pressed even to identify many of the events that she contemplates.

"If outward blessings be not as wings to help us mount upwards," Bradstreet states in one of the prose "Meditations Divine and Moral," "they will certainly prove clogs and weights that will pull us lower downward" (288). The "Meditations When my Soul hath been Refreshed" repeatedly enact such meditative ascents. She records her recovery from "a sore fit of fainting," for example, as "a support to me when I shall have occasion to read this hereafter and to others that shall read it when I shall possess that I now hope for, that so they may be encouraged to trust in Him who is the only portion of His servants" (251). Praying that she "never forget" God's "goodness, nor question" his "faithfulness to me," she deliberately preserves in verse an incident of deliverance as a stay against darker times that would inevitably come. As she confirmed elsewhere, "The remembrance of former deliverances is a great support in present distresses" (284). In the poem on the "fit of fainting," she enacts the "remembrance" by conflating biblical speakers into a voice that grace has made capable of grateful praise:

> O never let me from thee swerve,
> For truly I am Thine.
> My thankful mouth shall speak Thy praise,
> My tongue shall talk of Thee. (251)

The Canticles Bride's confidence ("My beloved is mine, and I am his" [Cant. 2:16]) and the Psalmist's gratitude ("My mouth shall speak the praise of the Lord" [Ps. 145:21]) blend into a neobiblical self suggestive of the poet's assured participation in Scripture promise. In the closeness of her biblical paraphrase, Bradstreet enacts commentator James Durham's advice that "We should consider the command we have, not only to praise, but to praise in these words of *David*, and other Penmen of holy Psalms." For Puritans such echoes of biblical voices were not mere literary borrowings, but warm confirmations of an identity built up from Bible promise. The more completely Bradstreet could absorb the Bible's moods and even words, the more fully she could achieve a self-reading as the referent of its prophetic colloquies.[13]

A neobiblical sense of self is equally strong in Bradstreet's response to affliction. While the Psalmist most often models her saintly gratitude, the Canticles Bride models her confessed need for Christic support. The Bride's diligent search for her Beloved—"By night on my bed I sought him whom my soul loveth: I sought him, but I found him not" (Cant. 3:1)—offered comforting biblical precedent for her own bouts with spiritual darkness: "In my distress I sought the Lord / When naught on earth could comfort give" (248). The poems that record illnesses gain in resonance from their echoes of the Bride's complaint that "I am sick of love" (Cant. 2:5). The spiritual ideal of the weak and lovesick Bride underlies Bradstreet's many references to her "hungry soul" (246), "wasted flesh" (248), "sinking heart" (249), "feeble spirit" (249), "Confusion" (270), "shame" (270), and every "weakness . . . Of body and of mind" (267). When she complains that "From side to side for ease I toil" (247), she invests her unease with biblical and hence salvific significance as an echo of the Bride's lament that "I sleep, but my heart waketh" (Cant. 5:2).

By repeatedly conflating biblical and psychological realities, Bradstreet incorporates even the worst of times into her hopeful self-reading as developing saint. "By night when others soundly slept" illustrates with particular clarity the extrapersonal dimension of her personal piety. Although it is the first of "Several Occasional Meditations," the poem leaves unspecified the event that prompted it other than defining it as an episode of spiritual darkness. The episode, as Bradstreet depicts it, is representative of all such moods as they inevitably descended on all believers:

> By night when others soundly slept,
> And had at once both ease and rest,
> My waking eyes were open kept
> And so to lie I found it best. (246)

That Bradstreet deliberately universalizes the event is clear from her invocation of a similar scene in the opening lines of the poem on the burning of her house:

> In silent night when rest I took
> For sorrow near I did not look
> I wakened was with thund'ring noise
> And piteous shrieks of dreadful voice. (292)

Such interchangeable descriptions underscore the poet's concern with grasping and teaching the redemptive patterns underlying all affliction.[14] In the house-fire poem, of course, Bradstreet is among the sleepers whose spiritual guard is down, and the loss of her house offers a harsh corrective against worldly security. In "By night when others soundly slept," however, she is fully awake, restless with the true Bride's yearning for the Beloved: "I sought Him whom my soul did love, / With tears I sought Him earnestly" (246). That the Bride's holy search provides a salvific context for wresting saintly possibility from despair is clear from the poet's assertion that God "bowed His ear down from above. / In vain I did not seek or cry." Reassured that "My hungry soul He filled with good," she voices the full gratitude of the saintly metaself:

> What to my Savior shall I give,
> Who freely hath done this for me?
> I'll serve Him here whilst I shall live
> And love Him to eternity. (246)

"By night" articulates the praise by which Bradstreet clarified her identity as an experienced pilgrim, as an individual embodiment of the paradigmatic saved soul. Like "As Weary Pilgrim," the poem strengthened her hope that Christ was creating just such an identity within her. Like "Pilgrim," too, it stood as a permanent record—a verbal Ebenezer—of a self-examination that succeeded.

Bradstreet's poems spoke as fully to her readers' experience of the faith as to her own. Her fundamental reasons for writing—meditating and teaching—intersected in a voice that not only stimulated her assurance as pilgrim but encouraged readers to achieve such assurance for themselves. Although her role as teacher is not often featured in discussions of her poetry, didactic aims were, from her own testimony, uppermost in her mind. Like the ideal parent celebrated in the elegies on her father and mother, she told her children that "I now travail in birth again of you till Christ be formed in you" (241). The family-oriented verse especially reveals her concern that her loved ones "gain some spiritual advantage by my experience" (240). Her autobiographical themes often reinforce the mistaken assumption that she wrote solely for self-expression, an assumption that usually underlies the view that she resisted Puritan modes of thought and writing. Her participation in these modes is further obscured when she is compared to more explicitly didactic poets like Wigglesworth and the elegists. But the directive to "win men's Souls to bliss," as Jonathan Mitchell described Wigglesworth's poetic goal, was as central to Bradstreet as it was to the doomsday poet. That her didacticism is more firmly connected to her personal life stems chiefly from the effect that her role as a Puritan mother had on her poetic vocation. Unlike Wigglesworth, whose broad themes were addressed to an equally broad audience, she drew lessons from her own experience for the benefit of readers whom she knew and loved.[15]

Despite Elizabeth Wade White's assertion that "the fulfilled and integrated woman" and "the somewhat self-conscious poet" rarely come together, the two roles converge in Bradstreet's pervasive concern with teaching. Her voice, especially in the family poems, embodies what Cotton Mather would later define as the character of the "virtuous Mother": "how ardent are her *Groans* as if she were even *travailing in Birth again*, that her Child may be washed in the *Laver* of the *New Birth* betimes!" Such a mother, Mather claimed, "is *a Teacher* to them all," an ongoing "*Example* of all Virtue that she sets before them." Through poetry Bradstreet made her life into just such an example to her family readers. As she wrote to son Simon, "Parents perpetuate their lives in their posterity and their manners; in their imitation children do naturally rather follow the failings than the virtues of their predecessors, but I am persuaded better things of you" (271). "Better things" could result, of course, from poems that articulated the humility and gratitude of a pious soul. We have seen that she recorded her recovery from "a sore fit of fainting" as a help "to others that shall read it when I shall possess that I now hope for, that so they may be encouraged to trust in Him" (251). The didactic blending of poet and parent also emerges in the poem "In Reference to her Children," where the image of the mother bird singing her brood to spiritual maturity integrates Bradstreet's complementary roles as mother and artist.[16]

In the domestic poems Bradstreet speaks as a family historian who, like all Puritan historians, seeks to reveal the providential significance of human events in order to stimulate a celebration of God's will. When daughter Hannah recovers from a fever, for instance, Bradstreet prays that she "remember" the deliverance "And celebrate Thy praise" (262). Elsewhere she asks God to put her son "in mind of what / Thou'st done for him, and so for me" in permitting his safe return from England (264). She anticipates her husband's return as an opportunity to repay God's "kindness" with praise and thanksgiving, to "serve Thee better than before / Whose blessings thus surmount" (268). Throughout these poems Bradstreet explicates the moral significance of domestic events as persistently as she uncovers the redemptive meaning of history in "The Four Monarchies." At her husband's recovery "From a Burning Ague," she urges him toward just such a reading of personal event:

> My thankful heart with pen record
> The goodness of thy God,
> Let thy obedience testify
> He taught thee by His rod.
>
> And with His staff did thee support
> That thou by both may'st learn,
> And 'twixt the good and evil way
> At last, thou might'st discern. (261)

By reiterating the correction and support that Simon has received, she encourages him and other family readers to develop equal proficiency in extracting salvific meanings from the events of their lives. As she tells her "dear children" in a prose meditation, she has recounted "the many sicknesses and weaknesses that I have passed through" so "that if you meet with the like you may have recourse to the same God who hath heard and delivered me, and will do the like for you if you trust in Him" (257). Repeatedly offering herself as a text illuminating the divine shaping of human lives, Bradstreet projects a self made useful to her readers, a model to imitate in their own celebrations and sorrows.

This ongoing concern with teaching narrows the often exaggerated gap between the ambitious Renaissance poet and the humble Puritan believer. Although Bradstreet speaks more to the visible than the invisible world in those poems that are more properly "Elizabethan" than "Puritan," such as the Quaternions, "The Four Monarchies," and the poems on Sidney, DuBartas, and Queen Elizabeth, all of her work exhibits a typical Renaissance—and "Puritan," in the view of the poet and her readers—mix of beauty and utility. Like most Puritans, she was convinced that a real poet, whether of public or private themes, was inevitably a teacher as well. "The Prologue" to *The Tenth Muse*, for example, places supreme value on a poet's capacity to sing the epic and historical—and hence inherently moral—themes "of wars, of captains, and of kings, / Of cities founded, commonwealths begun" (15). Her ironic concession that she cannot handle these topics certainly does not keep her from trying: her long treatment of "The Four Monarchies" comprises the bulk of the 1650 volume. Her equally ironic praise in "The Prologue" of those "poets and historians" who "set these forth" similarly mocks not the didactic subject matter but the prejudices of male literati who deny women's capacities to sing it. In mounting her attack, Bradstreet aligns herself solidly with Renaissance didacticism by voicing her admiration for "Great Bartas' sugared lines" through a "simple I" who appropriates the conventional self-deprecation of a Renaissance poet.[17] For all her humility, she assigns to the true poet an ability—here confirmed by her professed inability—to teach. Her "schoolboy's tongue" offers ironic evidence that she is still student and not yet teacher, not yet a full-fledged poet because she claims to lack the eloquence of Demosthenes, "that fluent sweet tongued Greek" who was the very type of the didactic orator.

"The Prologue" is itself a didactic exercise in which Bradstreet's authority as poet is explicitly repudiated but implicitly confirmed. Despite its light surface, it offers serious lessons concerning literary fashion, male prejudices, and the hyperbolic Renaissance conception of verse:

> And oh ye high flown quills that soar the skies,
> And ever with your prey still catch your praise,
> If e'er you deign these lowly lines your eyes,
> Give thyme or parsley wreath, I ask no bays;
> This mean and unrefined ore of mine
> Will make your glist'ring gold but more to shine.   (16–17)

The critique of literary pretensions thinly concealed beneath Bradstreet's ironic concession that "Men can do best, and women know it well" (16) turns on the contrast between her ostensible humility and the "high flown quills" of poetic fashion. Like any effective teacher, she carefully matches her lessons to her pupils' most basic assumptions. One of these is her readers' reverence for the Ancients. "But sure the antique Greeks," she wryly observes, "were far more mild / Else of our sex, why feigned they those nine / And poesy made Calliope's own child." Those who dismiss women poets had better be prepared to forgo the very foundations of Renaissance thought by conceding that "The Greeks did nought, but play the fools and lie." Perhaps because of the conventional nature of the war between the sexes, Bradstreet anticipates male reaction with uncanny accuracy. As a woman poet who is "obnoxious" or vulnerable "to each carping tongue / Who says my hand a needle better fits," she predicts that "If what I do prove well, it won't advance, / They'll say it's stol'n, or else it was by chance" (16). As if on cue, Nathaniel Ward's introductory poem to *The Tenth Muse* dubs her as "a right Du Bartas girl" (4), and his Apollo reacts with surprise "To see a woman once do ought that's good."[18]

Bradstreet reiterates the importance of teaching in "The Author to

Her Book" by playfully conflating her roles as parent, teacher, and poet into a witty self-portrait as mother to the "rambling brat (in print)" of *The Tenth Muse* (221). Despite the self-mocking allusions to her revisions—"rubbing off a spot still made a flaw"—the poem echoes the pride of authorship voiced in "The Prologue." Here, too, Bradstreet appropriates a poetic identity in opposition to the "high flown quills" chided in the earlier poem by repeating her endorsement of solid substance over literary fashion and posing:

> In better dress to trim thee was my mind,
> But nought save homespun cloth i' th' house I find.
> In this array 'mongst vulgars may'st thou roam.
> In critic's hands beware thou dost not come,
> And take thy way where yet thou art not known;
> If for thy father asked, say thou hadst none;
> And for thy mother, she alas is poor,
> Which caused her thus to send thee out of door.   (221)

On one level, of course, this too is a pose, as the speaker's humble domesticity masks considerable artistic pride. On another level, however, the poem articulates a secular parallel to the bond of humility and assurance that asserts itself time and again in the religious verse. Like "The Prologue," "The Author to Her Book" confirms what is at root a moral lesson: modesty is better than self-boasting, not least because of its rhetorical utility in anticipating and thus blunting any attacks by "critic's hands."

Apart from these satires of literary fashion, the most compelling evidence of Bradstreet's respect for edifying verse is the makeup of *The Tenth Muse* itself. In most of the volume she adopts the solidly didactic roles of natural philosopher and cosmologist ("The Four Elements" and "The Four Seasons"), psychologist and character writer ("Of the Four Humours" and "Of the Four Ages"), and redemptive historian ("The Four Monarchies"). Her underlying purpose in these poems, one shared by other cosmological literature of the period, is to expose the order underlying the intricate and shifting workings of the world—to show "How," as she states in the prefatory poem addressed to her father, "divers natures make one unity" (14). Concerned in "The Four Monarchies" with teaching the moral order of history, she takes as her major theme humanity's fall from a peaceful "golden age" in which "Man did not fondly strive for sovereignty" (73). The past, as she recounts it, is replete with moral correctives, and the sad litany of human affairs corroborates the biblical history of sin that breaks her meditative stupor in "Contemplations." Just as the religious poems mediate between Scripture and the reader, the Monarchies use rhyme and meter to enliven dry and difficult material from such sources as Raleigh's *History of the World* and Joshua Sylvester's translation of DuBartas's *The Divine Weekes and Works*. Bradstreet was not merely a "right Du Bartas girl" but an accomplished and learned Renaissance *and* Puritan poet, writing to teach as well as delight by conveying lessons that were at once accessible and edifying.[19]

Bradstreet's emphasis on the moral significance of cosmology and history parallels her search for underlying spiritual patterns in the religious poems. The didactic intersection of the secular and the sacred is perhaps clearest in the poems on Sidney, DuBartas, and Queen Elizabeth and in "A Dialogue Between Old England and New" — all of which articulate the poet's role as social commentator and critic. The tributes to Sidney and DuBartas reconfirm Bradstreet's view that the true poet teaches pious lessons. Sidney manifests the artistic ideal enunciated in "The Prologue" in his final rejection of the excesses of wit in favor of worthy themes and solid expression. Sidney's "wiser days," Bradstreet attests, "condemned his witty works, / Who knows the spells that in his rhetoric lurks, / But some infatuate fools soon caught therein" (189). Replicating Solomon's progression from base concerns to celestial themes, Bradstreet's Sidney exemplifies the Puritan belief that the real test of poetry was its moral and didactic utility. "He's a beetle-head," she asserts, who

> . . . sees not learning, valour and morality,
> Justice, friendship, and kind hospitality,
> Yea, and divinity within his book;
> Such were prejudicate and did not look. (190)

Bradstreet reconfirms the honored status of a poet who teaches in her praise of DuBartas's encyclopedic learning. But like Sidney, DuBartas is a consummate poet chiefly because a greatness of spirit and a "lib'ral nature" inform his poetic lessons (193). Bradstreet emulates this manner of teaching by asserting the elegiac commonplace that even the best and the brightest are no match for mortality. Gifted as Sidney was, "man is born to die, and dead is he" (190). DuBartas's passing similarly teaches that "Nature's law, had it been revocable, / To rescue him from death, Art had been able" (194). Since time cuts down both great and small, living — and writing — piously may offer the best revenge. A poet's "Fame" is commensurate with the edifying light that he or she brings to readers.

Bradstreet herself sheds such light in the poem "In Honour of that High and Mighty Princess Queen Elizabeth of Happy Memory." The

Queen's life and death yield lessons on the qualities of an ideal monarch, the great queens of history, the eschatological promise of England's glory, and the dignity of women: "Let such as say our sex is void of reason, / Know 'tis a slander now but once was treason" (198). Speaking as redemptive historian and prophet, Bradstreet confirms that England's former greatness, exemplified in the late queen, contrasts sharply with the sad state of a country that would be "happy, happy, had those days still been" (198). The lessons of sacred history are even clearer, however, in her most topical poem, "A Dialogue Between Old England and New; Concerning Their Present Troubles, Anno, 1642." Bewailing the "sad alarms" and "new woes" (179) of the Civil War, the poet has England confess to "my sins, the breach of sacred laws" (182). Railing against "Idolatry" and "superstitious adoration," she portrays an England in which so many "Church offices were sold and bought for gain, / That Pope had hope to find Rome here again." Bradstreet does not hesitate to point out the folly of a backsliding nation that "jeered" at New England for "flying for the truth." Recent events reveal the folly of mocking those "preachers" who "cried destruction to my wicked land" (183). Here, as in all of her verse, she asserts the inexorable force of God's will as the most important lesson that events in the world, whether personal or historical, could offer.[20]

Bradstreet's voice as poet-teacher assumes prophetic stature in the consolatory response of New England, the dutiful daughter convinced that "much good fruit" (185) would yet emerge from a renewed struggle against the mutual enemy of Old England and New, "Rome's whore with all her trumpery" (186). Like Wigglesworth, Bradstreet asserts sacred historiography as a framework in which present calamity anticipates future joy for "Abraham's seed": "For sure the day of your redemption's nigh; / The scales shall fall from your long blinded eyes, / And Him you shall adore who now despise" (187). This exhortation encapsulates the poet's lifelong search for broader contexts in which the divine significance of earthly events could be absorbed and shared. While the family poems place her life within the redemptive framework of the saintly pilgrimage, the historical verse reads political events into the world's pilgrimage toward the Latter Days. For Bradstreet as for Wigglesworth, history reconfirms on a grander scale the sufferings and promise inherent in an individual life. If interpreted in the same corrective light as private trials, England's upheavals could become harbingers of glorious "days of happiness and rest; / Whose lot doth fall to live therein is blest."

History, too, offered an Ebenezer of God's work in the world for those who could read it properly. If England perseveres as a collective pilgrim, "in a while, you'll tell another tale" (188). Bradstreet's ongoing concern with discovering and teaching the larger salvific structures informing lives and events resulted in a voice marked by a nearly indistinguishable blend of the personal with the paradigmatic. By conflating personal event with redemptive meaning, she intensified not only her own self-reading as hopeful saint but the redemptive experience of her readers. The degree to which they could identify with her pious yet accessible speaker suggested their possession of a scriptural faith shared by all saints. By dramatizing rather than merely describing saintly experience, Bradstreet extended the Ebenezer of her self-scrutiny as a blueprint by which readers could build their own monuments of felt belief.

CHAPTER FIVE

"Hidden Manna That the World Knows Not":

The Pilgrim's Inner Life

The profound influence of Puritan psychological models on Bradstreet's poetry reflects her view of writing as a vehicle for intensifying and teaching a redeemed experience of the self. Through autobiographical poetry, Puritan self-examination could be not only enacted but also made to yield more hopeful results. In her letter to her children she confirmed tastes "of that hidden manna that the world knows not." Poems could offer similar witness, and the clarity with which her verse proclaims the manna of the saint's joy (Rev. 2:17) makes her, as Roy Harvey Pearce once remarked, the "easiest of Puritan poets."[1] By connecting specific events in her life with the cycles of affliction and deliverance which she saw as their deepest meaning, she also sought to convey salvific experience as fully as possible to family readers whose second birth was her primary concern. Because *their* pilgrim identities hinged in part on whether they correctly understood hers, she took pains to clarify the redemptive significance of her life, speaking to their needs not as a spiritual superior but as a fellow sinner in need of the very lessons she imparts.

"The Vanity of All Worldly Things" is one of the most legible of these self-formulations. Like "As Weary Pilgrim," "Vanity" so clearly disappoints modern expectations for poetry that it has been read as an expression of pathology, "a low point in Anne Bradstreet's usually resilient spirit" which "marks the encroachment of the shadow that was to fall between the poet and her celebration of the world." But Bradstreet herself saw this "shadow" — the word echoes Eliot and a modernist aesthetic — not as an encroachment upon her spirit but as her manifest artistic and spiritual goal. Her stylized portrayal of the created realm must be considered a strength rather than a weakness in light of the otherworldly frame that she tries to achieve.[2] Bradstreet's identification with the world-weary Preacher of Ecclesiastes helps clarify her thought and speech as an earthly saint. As in "Pilgrim," self and Scripture conflate in the poet's assimilation of the Word as felt experience suggestive of her assured place in Bible prophecy:

> As he said vanity, so vain say I,
> Oh! vanity, O vain all under sky;
> Where is the man can say, "Lo, I have found
> On brittle earth a consolation sound?" (219)

Invoking a conventionally Puritan *contemptus mundi*, Bradstreet's litany of carnal attractions is so extensive and universal that neither she nor her reader can escape indictment. Although Elizabeth Wade White correctly maintains that "the depth of feeling which animates the poem is Bradstreet's own," that feeling is articulated through a biblicism so pervasive that the poet becomes virtually indistinguishable from the biblically shaped identity that she appropriates. Solomon and Bradstreet do not connect simply as source and borrower: they instead merge into a single humbled personality foretold in Scripture and fulfilled in the poet's experience. As Rosamond Rosenmeier observes, Bradstreet's indebtedness to Ecclesiastes is so profound that both she "and the Preacher are speaking through her voice."[3]

Bradstreet's identification with the Preacher intensifies her hope for the spiritual growth foreshadowed in Solomon. As we have seen, his movement from the worldly Proverbs through the cynical Ecclesiastes to the celestial Song of Songs was thought to anticipate the progress of all believers who learned to repudiate the pleasures of this life. By emulating Solomon's ascent, Bradstreet writes her way toward the meditative reward of all true pilgrims: a contemplation of the next life that "satiates the soul" and "stays the mind, / And all the rest, but vanity we find" (220). Such self-biblicizing reveals her relentless push toward the interior correspondence of self with Scripture suggestive of true belief. Dramatizing her conviction that no other verbal source could adequately convey the reward promised to the self that she seeks, she absorbs biblical prophecies of glory by making God's language her own:

> This pearl of price, this tree of life, this spring,
> Who is possessed of shall reign a king.

> Nor change of state nor cares shall ever see,
> But wear his crown unto eternity.   (220)

The pearl (Matt. 13:46), the tree of life (Rev. 22:2), the spring (Isa. 58:11), the celestial kingship of believers (Rev. 1:6, 5:10), the crown as a conflation of the crowns of life (James 1:12, Rev. 2:10), righteousness (2 Tim. 4:8), and glory (Isa. 28:5, 1 Pet. 5:4)—all define a self shaped nearly exclusively by the Word. By articulating Solomon's world-weariness within the broader framework of both dispensations, Bradstreet enacts an interior movement from Old Testament wisdom to New Testament faith.[4]

This systematic replacing of earthly with biblical identity offered readers an experiential model that was both current and eschatological. While the speaker's final calm dramatizes the conclusion of a successful meditation that the reader is invited to reenact, it suggests as well the happy outcome of an entire saintly life. What would ultimately "satiate" the soul, Bradstreet insists, was the celestial peace that would come to those who possessed the crown of life. Invoking spiritual rest both here and hereafter, Bradstreet, like Wigglesworth in "Vanity of Vanities," employs a two-part structure that mirrors redemptive duality, an inner turning from law to gospel and from sweeping conviction to consolation and Christian hope. The first stage subverts everything to which the carnal self clings. Worldly honor ends in death and oblivion; wealth brings "but labour, anxious care, and pain"; pleasure, "More vain than all," cannot keep the "conscience" from raging; beauty is "but a snare"; youth and age produce only "vice" and "rage" (219). Even "wisdom, learning, arts" are exposed by Solomon, "the wisest man of men," as "But vanity, vexation of mind." The stoic counsel neither to "laugh, nor weep, let things go ill or well" is "vain" because it requires humans to remain indifferent to their state. "While man is man," Bradstreet concedes, "he shall have ease or pain." Having exhausted the world's enticements, she voices the restlessness of every soul whose convicted conscience rages for peace:

> If not in honour, beauty, age, nor treasure,
> Nor yet in learning, wisdom, youth, nor pleasure,
> Where shall I climb, sound, seek, search, or find
> That *summum bonum* which may stay my mind?   (219–20)

The question leads to the speaker's recognition of an earthly realm defined not by logic and order but by paradox and confusion. In the illusory "real" world, nothing is what it seems: true honor can scarcely accrue to "beasts and sons of men" (219); the former king is "now a captive"; wealth brings pain; time changes beauty into ugliness; true wisdom leads only to a humbling recognition of ignorance: "he that knows the most doth still bemoan / He knows not all that here is to be known." Everything in the created realm amounts to less than nothing as the speaker finds nowhere on "brittle earth" to turn for solace.

Such anxiety, as Wigglesworth's poetry also demonstrates, created its own relief. Having dismissed all earthly attractions, Bradstreet lines out another route to a far different realm, "a path no vulture's eye hath seen" (220), and with the introduction of the "living crystal fount" of the water of life, her language becomes almost exclusively biblical. Once she rejects "brittle earth" as an ephemeral illusion (219), the remainder of the poem consists largely of a paraphrase of the twenty-eighth chapter of Job.[5] Bradstreet absorbs the biblical perspective by writing her own answer to Eliphaz's question, "Are the consolations of God small with thee? is there any secret thing with thee? Why dost thine heart carry thee away . . . and lettest such words go out of thy mouth?" (Job 15:11–13). Job's extended search for true "wisdom" and "understanding" (Job 28:20), labeled in the biblical text as a "parable" (Job 29:1), models the riddle-like structure of Bradstreet's paraphrase. Puritan readers knew full well, of course, the "path" that she is about to endorse, and the mock suspense generated by her repeated assertions of where "it" cannot be found would have prompted a knowing and therefore consolatory response:

> The depth and sea have said "'tis not in me,"
> With pearl and gold it shall not valued be.
> . . . .
> It's hid from eyes of men, they count it strange.
> . . . .
> But where and what it is, from heaven's declared;
> It brings to honour which shall ne'er decay,
> It stores with wealth which time can't wear away.
> It yieldeth pleasures far beyond conceit. (220)

The riddling defers the anticipated answer, thereby enabling Bradstreet to present the pilgrim path as the reader's own discovery. Biblical language and allusion become antidotes to mere thought: readers could "stay the mind" only by acknowledging the mind's inability to grasp the essence of the Word. Defining true wisdom as the repudiation of wisdom, Bradstreet distances her essential identity in the text from the self of carnal sense and reason and thereby stills the "vexation of mind" that plagues all earthly pilgrims. Asserting a biblical perspective for readers to seek as well, she demonstrates the carnal self's inability to soothe a raging "conscience" (219) by extolling something more permanent than the "brittle" world that such a self loves.

Despite its clear renunciation of a carnal perspective, "Vanity" articulates an assurance that does not veer into forbidden certainty. Far from asserting a definitive claim to the crown of life, Bradstreet instead casts the soul's final reward in the third person, a decision consistent with the humility that she both demonstrates and promotes. Her closing promise that the elect soul will "wear his crown unto eternity" (220) voices a relatively subdued anticipation of personal glory, especially in contrast to the more confident statements of assurance in Edward Taylor's private Meditations. But Bradstreet is not writing solely for herself and her God, and thus takes greater care to avoid provoking a dangerous security in her readers. Hoping for election but not presuming upon it, she places herself on equal spiritual footing with them. In its celebration of the generic "Who" and "his" of the redeemed soul, "Vanity" is a proclamation by one believer to another of a shared faith rather than an assertion of that faith by a spiritual superior. As the final line proclaims, "all the rest, but vanity *we* find" — Solomon, Job, Bradstreet, the reader, and every other soul who succeeds in rejecting the world and its charms. Puritan readers would find in "The Vanity of All Worldly Things" a model for locating their own "vexation of mind" within a redemptive struggle that drew hidden manna out of spiritual darkness. To seek something better than worldly contentment signaled a battle against the self of sense that would surely be rewarded with the crowns of election. In her Solomonic restlessness and Job-like faith, Bradstreet projected a self for readers not just to admire but to *become* as they assimilated the salvific hope voiced in the text.

In sharp contrast to the tranquil otherworldliness of "The Vanity of All Worldly Things" is the spiritual turmoil of "Contemplations." Indeed, the two poems seem to support the widespread critical assumption of two Bradstreets, one in tune with the demands of her faith and one who submits to those demands only with great difficulty. The experiential gap between the two poems, however, closes when they are read as complementary approaches to redemption. While "Vanity" invokes saintly identity as an inner ideal, "Contemplations" portrays it as an ongoing development, a dynamic process that continually activates the believer's meditative life. In terms of Puritan textual and spiritual identity, the two poems are not oppositive but sequential. While "Vanity" justifies the struggle by celebrating its outcome, "Contemplations" dramatizes that struggle by charting the process by which the holy war against sense and self was waged.

Its confessional surface has prompted some critics to see "Contemplations" as a hymn to God-in-nature or a celebration of the senses and the secular imagination, usually in support of the view that Bradstreet was a poet of divided concerns who experienced unusual spiritual difficulty. But the tensions articulated in the poem reflect psychological patterns that were considered inseparable from earthly belief. Puritans not only acknowledged a pull toward the world but insisted that such inclination was inevitably exposed by honest self-scrutiny. Nothing more fully characterizes Puritan self-exegesis than the worldliness that Bradstreet discovers and confesses. And nothing could be more consistent with the aims of Puritan meditation than her demonstration that the final vision of the "white stone" of Revelation could come only after an arduous battle against a sinful self all too easily seduced by the world's charms. By acknowledging her attraction to natural beauty, Bradstreet does not resist her faith so much as she confirms that the earthly experience of that faith was defined by resistance. Hers is not a cloistered virtue — the rich autumnal colors from which she must tear herself away are proof enough of that — but difficult and hard-won. The progression from Phoebus to Christ enacted in the poem dramatizes the continuing fight against world and self that defined Puritan interiority. As Bradstreet's most vivid poetic expression of the struggle toward assurance, "Contemplations" witnesses the spiritual challenge of peering beyond the visible manifestations of God's handiwork in order to glimpse something of the eternal vision afforded by saving faith.[6]

As a textual Ebenezer commemorating this process, "Contemplations" is the very opposite of a hymn to nature or even to God-in-nature. It is instead a dramatic record of Bradstreet's search for the identity that mattered most to her, the saintly metaself made capable of seeing beyond created things by the convicting force of the Word. Like most Puritan autobiographical texts, the poem enacts a pious movement from the creatures to the Creator and from the Book of Nature to the Book of Scripture. Recording a shift from natural to revealed religion that was the goal of all meditation, "Contemplations" invokes a process recorded as well in the poet's brief autobiography. "That there is a God," she writes to her children, "my reason would soon tell me by the wondrous works that I see, the vast frame of the heaven and the earth, the order of all things, night and day, summer and winter, spring and autumn, the daily providing for this great household upon the earth, the preserving and directing of all to its proper end" (243). But such arguments from design were accessible to all, damned as well as saved. The aroused believer wanted more, and the letter reveals Bradstreet's dissatisfaction with mere sensory proofs of the divine. How, she asks, could nature tell her that "He is such a God as I worship in Trinity, and such a Saviour as I rely upon?"

Nature could teach much, but not all. To relish God's handiwork was to perceive divine glory at its lowest level, without the full engagement of the will. The "dim Eye of Reason," Richard Steere confirmed in an extensive verse treatment of the proper uses of the world, offered "but Invitations to that fulness, / Of which by help of Faith we gain a Taste," "little Droppings" that provided mere hints of the "Ocean of Delight" afforded by grace. Thomas Shepard similarly insisted that "rational conviction makes things appear notionally; but spiritual conviction, really." "Reason," Shepard explained, "can see and discourse about words and Propositions, and behold things by report, and so deduct one thing from another; but the Spirit makes a man see the things themselves." Thomas Hooker would have agreed with Bradstreet's poetic confirmation that mere knowledge was not sufficient. After all, he remarked, "The devills in hell have this faith too." Had Bradstreet remained dazzled by the trees and the leaves, she would have attained a "notional" but not a saving sense of God's glory. As William J. Scheick points out, the "failure of the Book of Nature" in "Contemplations" reflects the Puritan distinction between prelapsarian *sapientia* and the much more limited *scientia* of fallen humanity. Because *scientia* depended "upon the senses for knowledge, through nature," Scheick argues, it was "inadequate for discerning truth or for attaining salvation." It is Bradstreet's meditative progress from *scientia* to *sapientia* that "Contemplations" records.[7]

Believers could not move beyond mind and sense without first recognizing that natural faculties unaided by grace could not grasp spiritual truth, a lesson that Bradstreet's speaker has forgotten at the beginning of the poem. Her awe at the wonders of nature seems orthodox enough: "If so much excellence abide below, / How excellent is He that dwells on high, / Whose power and beauty by his works we know?" (205). Despite her acknowledgment of God's creative power, however, she remains arrested at the sensory level, "Rapt . . . at this delectable view" (204). Attributing too much spiritual efficacy to nature, she celebrates the "glistering Sun" in a hymn as misdirected as it is fervent:

> The more I looked, the more I grew amazed,
> And softly said, "What glory's like to thee?"
> Soul of this world, this universe's eye,
> No wonder some made thee a deity;
> Had I not better known, alas, the same had I.   (205)

Not even the Bible can keep her from nearly worshiping the sun, which "as a bridegroom from thy chamber rushes, / And as a strong man, joys to run a race." The Bridegroom of Psalms 19, the immediate source of the image, was commonly seen as an allegory of Christ. Dramatizing her misguided contemplations by wrenching a well-known biblical image out of its proper interpretive context, Bradstreet underscores her sinful inclination to praise the wrong "son," the light of this world but not of the next. Like "Contemplations" itself, Psalm 19 opens by confirming that "The heavens declare the glory of God: and the firmament sheweth his handywork" (Ps. 19:1). But the Geneva Bible glosses these verses by explaining that nature offers divine lessons even to benighted souls: "The heavens are a scholemaster to all nations, be they never so barbarous." By saluting the physical sun so directly, Bradstreet confesses that her perceptions are no different from those of the unredeemed. Unable to see anything in nature that distinguishes her as an assured believer, she has not yet learned lessons deeper than those offered at nature's school.[8]

Scripture foretold that in the celestial Zion there would be "no need of the sun, neither of the moon, to shine in it: for the glory of God did lighten it, and the Lamb is the light thereof" (Rev. 21:23). That Bradstreet's speaker still *needs* the physical sun amounts to a confession of her sinful self. Instead of ascending to a transcendent realm by means of David's words, she has in fact descended, articulating her misplaced adoration in a parodic invocation of the Ave Maria: "Hail creature, full of sweetness, beauty, and delight" (206). Like Milton's Eve, who sings an adoring hymn to the Tree immediately after tasting its fruit, Bradstreet is nearly overcome by the glory of the creatures. Of course, she knows "better" than to worship a created object, however radiant, and immediately asserts the proper reading of the sun in a deliberate retreat from her "amazed" readiness to take the lower meditative path: "How full of glory then must thy Creator be, / Who gave this bright light luster unto thee? / Admired, adored for ever, be that Majesty" (206). But however clearly she voices the proper response, she does not yet *feel* it. Her thoughts cannot move from this world to the next until she attains a more profound humility than what she has so far expressed. Although she wants to glorify the Creator, she can as yet direct heartfelt praise only to the creation.

The speaker's spiritual flatness is clear from the result of her initial contemplations. Too enamored of the "pathless paths" of this world to break through to the next, her "mazed Muse" wishes to "magnify" the "great Creator" who has "decked" nature so "liberally"—"But ah, and Ah, again, my imbecility!" (206). Having gone as far as natural vision and eloquence can take her, she finds herself "Silent alone," isolated by mind and sense not only from God but from the very world that leaves her Muse so "rapt" and "mazed." Even the "merry grasshopper" and "black-clad cricket" "kept one tune and played on the same string, / Seeming to glory in their little art" (207). The contrast between nature's song and the speaker's muteness recalls Paul's command that "at the name of Jesus every knee should bow, of things in heaven, and things in earth, and things under the earth: / And that every tongue should confess that Jesus Christ is Lord, to the glory of God the Father."[9] Bradstreet's confession of a botched response to the injunction exposes the meditative dead end that she has reached: "Shall creatures abject thus their voices raise / And in their kind resound their Maker's praise, / Whilst I, as mute, can warble forth no higher lays?" Rather than bringing her closer to God, nature has left her even more distant. Initial meditative confidence and verbal facility sink in her humbling recognition that nature's revelations of supernatural excellence, already inherently limited, have come far too easily. Clearly, they have not yet worked their way from her head to her heart.

What is most interesting about "Contemplations" is that Bradstreet does not hide her confessed preoccupation with natural beauty, but makes it inescapably clear as the reason for her meditative failure. Having glorified nature and thus her own senses, she must confront the source of her blocked vision and eloquence in the biblical legacy of sin. Harsh legal lessons of Scripture, probed in stanzas 10 through 17, reveal the origins of her spiritual dullness not as mere historical analogy but as the immediate reason why her vision and speech are sadly limited. Her assertion that meditating on the Word "makes things gone perpetually to last" (207) confirms the eternality of Scripture as a convicting text. Present tense verbs throughout the biblical passages dramatize her inner replication of an unsettling identity exemplified by Adam and "bloody" Cain. With the killing of Abel "The virgin Earth of blood her first draught drinks, / But since that time she often hath been cloyed" (208). Wandering Cain, "His face like death, his heart with horror fraught," typifies all humanity, including the speaker, whose recognition of Eve as "our grandame" (207) links her inescapably with all of Adam's "progeny, / Clothed all in his black sinful livery, / Who neither guilt not yet the punishment could fly" (209). Bad as these Old Testament sinners are, Bradstreet regards herself and her contemporaries in even worse light. Moderns, after all, have even shorter lives in which to repent:

> Our life compare we with their length of days
> Who to the tenth of theirs doth now arrive?

> And though thus short, we shorten many ways,
> Living so little while we are alive;
> In eating, drinking, sleeping, vain delight
> So unawares comes on perpetual night,
> And puts all pleasures vain unto eternal flight.

At this point the speaker returns from Scripture with what John Lynen calls "a new and better state of consciousness."[10] Having had her nature-dazzled identity shaken by harsh biblical reminders of spiritual and perceptual limits, she is forced by Scripture to acknowledge her own "vain delight," the misguided rapture with nature that she has exposed within herself.

Bradstreet counters life's brevity with the memory of historical sin, which "makes a man more aged in conceit / Than was Methuselah, or's grandsire great" (207). Once impressions of sense are conquered by biblical memory as the Puritan source of all true wisdom, she begins to undergo the process by which the saved soul is distinguished from the rest of the creatures. As the speaker now concedes, nature is superior only when seen within a fallen perspective. Having envied "stones and trees" that seemed "insensible of time" (209), she is reminded by Scripture that the immortality of the elect is real while that of nature is illusory. Chastened and corrected by her excursion into the Bible, she now questions the very themes that she sang in the opening stanzas:

> Shall I then praise the heavens, the trees, the earth
> Because their beauty and their strength last longer?
> Shall I wish there, or never to had birth,
> Because they're bigger, and their bodies stronger?
> Nay, they shall darken, perish, fade and die,
> And when unmade, so ever shall they lie,
> But man was made for endless immortality. (210)

This revised view of humanity's relation to nature allows her to resume her meditations. Like Milton's Adam, whose vision of a redemptive future comes from Michael as spokesman for the Word, Bradstreet uses the Word to recover and internalize the redemptive past. Peering in opposite temporal directions, both learn the same lesson: the pervasiveness of sin in the world and in the self. Reinvigorated in her search for the evidence of things not seen, she is now able to root the beauties of nature more solidly in a gracious interpretive framework.[11]

With stanza 21, the poet's "contemplations" in effect begin anew:

> Under the cooling shadow of a stately elm
> Close sat I by a goodly river's side,

> Where gliding streams the rocks did overwhelm,
> A lonely place, with pleasures dignified.
> I once that loved the shady woods so well,
> Now thought the rivers did the trees excel,
> And if the sun would ever shine, there would I dwell. (210)

This description of nature is far more restrained than at the beginning of the poem: the "cooling shadow" of the elm contrasts sharply with the overwhelming, Babel-like oak of the opening stanzas, "Whose ruffling top the clouds seemed to aspire" (205). Similarly, the sun is now demoted from "this universe's eye" to a finite creature in a finite realm. Now convinced of her error in assuming that "the sun would ever shine," Bradstreet is determined to break through nature's mask to perceive the Son behind the sun. Why she now centers on the river rather than the trees becomes clear when she equates the "stealing stream" with the earthly pilgrim who perseveres in the quest for heaven: "'O happy flood,' quoth I, 'that holds thy race / Till thou arrive at thy beloved place'" (210). At this point she can use nature properly as an "emblem true of what I count the best" (211). The river is a frankly emblematic image that points beyond itself, inseparable from the pilgrimage that it represents: "O could I lead my rivulets to rest, / So may we press to that vast mansion, ever blest." No longer a distraction from divine glory but its visible analogy, the natural world has become a transparent, metaphorical revealer of its Creator.[12]

The Bible has made the world safe as a meditative object. Bradstreet, more casual toward nature because she no longer adores it, can now address the fish, those "wat'ry folk that know not your felicity," in witty, even playful terms:

> Look how the wantons frisk to taste the air,
> Then to the colder bottom straight they dive;
> Eftsoon to Neptune's glassy hall repair
> To see what trade they great ones there do drive,
> Who forage o'er the spacious sea-green field,
> And take the trembling prey before it yield,
> Whose armour is their scales, their spreading fins their shield. (211)

The vignette of "Thetis' house" can be as ornate as the poet wishes because the proper interpretive framework for all such vignettes has been solidly established. Given the efficacy of pious tears within that framework, the "wat'ry folk" are emblematic representations of believers who remain unaware of the redemptive significance of their trials. The elaborate language reflects the speaker's radically diminished view not just of nature's beauties but of herself as would-be visionary. The self-conscious metaphors ("wantons frisk," "Neptune's glassy hall," "spacious sea-green field") enact a gentle self-parody similar to that suggested by the "whole mines of gold" and "riches" of the East in the poem "To My Dear and Loving Husband" (225)—a parody whose target is the carnal vision and speech with which "Contemplations" had opened.

The poet can lampoon her earlier sensory excesses in part because her share in "Adam's livery" subverts any expectation that she can praise sufficiently. She can now cheerfully refer to her thoughts as a "thousand fancies buzzing in my brain" (211) in a more relaxed view of nature and language that culminates in the "sweet-tongued Philomel" (212), an image suggestive of the poet's recovered ability to sing praise as mindlessly—and salvifically—as a bird. Like the "wantons" frisking in the water, the nightingale finds validation in a spiritual significance inseparable from the image itself. Bradstreet's song to the bird, a poem within the poem, invokes a near-perfect harmony of the physical and the spiritual:

> "The dawning morn with songs thou dost prevent,
> Sets hundred notes unto thy feathered crew,
> So each one tunes his pretty instrument,
> And warbling out the old, begin anew,
> And thus they pass their youth in summer season,
> Then follow thee into a better region,
> Where winter's never felt by that sweet airy legion." (212)

This stanza, like all that follow the convicting scenes from Scripture, articulates the poet's identity as a counterpart to the untroubled bird, a Puritan singer of the "better region" promised to all sincere believers. As in her identification with a mother bird in the poem "In Reference to Her Children," Bradstreet handles the spiritualized nightingale deftly and lightly. Natural image now pulls in tandem with spiritual import. No longer at odds with each other, matter and spirit merge into a dual perception appropriate to the speaker's duality as a saintly metaself who loves this world dearly but learns to prefer the next.

"Contemplations" dramatizes a search for consolation beyond the world and the worldly self. Once Bradstreet accepts nature as a means to vision rather than its end, she describes a corrected view of mankind consistent with her revitalized assurance as an earthly pilgrim who recognizes the paradoxical nature of worldly creatures who can, through grace, transcend the world. The human condition is now embodied not in self-absorbed reverie but in a universalized restatement of the sin-caused panic of Adam and Cain:

> Man at the best a creature frail and vain,
> In knowledge ignorant, in strength but weak,
> Subject to sorrows, losses, sickness, pain,
> Each storm his state, his mind, his body break,
> From some of these he never finds cessation,
> But day or night, within, without, vexation,
> Troubles from foes, from friends, from dearest, near'st relation. (212)

Like the fish who remain unaware of their present "felicity," "this sinful creature, frail and vain, / This lump of wretchedness, of sin and sorrow" repeatedly ignores God-given opportunities for bliss (213). "Wracked with pain," humanity "Joys not in hope of an eternal morrow." Bradstreet reiterates the natural tendency to fixate on sensory reality in her final nonbiblical image: the mariner who "Sings merrily" during fair weather, "As if he had command of wind and tide, / And now become great master of the seas." Like the river, the fish, and the nightingale, the mariner is presented as allegory, a worldly "creature" used properly as a springboard to spiritual truth. When "suddenly a storm spoils all the sport, / And makes him long for a more quiet port," he mirrors not only the speaker's initial obsession with nature but the folly of all who cannot penetrate beyond "this world of pleasure":

> Fond fool, he takes this earth ev'n for heav'n's bower.
> But sad affliction comes and makes him see
> Here's neither honour, wealth, nor safety;
> Only above is found all with security. (213)

Bradstreet attacks the mariner's confusing of earth with heaven as an echo of her opening flirtation with the sun as a "deity." Having exposed and renounced her former identity as just such a "Fond fool" for nature, she rewrites herself into one of Paul's "fools for Christ's sake" (1 Cor. 4:10), a determined seeker of things *not* seen.

The final repudiation "of friends, of honour, and of treasure" (213) completes the poet's progression from historical to saving faith. By exposing a sinful self in order to intensify her experience as a saintly self, "Contemplations" dramatizes the ideal outcome of Puritan inner struggle.[13] In a prose meditation Bradstreet spoke to the dichotomy of outer weakness and inner strength that sustained the pilgrim during God-sent trials: "Who am I that I should repine at His pleasure, especially seeing it is for my spiritual advantage, for I hope my soul shall flourish while my body decays, and the weakness of this outward man shall be a means to strengthen my inner man" (255). Although "Contemplations" records a meditative episode of warm assurance, its conclusion makes clear that the poet's struggle was far from over. However vividly the poem proclaims a meditative victory of spirit over sense, the final stanza, with its reiteration of time's hold on the world, yields a hard-won lesson in humility that believers were to relearn for as long as they lived:

> O Time the fatal wrack of mortal things,
> That draws oblivion's curtains over kings;
> Their sumptuous monuments, men know them not,
> Their names without a record are forgot,
> Their parts, their ports, their pomp's all laid in th' dust
> Nor wit nor gold, nor buildings scape times rust;
> But he whose name is graved in the white stone
> Shall last and shine when all of these are gone.   (213–14)

The deprecating effect of the alliteration ("their parts, their ports, their pomp's") and the belittling phrase "all of these" reinforce a final dismissal of the same realm in which the speaker had initially gloried. In its place, of course, stands the Word, and Bradstreet's convicting assimilation of Old Testament sin is now rewarded with comfort derived from New Testament eschatology. All that remains at the end of the meditative pilgrimage recounted in the poem is the "white stone" of Revelation, on which there is "a new name written, which no man knoweth saving he that receiveth it" (Rev. 2:17).[14] Like the call for the Bridegroom that concludes "As Weary Pilgrim," "Contemplations" ends by witnessing the poet's desire to reaffirm her conformity with Scripture in speech as well as identity. The movement from sinful to saintly selfhood charted in the poem makes the concluding image not only appropriate but very nearly inevitable.

It is not often recognized that "Contemplations" was didactic as well as meditative in its aims. In addition to clarifying Bradstreet's assurance, it projected a voice appropriate to helping external readers anticipate their own "divine translation" from sinful to saintly self, from time to eternity, and from historical to saving faith. "Contemplations" led its readers through a sequence that was both convicting and consoling, difficult yet imitable. While the initially "rapt" speaker voiced a shallow faith still too easily distracted by the beauties of creation, her final vision dramatized the spiritual peace that Puritans believed resulted from a sincere struggle to transcend the world. That such a nature-stricken speaker could achieve a saintly perspective would have encouraged readers in their attempts to do the same.

As is the case with all of Bradstreet's poetry, the Puritan response to "Contemplations" depended on her ability to cast her own experience into generalized terms with which readers could identify. At the poem's beginning she enhanced the universal application of her inner turmoil with richly descriptive language that virtually ensured the reader's convicting descent into the realm of the senses:

> Some time now past in autumnal tide,
> When Phoebus wanted but one hour to bed,
> The trees all richly clad, yet void of pride,
> Where gilded o'er by his rich golden head.
> Their leaves and fruits seemed painted, but was true,
> Of green, of red, of yellow, mixed hue;
> Rapt were my senses at this delectable view. (204)

Despite a hint of unreality in the scene, the speaker's fixation with a nature that "seemed painted, but was true" transfers easily to the reader, who is also taken in by the lush description and thus made to feel an urgent need for the shift in perspective acted out in the poem. The speaker's "imbecility" in her attempts to render "higher lays" similarly echoes the dilemma of readers laboring under a lukewarm faith. In addition, Bradstreet casts the lessons of Scripture in a first-person plural that encompasses reader as well as speaker, both of whom discover in "Our life" their shared conviction as neobiblical sinners, "Living so little while we are alive; / In eating, drinking, sleeping, vain delight" (209). By confessing to a worldliness so appealingly and universally stated that readers could not deny their collusion, the poet directs them toward the repudiation of carnal identity that was the remedy. All of mankind, she stresses, "seems by nature and by custom cursed." No one can hope to reap any comfort from "youth, nor strength, nor wisdom" (210), qualities corrupted in Eden when Adam lost the "endless immortality" for which humanity was created. With the explicit reconfirmation that "Man at the best [is] a creature frail and vain, / In knowledge ignorant, in strength but weak" (212), the convicting force of guilt falls upon reader and speaker alike.

But melancholy was only the first stage of redemption, and the abrupt shift from nature to Scripture dramatizes the reader's only possible escape from similar spiritual paralysis. Like "Vanity" and "Pilgrim," "Contemplations" reaffirms the power of the revealed Word to keep in check the "fancies buzzing" (211) within all believers. In the letter to her children Bradstreet attested that "If ever this God hath revealed himself, it must be in His word, and this must be it or none. Have I not found that operation by it that no human invention can work upon the soul?" (244). To seek revelation outside of Scripture, she insists, was to court disaster: "Is there any story but that which shows the beginnings of times, and how the world came to be as we see?" By dramatizing a biblical escape from carnal limitations, "Contemplations" reaffirmed that there was no other "story" but the cycle of sin and redemption set forth in Scripture. Speaker and reader unite within the biblical metatext not simply because of the shared history it contains but because of the current psychological reality that it exposes.

A personal engagement with Scripture makes the believer not just "more aged in conceit" (207) but more wise concerning human nature. Bradstreet seals the bond between personal and historical sin by bringing the biblical Fall into the reader's present: it is through reading and remembering that the believer sometimes "seems to be" in "Eden fair." Sin thus emerges not as mere historical memory but as an ongoing state concurrent with the act of reading. The reader, too, "Sees glorious Adam" and "Fancies the apple" with him in the reading present; Eve sits "in retired place"; Cain "oft looks her in the face" (208) and "Bewails his unknown hap and fate forlorn"; Eve "sighs" at the loss of Paradise—all presented as *tableaux vivants* within the reading self.[15] The murder of Abel becomes a crime perpetually reenacted by each convicted soul: "His brother comes, then acts his fratricide; / The virgin Earth of blood her first draught drinks, / But since that time she often hath been cloyed." True to the poet's convicting aims, each biblical sinner becomes an Everyman of guilt and sorrow. Adam "like a miscreant's driven from that place, / To get his bread with pain and sweat of face" (207), while Cain invokes universal conviction "at the bar" (208), an emblem of every sinner who despairs of salvific hope. Cain, "His face like death, his heart with horror fraught," acts out the darkest spiritual condition of the Puritan self "Branded with guilt and crushed with treble woes" (208). Inseparably bound with the speaker to Adam's "progeny" (209), the reader confronts Cain as a biblical exemplum of his or her current anguish. The world's first murderer, who "neither guilt nor yet the punishment could fly," embodies the legal conviction that translates biblical history into redemptive insight.

The antidote to the Law that Bradstreet offers is the reader's potential escape from the sad cycles of decay and death that figure so prominently in the poem. Read in terms of Puritan self-experience, "Contemplations" generates an underlying urgency that contrasts sharply with its seemingly tranquil surface. The theme of temporality emerges in the very first scene, set at the end of a day in the waning of a year: "Some time now past in the autumnal tide, / When Phoebus wanted but one hour to bed" (204). The waning light invokes the impermanence of earthly life through an echo of the Psalms: "Mine eyes prevent the night watches, that I might meditate in thy word" (Ps. 119:148).[16] To the carnal senses, it seems that time will go on forever. Although the opening scene is dominated by the colors of dying leaves, nature seems to possess "no winter and no night" (205). After wondering whether the "stately oak" has seen "hundred winters past" or "thousand," the speaker tries to move from time to timelessness in her concession that "all these as nought, eternity doth scorn." But her meditative progress ends abruptly, and the sun, which runs its "swift annual and diurnal course" (206), pulls her back into time's grip. Indeed, it is the sun that creates and defines time: "Thy presence makes it day, thy absence night, / Quaternal seasons caused by thy might." The lessons from biblical history reinforce the reader's growing sense of being trapped within temporal decay. Just as general humanity has wasted the redemptive opportunities offered by sacred history, fallen individuals ignore the chance afforded by their lifetimes, a point underscored in Bradstreet's lament that moderns enjoy an even shorter "length of days" (209) in which to repent than their biblical ancestors. The pursuit of sin becomes a gamble against the coming of "perpetual night," and short as life is, the reader learns that "we shorten [it] many ways, / Living so little while we are alive." Such harsh lessons initially provoke an appropriately pessimistic reading of human temporality: while stones and trees seem "insensible of time," "man grows old, lies down, remains where once he's laid."

But the Word was eternal, and the poem offers the Bible as the reader's escape from the confines of a single lifetime. Once the biblical vignettes animate historical sin within the reading present, speaker and reader rediscover that "man was made for endless immortality" (210). Biblical promise ushers in the optimistic self-experience enacted in the remainder of the poem, and images derived from the natural world begin to assume a timeless quality consistent with their spiritual significance. The "stately elm," the "stealing stream" (210), the "wat'ry folk" frisking in the sea (211)—each assumes atemporality as an "emblem true" of a spiritual realm that now seems at least potentially attainable. The "sweet-tongued Philomel" (212), Bradstreet's most fully developed representation of nature viewed through redemptive lenses, lies completely outside of time: it "Reminds not what is past, nor what's to come dost fear." As harbinger of "The dawning morn" and guide through a "summer season," the nightingale points the reader toward a realm of endless beginnings, a "better region, / Where winter's never felt by that sweet airy legion." The nightingale parallels the poet, who also sings her readers from the temporal to the eternal. Emulating Philomel's encouragement to each of her "feathered crew" to tune "his pretty instrument, / And warbling out the old, begin anew" (212), Bradstreet encapsulates her chief artistic goal not just in "Contemplations" but throughout her verse. Poetry helped her translate temporal meditative experiences into timeless vehicles by which her readers could repudiate the Old Creature and "begin anew."

The closing proclamation that true "security" lies "Only above" (213) completes the conquest of temporal illusion by timeless truth. The created world that speaker and reader share is supplanted with a final emblem validated by its source not in nature or human invention but in Scripture: "Nor wit nor gold, nor buildings scape times rust; / But he whose name is graved in the white stone / Shall last and shine when all of these are gone" (214). Here, as in "The Vanity of All Worldly Things," the final bliss of the elect soul is couched in a third-person "he" that encompasses reader as well as speaker. Bradstreet's readers would recognize that the "white stone" came from the same verse in Revelation that extols the "hidden manna" sustaining the pilgrimage from time to eternity (Rev. 2:17). To taste this manna was to experience, however briefly, an unseen realm that time could not reach. Both "Contemplations" and the autobiographical letter reveal the poet's conviction that such tastes of the eternal were to be sought not in the world but in the Word. God, she told her children, "hath not left me altogether without the witness of His holy spirit, who hath oft given me His word and set to His seal that it shall be well with me." Against this "promise, such tastes of sweetness" afforded by the "hidden manna that the world knows not," she asserts that "the gates of hell shall never prevail" (243).

Bradstreet's confirmation in the letter that "it is the absence and presence of God that makes heaven or hell" (243) defines the true day and night of the believing soul. The poem's opening salute to the physical sun—"Thy presence makes it day, thy absence night" (206)—reveals a distressingly literal misreading of the dawning of the new day in the Song of Songs, when "the shadows flee away" (Cant. 2:17). The Canticles dawn, widely interpreted as the coming of the Gospel after the night of the Law, signals the removal of "whatever marres the immediat, full and satisfying injoying of Christ," commentator James Durham explained, "which as shadows, hide him from us, or darken him that we do not see him as he is."[17] The overall movement of "Contemplations"—from sun to Son, from earthly time to celestial timelessness, and from a world that conceals and darkens Christ to a world that illuminates Christic glory—confirmed a vision available only to the revitalized senses of an assured believer. Attesting to a perceptual shift of nature from mere object to divine emblem, Bradstreet promoted her own and her reader's experience of a self for whom darkness, decay, and time existed as harbingers of a pilgrimage already ended and a race already run.

If we apply modern aesthetic expectations to "Contemplations," we might well agree that "The defeat of Phoebus meant the defeat of Anne Bradstreet's imagination." But as John Lynen observes, the poem presents "no mere picturing of nature but a study of the experiential process" by which nature could be put to salvific use. By retracing the text's progression from the seen to the unseen and from the temporal to the eternal, its readers learned to rely on Scripture and not sense as the locus of a redeemed self developing within. Enacting an artistic and homiletic goal underlying all Puritan poetry, Bradstreet helped these readers "deeply groan for that divine translation" (213) from this world to the next, from self to Savior, from human words to the divine Word, and from corrupted sense to saving faith not as abstract doctrine but as the animating force of personal identity. This inner world, not the beauties of nature, comprises the real landscape of "Contemplations." The "autumnal tide" and "painted" leaves do not depict nature itself so much as a dangerously carnal vision of nature. While it is true, as Adrienne Rich comments, that Bradstreet's "landscape is more American than literary," that landscape is far more spiritual than American.[18] As backdrop for the poet's meditative and homiletic themes, the forest of "Contemplations" is finally no more naturalistic than Dante's dark wood, the enchanted forest of *Comus*, or the "banks of Lacrim flood" in her own debate between "The Flesh and the Spirit" (215).

While Bradstreet's imagery does not reduce to post-Romantic naturalism, neither does her voice reflect post-Romantic expressiveness. Josephine Piercy argues that "The Vanity of All Worldly Things" is the only poem in *The Tenth Muse* "that completely discards imitation and disguised emotions for a forthright, lyric expression of personal thought." But Bradstreet absorbs Puritan conventions of self-experience so completely, not just in "Vanity" but throughout her autobiographical verse, that she speaks most clearly in a role that Rosamond Rosenmeier has called "the Christian everyman." To recognize how profoundly these conventions shaped Bradstreet's poetic voice is not to suggest that she engaged in self-deception or hypocrisy. On the contrary, she recorded episodes in her spiritual life as honestly and clearly as she could, in language that allowed her to confirm and intensify her pilgrim identity as a means of strengthening religious assurance in herself and in her readers. As Cheryl Walker observes, "Contemplations" is a meditation "embodying the struggle that it serves (aesthetically at least) to resolve."[19] What we read in the poem is not the literal confession of an un-Puritan self but a thoroughly Puritan struggle in which such confession was indispensable.

As an embodiment of Bradstreet's artistic goals, the self projected in "Contemplations" manifests the paradigm of the saintly metaself as fully as Wigglesworth's pastoral speaker in "God's Controversy with New-England." Unlike Wigglesworth, however, Bradstreet does not address external events so much as she depicts an ongoing inner process that gave those events their redemptive significance. Rather than recording daily trials and triumphs in the believer's life, these poems enunciate the experiential framework in which trials and triumphs were to be interpreted. This framework receives situational expression in the occasional poems, most of which focus on those times when the pilgrim's faith was most sorely tested and the wisdom of God's ways seemed hardest to grasp. While "The Vanity of All Worldly Things" offers a general confirmation of the hidden manna that nourishes the assured self, "Contemplations" traces the meditative stages in such a self's becoming, the ongoing cycles of rebuke and reward by which grace shaped believers into true pilgrims. It would remain for other poems written in grief or anguish to witness how such a self coped with specific trials by which God nudged all pilgrims, sometimes against their will, along the redemptive path.

CHAPTER SIX

"Make Use of What I Leave in Love":

The Saintly Self on Trial

Puritans agreed that the redemptive cycles defined in "As Weary Pilgrim," "The Vanity of All Worldly Things," and "Contemplations" were most clearly seen in the specific burdens of individual believers. True saints, Wigglesworth affirmed, were "great Sufferers" who strove to bear such affliction "chearfully." "Nor must we think," he warned, "to ride to Heaven / Upon a Feather-bed." Believers found biblical precedent for personal suffering not only in Christ's Passion but in the Suffering Servant of Isaiah and the "black, but comely" Canticles Bride (Cant. 1:5), who was plagued with "spots & sinne," as a Geneva gloss explained, "but hath confidence in the favour of Christ." Puritans insisted that affliction could yield good results by pushing believers toward seeking Christ's power to effect their deliverance. What Bradstreet refers to in her "Meditations Divine and Moral" as the "practic part" of the faith consisted of coping with the daily trials that separated the sheep from the goats. Conceding that "Many can speak well, but few can do well," she insisted that "he is a true Christian that is a proficient in both." Afflictive events, however difficult to bear, strengthened redemptive proficiency by offering opportunities to repent and thus to realign inner identity with the normal patterns of belief. When Bradstreet addressed dark times in her verse, she wrote to test her proficiency in the daily practice of her faith and, if possible, to effect this realignment.[1]

In bad times and in good, Christian duty was the same: to praise divine wisdom for issuing the precise lesson that the spirit needed. Pious gratitude came more easily, of course, in times of mercy and thanksgiving, and the attitude dramatized in such poems as "For Deliverance from a Fever" is as straightforward as it is predictable. Yet Bradstreet's piety is not always so obvious when she writes about trials and suffering. In some poems she cannot fathom God's reasons for taking the life of a young child. In others, such as the famous poem on the burning of her house, she views the workings of Providence with numbed bewilderment. Sometimes she complains of a deadening weakness of spirit as well as flesh—hardly what one might expect from a Puritan mother teaching her children the proper pathway to heaven. Bradstreet's inability always to assimilate the comfort of doctrine, however, accorded fully with the Puritan belief that pilgrims could expect dark moods that evidenced the incomplete nature of their regeneration. The Psalmist repeatedly voiced an emotional upheaval to which all believers were subject, and Paul attested to similar conflict within those for whom "the body is dead because of sin; but the Spirit is life because of righteousness" (Rom. 8:10). If we ignore the salvific role of turmoil in Puritan inner life, we can misread Bradstreet's poems of struggle as expressions of unusual personal doubt rather than articulations of the psychomachia that defined earthly belief. Critics are certainly correct in finding psychological tension in poems like "The Flesh and the Spirit." But we distort the Puritan experience of such a poem if we label as "un-Puritan" Bradstreet's concessions that Flesh sometimes wins.[2]

By writing reenactments of inner struggle, Puritan poets also offered edifying models to their readers. The autobiographical thrust of Bradstreet's later work makes it easy to forget what her poems of doubt owe to her didactic aims, particularly her purposeful shaping of autobiographical material into clear demonstrations of how redemption worked in the believer's daily life. What she indicts in such texts is not the faith but her stubbornly human response to it. Constantly translating personal experience into what Karl Keller called "exemplary stories for her children," she articulated the very moods that would trouble those who most needed spiritual comfort—and consolatory poems.[3] In poetry that recorded difficult times, she spoke to her readers' doubts by revealing her own. By so doing, she encouraged their pilgrim identities through a voice defined not by pious superiority but by sympathy and commiseration.

As we have seen, Bradstreet commended two forms of divine guidance revealed in husband Simon's recovery from a "burning ague": "Let thy obedience testify / He taught thee by His rod. / And with his staff did thee support" (261). Sometimes, of course, the rod was far more evident than the staff. The deaths of loved ones, illness with little prospect of recovery, and the loss of a cherished home did not readily yield up God's purposes. Besides reminding believers of their need for divine help, trials like these kept them in "continual expectation," as Bradstreet wrote in a prose Meditation, of their hoped-for "change" (254) into celestial souls beyond all such pain. In the meantime, she confirmed, what "stays" the soul is faith that "God doth not afflict willingly, nor take delight in grieving the children of men; He hath no benefit by my adversity, nor is He the better for my prosperity, but He doth it for my advantage, and that I may be a gainer by it" (254). Elsewhere she admitted that she "can no more live without correction than without food" (257), conceding that God "grinds" his servants "with grief and pain till they turn to dust, and then are they fit manchet for his mansion" (275). Uniting these statements is Bradstreet's concern with subduing the pride that revealed a carnal identity who required God's strongest correctives. "Iron," she wrote, "till it be thoroughly heat, is incapable to be wrought; so God sees good to cast some men into the furnace of affliction and then beats them on His anvil into what frame he pleases" (277). For Bradstreet and her readers, the inevitability of suffering proved the corrupt nature of all earthly believers: "'I have seen an end of all perfection,'" she quoted from David, "but he never said, 'I have seen an end of all sinning.' What he did say may easily be said by many, but what he did not say cannot truly be uttered by any" (280). Every saint, she remarked, "stands in need of something which another man hath (perhaps meaner than himself) which shows us perfection is not below, as also that God will have us beholden one to another" (291).

Repeatedly internalizing the central lesson of Wigglesworth's "Riddles Unriddled," that children of light often felt engulfed in darkness, Bradstreet certainly "stands in need of something" in those poems that document spiritual difficulty. In a prose meditation she admitted that when God "seems to set and be quite gone out of sight, then must we needs walk in darkness and see no light; yet then must we trust in the Lord and stay upon our God" (282). Attesting to such walks in the autobiographical letter to her children, she confirmed the value of these tests of faith, "which most commonly hath been upon my own person in sickness, weakness, pains, sometimes on my soul, in doubts and fears of God's displeasure and my sincerity towards Him; sometimes He hath smote a child with a sickness, sometimes chastened by losses in estate, and these times (through His great mercy) have been the times of my greatest getting and advantage; yea, I have found them the times when the Lord hath manifested the most love to me" (242). Bradstreet's list of the events that have brought her the greatest salvific benefit reads like a subject index of the poems that manifest spiritual struggle. Sometimes she writes about "doubts and fears of God's displeasure and my sincerity towards Him" ("The Flesh and the Spirit"); sometimes she considers "sickness, weakness, pains" ("Before the Birth of One of Her Children," "Upon a Fit of Sickness," and many of the "Occasional Meditations"); sometimes she wrestles with the hard fact that God "hath smote a child with a sickness" (the grandchild elegies); and in one of her most famous poems she laments "losses in estate" ("Upon the Burning of Her House"). In each of these poems, Bradstreet counters her troubled spirit with an act of heartfelt confession by which speaker and reader alike achieve strengthened identity as a pilgrim struggling through the world.[4]

The debate between "The Flesh and the Spirit," a verse psychomachia recalling portions of Wigglesworth's "Riddles Unriddled" and Taylor's *Gods Determinations,* is one of Bradstreet's clearest formulations of the redemptive war between the New and Old Creatures within each pious soul. As the debate makes clear, fleshly yearnings and spiritual doubts could play a salvific role if believers acknowledged and opposed them. Brought to the "secret place" of meditation by the "Lacrim flood" of remorse (215), Bradstreet's speaker has been prepared by conviction to overhear and describe a struggle between sinful and saintly dimensions of identity that defined Puritan assurance. Consistent with the endless turmoil within all pilgrims, there is no possibility of reconciliation between the sisters. As personifications of carnal reason and saving faith, Flesh and Spirit can agree only to disagree, each strengthening her identity in opposition to the other. Bradstreet emphasizes the continuing nature of the debate with the broad topic that the sisters consider—"Things that are past and things to come"—and its eschatological source in Paul's promise that "all things are yours; / Whether . . . the world, or life, or death, or things present, or things to come" (1 Cor. 3:21–22).[5]

Having established the poem's psychological framework, Bradstreet's speaker drops out, leaving the sisters to reveal their own natures in speeches carefully shaped in accordance with theological expectation. Flesh mocks the meditative act itself, thereby subverting the very existence of the poem and the process that it both replicates and extols:

> Sister, quoth Flesh, what liv'st thou on,
> Nothing but meditation?
> Doth contemplation feed thee so
> Regardlessly to let earth go? (215)

The ironic fact that Flesh initiates the debate and the turmoil that it manifests reflects the salvific role of doubt in Puritan psychology. Appropriately, however, Flesh remains true only to what she can experience, repeatedly rejecting the evidence of things not seen. Applying reason and sense to matters of belief, she points up the paradoxes of the faith as seen from a carnal perspective. Why strive for intangible rewards "beyond the moon," she demands, when earth has more wealth "Than eyes can see or hands can hold" (216)? Matters of faith, which lie, as Spirit points out, beyond Flesh's "dull capacity" (217) are for the carnal sister mere "shadows which are not" (215). In her rejection of such intangibles, Flesh appeals, paradoxically enough, to the "sense" of Spirit and thus unwittingly employs a language to which Spirit's ears are utterly deaf.

The very predictability of Flesh's arguments—a litany of worldly attractions that echoes "The Vanity of All Worldly Things" and Wigglesworth's "Vanity of Vanities"—undermines the "True substance in variety" (215) that she promotes. Here, however, their dismissal is voiced not by one saint speaking to another but within a grace-split identity urged upon readers, who experience the poem as an overhearing of their own thoughts. On one level, of course, Flesh's catalog of earthly delights stimulates its convicting parallel within the reader's aroused conscience. By objectifying the carnal dimension through the very existence of the debate, however, Bradstreet separates the fleshly dimension from the reading self. Flesh's arguments, designed to *sound* seductive but not actually to *be* so, offer easy targets for the reader's scorn, in part because the attributes of "honour," "riches," and "pleasure" are so boldly and rapidly ticked off. But while Flesh cannot win the debate, she cannot really lose either—at least not in the narrative moment of the poem. Rather, the perspective that she voices is fated to remain until Flesh herself ceases to exist—until she is, as Spirit predicts, "laid in th' dust" (216) at the saint's death. Like Wigglesworth in *The Day of Doom*, Bradstreet dramatizes two hopelessly irreconcilable perspectives. Even though one dimension of the self could never wholly subdue the other while the elect soul was alive, Bradstreet showed readers that keeping a close ear to the endless give-and-take between the two was indispensable to their spiritual progress.

Flesh cannot win because the speaker possesses a lively Spirit to oppose her. Spirit's ability to "combat with" Flesh (216) begins when she acknowledges that "Sisters we are, yea, twins we be" (216). Once she recognizes her sister and thus accepts her share of guilt, Spirit repudiates her by insisting on the separateness that defined the true believer's inner duality. While Flesh repeatedly seeks to pull down the barrier between the two by sharing her pleasures, Spirit keeps alive the "deadly feud 'twixt thee and me" by redrawing the covenantal line that separates them:

> For from one father are we not,
> Thou by old Adam wast begot,
> But my arise is from above,
> Whence my dear Father I do love.   (216)

Spirit defines her "unregenerate part" as a vicious "foe" through a harshly unsentimental Puritan self-reading: "Thou speak'st me fair, but hat'st me sore, / Thy flatt'ring shows I'll trust no more" (216). Conceding that she has "oft" been made Flesh's "slave," Spirit enacts the salvific confession that gives her the strength to resist the sinful self's arguments. Flesh, like Milton's Comus, is a conciliator who tries to make peace by offering her sister the world. Spirit, by contrast, emerges as an active, vigorous fighter who is by far the less charitable character. Spirit's harshness is theologically necessary, of course, because she is fighting for her very existence. A soul with no inner split had given itself entirely over to the fleshly perspective. Deriving a "settled heart" from her determination *not* to settle for Flesh's reasonings, she refuses to be drawn into a logical exchange with her "flatt'ring" sister. By simply cutting off the debate, she fulfills the Psalmist's prophecy that "the mouth of them that speak lies shall be stopped" (Ps. 63:11). As she proclaims, "I'll stop mine ears at these thy charms, / And count them for my deadly harms."

Spirit's assertion of an "ambition" that "lies above"—an echo of the doctrinal endings of "As Weary Pilgrim" and "Upon the Burning of Our House"—may strike the modern reader as a flat response to Flesh's appeals to reason and sense. But in her allegiance to scriptural rather than sensual reality, Spirit lines out a meditative path consistent with her claim that the "word of life" is her "meat" (217). Fed by Scripture, her antagonism grows as she mounts one biblical response after another to Flesh's appeals. Recalling Paul's celebration of the final reward of true belief, when "Death is swallowed up in victory" (1 Cor. 15:54), she anticipates her "greatest honour" when she is "victor over thee, / And triumph shall with laurel head, / When thou my captive shalt be led" (216). Against earthly pleasures she opposes the "hidden manna" of scriptural joy invoked as well in Bradstreet's letter to her children. At times Spirit's speech reads like a catalog of biblical prophecies of gracious reward: the "royal robes" (217) of grace foreshadowed in the "wedding garment" of the elect (Matt. 22:12), the white raiment of the Lamb's Bride (Rev. 3:5), and the "crown not diamonds, pearls, and gold, / But such as angels' heads enfold," a conflation of the crowns of life (Rev. 2:10), glory (1 Pet. 5:4), and righteousness (2 Tim. 4:8) awaiting the Chosen. While Flesh offers the enticements of the world, what Spirit anticipates has meaning only within the boundaries of the Word.

Selecting "Eternal substance" (217) perceptible only to the eye of faith over the "True substance" (215) endorsed by Flesh, Spirit strives to "pierce the heavens and see / What is invisible" to her carnal sister (217). What she finally sees is John's vision of the New Jerusalem as set forth in Revelation 21 and 22. Invoking the biblical opulence of a heavenly city with walls of "precious jasper stone," "gates of pearl," and streets of "transparent gold" (217), Spirit lines out a realm that even Flesh would desire could she imagine it. Like the "white stone" in "Contemplations" and the Bridegroom's call in "As Weary Pilgrim," Spirit's description counters carnal reason and sense with Scripture as the source of the saint's faith. Agreeing that "Earth hath enough" of what Flesh wants (216), Spirit articulates the biblical promise that "men of the world" will "have their portion in this life" (Ps. 17:14) and not in the next. Too aware of the shortcomings of this world to remain content with such "trash," she holds out for the everlastingness of things not seen, and in her final rebuttal consigns to her carnal twin "the world and all that will" (218).

Like "Contemplations" and "As Weary Pilgrim," "The Flesh and the Spirit" assured readers that doubt could spur their spiritual growth if they opposed it with the persistence modeled by Bradstreet's Spirit. While Flesh helped them confront their own sin, Spirit strengthened their resolve to define themselves in opposition to that sin and thereby to assimilate the hope that a divided experience of self could bring. Readers who felt some measure of Spirit's otherworldliness could feel that her inner equivalent was winning the war for their own souls. The two sisters embodied an identity that Bradstreet made both pious and imitable by validating and encouraging the reader's difficult struggle toward belief. The debate warned readers that fleshly temptation would not end until they entered a realm where time would no longer be measured — where they would "have no need" of either sun or moon, where there would be neither "darksome night" (217) nor "withering age" (218). In the meantime, the self-division dramatized and stimulated by the text consoled them that even in their greatest spiritual turmoil God had not given them up for lost.

Bradstreet repeatedly incorporated her physical illnesses into the ongoing dichotomy of fleshly weakness and redemptive strength dramatized in "The Flesh and the Spirit." She made her sicknesses into necessary foils to divine power by reading herself as a latter-day Lazarus in whom, as Christ promised, "This sickness is not unto death, but for the glory of God" (John 11:4). The meditative and didactic utility of suffering doubtless influenced Bradstreet's choice of events to commemorate in verse. Throughout the poetry, physical affliction provides a special test of her ability to find redemptive patterns at work in her life. In poems like "For Deliverance from a Fever," the full cycle of suffering and deliverance could be clearly read in her recovery. But poems written before she recovered record her faith that the cycle would be fulfilled. In them we see her struggling to achieve an assurance that God would somehow put things right.

Two such texts are "Before the Birth of One of Her Children" and "Upon a Fit of Sickness, Anno 1632 *Aetatis Suae*, 19," her earliest extant poem. Reiterating Paul's affirmation that "the sufferings of this present time are not worthy to be compared with the glory which shall be revealed in us" (Rom. 8:18), both poems present the speaker's anxiety as a parable of the temporal frailty of all pilgrims. "Before the Birth," some "farewell lines" offered to her husband, contains Bradstreet's candid confession of a fear that she might someday be forgotten and that her children might be subjected to a "step-dame's injury" (244). Voicing no anticipated reunion with her husband in heaven, she nonetheless enacts a solidly Puritan self-reading through her endorsement of the central lesson of all elegies: "All things within this fading world hath end, / Adversity doth still our joys attend." Death, the wages of sin, is a "sentence past" that is "irrevocable, / A common thing, yet oh, inevitable."

Bradstreet hardly seems willing to go gently into that good night after only "half my days that's due" (224). Just as Flesh models human concupiscence, the speaker of "Before the Birth" voices natural fear. Although the prospect of death terrifies a self in whom "nature" expects a full lifespan, frank confession once again initiates redemptive recovery. Challenging her husband to bury her "many faults" and to cherish whatever "worth or virtue" she possesses, Bradstreet transforms wedded love into a vivid *memento mori*, a goad for Simon to behave and believe piously after her death: "And when thou feel'st no grief, as I no harms, / Yet love thy dead, who long lay in thine arms." In her closing plea for Simon to "kiss this paper for thy love's dear sake," she offers her death as proof that grief is always the price of love. Reconfirming the inevitability of "Adversity," the poem teaches, though more gently, the chief lesson of "The Flesh and the Spirit." While worldly love defined one's humanity, accepting the separation from what one loves was part of becoming something more than human, of moving from "this fading world" to the lasting realm of true belief.

In "Upon a Fit of Sickness" the nineteen-year-old poet similarly connects death's approach with the fulfillment of the Law: "For Adam's sake this word God spake / when he so high provoked" (222). Invoking the pious inversion of life and death that Wigglesworth develops in "Riddles Unriddled," Bradstreet anticipates the peace of a heaven "Where I shall have all I can crave, / no life is like to this." Seen from a celestial perspective, earthly life is a "bubble blast" "that always art a breaking, / No sooner blown, but dead and gone, / ev'n as a word that's speaking." Praying to be given "this grace" to accept God's "decree" and to use what little time remains for "doing good," she offers the poem itself as a good deed by urging the reader to seek the "profession pure" that she voices. Asserting her assurance as a saintly self, she renders death an "envious foe" with her boast that "The race is run, the field is won, / the victory's mine I see." Such confidence is theologically justified by the repudiation of carnal identity that the poem enacts. Like other Puritan self-elegies, such as Edward Taylor's "A Fig for Thee Oh! Death," the poem articulates her ability to imagine herself hovering between two worlds.

The good death that the young poet anticipates is identical to that which she later attributed to her parents. Her tranquil commemoration of a mother who spent her entire life "Preparing still for death" (204) and a father who was "fully ripe" and "timely mown" (202) was possible because both lives could be easily read in terms of redemptive paradigm. Not every death, however, revealed divine purpose so clearly, and the pilgrim's ability to reconcile human wishes with divine will was most taxed when the usual elegiac lessons were hardest to discern. Especially striking in this regard are the three poems on her grandchildren, in which she voices a resentment and anger antithetical to the pious resignation of "Upon a Fit of Sickness" and "As Weary Pilgrim." Even the rhetorical and didactic purpose of the grandchild elegies seems problematic: why would Bradstreet voice such bitterness to family readers who were also grieving? Although she admitted to her children that one of the times of her "greatest getting and advantage" was when God "hath smote a child with a sickness" (242), what "getting and advantage," either for herself or her readers, can be found in these poems? If ever her family readers needed consolation from her verse, it was now. Why would she give them stones instead of bread, such unsettling memorials when their spiritual need was greatest?

Nowhere, perhaps, does Bradstreet seem to convey greater ambivalence toward her faith than in the elegy on grandson Simon. The poem has often been read as an unsuccessful attempt to suppress a rebellious response to the child's death—to conceal personal doubt beneath conventional statements of dogma.[6] Like two sisters who preceded him, Simon has been rudely "Cropt by th'Almighty's hand; yet is He good" (237). The recitation of doctrine, too flat to be entirely convincing, sounds like a forced lecture to the self:

> With dreadful awe before Him let's be mute,
> Such was His will, but why, let's not dispute,
> With humble hearts and mouths put in the dust,
>   Let's say He's merciful as well as just.   (237)

What is most striking about the rebellion, however, is that it has *not* been suppressed. Instead, Bradstreet places it at the very center of the elegy, and although she recommends against questioning God's dispensations, she is hardly "mute." Nor does she seem to achieve any significant resolution of her grief. The most she can do is hope, however faintly, that her anguish will be soothed in the future, when Christ "will return and make up all our losses." For now she can only mark the contrast between her words of sorrow and the language of orthodoxy. As Randall Mawer observes, her exhortation to "say" that God exercises mercy along with justice contains a great deal of irony. Nor does her conclusion seem very convincing: "Go pretty babe, go rest with sisters twain; / Among the blest in endless joys remain." By reasserting the conventional language of grief, the closing lines, as Stanford notes, seem to convey "a settling back into dogma after her outburst of feeling." But rather than concealing her outburst Bradstreet forces her reader to confront it: the paradox of a merciless God of mercy is as explicit as it is inescapable. God lets children die—"yet is He good," and the inverted phrase seems as much a question as an affirmation of faith. Mawer correctly points out Bradstreet's concern with "psychology," with the "quest for resignation to God's will." But the disturbed speaker's relationship to her reader remains unexplained. Why would Bradstreet portray herself in such a light, especially in a poem written apparently to comfort herself and family members? Does the elegy reflect a loss of artistic control, an unwitting subversion of the very doctrine that the poet tries to defend?[7]

Answers to these questions emerge from the lessons that Bradstreet's family readers would likely have drawn from the distressed speaker. First, her reaction to the child's death embodies the Puritan demand for honest self-examination: there is nothing unorthodox in her concession that easy answers are no answers at all. Second, she dramatizes why believers needed to strive for abject humility in the face of God-sent trials. Speaking as a convicted soul who demonstrates through her numbness the futility of natural responses to tragedy, Bradstreet acts out the dangers and limits of self-reliance. She does not try to argue herself into accepting Simon's death. Instead, she dramatizes the willfulness of such arguments in the same manner as in "The Flesh and the Spirit," by abruptly cutting off her natural reaction to the loss in favor of doctrinal statement. It is the Flesh within, she concedes, that impedes her acceptance of God's will.

Like the poems on illness, the elegy on Simon offers a situational reenactment of the meditative process set forth in the Flesh/Spirit debate. The poem's movement from pain to doctrine reflects the speaker's attempt to overcome human words with the redemptive antidote of God's Word. Although the poem confirms the Puritan belief that human perspectives were to be directly confronted and openly acknowledged, it also reveals exactly how far such perspectives could go without divine help. If any change in the speaker will permit her to accept the child's death, that change will have to come *after* the narrative moment of the poem—and it will occur, Bradstreet suggests, in spite of human reason and not because of it. Seen in this light, her failure to derive full comfort from imagining the child "Among the blest" attests to her inability to overcome affliction without Christ's aid. While she confesses that Christ has not yet provided solace in this trial, she registers the hope that he someday would, thereby demonstrating the only possible recourse for an earthly pilgrim whose natural ability to make sense out of tragedy proves insufficient. As Mawer notes, the speaker focuses on God's power, not his mercy. In so doing, she manifests, rebellion and all, the psychology of the humbled believer for whom a "dreadfull awe" of the divine would simply have to do until the perfection of faith supplanted human dread with gracious love.[8]

The other family elegies, which also expose the unreliability of natural responses to tragedy, support Robert Daly's observation that for Bradstreet, as for all Puritans, "resignation to the will of God required a difficult and conscious act of her own will; to believe what one had not yet seen was something to be struggled for and achieved." The achieving, however, did not always follow from the struggle. In the elegy for granddaughter Anne the poet confesses a chronic human tendency to set her hopes "on fading things." As in the lament for Simon, she makes it inescapably clear that natural reason is the cause of her grief: "More fool then I to look on that was lent / As if mine own, when thus impermanent" (236). Although Mawer contends that the poem questions the faith, it instead concedes the speaker's inability to fulfill the demands of that faith.[9] The elegy for daughter-in-law Mercy, "Who might in reason yet have lived long" (238), also reveals the futility—and strength— of human expectations. Bradstreet comforts her son not by presuming to explain God's purposes but by conceding that such purposes must be accepted on faith:

> Cheer up, dear son, thy fainting bleeding heart,
> In Him alone that caused all this smart;
> What though thy strokes full sad and grievous be,
> He knows it is the best for thee and me. (239)

God's plan is vindicated precisely because it does *not* make human sense. By urging her son to take solace from the very Author of the tragedy, Bradstreet emphasizes that neither she nor her reader can grasp the spiritual significance of the loss without perceptions renovated by grace.

The inevitable conflict between human and divine perspectives on tragedy recurs in the lament for granddaughter Elizabeth. Here, too, Bradstreet makes no attempt to depict the child's death as being fair or reasonable, but instead underscores its irrationality if seen in merely human terms. As she asks the dead child, "why should I once bewail thy fate, / Or sigh thy days so soon were terminate, / Sith thou art settled in an everlasting state" (235). But the poem itself answers the question: sometimes God's reasons must remain beyond human comprehension. This suggests why the second stanza, with its images of senescence and decay, distinguishes between deaths that can be understood and those that cannot. While the elegies on her parents confirm that the death of mature plants was perfectly reasonable, human logic cannot so easily explain why "buds new blown" should "have so short a date." God took Elizabeth, a plant "new set," as a test of the survivor's ability to accept the loss as a magisterial act of "His hand alone that guides nature and fate." Once again refusing to ignore God's agency in the death, Bradstreet articulates the only solution for believers who learned that the Lord takes away as well as gives. Confessing her fallen tendency to invest too much love on the creatures—she addresses the child as "my heart's too much content"—she leans on the scriptural promise of "an everlasting state" even if she cannot yet take full comfort from the doctrine. The conventional elegiac language of the first stanza ("Farewell fair flower that for a space was lent") and the less than heartfelt allusion to the child's bliss in heaven become pious incantations that Bradstreet urges upon herself and her readers as the only possible salve for despair.

As Mawer points out, the elegy is "both orthodox and rebellious." But as is so often the case, it is Bradstreet's concern with teaching that enables these seemingly contradictory traits to coexist. As in the poem on Simon, she confesses doubt in order to promote faith. The forced resignation that Wendy Martin finds in the poem is not indicative of an unusually stubborn soul or expressive of "heresy," as Mawer contends, but was instead part and parcel of saintly experience. As John Weemse insisted in his handbook on Bible interpretation, believers who confronted such doubts were in good company indeed: "if thou complaine of doubting, how oft objected Christ that to his Disciples? yet commended their faith, believing but *radicaliter*." Although Daly finds genuine resignation in the poem and Mawer senses "outrage," the truth lies somewhere in between. Bradstreet concedes that the earthly saint must occasionally be resigned to rage, however impious such rage may seem. Until the soul's perfection in heaven, the earthly pilgrim simply had to accept the terrifying disparity between what Mawer calls the "cold grandeur" of God's will and the "hot agony" of human suffering.[10]

Despite their hard lessons, the family elegies display Bradstreet's remarkable sensitivity to the situations and readers that she addresses. Like Wigglesworth, she embodies an empathy central to Puritan preaching by enacting William Perkins's advice that the minister should always "include himselfe (if he may) in his reprehension, that it may be more milde and gentle." One could not teach what one did not feel: in another preaching handbook Richard Bernard agreed that "the gracious and zealous heart is an excellent Rhetorician" that "speakes to another what first it feeleth in it selfe; as it is affected it endevours to affect others."[11] Writing for family members whose grief at the children's deaths would be at least equal to her own, Bradstreet projects a voice that echoed her readers' presumed feelings. The grief that unites speaker and reader within the dark interval between affliction and deliverance confirmed that they were not alone in their bitterness. Far from reflecting an attack on the faith, conscious or otherwise, the elegies instead reveal Bradstreet's concern with addressing her family on their own terms as they faced the most difficult tests of that faith imaginable.

Bradstreet and her readers knew from the Sermon on the Mount that God "sendeth rain on the just and on the unjust" (Matt. 5:45). As texts designed to console herself and family members during times of God-sent rain, the family elegies do not reveal a response to the deaths that is any worse than normal. On the contrary, Bradstreet shows how predictably and depressingly normal she has turned out to be. Puritan readers would find in her confessions of an unreconciled self far more evidence of grace than may first appear. Learning to confront one's resistance to God's will was what gave such trials their redemptive possibilities. As Thomas Shepard attested, "the greatest part of a Christian's grace lies in mourning the want of it."[12] Bradstreet's troubled speaker offered dramatic witness to the "mourning" without which true piety could not exist.

In their belief that Christ came into the world to heal not the healthy but the sick, Puritans found edifying value in autobiographical texts only if the narrators perceived themselves, like Bunyan, as "the chief of sinners." Patterns of self-experience manifested in journals, conversion narratives, and spiritual autobiographies virtually dictated the projection of a weak and struggling self, not only to confirm the genuineness of the writer's humility and conviction but also to teach readers not to expect a perfected, doubt-free faith in their own lives. Bradstreet's autobiographical letter is typical in giving full play to the meditative and didactic benefits of discovering and confessing such opposition to God's will. Insisting that dark times presented the greatest opportunity for assessing the inner workings of faith, she advised her children to accept them humbly and gratefully. "If at any time you are chastened of God," she urged, "take it as thankfully and joyfully as in greatest mercies, for if ye be His, ye shall reap the greatest benefit by it" (242). As particularized confirmations of the salvific reading of affliction, Bradstreet's poems of trial repeatedly confirm that assurance could not be achieved unless believers confronted a sinful self for whom divine deliverance was absolutely necessary. In these poems the frank confession of sin becomes the fullest possible affirmation of orthodoxy, an affirmation acted out rather than merely described.

For such trials as the death of a child, full comfort sometimes had to wait for the perfection of faith that would come in the next life. The same was true of another category of affliction listed in the letter—those "losses in estate" that remind the saint of the transience of earthly wealth and happiness (242). This type of trial receives fullest expression in the famous "Verses Upon the Burning of Our House." Like the family elegies, the house-fire poem presents an experiential homily on the natural inclination toward worldliness. The first section of the poem, which records Bradstreet's frightened reaction to the fire, indeed seems more vivid and engaged than the doctrinal affirmations of the "house on high" at the end (293).[13] Her ambivalence is underscored by the poem's structure: if her appropriation of Job's stoicism in blessing "His name that gave and took" had been complete, the poem would have ended at this point. Instead, however, she must descend into the world of human regret in an extended litany of the "pleasant things" and family memories associated with her home. The overall effect of these memories is that of a catharsis attempted rather than achieved, and a second resignation expressed in a paraphrase of Ecclesiastes ("Adieu, Adieu, all's vanity") introduces a final section in which doctrinal abstractions replace images of human activity and regret. As in the family elegies, Bradstreet's concluding contrast between the earthly and heavenly houses, the latter "Framed by that mighty Architect," seems more a recitation than a certainty. In heaven, she tells herself,

> There's wealth enough, I need no more,
> Farewell, my pelf, farewell my store.
> The world no longer let me love,
> My hope and treasure lies above. (293)

If this final statement seems disappointingly flat, Puritan readers would certainly have approved of the meditative process that precedes it.[14] Acknowledging the pain that gave earthly burdens their corrective power, Bradstreet confesses an attachment to the world that vindicates Puritan definitions of earthly belief. By articulating her difficulty in devaluing the world while she is still in it, she enacts the experience of a convicted believer, torn between two realms and split by divided allegiances, who is forced to look toward the redemptive future for a final integration of self and a fuller understanding of God's ways.

Dramatizing the process as well as the power of self-abasement, Bradstreet made certain that her readers stood convicted as well. One way in which she universalizes her lessons, as Rosamond Rosenmeier notes, is by placing her experience within a millennialist framework derived from Job and Revelation. The sudden outbreak of the fire parallels such depictions of the Second Coming as the opening stanzas of *The Day of Doom*, and as Rosenmeier suggests, Bradstreet recounts her loss as a prelude to what lay ahead for all believers.[15] The reader's conviction is strengthened by the appealing and universalized memories that the poet associates with her home. Readers who sympathized with her losses—and the "pleasant things" that she selects assured that they did—would perceive their need for the lessons that she forces upon herself. In addition, they would recognize that she has at least tried to react properly to the fire, immediately calling out for God "To strengthen me in my distress / And not to leave me succorless" (292). Bradstreet's struggle to move from initial numbness to salvific pain, an effort intensified by her lament for cherished belongings, also fulfills the Puritan mandate to probe events honestly and at length to discover their deepest lessons.

Finally, the transfer of her attention to that other house, "purchased and paid for too / By Him who hath enough to do" (293), articulates her faith that deliverance from such trials was to be sought in Christ and not the self. That such a heartbroken speaker could call upon Christ would console Puritan readers. Whatever darkness they experienced was not to hinder their own appeals for divine aid.

The speaker is most fully exemplary in her hope for a biblically defined future even as she confesses to a sadly confused present. Bradstreet invokes broader redemptive contexts not only by presenting the fire as a foretaste of Doomsday but by studding the poem with scriptural echoes that enhance the universality of her situation. The key texts lead from the suffering of Job and the world-weariness of the Ecclesiastes Preacher to the eschatological promises set forth in John 14:2 ("In my Father's house are many mansions. . . . I go to prepare a place for you") and Luke 12:34 ("For where your treasure is, there will your heart be also"). The biblical metatext that lies only slightly beneath the surface of the poem reconfirms the essential futurity of a faith that centered not in what was felt and seen but in what *would* be felt and seen in the fullness of time. Bradstreet directs her search for resignation toward Scripture as the sole source of a saintly perspective for which all believers were to hope and pray. As a God-given link between fallen present and gracious future, the language of the Bible becomes a verbal formula to which she must cling precisely because she cannot yet fully internalize its promise. Insisting on the truth of Scripture testimony even when the evidence of God's blessing seems appallingly slim, she confirms, as she does in "Contemplations" and "The Flesh and the Spirit," that earthly substance was no match for biblical promise. The fire, if read as a neobiblical event, made sense in a way that it never could to the natural understanding. This was, of course, a lesson as much for her readers as for herself. They would have derived considerable comfort from her vivid demonstration of the perfectionist trap of expecting too much from a self still engaged in the difficult task of being alive. If the burning of a beloved home provoked a disturbing degree of bitterness and regret, one could at least take comfort that this was a world of probation and not perfection.

Bradstreet's view of life as an unending series of spiritual tests helps close the gap between the struggling speaker of these poems and such relatively more tranquil statements of faith as "The Vanity of All Worldly Things" and "As Weary Pilgrim." These texts do not project two Bradstreets, one anxious to embrace the faith and the other resisting its most basic tenets. Instead, they reveal a poet-teacher striving to internalize and demonstrate both dimensions of a Puritan metaself defined by the opposition of sin and grace, desire and fulfillment, earthly pilgrimage and celestial peace. Far from witnessing a falling in and out of belief, Bradstreet's shifts in mood from poem to poem merely confirm that a warm faith was more difficult to achieve at some times than at others. When her focus is general, as it is in "Vanity," "Pilgrim," and "Contemplations," inner turmoil is more evenly balanced with spiritual reaffirmation. But when her focus is more specific and situational—when she writes about events that expose the vast gulf between earth and heaven—she acknowledges that gulf clearly and honestly. In this lies Bradstreet's most basic accommodation to her readers. They would stand most in need of the consolation that she offers during episodes of sharp affliction, when they too felt that the Spirit had deserted them. At such times they would need to confront dark moods as evidence of human weakness, and they could best learn the rigors of self-conviction from someone who had not found all the answers, someone whose need for Christ's aid was every bit as pressing as their own.

It would be wrong to describe Bradstreet's speaker, whose confessed insufficiencies are inseparable from the spiritual lessons she is trying to absorb and convey, as a deliberately invented self. In poem after poem she forged what *she* saw as the very opposite of a fictive voice—an identity shaped not by human invention but divine truth. Her repeated conflating of personal experience with redemptive pattern reflects her efforts to identify and communicate what she thought was the deepest reality informing her life. Moreover, her experience could not benefit her readers unless she acknowledged sin and doubt as frankly and dramatically as she celebrated assent and assurance. As Jane Donahue Eberwein has observed, "Her poetry expresses, better than any other colonial verse, the human experience of Puritanism."[16] No other poet, not even Edward Taylor, offers a more vivid sense of how it must have felt to be a Puritan in the day-to-day world, constantly mediating between the sinful self that one *was* and the saintly self for which one constantly prayed.

It may well be that Bradstreet's work embodies the struggling Puritan metaself more clearly, and not less, because she was a woman. Although a number of critics interpret her difficulties with the faith as rebellion against the androcentric theological and political structures of her time, such difficulties comprised a normal and even mandated dimension of inner experience for all saints, male and female. For Puritan women, however, social expectation coincided more closely with theological ideals of humility and self-deprecation, and this congruence of spiritual and behavioral norms may have permitted women to internalize the selflessness of the humbled, struggling believer more easily than men.[17] Bradstreet's relatively muted articulations of spiritual joy, especially when compared with an assurance that is sometimes fairly trumpeted by Taylor, may reflect the impact of gender roles on the contrasting social situations of their work. Taylor's *Preparatory Meditations*, private exercises designed to intensify his own experience of doctrine, do not address external events or external readers and are accordingly much fuller in expressing the saint's inner triumphs. Many of Bradstreet's poems, by contrast, assume an added responsibility of edifying family readers consistent with her role as a Puritan mother. Throughout her poetry she is careful not to frustrate these readers by dwelling on an intensity of vision that was at best fleeting and rare. The poems that focus on afflictive events reveal her care, doubtless intensified by her intimate audience, not to talk down to readers who needed a message of sympathy from someone who shared their grief.

Rosenmeier aptly comments that Bradstreet's poetry was written to be "lived through," that the redemptive truth "will not be found in the words but beyond them, in the effects which the words will help to form in her readers."[18] Concerned with conveying that truth through a seamless blend of the confessional and the didactic, Bradstreet emerges as a poet in whom rhetorical purpose is far more evident than is often recognized—not, certainly, a naive artist who blurts out spiritual insufficiencies in an unintended contradiction of what she wants her poems to do. Like anyone instructed in the faith, her children had to learn that the earthly pilgrimage was defined not by perfection but by need. As the poem prefacing her spiritual autobiography suggests, she was determined to speak directly to that need through the work that she would leave behind,

> That being gone, here you may find
> What was your living mother's mind.
> Make use of what I leave in love,
> And God shall bless you from above. (240)

Perhaps seeking to counter the idealized memory of their mother which her children would inevitably retain, the poet assured them that she, too, underwent times of doubt and resistance, that her pilgrimage involved every bit as much pain as theirs.

What Elizabeth Wade White has called Bradstreet's continuing appeal as a "human being" sometimes obscures her identity as a *Puritan* human being. No other Puritan poet dramatized so clearly the orthodox conviction that "all have sinned, and come short of the glory of God" (Rom. 3:23). And none exploited more fully the redemptive possibilities of Paul's promise that "with the mouth confession is made unto salvation" (Rom. 10:10). As Richard Bernard confirmed, "contrition is wrought upon the acknowledgement of your own offences, and not by beholding the evils of other men." For Bradstreet this was how contrition manifested itself in poetry. Her verse demonstrations that, as Weemse attested, God's "grace may be perfitted through our weakness" resulted in a voice no less Puritan for its humanity, a voice that remains perhaps the most directly engaging in early American literature.¹⁹

Part Four

The Pilgrimage Absorbed:

Edward Taylor

Thy Crumb of Dust breaths two words from its breast,
    That thou wilt guide its pen to write aright
To Prove thou art, and that thou art the best
    And shew thy Properties to shine most bright.
    And then thy Works will shine as flowers on Stems
    Or as in Jewellary Shops, do jems.

— Edward Taylor, "Prologue" to the *Preparatory Meditations*

Chapter Seven

Apostle to a Naked Christ:

Gods Determinations for Pilgrim Readers

Ever since the rediscovery of his poetry in the 1930s, Edward Taylor has been isolated from his contemporaries. At first, this isolation was both theological and aesthetic. It took a while for modern criticism to accept the fact that he was really a "Puritan." He seemed far too good a poet for that, and much of the early commentary assumed that some form of unorthodoxy must have allowed him to write the way he did. Taylor's Puritan credentials had to be established largely from his prose, not his verse, and it was only after his conservative stance regarding the Lord's Supper became clear that we had to admit that nothing in his religion, at least, accounted for how different he seemed from Wigglesworth or Bradstreet. Taylor's aesthetic isolation, however, continues to be a major theme in the criticism. He is still commonly discussed as a poet writing "unto thy Praise alone" in an artistic and psychological vacuum. The unusual nature of the *Preparatory Meditations* has prompted many critics to give implicit assent to Karl Keller's comment that Taylor "knew how to play, even when it turned out to be his own game, not God's at all."[1]

Our nearly exclusive focus on the Meditations has prompted us to overstate the uniqueness of Taylor's poetic and meditative "game." By stressing his exceptionalism and thereby obscuring his participation in a poetic exemplified by "As Weary Pilgrim," we have overlooked the extent to which he shared fundamental spiritual and artistic codes with Bradstreet and Wigglesworth. We often forget, for instance, that he wrote a great deal of poetry besides the Meditations, all of which manifests a speaker-reader dynamic that also informs their work. *Gods Determinations* exploits homiletic techniques in common with such generalized articulations of the faith as *The Day of Doom*, "The Flesh and the Spirit," and "As Weary Pilgrim." His early attacks on the Restoration are closely aligned with such topical poems as "God's Controversy with New-England" and the "Dialogue between Old and New England." And his verse treatments of family events project a voice similar to the saintly spouse who speaks in Bradstreet's domestic poems. Such correspondences also suggest something not often recognized about the *Preparatory Meditations*. Redemptive processes embodied in Taylor's private poetry are identical to the meditative work that Wigglesworth and Bradstreet urged upon themselves and their readers. Beneath their more volatile surface, the Meditations record a search for the same essential identity articulated in "As Weary Pilgrim" and "Riddles Unriddled." Despite our tendency to read Taylor's meditative voice as personally and literally expressive, there is an extrapersonal dimension in that voice—a dimension shared with the speakers of most of Bradstreet's and Wigglesworth's poems. Even when Taylor wrote poems for which he would be the sole earthly reader, the paradigm of the saintly metaself exerted a profound influence on the sense of identity that writing helped him generate and sustain.

This is not to deny Taylor's originality as an artist, but to reconnect him more securely with the poetic theory and practice of his time and place. Like his contemporaries, Taylor wrote poetry as a means of assessing how strongly the salvific process lived within him. He forged a voice consistent with this aim, one in which the private and personal became virtually indistinguishable from the paradigmatic and biblical. He, too, saw poetry as a powerful tool for animating a pilgrim's faith within others, and his public verse manifests a sensitivity to situation and audience inseparable from the Puritan regard for preaching as a powerful agent of edification. Like Bradstreet, however, he wields an expressive power that sometimes makes us overlook his didactic aims. Although most Taylor criticism centers on the Meditations and consequently depicts a poet unconcerned with teaching or arousing external readers, a far larger body of his poetry reveals his artistic role as an apostolic witness who persuades readers that they must, in the words of the pastoral saint of *Gods Determinations*, rely "on a naked Christ alone" (444). This reader-centered verse reveals Taylor's full share in a poetic based on stimulating the active pursuit of redeemed identity in poet as well as reader. Although the public poems are rarely central to discussions of Taylor, they in fact provide the firmest basis for considering his relation to Puritan literary culture. Moreover, they serve as a fitting introduction to the Meditations because they articulate, though in more legible form demanded by their public situation, the same self-experience that was the goal of Taylor's private verse. To understand the Taylor of the *Preparatory Meditations*, a poet who turns away from the world in an exclusive soliloquy to Christ, we must first confront this "other" Taylor, the one who spoke to fellow pilgrims as fully and clearly as he could. Once we do so, we may discover that the private contemplative and the public poet are not so far apart as they first appear.

Taylor's earliest extant poem, sent in a letter "to my schoolfellow. W.M.," already exhibits the conflation of private self with saintly pattern central to the psychological and rhetorical conventions of Puritan verse.[2] Underlying the elaborate formula is a conventional Renaissance self-deprecation that translated easily into the Puritan insistence on artistic sincerity. Conceding that "my Muse be not addornd so rare / As Ovids golden verses to declare / My love," the young Taylor insists that "it is in the loome tyed / Where golden quills of love weave on the web" (4). The edifying Puritan speaker also emerges in "A Letter sent to his Brother Joseph Taylor & his wife after a visit," in which Taylor speaks less as a brother than as an Everysaint who reconfirms the need to stand "Rooted on Christ that noble rock alwa / Opposing all the waves of Satans Sea" (4).

The generic voice indispensable to stimulating redemptive response assumes more topical form in three other poems written before Taylor left England. In "A Dialogue between the writer and a Maypole Dresser," stylized debaters provide a close parallel to Wigglesworth's use of characterization in *The Day of Doom*. Functioning as a personification of error, the Maypole Dresser defensively reduces the charge that the maypole reflects "heathens games" to an absurdity: "What must we have no recreations; what / Must all our pastimes be by us forgot?" (7). Distorting the Writer's concession that "a lawfull recreation" is harmless into proof "that our may-poles are but recreations," the Maypole Dresser claims to serve both God and mammon: "We love the lord although wee love our play!" The gentle Writer, by contrast, speaks with compassion, wishing "rare compounds of happinesse" and begging his "Deare friends" to listen "Not for mine own, but for, your own dear sake" (5). Patiently explaining the maypole's origin as a monument to "Flora a whoreish strumpet in Rome" (6), he admonishes in love and not anger by invoking the authority of Scripture. Like the gentle narrator of Wigglesworth's "God's Controversy with New-England," the

Writer assures his opponent that "I do not you command to heare / Or hearken unto mee," but instead insists that "God commands, and mee thinks for his cause / You should disband the heathen rules and laws." The closing call to "repent / Yourselves of this, & for it now relent" (8) reiterates the Writer's pastoral concern by offering the "door of heav[en]" as reward for a corrected attitude. Equally legible spokesmen for truth and error debate in "An other answer," Taylor's response to a pamphlet denying Catholic responsibility for the Great Fire of London.[3] Although the pro-Catholic "Pamphlet" resorts to a theological version of sticks and stones by calling the Reformers "Hereticks" (8), Taylor's Protestant respondent is even less charitable, flatly dismissing the Catholic plea to "Return into your mothers lap" by retorting that "You know n't your Fathers house, therefore / Your Holy Mother is a Whore" (9). The harshness of Taylor's defender of orthodoxy, common in polemic works of the time, is consistent with the poem's attack on a Catholic straw man who represents all "Popish Fry" (13). Frankly exploiting Protestant suspicions regarding the fire, "An other answer" invokes the grim expectation that Rome would burn at the Latter Days in the fire that really mattered: "As London is," the speaker promises, "so Rome shall bee." Regardless of where they stood on such issues as vestments, the Prayer Book, Psalm singing, or even maypoles, Taylor's readers would have relished such an attack on "Satans Synagogue" (10).

The most elaborate rhetorical embodiments of sin and piety in Taylor's early verse are the "proud PRELATE" and the "Poor PROFESSOUR / Silenced on Bartholomew day 1662" who debate in "The Lay-mans Lamentation upon the Civill Death of the late Labour[ers] in the Lords vinyard." Framing what Norman S. Grabo calls a "mock elegy" for a godly ministry suppressed by the Act of Uniformity, Taylor invokes standard hagiographic formula in his lament for "our good news bringers" by depicting their loss as an undoing of saintly actions.[4] "Our Builders [are] raiz'd," he cries, "our Planters plucked up / Our Nources breasts are dry, there's not a Sup / Of Milke for Babes" (14). The piety of such "Sons of Thunder, & of Consolation" justifies the sorrow of "poore Children" who have lost these "Spiritual Fathers": "Alas! our Israels Glory is departed! / And God's own Arke is by Philistins carted." Taylor employs the common elegiac image of godly preachers as "fixed Stars that filled our Hemisphere / With brightest beames of light," now sadly replaced with the "foggy Metiors" and "bad Vapours" of "thin-soul'd Priests" (15). God "tip'd" the tongues of the dissenting clergy when they preached, "And when they pray'd, soe warme was their request / That sure the Spirit of fire was in their breasts." They were, in sum, Christ's "Thundring Legion," not hypocrites who were "in their pulpits Angels cleare, / And Divels Carnate when they were elsewhere." That their lives provided such "lively Comments of their Preaching" absolves the Professor from the Prelate's charge that "you too much Esteem" their loss. As the Professor insists, "Wee'll not Hyperbolize, & yet wee'll call, / Them next to Christ, our verie all in all" (16).

Taylor's suasive purposes lend a functionality to these stylized characters. The proud Prelate, attacking the Professor as a "whining Sectary" (14), flatly asserts that "Change is noe robbery" with a cold arrogance underscored by his persistent name-calling: "Foolish Fanatick, silly Scismatick, / Round-headed Fury, Crack-brain'd Lunatick" (14); "prattling Zealot" (16). The Prelate's argument finally reduces to sheer threat. "Wee have got power now," he boasts in his last speech, "How dare you prate / Wee'll Gag you if you prattle at this rate" (18). His perfect foil, of course, is the Professor, who represents all those who "went t' our Churches, big with expectation / Hoping to finde Elishas, but wee saw / Onely Elijahs Mantle stuff'd with straw" (14). That Taylor took pains to make the Professor seem both impassioned and reasonable is suggested by the concession that some conformists "May Possibly, bee found without the Leaven / Of Ignorance, or Scandal," though such traits occur in "hardly one in seaven" (16). Some were "lead a wry: / And did Conforme in hearts Simplicity," while others "wanted Courage" or "Coine." But these exceptions prove the rule: "Take out these few," the Professor asserts, "& every one o' th' rest, / Call you, not Parish Priest, but Parish Pest."

Despite the Professor's "desire, / Wholy to purge myselfe from Passions fire" and "all black Prejudice" in order to "paint" the conforming ministers "in their colours right" (16), his "Calmly" rendered "Charactar" is every bit as stylized—and in the Puritan view, accurate—as the idealized description of the dissenters. Calling the conformists "Ill Beasts: Dombe Dogs: Blinde Leaders of the blinde," he claims that "My Inke's not black enough for to discribe" the true believer's "sad Dilemma" of having to choose to "Displease your God, or else displease your King" (17). Through the Wigglesworth-like strategy of placing the reader between two diametrically opposed ministries, Taylor makes the proper choice an easy one: "men of Conscience need not long to muse / What in this case to leave, & what to choose." Despite the standard call to "Save us, Lord, save us, from this Generation" (18), Taylor offers none of the optimism that usually concludes the New World jeremiad. Nor does he join Bradstreet in restating the motherland's potential as the New Zion. In the two decades that had passed since Bradstreet's "Dialogue between Old England and New," Puritan control of England had come and gone. New England, however, still held promise for a continuing Reformation, and not long after writing "The Lay-mans Lamentation" Taylor would be there himself, taking up Elisha's mantle in emulation of those sons of thunder and consolation whose silence he mourned.

Taylor's most extensive verse polemic against sin in the world is the *Metrical History of Christianity*, an unfinished epic of some twenty thousand lines written probably during the first decade of the eighteenth century. Taylor's *History*, like Wigglesworth's "God's Controversy with New-England" and Bradstreet's "Four Monarchies," features a prophetic speaker who stresses the moral significance of earthly events. Like Wigglesworth and Bradstreet, Taylor enacts a self-humbling that points up the sublimity of his theme. Repeatedly he confesses that "by my blundrings oft the strings do fall / Or else my bluntness doth thy beams begall / Lord help me then." Although Providential history "deserves a pen Divine," he must resort to far more mundane tools: "But now my quill attempts it as I stand / With Candle light and Lanthorn in my hand." Like all Puritan poems, however, the *History* derives its artistic worth from the redemptive "Truth" that it sings, whose "blaze," Taylor insists, "Will grace the shine the more and bless the Phrase."[5]

As the "Phrase" is blessed, so is the phrase-maker. At once humbled and enobled as a neobiblical seer who grasps God's design even in the darkest times and events, Taylor appropriates an identity whom faith has "made receptive," as Keller notes, to history as "something to be read as proof of one's faith."[6] This self-affirming dimension of the *History* is especially clear from Taylor's goal of extending biblical vision to post-biblical times, a mission that he sees as frankly heroic. Depicting himself as a ship captain guided by divine light through the murky past, he resolves to share "truth's Optick" with the reader, to find in "the Soile / Of Holy Truth, the beams of Some rich mine" and to "out quoile / Before your Eyes that you may see their Shine" (398). Taylor re-voyages time as a self able to pierce through "darksom dayes" to grasp the "Shine" of "Prophetick Truth" revealed only to God's messengers. By recounting God's story, he seals his identity as a participant in that story. Indeed, it sometimes seems almost as if divine glory will not fully exist until he tells it. He admits, for instance, that divine "Justice" is hard to discern in the "dark pitchy night" of Henry II, when she seems to have "No hands, or hands polluted, and not white" (387). But a closer, grace-informed reading of the times allows him to reveal "How on her glorious Bench in Robes all Bright / More White than Snow, She Sits dispensing right" (387). Like the biblical prophets, Taylor exposes secrets accessible only to an understanding renewed by faith. When he asks Justice to "give thy hand, / That I may shew it White, though some think tand" (262), he justifies God's ways to benighted man by enacting a godly reading of human history.

In each "Century" his prophetic speaker reveals the "Shine" of divine "Grace," "Justice," "Efficiency," "Patience," and above all, "Truth." Offering his text as "our Looking Glass" reflecting the "face" of God's will (382), Taylor repeatedly invokes the faith that makes him Truth's instrument despite his "maimed Sapphicks" and "dull Pentameters":

> I in thine Honour do ingauge my quill
>   My very Heart I truely mean.
> These muddy puddles do fulfill
>   Thy Holy breathed Veans. (314)

As the heart/quill equation suggests, the *History* is as much a spiritual exercise as Taylor's more private verse. By articulating a salvific humility that unlocks Truth's deepest secrets, he asserts an assured intimacy with the divine force that affords privileged insights reserved for true seers: "Sweet Truth I now get ore thy Garden Style / To View thy flowers in their bright Shine" (356); "Prophetick Truth most brightly doth display / Its beams in this Dark night and Such I'le name" (398). To a self empowered by prophetic vision, narrating history is inseparable from praising God. Taylor recounts "Divine Efficiency" in the tenth century, for instance, "That God may have the Honour of the Same" (351). God's work in the ninth century similarly "makes my Hymns thus toote" (319). And in a recurring image, the poet harvests the "beams" of Justice for God's glory and the reader's edification: "Which gathering up, in Sheaves, I'le binde and shock / The Glory of thy harvest to unlock" (344). By dramatizing the effects of Providence upon a prophetic self, Taylor collapses all of time into a spirited reconfirmation of divine control despite the chaos apparent to merely human perception. Even when she "seem'd as she would take a nap" (114), Justice is still vigilant: "Wickedness" finally provokes her, and she "Sends flashes" that "through these Chincks of Providence shine bright" (114). By repeatedly depicting the renewal of "Justice that dorment seemd to lie" (178), Taylor, like Wigglesworth, confronts his readers with historical time as a fragile medium in which divine anger could "start" at any moment: "Now it darts / Its fiery beames and from her Chamber flies / And to this darksome age she doth thus say / Hoe, hoe, my Glory comes to tend your day" (178).

Such revelations could be exposed only by an heir to those biblical and post-biblical witnesses to the divine pattern concealed in human events. Taylor's role in the *History* echoes that of John on Patmos, "Whose Golden Pen so cleare doth write / Those Glorious Visions that did light / Before his Eyes in open Sight, / That 't us assails" (9). John's text, obscure to nonbelievers but "cleare" enough to those who read it with the eye of faith, animates Taylor's own perceptual and homiletic mission: how can he *not* write when "Glorious Grace breaks forth to greet / Us with such gales?" (9). John Chrysostom offers similar precedent for Taylor's explication of God's "Efficiency" in human affairs: "John Chrysostoms holy Pulpit flung / A silver drill of Rhetorick which run / The Macedonian heresy a drift" (132). And the Venerable Bede brings the gift of prophecy closer home, to the English nation. Bede "In sermons did the Holy texts Expound," and "Turn'd Psalms, Johns Gospell, other books imbrac'd, / Into his Native tongue, before all grac'd" (241).

What unites Taylor with these figures is his ability to translate the past into current redemptive experience. His underlying thesis is that Providence controls human events now no less than in the past, in bad times no less than in good. The chief burden of the *History* is to clarify "Bright Justice" "untill thy Glory blaze / Before their Eyes that deem thee dead these dayes" (301). Like Wigglesworth's "God's Controversy," the *History* traces a struggle between sin and grace identical to the redemptive turmoil within the individual soul. Taylor's epic "Looking Glass" (382) reflects not only God's plan for the world but the cycles of individual belief. The timelessness of "Christs sparkling Image," which "shines / Through these Choice Persons Lives and Lines" (11), links a Primitive Church of Edenic purity with the individual assurance articulated in the *Preparatory Meditations* and the closing lyrics of *Gods Determinations*. The early "Saints rising up in Churchhood" receive spiritual benefits that congregational worship continued to offer: their "Officers" shine "like Angells," "Or like the Stars in glories line / And flame forth Rayes of Light Divine / In holy Wayes." Taylor further conflates the historical and personal dimensions of salvation by describing past corruption in language echoing the agonies of a convicted soul. Tenth-century "Cruelties," for example, fly "In Bloody Colours, and in flames that try / What mettall Heaven's made of, in deep groans" (382). The rise of "superstition," by which Taylor invokes present sin as much as historical error, persists to the narrative present in the "dawbings" and "ditchy doings" (163) of "Romish trash" (274). Indeed, all of Taylor's references to Rome, including the predictable appearance of Pope Joan as an emblem of papal corruption (285–86), enhance the presentation of history as "a drama of opposites," a sin-grace dichotomy of outer ceremony *versus* inner belief. Like the Maypole Dresser, the proud Prelate, Satan in *Gods Determinations*, and conviction itself, the Roman Church unwittingly plays a salvific role in Taylor's historiography as the institutional sin by which Reformed grace achieves clearer definition. Rome repeatedly provides the darkness indispensable to Taylor's celebration of the "radient beams of blessed Gospell light / That fly from Holy Lips of true Divines / Not muddied with the dirt of sinfull times" (319).[7]

By exposing the corruption of "sinfull times," the *History* enacts a communal confession of sin that corresponds to the private confessions dramatized in the Meditations. Forcing himself to tell the story of Rome's ascent, Taylor articulates the remorse of a believer caught in enough "lies" "to crush and break the back / Of my poore pen" (337). Like Bradstreet, who uses biblical history in "Contemplations" to sharpen her conviction of personal unworth, Taylor offers post-biblical history as a confirmation of depravity's iron grip on the world and the self. What Donald Stanford has called Taylor's "morbid interest in torture and pain" reflects the poet's belief that if time and the world were ever to regain value as sources of redemptive lessons, historical sins of the tribe had to be acknowledged as openly as private sins of the heart. As in Bradstreet's poems of affliction, however, confessed darkness leads to a rediscovery of light. Even when Taylor apologizes for the corruptions that he relates, he confirms that history's harsh tonic offered a cure that led to spiritual healing. To this end he and his reader drink the "swill" of past atrocities as a salvific purgative: "And for the reader's sake a drop or more / I now attempt to vomit as before" (149). As Stanford notes, "it is difficult to understand how the same poet could write" such a *History* and yet so vividly convey "the sweetness of God's grace" in the Meditations and *Gods Determinations*.[8] But like Bradstreet and Wigglesworth, Taylor believed that an unflinching confrontation with sin made redemptive sweetness possible. Moreover, Taylor's story of the world's "swill" unites speaker and reader on the proper side of the redemptive fence. Here is sad truth, Taylor constantly states, which we must confront for our own good: "now," he warns, "my pen doth weep to lay before yee / The Dismall things it finds: attend the story" (127).

Presenting the world's "story" as a salvific goad, Taylor speaks as an exemplary saint whose joys and sorrows are inseparably joined to the glorious victories and temporary setbacks of Providence. When the gospel light dims, so does he: "I therefore Change my verse and bring out Rhimes / Tunde to the Melancholy Shape of Times" (193). Redemptive triumph similarly generates its own language and response. When Taylor recounts the victories of the faith he cannot "choose but make my Feet / Ware Sapphick Slippers when this sweet / And Glorious Grace breaks forth" (9). In his varied responses to the "Shape of Times," Taylor's speaker consistently offers the past as a test of current spiritual response. His narrative turns the ups and downs of Church history into atemporal and ongoing redemptive challenges issued by a self fashioned in emulation of the Protestant martyrs, who "in Canterbury flame / Were burnt all Singing Psalms as voide of Pain" (408). Taylor, too, sings "Psalms" of God's work in the world by presenting a story that would someday be "voide of Pain"—an unfolding revelation of a divine "Efficiency" that would finally replace all suffering with gracious delight. Throughout the *History* he unravels the threads of divine Justice through time as a means of helping redemption along, of lending "to Graces web a brush" (144). Taylor the redemptive historian speaks as a saintly metaself who manifests, not only in his grand theme but in his ardent desire to tell it, the irresistible force of Providence in human lives. Assuring his readers that God was alive not just among the Apostles, the Fathers, and the martyrs, but in their own time, Taylor hoped to persuade them that the sweep of history proved God's concern for their salvation as well.

Whether he denounces a lukewarm English church or the corruption staining the broader history of Christianity, Taylor repeatedly grounds historical events in a sin-grace duality in which turmoil reflects a fulfillment rather than disruption of the divine plan. An identical dynamic informs his extended treatment of redemption from the inside. While the *Metrical History* recounts world events from the hopeful perspective afforded by faith, *Gods Determinations Touching his Elect*, Taylor's best-known public poem, encourages a correspondingly optimistic view of personal identity. Like the Professor of the "Lay-mans Lamentation" and the prophetic speaker of the *Metrical History*, the "Soul" whose conversion is narrated in the poem embodies the generic traits of the saved self. This time, however, Taylor turns from external event and controversy in order to focus more directly on private religious experience.

An internal epic treating the pilgrim's progress from self-doubt to assurance, *Gods Determinations* differs sharply in approach from that other American Puritan epic, *The Day of Doom*. While Wigglesworth's sinners embody a variety of doctrinal errors, Taylor creates a single "fictive" character who manifests only one fault: he is too timid to assert his probable share in salvation. These differing strategies most likely reflect a contrast in how the two poets defined their intended readers. While Wigglesworth addressed a broad audience of believers and nonbelievers alike, Taylor directed his efforts toward those who, like Soul, believed the Word but hesitated to claim its redemptive promise. Unlike Wigglesworth, who wrote for publication, Taylor seems to have written for members of his congregation—one senses this when he has divine Mercy predict that "Some will have Farms to farm, some wives to wed: / Some beasts to buy" (394–95)—whose spiritual troubles he knew from his pastoral dealings with them. While Wigglesworth aimed his message at what preachers called a "mingled" or "mixed" people, Taylor could assume that most of his readers would eventually manifest the signs of saving grace. What held them back was not the full range of human perversity, stubbornness, or rebellion, but anguish at the sin that they found within.⁹

Although Wigglesworth and Taylor might almost seem to depict two different Puritanisms, the two poems instead reflect the standard homiletic assumption that the Old Creature and the New required very different appeals. As John Weemse put it, "Application of Doctrine stands either in rebuke, or consolation to a sinner; under which two, all other Doctrines or instructions are included." This dual function of preaching corresponded to a duality within the earthly believer and within the Bible itself. As the "two-edged sword" capable of discerning "the thoughts and intents of the heart" (Heb. 4:12), Scripture could either convict or console, depending on the believer's inner state. The biblical prophets modeled this duality inherent in preaching the Word. In his *Arte of Prophecying*, William Perkins encouraged ministers to emulate "the manner of the Prophets in their Sermons, to denounce judgements and destruction to the wicked: and to promise deliverance in the Messias to those that doe repent." These two modes of preaching animated the salvific roles of the two dispensations and of their inner parallels, the sinful and saintly dimensions of redeemed identity. As Perkins explained, "when the word is preached, there is one operation of the Law, and another of the Gospel." Convicting legal lessons necessarily preceded the consolations of the Gospel. Those who had "knowledge, but are not as yet humbled," Perkins advised, were to be pushed toward the "legall sorrow" of realizing that they could not fulfill the Law on their own. To such "hard-hearted" hearers "the Law must bee denounced with threatning, together with the difficulty of obtaining deliverance until they be pricked in their heart." Believers already "humbled in part" were to be handled more gently: "Let the Law bee propounded, yet so discreetly tempered with the Gospell, that beeing terrified with their sinnes, and with the meditation of Gods judgement, they may together also at the same time receive solace by the Gospel." Hampered more by timidity than pride, such hearers could receive "the law without the curse." Since they had already partly achieved the broken heart preparatory to the coming of grace, they deserved an application of Gospel comfort appropriate to their more advanced spiritual condition.¹⁰

Wigglesworth's poem functioned primarily as a "sentence of the Law" that spoke, as Perkins defined it, "of Perfect inherent righteousnes, of eternall life given through the workes of the Law, of the contrary sinnes, and of the curse that is due unto them." Propelling his readers toward the fulfillment of the Law at Judgment, Wigglesworth urged conviction on those whose spiritual growth was either stunted or neglected altogether. Seeking to encourage godly remorse, he articulated a comprehensive attack on depraved thinking by depicting those who would find themselves "At Christ's left hand."[11] *Gods Determinations* dramatized the gentler operation of the Word for those further along the redemptive path, sincere believers whose sense of conviction was so acute that it hampered their assurance of salvation. Depicting redemptive turmoil from the perspective of the saved, Taylor presented a "sentence of the Gospel" that treated, as Perkins explained, "Christ & his benefits" and "faith beeing fruitfull in good workes: as, Joh. 3. 16." The verse that Perkins cites as the archetypal gospel sentence—"For God so loved the world, that he gave his only begotten Son, that whosoever believeth in him should not perish, but have everlasting life"—provides the thesis of *Gods Determinations*, a thesis encapsulated when Taylor's pastoral Saint advises Soul to rely "on a naked Christ alone" (444).

Like Wigglesworth in *Meat Out of the Eater*, Taylor writes for an already contrite audience, and thus casts the reading self in the most optimistic terms possible—a strategy antithetical to that enacted in *The Day of Doom*. While Wigglesworth devotes most of the doomsday poem to the arguments of the damned, Taylor quickly dismisses the vast legion of the unregenerate to "eternall woe" (400). The rest of *Gods Determinations* explores the self-doubt that keeps the various ranks of the elect from accepting their vocation. Taylor's evangelical emphasis does not, however, minimize the importance of conviction: the first twenty-two lyrics vividly depict the terror of true remorse. But Taylor places conviction at the beginning of time and not at its end, when repentance came too late. The redemptive process starts when his generic hero-Soul, prefigured in Adam, absorbs the historical Fall: "Man at a muze, and in a maze doth stand, / While Feare the Generall of all the Band / Makes inroads on him" (389). Like Cain in Bradstreet's "Contemplations," Taylor's paradigmatic Soul "quickly Findes God stand as Enemy" (389), quaking "As if each Word he was about to make, / Should hackt a sunder be" (398). Accepting his inability to defend himself, Soul embodies the legal conviction that makes possible the gracious influences described in the rest of the poem. While Wigglesworth's sinners apply carnal reason to a futile debate with the Law personified, Soul turns immediately to Christ "for Succour" as a self split by grace:

"in my soul," he confesses, "my soul finds many faults. / And though I justify myself to's [Satan's] face: / I do Condemn myselfe before thy Grace" (413). Taylor's readers would immediately recognize Soul's conviction as genuine. By crying out for Christ's help, Soul initiates the same escape from legal sorrow that the poem offered the reader.[12]

Taylor repeatedly affirms that severe attacks of conscience may well signal the workings of grace. Encouraging the reader's hope as a self on the verge of such rehabilitation, he presents "low" spirits (398) as a prelude for the gracious influences that follow. Even as the evidence of salvation continues to mount, Soul remains acutely aware of his sin. Although he is able to imitate Christ by telling Satan to "begone therefore" (413), he cannot deny Satan's accusations of unworth. The contest in humility that engages the second and third ranks, each claiming that "Its worse with us" (427), gently mocks the overly scrupulous reader's obsession with personal insufficiency. Even toward the end of the poem, as the evidence of election becomes unmistakable, Soul retains salvific humility: "What I such Praises sing! How can it bee? / Shall I in Heaven sing?" (457). As Soul undergoes the transformation from sinful to saintly identity, the closing lyrics fulfill Mercy's promise when the redemptive plan was being hammered out by the divine dispensations: "When any such are startled from ill, / And cry help, help, with tears, I will advance / The Musick of the Gospell Minsterill" (396). The comfortable effects of the Gospel ministry/minstral signal a shift from fear to joy emphasized by a second "Preface," in which Saint begins to provide pastoral counseling appropriate to believers who doubted not the Word but themselves. The "Want of Grace" (433) that Soul protests at this point stems, as Taylor makes clear, not from Christ's anger but from the same mistakenly dark self-exegesis that kept readers from their own assurance.[13]

Taylor is no more conciliatory than Wigglesworth toward the products of unregenerate thought. As the pastoral Saint affirms, "Faith will stand where Reason hath no ground" (436), and Satan's "Accusation of the Inward Man" confirms that "The Understandings dark, and therefore Will / Account of Ill for Good, and Good for Ill" (409). But because *Gods Determinations* depicts a successful vocation, Taylor is able to portray what Thomas Shepard called "a renewing of the whole man" in Christ's promise that grace will "Change / Those fond Affections that do range / As yelping beagles" (416) after the satanic "Cur" (415). Thomas Hooker confirmed the same lesson that Wigglesworth underscored in *Meat Out of the Eater*: although children of light may be "clouded with the darkness of their sins," they are "never overwhelmed with darkness, but they should be able to see their sins, and to see a way out for them, in which they should walk." While *The Day of Doom* emphasizes initial conviction, Taylor follows Hooker's "way out" to its consolatory end in conversion and church membership. And while the doomsday epic pits man against God in order to demonstrate the futility of self-reliance, *Gods Determinations* pits God and man against Satan through a dialectic prefigured in the "Dialogue between Justice and Mercy" and clarified by the struggle between sin and grace within the gracious soul. This new alliance, sealed in Christ's exhortation to "Fail not: my Battells fight" (418), encourages the reader's rehabilitated view of the role of both dispensations in effecting salvation. So complete is the perceptual harmony of Justice and Mercy that in the "Dialogue" they exchange their customary roles. Mercy at one point warns that "little Sins, but little pardons have," while Justice urges the "Humble Humble Soule" to "Cheer up, poor Heart, for satisfi'de am I" (397).[14]

Gods Determinations also promotes a redeemed view of time, one in which the Fall is eternally reenacted within remorseful believers: "Although we fall and Fall, and Fall and Fall / And Satan fall on us as fast," Christ "purgeth us and doth us call / Our trust on him to Cast" (420). By forcing the reader's identification with Adam as prelude to a hopeful identification with the redeemed, Taylor depicts salvation as a continuing process as well. "All this I'le do," Mercy promises, "and do it o're and o're" (392). And because grace makes earthly time useful, the initial focus in "The Preface" on creation and natural beauty presents the world as a realm that still has redemptive value. While *The Day of Doom* offers an atemporal vision—earthly time has in fact ended—that ruptures the reader's comforting ties with the world, *Gods Determinations* depicts a hopeful present well stocked with spiritual aids for those who walk "in the suburbs here of bliss": "These are Gods Way-Marks thus inscrib'd; this hand / Points you the way unto the Land Divine" (449). Wigglesworth invokes the future to undermine the present, but Taylor celebrates the present as harbinger of a glorious future. Calling the Judgment the greatly desired "pay day" of the elect (392), he counsels patience, not panic: "Judge not this Web while in the Loom, but stay / From judging it untill the judgment day" (449). Doomsday, William Ames affirmed, would "dispense the greatest terror among the ungodly and the greatest joy among the godly."[15] Prompting his readers to adopt the gracious view of the Judgment as their own, Taylor concludes *Gods Determinations* not with the end of the world but in the here and now of the developing saint, set in "this Curious Garden" of the visible church and its ordinances (454). An institutional recapitulation of Eden, the church provides the reader with a second "beginning," an experiential renewal that extends beyond the poem itself as the joys of the covenanted New Creature supplant the natural world and the Old Creature described in the first "Preface." As the poem closes, the garden of the visible church is ready to take up where the text leaves off, with the ordinances poised to offer continuing nourishment and support to the saintly identity that Taylor has animated.

Repeatedly encouraging a gracious response to Scripture, Taylor urges the reader to internalize the Puritan belief that the Word is "facile and comfortable," as Thomas Hall put it, to those who "are of a semblable disposition to it." The Bible became "facile" through a redeemed understanding of its Christocentric unity, a unity that Taylor dramatizes throughout the poem. When, for example, Mercy foretells the stubbornness of the elect in resisting salvation—"And I may stand untill the Chilly Dews / Do pearle my Locks before he'l stand on mee" (394)—Mercy's offer recalls "the voice of my beloved that knocketh, saying, Open to me, my sister, my love, my dove, my undefiled: for my head is filled with dew, and my locks with the drops of the night" (Cant. 5:2). The identification of Mercy with the Canticles Bridegroom also suggests the eschatological restatement of Christ's persistent love in Revelation: "Behold, I stand at the door, and knock: if any man hear my voice, and open the door, I will come in to him, and will sup with him, and he with me" (Rev. 3:20). This text lends deeper resonance to Taylor's image by connecting the knocking of Mercy/Bridegroom/Lamb with the Lord's Supper ("I . . . will sup with him"). The ability to grasp such connections helped Taylor's readers feel an inner conformity with the Bible text. Christ's promise that "I am your own, and you are mine" (405) encouraged their assimilation of the true Bride's claim that "My beloved is mine, and I am his" (Cant. 2:16; also 6:3 and 7:10). Although this covenantal bond is later aped by Satan, who addresses the "Inward Man" with unsettling familiarity—"how do yee: You and I Embrace" (410)—the final lyrics reconfirm the mutual love of reader and Savior foreshadowed in biblical imagery: "So God is theirs avoucht, they his in Christ. / In whom all things they have, with Grace are splic'te" (456).[16]

The consolatory framework of the Song of Songs consistently informs the perception of Christ that the poem offers. While the Christ of Justice depicted in *The Day of Doom* was designed to strike terror in the unregenerate, *Gods Determinations* presented its readers with a Christ of Mercy appropriate to animating the affections of a saved soul. Taylor urges the reader's love for Christ in his manifestation as the Bridegroom by depicting Mercy as a pre-Incarnate Christ who "breaths out perfumed reech / And doth revive the heart before it breaks" (391). In her promise to "Wooe them long" (395), Mercy echoes the Bridegroom's invitation to "Rise up, my love, my fair one, and come away" (Cant.

2:10): "My Dove," Mercy calls, "Come hither linger not, nor stay" (398). And the Christ who belittles Satan as a broken-toothed "Cur" becomes a divine lover who administers redemptive salve to Soul's—and the reader's—convicted conscience:

> Peace, Peace, my Hony, do not Cry,
> My Little Darling, wipe thine eye,
>   Oh Cheer, Cheer up, come see.
> Is anything too deare, my Dove,
> Is anything too good, my Love
>   To get or give for thee?   (414)

Shepard insisted that the elect, fired with holy love, would "Come first for Christ himself, and then . . . for all his benefits." Taylor incorporates the Canticles allegory into his readers' experience of a Christ whom they would surely love for himself alone, a Christ who "Hath Bowells melting, and Expanded arms: / Hath sweet imbraces, Tender mercy free" (449). Such a portrayal could only intensify their desire to join with Soul as "the Lambs espoused Wife" (453)—to internalize the Christic intimacy that the poem held out to them.[17]

Sin, by contrast, is carefully separated from and opposed to the reader's essential identity. Although Taylor's narrator confirms that "Nothing man did throw down all by Sin" (388), military imagery portrays depravity as an invasion that can potentially be repulsed. Taylor's Satan, revealed as the real source of excessive scrupulosity, extends the consolatory distancing of sin from the reader. Satan can wrest fear even from the consolatory language of Canticles, as when he challenges the second rank whether they exude "An Aromatick Spicery most sweet. / Is't so with you?" (422).[18] But faith reduces Satan to a harmless figure who instills remorse and thereby assumes an unwitting role as an agent of salvation. By stressing Satan's ultimate impotence, Taylor encourages an experience of self that contrasts sharply with that instilled by *The Day of Doom*. Wigglesworth, challenging his reader in "A Short Discourse on Eternity" to count the grains of sand, the "Atomes of the Air," every hair on "Man and Beast," and all the motes of "Dust," warns that "Yet shall the Years of sinners tears, / the Number far surmount" (68). But Taylor draws from the fallibility of human faculties another lesson altogether. At the conclusion of *Gods Determinations*, mind-boggling numbers invoke not the endlessness of suffering but "Our Insufficiency to Praise God suitably, for his Mercy." If "Heaven, and Earth be Atomizd" (451) and if each atom itself formed a little "World" of men; if each saint had as many tongues as these men would have; if each tongue could produce numberless "Songs of Praise"; and if each of these songs contained numberless "Tunes most sweet"—"Our Musick would the World of Worlds out ring / Yet be unfit within thine Eares to ting" (452). Considered within the perspective offered by grace, the disparity between man and God brings wonder rather than shame. As *Gods Determinations* closes, Taylor invites his readers to join the song of the redeemed despite their failings, not in a remote eschatological future but in their experiential present.

The final lyrics, which parallel Taylor's own devotions in the *Preparatory Meditations*, demonstrate how grace could animate a tongue stilled by self-doubt.[19] Taylor's saint sings despite the "Lisp" of depravity and thereby provides an exhortative model by which humbled believers could move from spiritual paralysis to a full-voiced "Admiration" of the church and its head. The speechlessness of conviction dramatized early in *Gods Determinations* ends in the fullness of meditative praise, and as the representative saint finds his voice, humbled readers are urged to join their own with others already in the covenantal coach. To those "few" who are still "not in," who walk alongside the coach as "Travellers afoot" (459), Taylor gives every assurance that they will soon find themselves joyfully riding and singing along with the rest.

Within the chronology of sacred history *Gods Determinations* precedes *The Day of Doom*: creation and the earthly joys of belief antedate the world's destruction and the fulfillment of those joys at doomsday. In soteriological terms, however, the poems reverse their positions. The private doomsday of conviction analogous to the final Judgment had to be endured before life in the world could be seen as a prelude to celestial bliss. Christ could indeed, Hooker attested, "change a proud and unbeleeving heart into a beleeving heart: but he must first destroy the power of unbeleef before he can bring in faith."[20] In terms of Puritan inner life, *Gods Determinations* thus begins where *The Day of Doom* ends. Believers who recognized their insufficiency under the Law were ready to see the world and the self as Taylor portrays them. Taylor's dramatic-narrative structure, his linking of private and communal redemptive contexts, perhaps even his selection of a poetic form—all were probably suggested by Wigglesworth's epic, which had been a best-seller for some twenty years. But as his title makes clear, Taylor wished to show the redemptive schema not as it applied to all mankind but only "touching his Elect," a narrower focus that allowed a much fuller expression of "the Comfortable Effects thereof."

Taken together, the two poems demonstrate that the eternal verities of doctrine were, when framed for various readers and hearers, anything but absolute and static in form and expression. Between Wigglesworth's stubborn reader and Taylor's timid reader lay a continuum of souls at every stage of salvific development, in need of diverse and ever-varying proportions of legal conviction and evangelical consolation. As Richard Bernard confirmed in his manual for preachers, the varied spiritual needs of diverse hearers made it necessary for a minister to "preach to the penitent with love, rejoicing at their conversion, [and] to the obstinate sharply, yet also with grief, for that they will not bee reformed." Both modes of preaching were, of course, mutually interdependent, and the prevalence of "love" or "grief" depended on the current state of the hearer's soul. We have seen that despite the predominantly dehortative message of *The Day of Doom*, Wigglesworth's stress on eschatological justice stimulated the reader's search for mercy in the experiential present: "Whoever sought heav'n as he ought," Christ asks in the very act of Judgment, "and seeking perished?" (48). Nor does Taylor minimize the Law in his exposition of Gospel mercy. His theology was certainly no softer than Wigglesworth's, and *Gods Determinations* is no more egalitarian than *The Day of Doom* in its definition of the saved. Moreover, Justice and Mercy pursue the elect soul with frightening relentlessness, and even the comforting "Christs Reply" underscores the pain of submitting to the divine will: "If in the fire where Gold is tride / Thy Soule is put, and purifide / Wilt thou lament thy loss?" (418). Despite their contrasting strategies, Wigglesworth and Taylor were united as public poets in their concern with adapting their message to the reader's spiritual needs. If those needs were ignored, preachers—and preaching poets—were accountable for far more than a mere failure of eloquence. "For we must remember," Bernard confirmed in a warning that the Puritan poet took to heart, "that we have a flocke to feed; their bloud to anser for."[21]

Despite its obvious strengths as a persuasive text, Taylor never published *Gods Determinations*. He may have felt that the poem, if circulated beyond his pastoral charges, might prompt those who were not ready for its comforting message to embrace that message prematurely. Puritan preachers considered unmerited consolation to be a real danger. "He that heales overly," Hooker warned, "hurts more than he heales; Are there not many to be humbled?" Shepard similarly cautioned that "If ministers shall preach the remedy before they show misery, woe to this age, that shall be deprived of those blessings which the former gloried in, and blessed the Lord for."[22] Given the poem's appropriateness for contrite readers, Taylor probably made a fair copy not for formal publication but in order to circulate the manuscript privately to those in his congregation who seemed, based on his pastoral dealings with them, to deserve its consolation. Many may have been called, but unlike *The Day of Doom*, *Gods Determinations* was intended for those few who seemed most likely to be chosen.

CHAPTER EIGHT

"BOTH WAYES BORN": EDWARD TAYLOR AS

WEARY PILGRIM

In *Gods Determinations* and the *Metrical History of Christianity* Taylor addressed two different but complementary arenas of redemption, the psychological and the historical. Despite their contrasting concerns with the internal and the external, both poems helped readers grasp the salvific utility of conflict. Just as historical afflictions furthered God's plan for the world, inner turmoil pushed the individual believer toward a warmer experience of the faith. At the opposite pole from these reader-centered poems are the *Preparatory Meditations*, vehicles for Taylor's private exploration of his own struggles as an earthly pilgrim seeking signs of inner congruence with the saintly metaself. Between the public poetry and the Meditations lies a third body of verse that combines elements of each. At once situational and introspective, these "occasional" poems record Taylor's self-exegesis as he reacts to specific events in his life. While his work is closer to Wigglesworth's when he speaks as sacred historian and pastoral counselor, he most resembles Bradstreet when he contemplates the joys and sorrows of daily life in terms of the cyclical patterns suggestive of assured belief.

Like Bradstreet, Taylor responds to his world with a voice reflecting his search for an identity shaped by salvific experience. Because that identity was defined by inner doubleness, the occasional verse enacts the same struggle that he urges upon spiritually timid readers in *Gods Determinations*. "Resolve the matter," he scolds himself in one of these poems, "Stay thyselfe or Goe. / Be n't both wayes born." Ironically, the hesitation that these lines convey keeps him from feeling redemptive doubleness as fully as he'd like. In theological and experiential terms, confirmation that he has been born "both wayes"—in grace as well as in sin—is what he most desires. By articulating Taylor's reaction to external situation and event, the occasional verse may have released him, as Thomas M. Davis suggests, to pursue the exclusively interior direction of the *Preparatory Meditations*. While the Meditations enact redemptive self-scrutiny in the timeless realm of heavenly contemplation, the occasional poems root Taylor's pilgrim identity in his immediate time and place. A college exercise, the discovery of giant bones, the behavior of insects, a devastating flood, a rainstorm, courtship and marriage, family tragedy, the deaths of saints, a spinning wheel, an episode of spiritual dullness—all become catalysts for a textual identity chastened and elevated by divine guidance. Like Bradstreet, Taylor does not write simply to record the events of his life. Instead, he joins her in celebrating such events as "occurrants" that mark the clarity of his assurance as a pilgrim journeying toward the better world to which they pointed.[1]

One of the earliest of these occasions produced "My last Declamation in the Colledge Hall," Taylor's contribution to a standard exercise in which Harvard students defended the five senses and the four languages: Hebrew, Greek, Latin, and English. In deference either to his college reputation as a poet or to his more advanced age, Taylor was assigned English, a greater challenge than defending ancient tongues enshrined in Scripture or the classics. As in the *Metrical History*, the poet's confession of unworth underscores the sublimity of his theme: "Oh! that my CAN could cask my WILL that I / My Native Speech aright might Dignify" (25). The distinction between "CAN" and "WILL," which anticipates the self-splitting later embodied in the spiritual struggle of the Meditations, enacts a humility that makes the poem possible. Once preliminary self-deprecation ends, Taylor sings the charms of English with what Thomas H. Johnson calls a "frivolous and playful spirit" appropriate to the occasion as an exercise of "undergraduate wit." The "heavy humor" that Norman S. Grabo finds in Taylor's grammatical and linguistic puns does not obscure a real reverence for "Speech" as "the Chrystall Chariot where the minde / In progress rides, Cart rutting of the Winde" (25). In the "Declamation" human words hold center stage, but when they later share that stage in the Meditations with the divine speech of Scripture, with what Taylor would call "the Winde thy Word displai'th," the sad limitations of language will be fully exposed. In light of poems yet to come, the confident speaker of the "Declamation" sounds like an undergraduate who has not yet fully confronted either the fallen self or the verbal inadequacy that confirmed its corruption.²

Taylor's response to the world around him is more fully represented in four poems dealing with nature, a strikingly small number for so prolific a poet. These pieces show, however, why Taylor never became a nature poet: like Bradstreet and Wigglesworth, he was far less interested in the world than in what the world revealed of the divine schema. While the *Metrical History* presents historical events as moral parables that further the saint's pilgrimage, natural events assume a similarly iconic role in these poems as emblems of God's creative power. And while the Meditations consistently shut out nature except as a source of metaphors for sin, these poems turn the observation of nature into another occasion for deciphering God's work in the world and in the self. Taylor's last poem on a natural topic, unfinished verses on mastodon bones unearthed in 1705 at Claverack, New York, illustrates with particular clarity his textual role as an exegete of divine Creation. Adopting the contemporary theory that the bones belonged to one of the "giants in the earth in those days" (Gen. 6:4), Taylor immediately pays homage to the force behind all such wonders of the visible world in an echo of Bradstreet's "Contemplations." Saluting the "Glorious One" who "plantdst the Tree of Nature to mentain / The glorious acts of Nature in the Same," he begins his account of the extraordinary by acknowledging God's glory in nature's ordinary operations, which "None ere can Stop" "Save thou alone" (211). Taylor's "Tree of Nature," from the "melancholy Rocks" at its roots to the "Sparkling Gems that mock the Sun & 'ts Shine" (212), reveals a divine order that gratifies every sense. Vegetative life offers "a Paradise of speckld Spots, / Of Orient flowers" and "rich perfume" that "kiss our nose, & eyes," while "Sensitive" life provides, in the songs of birds, "Sweete musicke for our Eares." But for Taylor, as for Bradstreet, the real value of natural beauty lay in its reflection of the divine. Taylor reads nature as he reads history, God's "bright selfe to view, / As in a Looking Glass." For him these bones reconfirm not simply the biblical giants or the Indian legend of a "Mighty Don" (215), but the infinite possibilities of divine creative power.³

Taylor's other nature poems similarly read the world as a meditative text. "Upon a Wasp Child with Cold" presents a neatly framed emblem whose homiletic possibilities rest on the frank anthropomorphizing of a wasp that warms "Her petty toes, & fingers ends" in the sun after a "Northern blast" (104). Taylor makes it impossible to read his depiction as anything but a conceit. In her slow ritual of recovery, the wasp acts "As if her little brain pan were / A Volumn of Choice precepts cleare";

"As if her velvet helmet high / Did turret rationality"; "As if her Pettycoate were lin'de, / With reasons fleece"—as if she embodied Puritan rationality in "Her warm thanks offering for all" (105). Numbed by the wind and warmed by the sun, the wasp, like the true believer poised between legal conviction and the warming love of the Sun of Righteousness (Mal. 4:2), becomes "A Scho[ol] & a Schoolmaster" that teaches how "A nimble Spirit" who minds "Her worke in e'ry limb" can become a meditative "Lather" of ascent to God. Her imputed actions represent an identity that Taylor absorbs by "Acting each part though ne'er so small / Here of this Fustian animall." In his movement from natural conceit to "An Heavenly musick furrd with praise," the poet does in fact what the wasp seems to do in fancy. In "Contemplations," as we have seen, Bradstreet confesses her inability to praise God properly, even though the "merry grasshopper" and "black-clad cricket" seem to have no trouble doing so. In the Meditations Taylor, finding himself similarly unable to participate in nature's celebration of the divine, stands "Blockish, Dull, and Dumb" while the "Bird" and the "little Bee" offer grateful praise.[4] Here, however, Taylor starts from the emblematic view of the world that Bradstreet achieves only toward the end of "Contemplations." Voicing a desire that God "cleare my misted Sight that I / May hence view thy Divinity," he performs an exegesis of nature that confirms a gracious ability to use the world properly.

Taylor's careful balancing of natural event with redemptive meaning is even more explicit in "Upon a Spider Catching a Fly," in which five stanzas of natural description precede five stanzas of spiritual interpretation. For Taylor, nature embodies the physical/spiritual duality of the saintly metaself writ large, a view that enables him to incorporate the two dimensions of the created world, as object and as emblem, into the meditative episode he records. That episode begins in the same way as Bradstreet's in "Contemplations," with careful observation of a natural realm that is already partly allegorized. The spider, an "Elfe" whose chief "ploy" is not its web but its craftiness, gently taps a "pettish wasp" as if it were "affraid" that "he Should pet, / And in a froppish, waspish heate / Should greatly fret / Thy net." But a "Silly Fly" receives quite different treatment: the spider "by the throate tookst hastily / And 'hinde the head / Bite Dead" (103). Taylor offers two readings of the event. The first is a simple warning against pride: "Strive not above what strength hath got / Lest in the brawle / Thou fall" (104). The second and deeper lesson emerges in his announcement that Satan is "Hells Spider" who spins nets "To tangle Adams race / In's Stratigems / To their Destructions." The only escape from the web of "venom things / Damn'd Sins" is to counter Satan's wiliness with faith in God's power to "Communicate / Thy Grace to break the Cord." This shift from seeing to interpreting assumes a spatial parallel as Taylor moves his vision from the earth to the air. The ominous parable of vulnerable insects leads to his self-reading as a grateful singer of praise, perched like a nightingale "In Glories Cage," singing "thankfully, / For joy." Like Bradstreet, Taylor chooses the nightingale as an emblem not only of a meditative flight above the dangers of this world but of a grace-given ability to sing the songs of the next. In the "we" who grasp the spider's lessons, Taylor's cool observation of natural struggle and death dramatizes a gracious perspective in which struggle and death could both be transcended.

Like Bradstreet, Taylor concedes that the lessons afforded by this world were not always so easy to absorb. "Upon the Sweeping Flood" enacts a darker reading of nature consistent with the convicting uses of affliction. While the poem on the wasp moves easily from natural event to confident praise, the meditation on the flood moves from natural disaster to a heartfelt confession of sin.[5] The flame "Which did dissolve the Heavens above / Into those liquid drops that Came / To drown our Carnall love" might have been "quencht" had the speaker and his readers "had a tear" of remorse to shed (109). Far from being in harmony with nature, humanity has made "th'Heavens Sick" and caused the skies to "purg & Vomit See / And Excrements out fling." While the wasp poem offers praise in gratitude for a meditative ascent, the poem on the flood enacts a "tear" to assuage divine anger. By convicting himself and the reader of "Carnall love," Taylor, like Wigglesworth in "God's Controversy with New-England," models a repentance suggestive of an affirmative movement that extends beyond the text itself. The poem ends with no transformation of speaker and reader into selves in whom God is well pleased. On the contrary, the contrition prompted by heaven's angry purging suggests a reconciliation possible only *after* the poem's narrative present.

The power of confession emerges even more clearly in the poem usually called "When Let by Rain," a Herbert-like treatment of spiritual self-doubt that replicates Soul's dilemma in *Gods Determinations*.[6] Hesitating whether to "Stay thyselfe or Goe," Taylor portrays himself as a "Flippering Soule" caught between the "Nippers" of inaction and action, fear and faith, sin and grace (102). Like the wasp, the spider, and the flood, the rain propels him toward the central question of Puritan experience: is he saved or not? The resulting self-reading exposes the ambivalence of all souls who, split by sin and grace, are "both wayes born." As in Herbert's "The Collar," the stakes are especially high: as a minister, Taylor must either win the "Coate" of his "Surplice" or be won by the "Coate" of his flesh. It soon becomes apparent, however, that the real issue is not Taylor's election but the intensity of his response to it. With bitter self-irony he asks, "Is this th' Effect / To leaven thus my Spirits all?" Incapable of praise, his heart, a "Crabtree Cask" and a "Verjuicte Hall," may prove to be like "Bottle Alle, whose Spirits poisond nurst / When jog'd, the bung with Violence doth burst." In paradoxical imagery appropriate to a soul at war with itself, explosive liquid leads to raging fire in the terrifying possibility that he will become "A sparkling Wildfire Shop" that yields all heat and no light, a soul animated only by "dull Spirits."

In the final stanza Taylor recovers by reconsidering the meditative episode in the context of larger patterns informing his entire spiritual life. As a result, he transforms the occasion of "One Sorry fret," now cast in the past tense as an "anvill Sparke" that "almost set / The house on fire" (103), into evidence of salvific turmoil. Assured that he is Christ's "Temple" after all, he concedes that he was "almost" overcome and thereby reasserts a faith that has survived the test recorded in the poem. Like Bradstreet, he derives consolation from spiritual doubt and hesitation through the biblical promise that God "sendeth rain on the just and on the unjust" (Matt. 5:45). By locating his initial panic within an experiential continuum shared by all believers, Taylor rewrites the weakness of the "building" of his Outer Man into evidence of genuinely enflamed affections: "Such fireballs droping in the Temple, Flame / Burns up the building: Lord forbid the Same" (103). Through writing, Taylor turns the episode into a harbinger not of insurmountable sin but of the psychic wear and tear that grace exacts of all earthly pilgrims. In its unsettling force and hopeful conclusion, "When Let by Rain" articulates his intense desire to internalize a saved identity sought by all sincere believers. While the final outcome of this search could not be absolutely clear to him, the urgency with which he pursued it brought its own comforts.

Bradstreet-like invocations of redeemed experience recur when Taylor takes up domestic themes. Replicating her balance of earthly with heavenly love, his courtship poems to Elizabeth Fitch unite spousal devotion with a rededication to matters of the spirit. As he insists in a letter accompanying one of these poems, earthly love must not be permitted to overwhelm heavenly: "I send you not my Heart: For that I hope is sent to h[ea]ven long since" (37). Once again speaking as a self divided by flesh and spirit, he assures Elizabeth that "the most" of his heart "that is allowed to be l[ay]ed out upon any Creature, doth Solely, & Singly fall to your share." "Conjugall Love" must be subordinated to what it "represents": the "respect which is betwixt Christ & his [Church]" (38). The poem itself, "This Dove & Olive Branch to you," which he would later call the "Preface to our True Love Knot" frisking "in Acrostick Rhimes" (111), reiterates the brief sermon of the letter: "THE RING OF LOVE MY PLEASANT HEART MVST BEE / TRVELY CONFIND WITHIN THE TRINITIE" (40).

This conflation of domestic and spiritual vocations is reconfirmed in a second poem to Elizabeth, "Were but my Muse an Huswife Good." Offering an "Eccho" to her love, Taylor voices a humility mandated of spouse and believer alike: "I no Rowling Phansy have to run, / Nor She Such Silken Huswifry ere Spun" (42). Although his "Coarse Iämbick" provides verbal confirmation of the limits of earthly attachments, he confirms with Bradstreet that once Christ's "Shine" is safely embedded in love's "Web of fulgent gold," the two loves become complementary and not oppositive. If the balance is upset and "Duty, Faith, & Love be ragged worn," even such a "golden web" can become "As black as Hair-Cloth made, all Snick Snarld run" (43). Taylor's pledge to keep the proper balance serves to absorb his and Elizabeth's love into their faith: "lets by walking right," he exhorts, "Loves brightest Mantle make Still Shine more bright / For then its glory Shall ascend on high / The Highest One alone to glorify." As in Bradstreet, the mystical marriage validates the earthly marriage, and the Canticles Bride's claim that "My beloved is mine, and I am his" (Cant. 2:16) offers sacred precedent for earthly love: "Thine whilst Mine Own: & yet mine Own whilst Thine / Thou being Mine alone, I'm Thine, & Mine."

Although wedded joy provided a comforting link between this world and the next, family sorrow revealed how different the two realms really were. As Taylor conceded in "Were but my Muse an Huswife Good," "Cares, & Crosses too amongst these meet, / Like Vineger which Sugar makes more Sweet" (42). Six years later, after two infant daughters had died, he wrote a poetic reconfirmation of this lesson so effective that Cotton Mather reprinted two of its stanzas at the end of a sermon on the proper handling of grief.[7] In "Upon Wedlock, & Death of Children," Taylor's struggle to achieve a redeemed view of death starts from an ostensibly redeemed view of wedded love. His family, depicted as an extension of divine decree, seems an institution as much of heaven as of earth:

> A Curious Knot God made in Paradise,
>   And drew it out inamled neatly Fresh.
> It was the True-Love Knot, more Sweet than spice
>   And Set with all the flowres of Graces dress. (106)

By celebrating the biblical origin of his family in Eden, Taylor sets himself up for his own Fall. Wedded love indeed originated in the Garden, but family tragedy began there too, in the sin by which "wedlock" and "death" became inseparably bound. Into Taylor's post-Edenic family "an Hellish breath" intrudes (107), and in order to absorb the loss of children in the New Eden he must, like Bradstreet in "Contemplations," return to the Old and grasp the full legacy of the first parents. However set with gracious "flowres" his family might be, he must learn that it mirrors not just pre-Fall bliss but Postlapsarian suffering. Having confessed his human tendency to confuse earth with paradise, the poet must convict himself in the sin that causes each and all deaths.

The gap that grief exposes between Taylor's will and God's is suggested in his confession that the death of "this flowre" Elizabeth at one year of age "almost tore the root up" of her father (107). The heartbreak came because the hour of grief was "unlookt for" in a human forgetting of that other, darker legacy of the first marriage. The epicyclic structure of the poem makes clear the pilgrim's ongoing need for such God-sent punishments. At the first death Taylor articulates a pious response to the loss of a child: "Lord take't. I thanke thee, thou takst ought of mine, / It is my pledg in glory, part of mee / Is now in it, Lord, glorifi'de with thee." This seems a clear resignation to God's will: by "pausing on't," Taylor has made sense of the tragedy. But the death of Abigail some five years later finds him equally unprepared, as revealed by the graphic depiction of "the tortures, Vomit, Screechings, groans, / And Six weeks Fever" that "would pierce hearts like Stones." Such heartbreak, Taylor concedes, is a consequence of the fact that "nature fault would finde" with God's dealings. In a renewed conviction dramatized by a second resignation, he again resolves to turn from a response of "nature" to a gracious acceptance of what God has wrought:

> Griefe o're doth flow: & nature fault would finde
>   Were not thy Will, my Spell Charm, Joy, & Gem:
> That as I said, I say, take, Lord, they're thine.
>   I piecemeale pass to Glory bright in them.
>   I joy, may I sweet Flowers for Glory breed,
>   Whether thou getst them green, or lets them Seed. (107)

As he confesses his need to trust in a Providence that he cannot understand, Taylor embraces God's will as his "Spell Charm, Joy, & Gem," images suggesting an almost talismanic use of redemptive language. Like Bradstreet, who urges herself and her readers to "say" that God is "merciful as well as just," Taylor clings to the language of orthodoxy as a means of striving for the perspective that it expresses. At the second death he appropriates the pious words that had allowed him to sustain the first: "as I said, I say."[8]

Reversing the usual elegiac transfer of divine glory from deceased parents to their children, Taylor claims a share in grace from his now-sainted daughters as his "pledg in glory." Like the poem itself, they become offerings—"take, Lord, they're thine"—that confirm his struggle to sacrifice what the natural self loves. Offering no reason for the deaths beyond God's desire for sweet flowers, Taylor, like Bradstreet, finds in the very irrationality of the loss a sharp reminder that God's will was to be accepted even if it could not be explained. Death somehow had to be rewritten into victory, transformed in the believer's imagination from a "Hellish breath" to the act of "a glorious hand." As if to remind himself that a merciful Lord gave as well as took away, Taylor is careful to record the births of Samuel and James, who have not died. Although he seems to assert a perspective more yearned for than achieved, he verbalizes a saintly desire to feel the rightness of God's dealings. Even if "joy" was the last thing that he actually felt, writing the poem initiated a pilgrim's search for divine help in order to feel it.

When his wife died seven years later, Taylor marked the occasion by transforming grief at the loss of a beloved saint into a celebration of sainthood itself. Parts 1 and 2 of "A Funerall Poem upon the Death of my ever Endeared, & tender Wife Mrs. Elizabeth Taylor" take up a problem treated extensively by all Puritan elegists: what does the deceased's translation to glory reveal about the survivors? Before Taylor can focus on Elizabeth's saintly traits in part 3, which follows the conventions of the formal, public elegy, he must first achieve the humility necessary for absorbing the redemptive lessons of her life. He dutifully asks not only Christ's permission to create "this little Vent hole for reliefe" (110), but also Elizabeth's, that she might "Spare me thus to drop a blubber'd Verse / Out of my Weeping Eyes Upon thy Herse" (111). And although he does not wish to "repine" (110), repining is precisely what he must do as the first step toward pious resignation. Parts 1 and 2 project a fallen, convicted self whose grief exposes the sad gap between human desire and divine will. Far from severing their "True Love Knot," Elizabeth's death confirms that "My heart is in't & will be Squeez'd therefore / To pieces if thou draw the Ends much more." The deaths of five children, "arrows" striking his "bowells," were bad enough, but now the arrows of affliction "Do Strike & Stob me in the very heart." As in "Upon Wedlock," Taylor speaks as an all-too-human vessel that must be vented or it will "burst." That it is his sinful dimension which *needs* this poem is clear from the sense of forced supplication that he voices. Although he sorely misses his "bosom Friend" and "Comfort," "Yet my Lord, I kiss thy hand."

Part 2 reflects Taylor's pursuit of a ritual of grieving by which he can transcend the mere venting of emotion. Denigrating the poem itself as a conventionally "mournfull Song" that testifies to fallen need (111), he contrasts the "Acrostick Rhimes" of his courtship poem with his renewed recognition of the bond of love and death. Love that began with poetry must end there as well, "with Poetick knocks" that "Break a Salt teare to pieces as it drops." Taylor justifies the poem as an outlet for the same grief that inspired the prototype of all elegies, David's "Poetick gusts" over Jonathan and Saul (2 Sam. 1:19–27), a passage that he, like Bradstreet, paraphrased in verse. Anxious to assert his right to write, he claims secular precedent as well: "Do Emperours interr'd in Verses lie? / And mayn't Such Feet run from my Weeping Eye?" Although he embraces a "Dutie" that "lies upon mee much," his real mandate is to move from grieving self to gracious framework, to break through his own sin in order to celebrate and preserve Elizabeth's sanctity. Like David, he must commemorate her life by rewriting it into a legible redemptive text for those who remained behind. If he were to "naile" her virtues "in thy Coffin" by *not* writing, "How shall thy Babes, & theirs, thy Vertuous shine / Know, or Persue unless I them define." This revised goal of proclaiming her life as an embodiment of grace enables Taylor to transcend his "Black Black Theme" and the self-indulgence that he sees reflected in his grief. The poem will be validated, he now attests, not by his "blubbering" performance but by her sanctity. "Thy Grace," he assures her, "will Grace unto a Poem bee / Altho' a Poem be no grace to thee" (111).

Despite Taylor's claim that "in Salt Tears I would Embalm her Clay," what he actually embalms is Elizabeth's "Noble part" as a saintly self who leads him from purgative venting to redemptive celebration (110). Convinced that she now enjoys a redeemed view of death still unavailable to him, he portrays her as gently chiding his need "at my Grave to Sing" (111). Hagiographic ritual replaces the mere expression of grief, and with part 3 Taylor begins a relatively impersonal description of her saintly identity. Promising "Bright Saints, & Angells" that he will not "abuse" their ears with empty "Hyperboles," he demonstrates that no praise of an elect soul could possibly be hyperbolic. Back-reading Elizabeth's life in light of her final glory in heaven, he draws what Grabo has called "an idealized portrait of the Puritan wife—one to be emulated rather than known."[9] She was, Taylor confirms, "Her Husbands Joy, Her Childrens Chiefe Content. / Her Servants Eyes, Her Houses

Ornament," emanating a "Shine as Child: as Neighbour . . . As Mistriss, Mother, Wife" (112). Like Bradstreet's parents, Elizabeth emerges as a saintly icon offering lessons for all—a transformation that has been effected, in Taylor's view, not simply by his rhetoric but by death itself. In keeping with his reverence for what she has become, he keeps his distance by referring to himself in the third person. Seeking to embalm her in the most edifying form possible, he speaks part 3 less as a widower grieving for his wife than as an exegete who proclaims the spiritual message of all such sainted lives.

Consistent with this goal, Taylor presents Elizabeth's "Walke With God" as the central fact of her entire life, including her childhood as "a Tender, Pious Bud / Of Pious Parents" (112). Appropriately "Obedient, Tender, Meek," Elizabeth undertook a pilgrimage that retroactively sanctifies her adult roles as well. As a neighbor she was "ever good," enacting a compassion suggestive of the Canticles Bride, whose "fingers" drip "sweet smelling myrrh" (Cant. 5:5): Elizabeth's "Fingers dropt with Myrrh oft, to her power." As mistress she embodied the divine balance of justice and mercy: she "Remiss was not, nor yet severe unto / Her Servants: but i' th' golden mean did goe." Most important, as mother she emulated Christ's mercy toward the elect: her "bowells Boiled ore to them that bee / Bits of her tender Bowells." Warmly embracing her chief responsibility as a Puritan parent, she taught her children "The Law of Life," giving "Correction wisely, that their Soules might Live" (113). As in Bradstreet's marriage poems, Elizabeth's spousal traits are inseparable from her sanctity. Taylor's catalog of her virtues portrays not just Elizabeth but the effects of grace upon her: "As Wife, a Tender, Tender, Loving, Meet, / Meeke, Patient, Humble, Modest, Faithfull, Sweet / Endearing Help, she was." Elizabeth, as Taylor embalms her, perfectly illustrates the godly balance of divine and human love that he had extolled during their courtship. Although "Of Earthly things" her "Husbands pleasure" came first, spiritual matters clearly took overall precedence. In every aspect of her life she was Taylor's "Faithfull Yoake Mate, in Christ's Cause."

Because Taylor's underlying purpose is to celebrate Elizabeth's glorification, he saves his fullest treatment of her "Noble part" for last, reordering the sequence of her life to stress redemptive rather than worldly chronology. The apex of her inner life was her conversion, and he accordingly ends the poem with an account of her struggle as "a Reall, Israelite indeed" (113) who undergoes the classic inner story of doubt, struggle, and triumph. Her conviction in sin was both harsh and genuine: "that Smart, / She then was under very, few did know: / Whereof she somewhat to the Church did Show." By describing her preparation for conversion in the present tense, Taylor makes her inner struggle correspond to the experience of reading the poem: "Repentance now's her Work"; "Faith, carries her Christ as one of his." Her preparation, in which "She's much in Reading, Pray're, Selfe-Application," manifests a proper balance of hope and fear by which she "Holds humbly up, a pious Conversation." When she finally "makes profess[ion]" to the Westfield Church, the event culminates a spiritual process fully embodied in the text as well as in her life. After a brief recounting of the fruits of her faith, especially her "gracious Speech," Taylor abruptly concludes by recording her love of Wigglesworth's best-selling manifesto of the redeemed perspective: "The Doomsday Verses much perfum'de her Breath, / Much in her thoughts, & yet she fear'd not Death" (114). *The Day of Doom* appealed to those whom faith allowed to foresee the final dispensation of God's Justice with wonder and not terror. Taylor depicts Elizabeth as just such a soul. Convinced that "Justice can do no wrong," she anticipated the end — her own and the world's — with the confidence of an assured believer.

"A Funerall Poem" must have helped strengthen the faith that it extolled. Obviously, Taylor's confidence that Elizabeth now "Swims in bliss" (110) brought him incalculable comfort, just as it always has to survivors. His determination to commemorate her glorification must have been reinforced by the duty to teach their children the salvific lessons of their mother's life. Taylor's family needed to perpetuate Elizabeth's most valuable and comforting identity as a true "Israelite." By writing "A Funerall Poem," he made certain that his wife's efficacy as guide to "thy Babes, & theirs" would continue (111), thereby enhancing his own sense — and his children's — of a "Noble part" that would follow her to glory. Although a beloved wife and mother was gone, the redemptive schema lived on. Her life, retold as a clear embodiment of that schema, provided its most decisive and intimate proof.

Taylor's nine other elegies apply the experiential dynamic of the family poems to a communal framework. Exploiting the conventions of the Puritan elegy to the fullest, they point up the relation between elegiac form and a ritual of mourning crucial to Puritan identity. "*The Meditation of Death*," Edward Pearse insisted in a treatise that Taylor owned, "greatly promotes our Spiritual Life; therefore walk much among the Tombs, and converse much and frequently with the Thoughts of a dying hour." It was with good reason that Puritans took this advice to heart. Death clarified the relation between the carnal self of the earthly present and the saintly self of the celestial future by providing the precise point at which one identity completed its transformation into the other.[10]

Like other Puritan elegists, Taylor sought to reveal the redemptive meaning of death by performing a sacred duty adumbrated in David's lament. As he tells the deceased Samuel Hooker of Farmington, "It surely would / Be Sacraledge thy Worth back to withhold": when "brave Jon'than" dies, shall "David's place be empty? Sling ly by?" (116). But the duty to commemorate Hooker is impeded by natural grief, which "when Greate / And geteth vent," speaks in "Non-Sense sobs" (116). As the poems on Elizabeth and their daughters also made clear, natural grief was sinful precisely because it *was* natural—an inescapable reminder that "nature" could offer neither consolation nor explanation. In the public elegies, the deceased's apotheosis as a saintly self who, like Increase Mather, "chose not the World to seeke" (247) sharpens the contrast between natural anxiety and gracious peace. As Taylor confirmed at the death of Richard Mather, "our losse, its grea[t]; whilst we are thus / Above with him" in our thoughts, "he's not below with us" (20). The peace of the dead underscored the turmoil of the living by convicting survivors in a self-centered panic at their own fate: "Unworthy We, oh Worthy he," Taylor wrote of Deputy Governor Francis Willoughby (22). Moreover, to celebrate someone else's joy presented a real challenge to the survivor's Christic selflessness. Willoughby's death virtually forces Taylor to move beyond self-pity to "count / [H]ow his great Gain, doth our great loss Surmount" (24). To be outstripped in glory by a departed saint was a humbling blow, as Taylor's final words to President Chauncy of Harvard suggest:

> Well, Chauncy, well, thou, where thou wouldst be, art.
> We Sink in Sorrow, judgment, & the Darke.
>   In middst of all the Combat pray do we
>   Inable us, oh Lord, to Shine as Hee.   (35)

Thinly veiled envy for the dead underscores the deceased's role as a dehortative model. What we struggle to glimpse through a glass darkly, Taylor admits, this saint who was lately among us now enjoys face to face, eternally.

Envy, fear, and heartbreak could hardly result in proper commemoration. As the Hooker elegy confirms, "Tears are a Dress / Becoming us, come they not to excess" (122). But as in the poem to Elizabeth, Taylor is able to "keep due measure" by remembering that his real duty is not to grieve for the letter of the deceased as an individual but to celebrate the spirit of the deceased-as-saint. His real subject is not Samuel

Hooker but "God in him" (121), not Zecharia Sims of Charlestown but the "aged Nazarite" that faith has made of him (22). We have already seen this focus on redeemed identity in Taylor's poems of intense personal loss. While parts 1 and 2 of the "Funerall Poem" wrestle with the problem of grief and its proper expression, part 3 examines what made Elizabeth "a Reall, Israelite indeed" by enumerating those traits that she shared with all redeemed souls (113). And while Taylor idealizes sister-in-law Mehetabel Woodbridge as a "Gentlewoman neate, accomplish't, true," his deeper interest lies in "Her Inward man," "a Storehouse of rich ware" and "Sanctifying Grace, that made all fair" (125).

The shift from outer to inner man allows Taylor to move the elegiac ritual from legal to evangelical discourse, from the confession of sin to the celebration of piety. Samuel Willard, in a funeral sermon for mintmaster John Hull, insisted that "there is no greater Argument to be found that we should excite our selves to mourne by, then the remembrance that they were *Saints*"; "this, this outshines them all; that he was a Saint upon Earth." Taylor, like most Puritan elegists, consistently generalizes his subjects, absorbing the details of their lives into broad portraits of the saintly metaself. Like Urian Oakes, who embalmed Thomas Shepard II as a "Scripture-Bishops-Character," Taylor does not lament the dead so much as he memorializes their sanctity. His physical description of Samuel Hooker, "in Person neat, of lesser Sise, / With Ruddy Looks, & with quick rowling eyes," moves rapidly into a spiritual portrait that recalls the godly ministry mourned in the "Lay-Mans Lamentation":

> His Head a Magazeen of Wisdom rich,
> With Spirits fand from foggy Vapoers which
> Do Reason cloud: a Fine Spun Fancy, Quick,
> Producing Notions brave, & Rhetorick. (117–18)

Hooker's essence, as Taylor distills it, exemplifies a *via media* of faith: he was "Grave, not Morose. Courteous, yet did Comand / A Distance due; & by a gentle hand" (118). He was, in short, a "steady" saint, "Not on, & Off." Back-read in light of his presumed glorification, Taylor's Hooker, whose "Shining Beams did fly to lighten all" (117), becomes nothing less than "a bit of Christ" whose gracious "Chrystallizing" has made saint and Savior virtually indistinguishable:

> An Orb of Heavenly Sunshine: a bright Star
> That never glimmerd: ever shining fare,
> A Paradise bespangled all with Grace:
> A Curious Web o'relaid with holy lace

> A Magazeen of Prudence: Golden Pot
> Of Gracious Flowers never to be forgot
> Farmingtons Glory, & its Pulpits Grace. (123)

Omit the last line and the images could describe the Christ of the *Preparatory Meditations*. True saints, William Ames affirmed, received "the bestowal of total perfection" of the soul at death. In keeping with his assumption that death and grace had perfected Hooker's Christic identity, Taylor sealed with language precisely what he thought had occurred in gracious fact.[11]

The communal conviction resulting from the loss of such souls yields the standard elegiac images of shared disaster. Praying that Hooker's death "be n't an Omen of our Fate / Foreshewing our apostate following State" (121), Taylor mourns Hooker's "Strenth," "Potency," and "Congregationall Artillery": "We need the Same; & need it more & more. / For Babels Canons 'gainst our Bulworks roare" (116). John Allen of Dedham is a broken "Stud," a "Stake pluckt out / Out of its place" (30–31); Willoughby's passing signals the waning of "our Garden," from which "[We]e cannot spare of what remains yet, any" (24); Sims is a fallen "Pillar, & a Builder who / [Both built], & long up[held] the building too" (21). Sims's death warns that "our Israels glory waxeth thin": "Our Motto write in teares, that all may View it, / That Predicates our Glory greate is FUIT." A poet with Taylor's ear surely intended the bitter sound of the Latin verb when read as an English pun.

Like all elegists, however, Taylor seeks not only to commemorate the dead but to stimulate redemptive experience within the living. Communal conviction initiated such experience. Although the saint's separation from the living dramatized a rupture between this world and the next, it also reinforced hopeful ties between the two realms. With the repeated claim that one of us is now in heaven, the reader's time and place become the starting point to saintly glory. By urging a personified New England, Connecticut, and Farmington to grieve for Hooker, Taylor thus transforms physical residence into spiritual orientation. His call to "Let Harvard mourn" celebrates Chauncy as a link to heaven (34), and had Willoughby not died "[H]e yet had stood within our garden, pal'd" (24). With David Dewey's sudden removal from "our Deaconry laid void" to new "work" in heaven, the reader's here and now are elevated to redeemed status as the glorified saint's there and then (83).

Extolled as a paradigm of the holiness that survivors hoped to achieve, the deceased displayed, if they proved faithful, their future selves — a completed version of an inchoate identity that they constantly sought to confirm. By celebrating the dead as embodiments of this identity, Taylor presents the difference and sameness between living self and dead saint as an oscillation of sinful and saintly tendencies within survivors. Sorrowful present and hopeful future meet in a balance of grief and joy that echoes the sin/grace duality of redemptive experience. While one self stands convicted in sin by death and sorrow, another finds consolation in the salvation confirmed in the deceased. At Richard Mather's passing, Taylor asserts, "we[e griev]ing d[o] / Leave him in Joy, & joy th[at i]t is so" (20). Because it is a pilgrim's experience of the faith that unites the dead with the living, Taylor is careful to point out that the deceased underwent the same struggle now plaguing survivors. In life Hooker's soul had been "A Stage of War, Whereon the Spirits Sword / Hewd down the Hellish foes that did disturb" (117); Dewey's earthly self had also been, like the carnal dimension of all believers, a "Seat of Sin, Corruption's nest"—a self by definition "True only to Untruth" (83).

The deceased's splitting into body and soul reinforces the correlation of the grief/joy duality of mourning with redemptive doubleness. Having performed his duties as deacon "Untill thy Person was dichotomiz'd / By death's sharp Sword," Dewey is both "parted and departed": his body and soul now "standeth part from part" "As doth the *Zenith* from the *Nadir* stand" (83). The conflict of bitterness and piety set in motion by the elegy is resolved not just in the immediate peace of the dead but in the reunion of their bodies and souls in the fullness of time, a reward that Taylor underscores in the final "repair" of Dewey, whose "Person spoild while 'ts parts asunder are" is made whole by grace (84). Richard Mather similarly embodies a cessation of inner turmoil, an escape from carnal selfhood that removes him from "Satan gain Shot, freed from Sin" (20). Through these portraits Taylor projects a peace that is at once eschatological and current. The saint's final reward mirrors the meditative peace of readers able to work through their own sin/grace struggle toward gracious resignation.

Explicating his subjects as legible paradigms of saintly experience, Taylor rewrites them into Bibles in miniature who, like the Word itself, both convict and console the reader. As a legal text, the deceased convicts by the radical otherness of celestial perfection and by the simple fact that his or her death is the wages of sin. But while the saint's death reminded survivors of the God of Justice, the saint's glory bound them more closely to the God of Mercy. Taylor's focus on saintly traits shifts his explication from the Old Testament of the deceased-as-text to the New. Like a preacher mediating between the human sin that caused the saint's death and the divine grace that animated the saint's life, he transforms his subjects into anticipatory emblems of hope, new links to the hereafter. As Taylor's Hooker assures the reader, "In Faith, Obedience, Patience, walk a while / And thou shalt soon leape o're the parting Stile, / And come to God, Christ, Angells, Saints, & Mee" (122).[12]

By praising the dead as emblems of sanctity, Taylor changes himself from a blocked writer into the fluent reader of texts already written by God, found poems of grace that needed only to be explained, not invented. Ames insisted, as we have seen, that "the word of God dwells bountifully in the faithful," who "are transformed into its form and pattern." As a reader of this "form and pattern" in the deceased, Taylor exchanged the burden of artistic creation for a mode of prophetic discovery. As he asks Hooker, "Shall thy Choice Name here not embalmed ly / In those Sweet Spices whose perfumes do fly / From thy greate Excellence?" (116). Echoing Willard's advice to "embalm the memory of the Saints with the sweet smelling Spices that grew in their own Gardens," Taylor overcomes the performative pressures of elegiac duty. Because the deceased had already been embalmed with grace, all that remained was to seal with words what faith had already accomplished — to make public the work that God had secretly wrought within the soul of the departed. When Taylor looks *only* in his heart and writes, he finds a grieving spirit stung by God's will. But when he turns from wounded self to the deceased's virtues, he recovers the faith necessary to a proper embalming. As in the poem to Elizabeth, it was the dead saint — or more properly, sanctity itself — and not the living speaker that validated the poem as an instrument for spiritual gain.[13]

Taylor's elegiac movement from fallen speaker to gracious theme, from how this death affects him to what he can read in the deceased as the embodied Word, enacts a ritual that mere self-expression could not satisfy. As Ruth Wallerstein once remarked in reference to *Lycidas*, "there were two griefs, the personal grief which kills, [and] the grief of repentance leading to God." By exposing the former in order to achieve the latter, Taylor, like other Puritan elegists, rewrote himself from a passive victim of God's punishment into an active celebrant of redemption. The elegiac duty has been made performable, he attests, by Increase Mather's virtues as saint rather than his own eloquence as poet: "When many left Christ's holy word thou stoodst fixt to 't / Which makes my gray goose quill commence thy poet" (248). Some ten years earlier he claimed in the *Preparatory Meditations* that the celebration of the Lord's Supper "makes me thus a Poet." Like the Sacrament, the idealized saint could make the pilgrim soul sing with gladness. No praise was too great for a soul fashioned and perfected by saving grace. Such a soul, after all, was God's greatest work in the world.[14]

Taylor's elegies transform the verbal conventions of mourning into useful, even indispensable vehicles for channeling raw emotion into pious activity and a comforting identification with the holy dead. As he tells his readers, weeping for Hooker "is honour due from you. / Yet let your Sorrows run in godly wise / As if his Spirits tears fell from your eyes" (123). Don't simply grieve *for* Hooker, he insists: you must grieve *like* him—like someone who has already achieved the perspective on death and dying now enjoyed by the deceased. The shift from sinful self to saintly Other allows Taylor to mourn the Christic dead as Christ Himself wished to be mourned. "*When the Saints die*," Willard warned, "*beware of irregular Mourning*: though we are to lament their Death, yet we must beware that it be after the right manner . . . after the same Language that Christ did to those weeping Women."[15] The text to which Willard refers, Christ's admonition to "weep not for me, but weep for yourselves, and for your children" (Luke 23:28), defined Taylor's efforts to transform tears of natural heartbreak into tears of salvific remorse. Holy deaths, he confirmed at the passing of Increase Mather, are "stings" designed to make "Sinners" feel divine "Smart: repent then e're it be too late / Less thou eternally smart in the horrid Lake" (247). The helplessness of grieving for Hooker is similarly transformed into an opportunity to "weep thy Sins away, lest woe be nigh": "Watch, Watch thou then: Reform thy life: Refine / Thyself from thy Declentions. Tend thy line" (120).

The greatest practitioner of useful grief, in the Puritan view, was Christ himself, who wept at Lazarus's death but then effected, through faith, his resurrection—an act equivalent to the verbal and spiritual ritual that Taylor pursues. Drawing his readers into this ritual by testing their ability to celebrate the deceased's joy and thus to escape from the dark glass of sin and self, he admits that the loss of Richard Mather "would sinke us if [w]e did not spie, / That whilst we drown in griefe he swims in Joy" (20). Like their subjects, Taylor's elegies provide touchstones for assessing the reader's perspective on dying. The celestial Chauncy articulates the challenge posed by the text when he asks, "Who'de feare the Grave? Death's but the golden Doore / Wherein we must unto bright Glories Shore" (35). Like Bradstreet, Taylor turns physical death into a telling index of spiritual health: "Go see thy Freckled Face in Gospell Glass," he urges New England at Hooker's death, "Go feele thy Pulse, & finde thy Spleen's not well" (119).[16]

Like the writing of Church history, the task of turning a saint's death into a "Gospell Glass" of self-revelation demanded a prophetic voice. As a witness to the deceased's grace, Taylor offered his poems not as literal biographies but as neogospels that proclaimed the *kerygma* of the saint's life. Just as the deceased Chauncy had diffused grace "by Pattern" in his life, the poet diffuses the redemptive message of Chauncy's life (33). Similarly asserting that Increase Mather "with thy pen hast played Christ's intrest Dear: / And hast recorded his blesst doings here," Taylor replicates Mather's verbal activity by recording the piety of God-in-Mather for "future ages to behold" (248). By speaking as an apostle to the now-Christic deceased, he exchanges self-referential stasis for a verbal celebration of the saintly death as an emblem of the victory still possible for the living. Mehetabel Woodbridge calls for "one more Pray're" as if "She should be where she would bee" (126). And Samuel Hooker anticipates the separation from his carnal element by stating that his hands and arms "are Dead, you see, and I / Have done with them" before he pours out "His Soul on Christ" (119). Like other elegists, Taylor shared in these final victories by erecting verbal monuments in fear and in hope. John Allen's death provokes a roll call of the "Spirituall Gamesters" who have "slipt away," leaving speaker and reader in need of a "Fencing Schoole" to keep up the good fight. Taylor's sense of abandonment prompts him to ask "Shall none / Be left behind to tell's the Quondam Glory / Of this Plantation?" (31). Fear transmutes into hope as the poem answers its own question. Taylor is still here—and the glory of the plantation increases with each saint that he embalms.

In three other poems usually classified as "occasional," Taylor enacts psychological patterns identical to those stimulated and confirmed by events in the earthly pilgrimage. In these poems, however, he responds to inner rather than outer episodes, isolating himself from history, nature, society, and family in order to seek assurance in a private colloquy of self and Savior. "Huswifery" is the most famous—and least characteristic—of these meditative poems. "Huswifery" and "An other upon the Same," a condensed reworking of the same theme and images, display none of the struggle that marks the *Preparatory Meditations*. Instead, they embody Taylor's tranquil exploration of a single conceit: the speaker as a spinning wheel on which God weaves the "Holy robes" that he hopes to wear in glory. The calm tone of "Huswifery" is reinforced by Taylor's unified development of the figure in what is usually called the "metaphysical" style:

> Make mee, O Lord, thy Spining Wheele compleat.
>   Thy Holy Words my Distaff make for mee.
> Make mine Affections thy Swift Flyers neate
>   And make my Soule thy holy Spoole to bee.   (105)

Carefully working out the conceit, Taylor begs for his "Conversation" to become Christ's "Reele"; he wants to be made "thy Loome" on which "thy Holy Spirit" winds "quills"; he asks that the divine "Ordinances" become his "Fulling Mills" (106); if he is decked out by God's huswifery, the "Shine" of his renewed faculties will "fill / My wayes with glory and thee glorify." In the final couplet his transformation remains hypothetical. If what he imagines comes true, "Then mine apparell shall display before yee / That I am Cloathd in Holy robes for glory." The image, a conflation of the biblical "wedding garment" (Matt. 22:11–12) with the "white raiment" of the elect (Rev. 3:5), anticipates the total remaking of identity that he seeks: "Then cloath therewith mine Understanding, Will, / Affections, Judgment, Conscience, Memory / My Words, & Actions." Although the "Shine" of redemption celebrated as historical fact in the *Metrical History of Christianity* is here internalized as salvific hope, "Huswifery" remains a statement of desire rather than fulfillment. Its even tone, intricate images, and hypothetical ending all suggest a definition of spiritual goals rather than a record of meditative experience.[17]

While "Huswifery" and its sequel celebrate what grace could do for Taylor, "The Ebb & Flow" conveys what it actually *does* to him, how gracious influences feel to a self being formed into the identity that "Huswifery" extols. As *Gods Determinations* and the family elegies also make clear, this process was as turbulent as its imagined conclusion was peaceful. Appropriate to his rigorous self-examination, Taylor begins the poem with *his* beginning as a sharer in these cycles, as a soul freshly animated by the spark of divine grace:

> When first thou on me Lord, wrought'st thy Sweet Print,
>   My heart was made thy tinder box.
>   My 'ffections were thy tinder in't.
>   Where fell thy Sparkes by drops.   (109)

Taylor's memory of his conversion, an inner parallel to the Edenic vision of the family that opens "Upon Wedlock, & Death of Children," results in a nostalgic lament for his own Golden Age of the spirit, when "Those holy Sparks of Heavenly Fire that came / Did ever catch & often out would flame." Like the corrupted world in the *Metrical History* and the afflicted family in "Upon Wedlock," the speaker has endured a personal Fall, an inner descent from initial zeal to a relatively more mundane spiritual life. His meditative "now" is decidedly less fervent than when he first felt Christ's "Sweet Print": "I finde my tinder scarce thy Sparks can feel / That drop out from thy Holy flint & Steel." Yet even though he disparages his lack of spiritual intensity as a "Censar trim" rather than a more volatile "tinder box," he still remains "Full of thy golden Altars fire." As in "When Let by Rain" and the *Preparatory*

Meditations, Taylor's election is not at issue, only his inability to experience its effects as fully as he would like. His relatively cool affections reveal an "ebb" of the spirit that was an inescapable part of the expected cycles of belief.

Spiritual flatness prompts Taylor to question whether "thy fire in mee" is "a mocking Ignis Fatuus, / Or lest thine Altars fire out bee, / Its hid in ashes thus" (109). But anxiety quickly brings its own resolution by triggering the balance of fear and hope central to redemptive experience. That balance is restored when he concludes that Christ's "Sweet Print" was definitely upon him. The saints would persevere—and his memory of "thy fire in mee," however faint it now seems, reinvigorates his faith. As with the "Flippering" speaker of "When Let by Rain," self-doubt generates its antithesis in saintly hope. The final couplet reasserts the "flow" of a pilgrim's inner life by locating the meditative event within broader cycles that were deeply affirmative. God has blown away such "ashes" before, and will surely do so again: "Yet when the bellows of thy Spirit blow / Away mine ashes, then thy fire doth glow." Having placed a discouraging episode within the continuum of salvific experience, Taylor closes with an upswing of the saintly cycle. In its confirmation of redemptive purpose for the dark night of the soul, the poem dramatizes an ability to turn affliction into joy by locating moments of doubt within a gracious framework that encompasses darkness as well as light. Had he written only about the "ebb," he would have told only one side of how redemption felt—and he would have gone only halfway in recovering the sense of self that he pursued.

Although its "occasion" is internal, "The Ebb & Flow" illustrates an artistic and spiritual dynamic informing all of the poems that record Taylor's pilgrimage through the world. Translating the peaks and valleys of his life into classic Puritan confirmations of hope and fear, he repeatedly exposes a sinful self plagued by grief, doubt, and spiritual dullness. But like Bradstreet's confessions, Taylor's also affirm a self filled with righteous anger and impatience at the sluggishness of his Old Creature. As we shall see, it is this same dual identity, animated by the ebb and flow of assurance, who speaks the *Preparatory Meditations*—who constantly strives to separate his essential self from a dumpish, mortal dimension that just as constantly reasserts itself in weakness, sin, and flawed song. Taylor's carnal dimension cannot feel Christ's presence with enough intensity, cannot generate sufficient horror at his sin, and cannot successfully transform human words into effective praise. But the very existence of such complaints gave warm evidence of a self rent by grace and contrition, a self willing to fight the sinful element that faith had turned into a mortal enemy.

Although the occasional poems provided clear opportunities to wage this war and assess the results, Taylor's self-description as a "Censar trim" suggests his awareness that the continuing mandate to oppose the fallen self demanded an ongoing and regulated form—a ritual form, though he would have abhorred the term. In the early 1680s, the probable time of the occasional poems, he began another poetic project that would occupy him for over forty years, a project that would force him constantly to reenact the experience recorded in "The Ebb & Flow." In keeping with the privacy of this ritual, he firmly shut out the distractions of the world. History, nature, ministerial colleagues, family, Westfield, his congregation—all were burned off, to use a Taylorian phrase, in his determination to concentrate on what he hoped was his essential and permanent self as a weary but struggling pilgrim.

Chapter Nine

"This Crumb of Dust": Pilgrim Voice

and Christic Reader in

the *Preparatory Meditations*

Although the *Preparatory Meditations* have established Edward Taylor as early America's finest poet, critics have always found serious artistic blunders in these unusual poems. Taylor will suddenly drop one image for another with little development of either; he often extends biblical images and typological parallels to the point of tedium; his violent mood swings keep us constantly off balance; his extreme self-deprecation sometimes seems histrionic and even unintentionally comic. These assessments are common despite the widespread recognition that Taylor wrote the Meditations as private records of his spiritual life, not "works of art" for poetry lovers. Still, he breaks so many of our aesthetic rules that we have trouble determining what rules, if any, he follows. Because he seems to make so few concessions to external readers, we sometimes conclude that he could not or would not do so.[1]

This assumption might seem true enough for the Meditations. But as the public and occasional poems make clear, Taylor did not always write in a vacuum. We have seen that poems as diverse as the *Metrical History* and the elegy on his first wife invoke strategies for drawing readers into a search for grace similar to those exploited by Wigglesworth and Bradstreet. While we can certainly argue that he was a better poet than they, he was not a different *kind* of poet. All of his verse, public as well as private, articulates and encourages the same underlying experience of self stimulated by the work of other Puritan poets. Taylor, like his contemporaries, wrote and judged poems in accordance with their usefulness in provoking a sharper sense of an identity that all believers sought. This was as true of doomsday epics published for a mass audience as for meditative exercises written for no one else to see.

The identity fostered by the Puritan experience of poetry was not autonomous. It was always conceivable only in relation to the Christic Other, both in its general makeup and in its revelation at particular meditative moments. In this sense, the *Preparatory Meditations* were not written in a vacuum, any more than such reader-sensitive poems as *Gods Determinations* and the elegy on Samuel Hooker. Even in his most private poems, Taylor had a "reader" firmly in mind: a Savior sharply defined by Puritan Christology, with clear expectations regarding those who approached him in prayer or in prayerful poetry. Given the Puritan poet's hope that verse might be the "living sacrifice, holy, acceptable unto God" commanded by Paul (Rom. 12:1), it seems legitimate to ask what the Christ in Taylor's imagination demanded as a "reader" and what effect such presumed demands had on the verse. The degree to which the poet played a theological role determined by his Christic audience makes it more difficult than we usually concede to locate the "real" Edward Taylor in the Meditations. By verbalizing the self-deprecation demanded by his faith through poems described in the "Prologue" as "Slips slipt from thy Crumb of Dust," Taylor struggled to find a voice consistent with the identity that his faith encouraged him to seek. As Charles Lloyd Cohen points out, Puritans achieved the "peace of conscience" that signaled assurance "by re-enacting the actions and affections associated with coming to believe." Those affections, as we have seen, witnessed a self in whom carnal and gracious tendencies were locked in constant struggle. The Meditations witness Taylor's search to internalize this struggle. The various moods that they record signal his participation in the full range of redemptive self-experience as his theology defined it.[2]

These verse embodiments of a saintly metaself's devotion to Christ were neither contrived nor cynical. While it is one thing consciously to adopt a persona, it is quite another unconsciously to absorb modes of self-perception and expression fostered by one's cultural milieu. Puritans constantly merged private identity with redemptive paradigm whenever they examined themselves for signs of grace. The nature of those signs and of the saved identity that manifested them was perfectly clear, even if the final existence of that identity within the believer had to remain problematic. Like all Puritans, Taylor knew precisely the self that he hoped faith was animating within him. In the Meditations, as in the occasional poems, he intensified his spiritual experience not by deliberately replacing one self with another, but by speaking like the self that his faith made him pursue. Poetry helped strengthen his assurance of a Christian "hope" that served not only as the "anchor of the soul, both sure and stedfast" (Heb. 6:19) but as the anchor of poetic voice and textual identity. Moreover, Taylor had an equally clear conception of the Christ for whom he wrote and of the manner in which the divine reader was to be petitioned. "Acting" a part, to use Karl Keller's term, within the drama required by his faith, he was convinced that he was being watched, heard, and judged on how sincerely he wanted a redeemed identity. Only one "reader" mattered in Taylor's spiritual exercises of a saved self. His most puzzling artistic "Slips" stem from the fact that he was acting *for* someone—and it wasn't the ordinary reader of poetry.[3]

Taylor's exclusive concentration on a Christic reader lends his private verse a rhetorical and communicative dimension that is usually overlooked. Like other, more obviously "Puritan" poems, the Meditations fulfilled the three uses for singing set forth in James Durham's popular commentary on the Canticles, which Taylor owned and frequently consulted, especially in his later years: "Glorifying God, and making his praise glorious," "edifying others with whom we join," and "studying edification our selves" to "our own chearing and refreshing."[4] The goal of "Glorifying God" emerges immediately in the "Prologue" with Taylor's pledge "To Prove thou art, and that thou art the best / And shew thy Properties to shine most bright." Although the goal of "edifying others" may seem irrelevant to private poetry, Taylor could "edify" the Christ in his mind by trying to be the kind of soul in whom Christ would take delight. This goal in turn reflects Durham's third benefit of singing, self-edification. Like most meditative writers, Taylor edified himself by monitoring his own expression for signs of his spiritual status. He could not do this without also monitoring Christ's probable response to that expression. Christ and Taylor are in this sense inseparable as "readers" of these poems: how Taylor "acts" in a given Meditation determines, in his mind, how Christ will "read" him. Christ's predicted response in turn shapes Taylor's own reading of the poem and of the self that it reveals. The result is an ongoing search for clearer definition as a saved self capable of imagining a personal transformation from a "Crumb of Dust" into an elect soul.

The Meditations project a repudiation of carnal selfhood appropriate to Taylor's conception of their aims and reader. Their one constant tie to this world was the Sacrament that sealed the poet's participation in the next as a glorified saint. In their emotional volatility and verbal play, they join "The Ebb & Flow" in defining their speaker nearly exclusively in terms of redemptive psychological patterns. In his private verse Taylor, like Bradstreet, absorbed and articulated an identity that he sincerely hoped was his: the saintly metaself shaped by the interior ebb and flow of sin and grace. This was a self constantly being destroyed and rebuilt by the power of the Word, a self repeatedly offered up to the Christic reader as a means of opposing the fallen identity that the poet repeatedly confesses. Whether in response to external occasion or to inner spiritual event, poetry helped Taylor imagine a self defined by holy longing, pious persistence, and an unquenchable will not simply to believe but to speak that belief as clearly as possible to himself and to his Lord. By speaking like a saint, he intensified his hope of being one.

The Christ addressed in the Meditations, alive in the poet's spiritual present but timeless and placeless in relation to the external world, matches the eternal identity that Taylor seeks in the poetry. The "Prologue" to the Meditations makes it clear that if Christ chooses to "Inspire" Taylor until he reflects back divine glory, "then thy dust shall live." The poet must experience himself as mere dust in order to become "*thy* dust," an assured self capable of reading present sin as a sign of future glory. Taylor embodies his desire to "live" eternally by projecting himself into the timeless framework of his Christic reader, the atemporal realm of heaven and Scripture. When he contemplates the Incarnation, "Wove in the golde Loom of Humanity," he consistently addresses a celestial Savior reigning in heaven, not the earthly teacher of the Gospels (2.128). Even when typological themes predominate, as in the long sequence that opens the Second Series, the elaborate details of biblical history never overshadow their fulfillment in the eternal Antitype with whom the poet hopes to connect.

Because the timeless Christ was perceptible only to an equally timeless self, Taylor rigorously suppresses virtually every detail of his external life. What remains is a continuing reenactment of the inner experience voiced in *Gods Determinations* by Taylor's hero-Soul, an experience that repeatedly generates the emotional pitch of a meditative speaker who begs "that thy Love might overflow my Heart! / To fire the same with Love: for Love I would" (1.1). Such vehement expression, especially when contrasted with other Puritan poems, reflects the closed system of poet and Savior that the Meditations address. While Wigglesworth published systematic treatments of doctrine for a wide readership and Bradstreet wrote chiefly to instruct and console family readers, Taylor's Meditations invoke the most exclusive sense of audience conceivable to a Puritan. Freeing himself from the spiritual needs of external readers, whether family or parishioners, conscience-stricken saints or willful backsliders, the Taylor of the Meditations turns the Puritan imagination in upon itself, pushing it to such experiential and artistic extremes that his voice seems almost modern in its psychological complexity and expressiveness.

But the *Preparatory Meditations* are not modern poems. When Taylor makes their purpose explicit, he lines out a goal linked not to making objects of beauty but to enacting a decidedly Puritan scrutiny of the self:

> Thou bidst me try if I be in the Faith,
>   For Christ's in me if I bee'nt Reprobate.
> Thou me dost Check if ignorance displaith
>   Itself in me. And I know not my State.
> A Reprobate my Lord, let not this come
> On mee to be the burden of the Song.   (2.155)

Even though Taylor could not "know" his "State" definitively, the ritual embodied in the poetry suggested the antithesis of a "Reprobate" song. His ongoing attempts to "try if I be in the Faith" enact the salvific tension of uncertainty and desire inherent in the saintly self. This identity, equivalent to what Keller has called the "mythic self" of the Meditations, witnesses Taylor's "incessant endeavor," as William J. Scheick observes, "to assert his self and to appraise that self's relation to the 'Sacred selfe'" of the saved soul. Taylor, no less than his contemporaries, participated in modes of self-perception consistent with theological expectation. Poetry helped him generate an assurance sought by all believers "through the narration," as John Owen King argues, "of their own psychological experience, narratives that build experience according to formulas established in the Puritan generation of John Bunyan." Writing as a self capable of turning his "Pen unto thy Praise alone," as a "Crumb of Dust" convicted in sin and thereby potentially saved ("Prologue"), he used poetry as a vehicle for confirming the existence and growth of his New Creature. In their fervent invocations of this ideal self, the Meditations are spiritually but not literally autobiographical. They do not record who Taylor *was* so much as they witness the self that his faith compelled him to seek.[5]

The Meditations project the self that Taylor thought Christ wanted him to be. His desire to make Christ his "lovely marke" (2.49) — to have his "poor Creaking Pipe / Salute thine Eare" (2.23) — helps shape his voice as the true "living sacrifice" he thought his divine reader demanded. Christ would want to read clear evidence of his "delight," as Paul phrased it, "in the law of God after the inward man" (Rom. 7:22). In particular Christ expected to find the sincere struggle by which the inner man was sustained and nourished. Whether at the believer's initial conversion or during the search to reconfirm this vocation in moments of assurance, the Christic reader would have little patience with smooth verses or a placid soul. As we have seen, Thomas Shepard linked spiritual growth with a willingness to "war and wrestle," to oppose the sinful self convicted under the Law with the gracious self wrought at conversion. William Ames confirmed that this "spiritual war" wrought "a daily renewal of repentance" and an ongoing reaffirmation of the "double form" that marked all true believers, "that of sin and that of grace." True belief, Taylor told his congregation in a *Christographia* sermon, was "the Same in one as in all, and the Same in all as in thee." Ames agreed that "Inasmuch as faith is in each believer individually it is in the form of those that are called." Taylor, however "Hide bound" in the flesh (1.22), repeatedly strives to rewrite himself into this "form"—to experience himself as the double-sided personality whom Christ would save.[6]

Sincere remorse was the identifying mark of a soul destined for heaven. "God is forced to make us feele this," Hooker insisted, "that we may be severed from our sinnes, and be subject to him in all obedience." Shepard agreed that compunction effected a "Separation from sin" by cutting "the sinner off from that evil that is in him." When Taylor bewails his sins—those "Bubs hatcht in natures nest on Serpents Eggs" (1.39)—he defines them as entities separate, or at least separable, from the essential self who speaks in the poetry. Although he "cannot kill nor Coop them up," he firmly declares them to be the Other. Constantly reenacting this meditative self-division, his litanies of self-loathing constitute an inner application of the homiletic principle, voiced by William Perkins, that while "the curse of the law is not to be urged against the person that is righteous and holy in the sight of God, yet it is to be urged against the sinnes of the person, which are remaining." When Taylor levels the "Two-edg'd Sword" of "Righteousness" against himself, the sword that cures "the Sinner" but "kills Sin right" (1.17), he incorporates his sin-consciousness into redemptive doubleness. As Puritan autobiographical texts repeatedly attest, such self-disgust made Taylor's salvation more probable, not less. Like Bradstreet, Taylor dramatizes Shepard's claim that "the greatest part of a Christian's grace lies in mourning the want of it." By lamenting the "Bubs" of his carnal nature, he voices the "Mortification, Selfe Denial" that he recommends to his hearers in the *Christographia*, a self-loathing that shows his Christic reader his salvific need to be heard and pardoned.[7]

Taylor feels most threatened when he cannot perceive this self-splitting—when he feels neither the pain of heartfelt conviction nor the joy of a comfortable assurance: "But oh! my streight'ned Breast! my Lifeless Sparke! / My Fireless Flame! What Chilly Love, and Cold?" (1.1). The ultimate horror was the antithesis of saintly doubleness, the "lukewarm" faith, "neither cold nor hot" (Rev. 3:16), from which he begs to be released: "Lord blow the Coal: Thy Love Enflame in mee." Throughout the Meditations he repeatedly complains that his saintly self-perception is not sharper:

> Lord! read the Riddle: Shall a gracious heart
> The object of thy love be sick of Love?
> And beg a kiss under the piercing Smart,
> Of want thereof? Lord pitty from above.   (2.96)

Given what Taylor thought Christ expected from him, such dissatisfaction with his meditative intensity had comforting as well as convicting implications. As Shepard maintained, God actually "shows mercy" to believers by "withholding much spiritual life and letting them feel much corruption." Dull spiritual vision was an expected result of this withholding. If the difference between yearning and fulfillment were blurred and special meditative glimpses of the divine became commonplace, the believer would not strive for a closer communion with Christ. If earth already seemed like heaven, what punishment had sin really brought?[8]

The very strength of Taylor's yearnings helped generate his redemptive hope. Canticles commentator John Collinges attested that "The Souls earnest desire to taste the sweetness of Christ, and trouble and impatience because it cannot attain what it truly longeth and thirsteth after, is a good evidence that the Soul hath tasted of the fruit of Christ; and that his fruit is sweet to the believers taste." Constantly vacillating between frustration and fulfillment, Taylor acts out a war against carnal identity that keeps him suspended between sin and sanctity, between conviction and consolation, and between the self that he is and the self that he seeks. Immediately after his plea for the kiss he recovers his bearings as a still-earthly believer: "But listen, Soule, here seest thou not a Cheate. / Earth is not heaven: Faith not Vision." He "wants" holiness in two senses: he lacks it and he desires it. In his repeated affirmations of contrition and desire, he articulates with language the self that he hoped Christ was nurturing in him through grace.[9]

In a dynamic also invoked by Soul's speeches in *Gods Determinations*, the speaker's complaints against sin ally him with Christ against a common enemy: Taylor's sinful self. Through self-dichotomizing he internalizes the redemptive push and pull of the Law and the Gospel: each poem becomes an auto-sermon in which, as John Weemse described the ideal sermon, "the gift of thundering must come first, and then comes the gift of consolation." Like Bradstreet's gentler self-remonstrations, Taylor's thunderings against his carnal self articulated his faith in Paul's promise that "with the mouth confession is made unto salvation" (Rom. 10:10). In addition, extreme self-deprecation demonstrated his saintly desire to adopt the Christic reader's view of sin as his own. Not only do I see my sin, Taylor repeatedly tells Christ, but I hate it as much as you do. "Was ever Heart like mine?" he asks, "My Lord, declare. / I know not what to do: What shall I doe?" (1.40). The irony, of course, is that Taylor was already doing it: confession both sharpened and eased his sin-consciousness. Despite Keller's comment that Taylor could "enjoy" the process, it is wrong to suggest that the poet did not take his self-attacks seriously. Puritans insisted that to the soul adopted by Christ and thereby made more like him through the transforming power of grace, sin would seem every bit as horrifying as Taylor portrays it in the poetry. Sin was Christ's Other — and Taylor is careful to make it *his* Other as well.[10]

Speaking as a self defined by contrition and thus located at the center of the same paradoxes of belief that Wigglesworth explored in "Riddles Unriddled," Taylor exploits the gap between fear and hope as an experiential abyss into which he aggressively and repeatedly leaps. There is seldom any real tranquillity in the Meditations because he was not seeking it. Instead, he repeatedly centers on his paradoxical experience as "A Dirt ball dresst in milk white Lawn" (1.46). Paul's condemnation of "our vile body" (Phil. 3:21) prompts him to confront his sinful/saintly makeup as an "Angell bright" dwelling in a "Swine Sty" (2.75). The voice of the Meditations is conflicted because conflict defines the identity that Taylor seeks. The gracious psychomachia exemplified in the plea for the Bridegroom's kiss by a dual self who lives in the "Vale of tears" but seeks the "mount of joyes" (2.96) provided a salvific and thus comforting framework for the various moods recorded in the poetry. Taylor's manifest impatience with the few "Crystal drops" available to earthly believers signaled a hot soul, not a lukewarm one.

What Taylor attacks is not his essential identity but the carnal element which keeps clogging that self's vision and fettering that self's tongue. The "Bubs" that he confesses were "hatcht" in "natures nest," in a worldly self he both clarifies and repudiates through the act of writing. Taking up Satan's role in *Gods Determinations*, these confessed sins help Taylor define himself as much by his opposition to depravity as by his immersion in it. By renouncing his sins, he defines them as only half of his total personality — and the *other* half that rails against them comprises the actual voice of the Meditations. Taylor's redemptive duality also emerges in the fact that his flaws often stem not from the sinful self that he seeks to escape but from the weakness of the saintly self developing within him. When he complains, for instance, of "Tattling" (1.21) or of uttering a "Lisp of Non-Sense" like a helpless child (1.17), he apologizes for the feebleness of a New Creature that he thinks he has glimpsed. This optimistic self-reading helps explain why Taylor sometimes describes his shortcomings in an almost affectionate manner, as inverse revelations of "thy new Born babe in mee" (2.111). Lamenting his inability to savor Christ's glory, he confesses to having only "Child affections" (2.118); elsewhere he longs to be nurtured as Christ's "Spirituall Babe" (2.150).

The consistent appropriateness of the images with which Taylor animates textual experience indicative of true belief suggests that the poetry is best seen as ritually rather than psychologically realistic. The "Bubs" cited above, for instance, fittingly anticipate a celebration of Christ as "advocate" for sinners (1 John 2:1). After conceding that he deserves to be handled "In Wrath," Taylor sees "a twinckling Ray of hope / Methinks I spie thou graciously display'st. / There is an Advocate: a doore is ope" (1.39). The "advocate" text could scarcely be treated without a full confrontation with depravity: without the "Bubs" of sin, there would be no need for the Christic defense. Language that seems at first glance to convey sheer outburst is, on closer examination, indispensable for assimilating the miracle of election: "Oh! Dear bought Plea, Deare Lord, what buy't so deare? / What with thy blood purchase thy plea for me?" As the poem shifts from the convicting imagery of sin to the consolatory imagery of purification, Taylor's initial deprecation of his "Dregs" and "Bubs" becomes a confirmation rather than a denial of salvific patterns within his soul.

My point is not that Taylor did not actually feel these moods, but that his expression of them, however vehement, is inseparable from the salvific ritual embodied in all Puritan poetry. The Meditations do not convey raw experience but Puritan modes of perceiving and expressing that experience. There is consistent spiritual method to Taylor's apparent madness as he carefully links his confessions of unworth to the text or doctrine at hand. He complains, for instance, that he is "denos'de" (1.3) and thus cannot smell "thy good ointments" (Cant. 1:3); he wants an "appitite" (1.11) for the eucharistic "feast of fat things" (Isa. 25:6); his "Blunted Tongue" (1.21) impedes his participation in the divine praise of Christ commanded of all beings (Phil. 2:9); he is "base and Froward" (1.23) in response to the Bridegroom's suit to "my spouse" (Cant. 4:8); his carnal nature as "a Flesh and Blood bag" contrasts sadly with the "new creature" (2 Cor. 5:17) arising from David's stock (1.30); his "Stupid Heart" (1.36) cannot comprehend the promise that all "things to come" are yours (1 Cor. 3:22); his "Skeg" (1.46) is unfit for the "white raiment" (Rev. 3:5) of the elect.

The Meditations of the Second Series, especially the typological sequence, present an especially direct correlation of self-deprecatory image with biblical text. Perhaps for this reason Taylor's confessions of sin seem less intense as the Meditations progress. He is an empty "Shell" (2.14) in contrast to Christ, "in whom are hid all the treasures of wisdom and knowledge" (Col. 2:3); he is a "Thistle, Bryer prickle, pricking Thorn" (2.18) unfit for sacrifice on Christ's altar (Heb. 13:10); in response to the "greater love" of Christ (John 15:13) he wonders "Should Gold Wed Dung, should Stars Wooe Lobster Claws" (2.33); he is a "Mite" (2.48) antithetical to "the Almighty" (Rev. 1:8); "sick" and "dry" (2.60[B]), he longs to receive "spiritual drink" (1 Cor. 10:4); plagued by "Lythargy, the Apoplectick Stroke: / The Catochee, Soul Blindness, Surdity / Ill Tongue, Mouth Ulcers, Frog, the Quinsic Throate" (2.67[B]), he begs for Christ to come "with healing in his wings" (Mal. 4:2); he is "black" (2.69) in contrast to the Christic "lily of the valleys" (Cant. 2:1); "Swinelike" (2.77), he wallows within the "pit wherein is no water" (Zech. 9:11); he fears that Christ's "prooning Hook" (2.144) will cut him out of the "garden" of the elect (Cant. 6:11); he is a "sorry Crickling a blasted bud" (2.161A) in contrast to Christ, who is "as the apple tree among the trees of the wood" (Cant. 2:3).

These self-attacks are too carefully worked out to be read simply as autobiographical expressions of a guilt that overwhelms him. Taylor fully expects to discover and confess sin in every poem he writes. While the difficulties that he records were real enough to him, their consistent accord with biblical adumbrations of the pilgrim soul underscores the ritual dimension of Taylor's self-readings. Had he been unable to confirm and articulate his assurance in the poems, it seems unlikely that he would have kept writing them. For all their disparagement of a fallen self, these poems of self-discovery provided a means of simultaneously sharpening his awareness of sin and breaking the spiritual paralysis that such awareness could bring. In their formal and thematic consistency, they reflect four decades of intensifying through poetry an identity clearly "readable" by Christ—and therefore, Taylor hoped, acceptable to him as well.

Although Paul confirmed that "There is none righteous, no, not one" (Rom. 3:10), Puritans insisted that conviction in sin was only one side of redeemed self-experience. "Its a shame," Taylor warned his congregation in the *Christographia*, "for thee to ly Sulling thy Glass with Sighs, and plastering thy Cheeks ore with teares for feare thou shouldst be Condemned for thy sins." Refusing in his private verse to accept this stasis of self-doubt, Taylor repeatedly acts, as Scheick observes, "*as if*" he is saved.[11] The verbal activity that the poetry effects was the antithesis of meditative sighing. While sin-consciousness confirmed Taylor's need for Christ as his "reader" and healer, tentative affirmations of assured belief demonstrated his faith in Christ's power to read and to heal. The search for such assurance provokes Taylor's constant internalizing of biblical themes: he tries on the "Wedden Garment" (1.23) of the redeemed; he basks in the reflective glow of the Old Testament types; he marvels at his potential identity as Christ's Bride; he celebrates his participation in the Lord's Supper as a seal of his assurance. Such concretions of holy desire enable him to counter self-loathing with a hope that suggested his saving faith in the Christic reader: "Hold up this hope. Lord, then this hope shall sing / Thy praises sweetly, spite of feares Sad Sting" (2.46).

This ongoing balance of hope and fear suggests Taylor's pursuit of an *imitatio Christi* in identity as well as perspective. Christ was, he insisted in the *Christographia*, "the best Example that can be," a "Coppy written by the pen of perfect Manhood, in the Unerring hand of Godhead." As he urged his congregation, "wilt thou not endeavour to Write by this Copy?" Like the saved soul, Christ had what Ames called a "double presence" in which the divine and human parts remained "distinct" and not "mixed." Weemse similarly maintained that "There was a fight betwixt Christ his *velleitas*, and *voluntas*; as there is in thy selfe betwixt sinne and grace." By voicing an identity split by salvific turmoil, Taylor rewrites himself by the "Copy" of the dichotomous *Theanthropos*, thereby clarifying his experience as a vastly inferior twin of his Christic reader. The "sweet Content" that he records in "The Experience" becomes in "The Reflexion" a link between the double-sided speaker and his Savior, who "Pearle-like" stands " 'Tween Heaven, and Earth." Between heaven and earth, between grace and sin, between spirit and body—all describe the position that Taylor occupies in the Meditations. Locating himself at the center of these polarities, he mimics the duality of the God-man, in whom "Each natures Essence e're abides the same" (2.44). By so doing, he enhances his sense of participating in what he describes in the *Christographia* as the "mutuall Filling each other" enjoyed by Christ and the believing soul.[12]

Although the persistence of sin kept the petitioning speaker and his Christic reader apart, the confession of sin brought them closer together. In his preaching manual John Wilkins distinguished between sins of "infirmity" and sins of "wilfullnesse and frowardnesse." Preachers should "accordingly," Wilkins reasoned, proportion "the severity of our reproofe." However severely Taylor berates himself, he repeatedly asserts his "infirmity" as a split self by writing the good fight that turns sin into the Other. But because he is still earthbound and must also see Christ as the Other, Taylor positions himself squarely in the middle as a self rudely great and darkly wise—right where he was certain Christ wanted him to be. Claiming as psychological reality what Bradstreet dramatizes as allegorical debate in "The Flesh and the Spirit," Taylor administers to himself the mixture of legal warning and gospel "solace" that Perkins recommended for those "humbled in part."[13] Each half of his double self thereby gains sharper definition in contrast with the other. As we have seen, the "Bubs" lamented in Meditation 1.39 reveal a gracious need for the Christic Advocate. The special meditative episode remembered in "The Reflexion" is similarly tempered by dark pleadings issuing from the speaker's "dull Heart" and "black Velvet Mask." Careening between hope and frustration, Taylor makes his duality impossible for Christ to miss. If I am saved, he repeatedly asserts, this sinful identity that I hate will be as distant from me in fact as I am now trying to make it in word.

Such confessions ensured the sincerity of his pleas for grace. Hadn't Christ promised that the door would open to any who knocked sincerely? As Taylor assured his congregation, "he refuseth none that Comes to him."[14] Salvific optimism achieves especially full expression in "The Experience," a rare account of a specific spiritual episode that apparently occurred during the Sacrament. Taylor's memory of "that Flame which thou didst on me Cast" leads to an unusually bold assertion of assurance:

> I'le Claim my Right: Give place, ye Angells Bright.
>   Ye further from the Godhead stande than I.
> My Nature is your Lord; and doth Unite
>   Better than Yours unto the Deity.

Scrupulously avoiding un-Puritan presumption, Taylor bases his "Claim" not on performance or merit but simply on Christ's assumption of human "Nature": even the angels did not receive such honor. That the intensity of vision does not last further underscores his inherent unworth: "I praise thee, Lord, and better praise thee would / If what I had, my heart might ever hold." When he reconsiders the event in "The Return" and "The Reflexion," he invokes the same tension of gratitude and longing. After expressing a saintly desire to be "in Heaven above with thee," "The Return" reiterates the theme of "The Ebb & Flow" by extolling the Ordinances as a more restrained but reliable source of assurance: "But I've thy Pleasant Pleasant Presence had / In

Word, Pray're, Ordinances, Duties; nay, / And in thy Graces, making me full Glad." Taylor's reconfirmation of the ordinary fruits of grace "In Faith, Hope, Charity" renews his confidence "That thou hast been on Earth below with mee. / And I shall be in Heaven above with thee."

Why Taylor retreats from transcendent vision to devotional ritual becomes even clearer in "The Reflexion," where the inevitable "return" from "sugar sweet" meditative intimacy brings pain as well as comfort:

> Shall Heaven, and Earth's bright Glory all up lie
>   Like Sun Beams bundled in the sun, in thee?
> Dost thou sit Rose at Table Head, where I
>   Do sit, and Carv'st no morsell sweet for mee?

The episode commemorated in the titled poems seems to have prompted Taylor's search for a verbal ritual by which to concentrate and regulate his meditative efforts. From this point on the Meditations no longer *describe* a colloquy with Christ: they instead *become* that colloquy, functioning as inner reenactments of the "Word, Pray're, Ordinances, Duties" and "Graces" by which the poet's hoped-for identity as Puritan metaself was continually fostered and sustained.[15] Such verbal duty acknowledged a necessary shift in the fulfillment of his spiritual desire to the eschatological future. As he reconfirmed nearly thirty years after the event recorded in the titled poems, a few "Crystal drops while here may well suffice" (2.96). It was indeed possible, as a lifetime of poetic and meditative activity attested, that "Such as enjoy thy Love, may lack the Sense / May have thy love and not loves evidence." Although Taylor lacks "Spectacles to prove / Thou lovest mee" with absolute assurance, all of the poetry anticipates a time when "I shall at last see Clear. / And though not now, I then shall sing thy praise. / In that thy love did tende me all my dayes."

Taylor's self-readings as pilgrim probe the degree to which "loves evidence" animates a *feeling* self who responds to doctrine and Scripture with the rejuvenated senses of the New Creature. Repeatedly pushing himself beyond a merely intellective apprehension of Christ, he does not try to resolve the paradoxes of faith in rational terms. Instead, he constantly brings them to the surface in a Wigglesworth-like undermining of his own carnal reason. Heeding Shepard's warning against the "understanding's arrogancy," Taylor consistently internalizes and articulates Puritan expectations regarding the limits of human rationality. "Things styld Transcendent," he admits, "do transcende the Stile / Of Reason, reason's stares neere reach so high" (2.44). But as Wigglesworth made clear in *Meat Out of the Eater*, this did not mean that reason was not to be exercised to the fullest. At one point, for example, Taylor puzzles over the proper interpretation of the teeth of the Canticles Bride. Are they the Church's "Arguments that do destroy her Foes"? Are they ministers who "dress" the Word for their flocks? Or do they represent the spiritual "Chawing" of meditation? (2.138). In a validation of right reason enlightened by faith, he confidently chooses the third reading. When he considers Christ as the "root and the offspring of David" (Rev. 22:16), however, reason serves him less well: "How then is Christ the Root, and Offspring bright / Of David, Shew, come, read this riddle right" (2.113). Taylor similarly bows to extrarational mystery when he tries to reconcile Christ's identity as "Abraham's Seed, and Isaac too" with "That One and Only Seed" extolled by Paul (Gal. 3:16): "How can this bee? Paul certainly saith true. / But one Seed promisd. Sir this Riddle read" (2.5). And reason barely resolves the ambiguous "Sense" of the Canticles statement that "My beloved is gone down into his garden" (Cant. 6:2). How, Taylor asks, can Christ simultaneously leave and remain in his garden? The text seems to reveal a "Sense that saith, and that unsaith the same" (2.129). Speaking as a believer humbled by biblical enigmas, Taylor stumbles over dark passages whose standard readings he knew full well. Indeed, he almost seems to be playing dumb, reducing his exegetical sophistication as a scholarly pastor to that of any soul willing, as Paul commanded, to "become a fool, that he may be wise" (1 Cor. 3:18). By so doing, he dramatizes Perkins's statement that even though the Bible is often "flatly contrary to the reason and affections of men, yet it winneth them unto it selfe." He also confirms the power of Scripture to expose his rational and thus carnal limitations.[16]

Beyond the limits of reason lay the wonder inseparable from true belief and evidenced by a gracious congruence of the Word with Taylor's heart. "What Golden words drop from thy gracious lips," he exclaims of a Canticles text, "Adorning of thy Speech with Holy paint" (2.138). Elsewhere he calls the promise that all things "are yours" (1 Cor. 3:22) a "Golden Word! Lord speake it ore again. / Lord speake it home to me, say these are mine" (1.32). Sometimes he voices gracious awe of the Bible by reducing its complexities to a ritual chant, as in his response to the Bride's claim that "My beloved is mine, and I am his" (Cant. 2:16): "Thine mine, mine Thine, a mutuall claim is made. / Mine, thine are Predicates unto us both" (2.79). Or again, in response to Paul's statement that "God also hath highly exalted him" (Phil. 2:9): "Sing Praise, sing Praise, sing Praise, sing Praises out, / Unto our King sing praise seraphickwise" (1.20). Here Taylor abandons his own words in imitation of the meditative ecstasy of the Psalmist: "Sing praises to God, sing praises: sing praises unto our King, sing praises" (Ps. 47:6). Sometimes the chant underscores Taylor's rejection of any physical dimension whatsoever of the biblical image at hand, as when he sings the "Spirituall" significance of the "white and ruddy" Bridegroom (Cant. 5:10):

> Hence purest White and red in Spirituall Sense
>   Make up thy Beauty to the Spirituall Eye.
> Thus thou art object to love Spirituall. Hence
>   The Purest Spirituall Love doth to thee high.   (2.116)

However flat such repeated abstractions may seem to a modern reader, they showed the Christ in Taylor's mind that he had avoided reading this enigmatic text carnally. Such submissions of human thought to biblical promise articulated the selflessness that Christ demanded of him. When he contemplates the "place" that Christ prepares in heaven (John 14:2), the Word overpowers his human words and sensibilities altogether: "Reason, lie prison'd in this golden Chain. / Chain up thy tongue, and silent stand a while" (1.41).

Taylor seeks ever clearer evidence of his transformation into a self upon whom Christ bestows "Thy Grace, thy Justice, Life": "Make such a Change, my Lord, with mee, I pray. / I'le give thee then, my Heart, and Life to th'bargen" (2.34). Constantly straining to *feel* this "Change" and to express it in a manner fit for divine ears, he begs Christ to

> New mould, new make me thus, me new Create
>   Renew in me a spirit right, pure, true.
> Lord make me thy New Creature, then new make
>   All things to thy New Creature here anew,
>   New Heart, New thoughts, New Words, New wayes
>   likewise.
>   New Glory then shall to thyselfe arise.   (1.30)

In his quest to be refashioned as the saintly metaself, he strikes the redemptive balance between conviction and consolation, between present yearning and future fulfillment. Within this balance he repeatedly juxtaposes petition, hope, and assurance, often within a single poem and sometimes within a single stanza:

> Oh! Happy me, if thou wilt Crown me thus.
>   Oh! naughty heart! What swell with Sin? fy, fy.
> Oh! Gracious Lord, me pardon: do not Crush
>   Me all to mammocks: Crown and not destroy.
>   Ile tune thy Prayses while this Crown doth come.
>   Thy Glory bring I tuckt up in my Songe.   (1.44)

Salvific desire, midway between humility and confidence, becomes the experiential intersection of Taylor's fear and love. By anticipating better praise contingent upon his election—"if thou wilt Crown me thus"—he transforms present anxiety into salvific hope: "If on this Angell fare I'm fed, I shall / Sing forth thy glory with bright Angells all" (2.60[A]); "If with thy precious robes will't dress me here / My present tunes shall sing thy praise when there" (2.94); "Accept I pray and what for this I borrow, / I'le pay thee more when rise on heavens morrow" (2.153). Through his fervent and persistent confessions that "I cannot sing, my tongue is tide. / Accept this Lisp till I am glorifide" (1.43), Taylor half perceives and half creates the very identity that he seeks.

Taylor activates this self-experience by closely monitoring the senses of his inner man. Clogged by the "Worlds ill sents," his nostrils must be cleansed before Christ's odor can penetrate his spirit: "All things smell sweet to mee: / Except thy sweetness, Lord. Expell these damps" (1.3). Pleas for renewed sight, prominent throughout the Meditations, evince his desire to see with saintly eyes: "What Beam of Light wrapt up my sight to finde / Me neerer God than ere Came in my minde?" ("The Experience"); "Enoculate into my mentall Eye / The Visive Spirits of the Holy Ghost" (2.72); "give my Souls Cleare Eye of thee a Sight / As thou shinst its bright looking Glasses bright" (2.125); "Grant me thy Spectacles that I may see / To glorify aright thy glorious Selfe. / And see this Saving Faith grafted in mee" (2.155); "Lord ope mine eyes to se thy glory bright / And tune thy praise in beams of glorious light" (2.158). Repeatedly straining to sharpen his inner sight, he seeks a Christ visible only to the eye of faith:

> The bodies Eyes are blind, no sight therein
>   Is Cleare enough to take a sight of this.
> Its the internall Eye Sight takes this thing
>   This glorious light the Sin blind Eye doth miss. (2.147)

Since only Christ could provide the "Eye salve" (2.147) needed to see him, whatever Taylor *does* see of him reinforces the poet's pilgrim identity. The ongoing tension in the poetry between seeing and not seeing reinforces the holy splitting that gave evidence of such a self. Although his vision must remain partially blocked by the dark veil of the flesh, his saintly possibilities emerge in fleeting meditative glimpses of a Christ whose "Love" plays "bow-peep with me here" (2.96).[17]

Because the Lord's Supper nourished the saved identity that the poetry was written to animate, the Sacrament offers Taylor's most frequent and immediate stimulus for a self who must continually "goe

Fasting" in the world "Untill thou hast an Appitite afresh" (1.11). As fare reserved for the New Creature, the Supper provided an ongoing institutional vehicle for revivifying Taylor's self-perception as "Dead Dust" made fit through grace to "eate Living Bread" (1.9). Expressions of gratitude for the self seated at the Table, the poems witness his ability to "say Grace" "o're this Feast Continually" (1.11) by offering thanks not simply for the rite but for the identity that it reaffirms within him: "When with this Paschall bread and Wine I'm brisk / I in sweet Tunes thy sweetest praise will twist" (2.71); "Eate at thy Table, and drinke too shall I? / Then O're this Feast, I will say GRACE for joy" (2.86); "When with thy Fare my Vessels fill to th'brim, / Thy Praise, on my Shoshannims, Lord, shall Ring" (2.91). Taylor consistently links his voice as poet with his identity as a pilgrim nourished by Christ's body and blood. The Supper "well Concocted will make joy up start, / That makes thy praises leape up from my heart" (2.106). The symbiosis of poem and Sacrament which pervades the Meditations provokes Taylor's search for language appropriate to the self that the Supper was meant to feed. In turn, finding that language in private poems of praise intensifies his assurance as a soul called to a rich spiritual feeding: "And with these Guests I am invited to't / And this rich banquet makes me thus a Poet" (2.110).

The interdependence of the poetry and the Supper ensured the consistency of a private ritual that Taylor pursued for over forty years. The most immediate trace of his search for repeatable structures through which this ritual could be enacted is the prosodic sameness of the Meditations, all written in a single rhyme scheme, meter, and stanza form. Larger elements also reveal Taylor's rage for order. The First Series, which was probably intended to be open-ended, contains several clusters of Meditations based on a single theme: the Lord's Supper (Meds. 8–11); the typical offices of priest, prophet, and king (Meds. 14–17); the crowns of life, righteousness, and glory (Meds. 43–45). Other clusters focus on single Bible texts: Philippians 2:9 (Meds. 19–22); 1 Corinthians 3:22–23 (Meds. 31–37); 1 John 2:1–2 (Meds. 38–40); and Matthew 25:21 (Meds. 47–49). The subunits of the Second Series are even more pronounced: they include the sequence on Old Testament types (Meds. 1–30, although typological themes extend well beyond this unit); the "Christographia" poems dealing with the nature and qualities of Christ as Antitype (Meds. 42–56); the poems attacking the sacramental innovations of Solomon Stoddard (Meds. 102–11); and the final sequence on texts from the Song of Songs (Meds. 115–65, excepting four poems). These are only the major subunits; most of the other poems align themselves as well into short sequences.¹⁸

These structures reflect Taylor's attempts to transform the anxiety of Puritan self-examination into a difficult but ultimately comforting devotional ritual, a "duty" that "raps" on the door of his soul and demands "Verse" (2.30). In their very existence, the poems manifest his assurance that "I want a power, not will to honour thee" (2.38). Denying any "power" to write, he repeatedly demonstrates his "will" to do so through dramatic affirmations of a humble self who "fain would prize thee, Lord," but can find no "pretious matter" in his heart (2.42). As verbal proofs of salvific desire, the poems point to the deeper sacrifice that Taylor seeks to offer: his entire being. "Lord thine Altar make mee," he begs, "Then sanctify thine Altar with thy blood: / I'l offer on't my heart to thee. (Oh! take mee)" (2.82). Poem and speaker emerge as twin sacrifices whose validity hinges on the warmth of Taylor's affections. His frequent references to "cold" affections—his "Fireless Flame" and "Chilly Love" (1.1)—suggest his conception of the poetry as an ongoing self-sacrifice that confirms his quasi-typological relation to Christ. Just as the types foreshadow the Incarnation, the Meditations foreshadow, however darkly, the celestial intimacy with Christ that is his goal.

While heaven is Taylor's target, the Old Testament types are his precedent. His last Meditation reconfirms a pervasive link between his flawed self and song and the burnt offerings of his spiritual forebears: "I do bewaile my heart hath little of this / Thee to assail therewith, but oh the Smell / Of such a gift, that thou art pleast with, yes" (2.165). The ceremonial types are, in Taylor's view, the most immediate biblical precursors of the poetry. At several points, for instance, he asserts that he can praise if Christ will "Circumcise" his "Mammularies" to divine sweetness (1.3) and sharpen the perception of the "Circumcised Eare, and Souls piert Eye" (2.125). His most extensive treatment of circumcision clarifies the relation between Old Testament rite and meditative ritual. Begging Christ to "pare off, I pray, what ere is bad" and "Circumcise my Heart, mine Eares and Lips," Taylor fulfills the ceremony not just in his baptism but in his desire to be pared off from the Old Creature within by Christ's "Covenantall blood" (2.70). While baptism offers the institutional completion of the type, its inner fulfillment is clearly spelled out in his desire to be made "thy Nazarite by imitation / Not of the Ceremony"—not by the legal rite of circumcision but by his gracious imitation of Christ "In Holiness of Heart, and Conversation" (2.15). Taylor's request to have his senses "Circumcised" exemplifies his use of Old Testament prefigurations of the spiritual obedience that he seeks. The legal form of the ceremony is superseded by the only ritual with any efficacy under the New Dispensation: returning grateful praise to the Christic Antitype. Taylor asks Christ to

> . . . bed mee in thy Circumcisions Quilt.
> My wounds bathe with New Covenantall blood.
> My ears with Grace Lord syringe, scoure off guilt.
> My Tongue With holy tasled Languague Dub.
> And then these parts, baptisde thine Organs keep,
> To tune thy Praise, run forth on golden feet.   (2.70)

In acts of praise Taylor recapitulates the spirit of biblical ceremony even as he repudiates its letter. He can thus perform his inner rite while denigrating that rite as performance, repeatedly validating the poems as expressions of gracious need but deprecating them as products of human sin. Taylor saw this poetic ritual, like the Sacrament, as a rite of love and not fear, a performing of the Law without any expectation that legal obedience—or fine writing—would save him.[19]

Taylor was hardly alone in his internalizing of biblical ceremony. Samuel Mather argued that burnt offerings were fulfilled in "the Persons of Believers, who (through Christ) are sanctified and cleansed to be a pure Oblation or Meat-Offering unto God." Self-sacrifices could not possibly be efficacious, however, on their own merits. As typologist Thomas Taylor warned, "The sweetest Manna becomes a rottennesse and a savour of death to carnall professors." What made any spiritual sacrifice acceptable was the faith evidenced by heightened affections. Accordingly, when the poet Taylor considers the morning and evening sacrifice of lambs (Num. 28:4–9), he immediately redefines the rite in terms of inner response. Depicting his heart as "A Pouch of Passion" plagued by a consuming fire of guilt rather than a purifying fire of atonement, he concedes that he is a tainted sacrifice unfit for Christ, "a Dish of Dumps: yea ponderous dross, / Black blood all clotted, burdening my heart" (2.25). His heart, "the Temple of the God of Flies," reconfirms his unacceptability before the Law: his fancy is "a foolish fire enflam'd by toys / Perfum'de with reeching Offerings of Sins." Intentionally writing himself into a legal corner and thereby reconfirming the primacy of Christ's sacrifice as the true Lamb, Taylor virtually forces himself to shift from legalistic performance to the inner piety of "my Pray're each morn and night." Reasserting his need simply to believe and obey, he identifies "My morn, and evening Sacrifice" with the spiritual work demanded of all earthly pilgrims: he comes "On bended knees, with hands that tempt the Skies. / This is each day's atoning Sacrifice." This humble approach to "mine Altar Christ," which recapitulates the Psalmist's plea to "Let my prayer be set forth before thee as incense, and the lifting up of my hands as the evening sacrifice" (Ps. 141:2), turns the activity of writing into evidence of Taylor's dependence on Christ in meeting the requirements of the Law. As Mather insisted, Christ is the "Sacrifice and the Priest, and the Altar; he is all in all: Go with him into the Presence of God, and present him to the Lord by Faith: And the Sacrifice that he hath offered shall be accepted for thee."[20]

Old Testament ceremony also links Taylor's verbal sacrifices more closely to the Supper, since both are foreshadowed in the same sacrificial imagery: "Here is Atonement made: and Spirituall Wine / Pourd out to God: and Sanctified Bread / From Heaven's givn us" (2.25). The underlying unity of poetic and eucharistic sacrifice enhances Taylor's sense of an identity whom grace has made capable of participating in both:

> I'le tend thy Sabbaths: at thine Altar feed.
> And never make thy type a nullitie.
> The Ceremonies cease, but yet the Creede
> Contained therein, continues gospelly.   (2.25)

That the poems themselves were written to fulfill the scriptural demand for inner sacrifice is evident from their repeated expressions of gratitude for the Supper. God sends "Atoning Efficacy," Taylor confirms, to grateful "Sinners in this path, and grace here stills." By asking Christ to "Still this on me untill I glory Gain," he replicates the New Testament rewriting of Old Testament ceremony into the simple command to glorify God through Christ: "By him therefore let us offer the sacrifice of praise to God continually, that is, the fruit of our lips, giving thanks to his name" (Heb. 13:15). Taylor's play on the ambiguity of "stills" (instills/distills) suggests the heat of a sacrifice made acceptable *to* Christ *by* Christ, an efficacious meditative fire that conquers the "foolish fire enflam'd by toys" that had plagued him earlier in the poem.

Like all the Meditations, the poem on the burnt offerings confirms Mather's statement that such sacrifices atone "for those continual daily Sins, and sinfulness of our Hearts and Natures."[21] Through poetry, the Old Creature could be consumed, or at least burnt back a little. Despite Christ's abrogation of the ceremonial types, their spiritual counterparts—the Sacrament, the Word, and meditation—continued to sustain truly humble souls. As Taylor claims, "A Spirituall Ordinance the Type suspendes / And Onely owneth Spirituall Qualities / To have a right thereto" (2.103). The ceremonies were perpetuated in the prayers and meditations—and meditative poems—of believers whose "Spirituall Qualities" allowed them to perform such duties in love and not fear. Although Taylor denigrates absolutely the written products of his private ritual, he vindicates the process of writing them as an antitypical equivalent of purification rites set up to guide his biblical predecessors on their pilgrimage to the Promised Land. Those rites, reinterpreted and reenacted "gospelly," helped him savor his own journey to the heavenly Zion.

The efficacy of Taylor's sacrifices depended, in his view, on the sincerity of his contrition and the purity of his heart. This theme recurs throughout the Old Testament, first in the contrast between Cain's rejected offering and the "respect" that God accords Abel's (Gen. 4:4–5), but most notably in Saul's unacceptable sacrifice and subsequent rebuke by Samuel: "Hath the Lord as great delight in burnt offerings and sacrifices, as in obeying the voice of the Lord? Behold, to obey is better than sacrifice, and to hearken than the fat of rams" (1 Sam. 15:22). Puritans consistently linked the divine preference for heart over deeds with the Gospel's supplanting of the Law. A merely legal sacrifice was less than nothing: "The sacrifice of the wicked is an abomination to the Lord: but the prayer of the upright is his delight" (Prov. 15:8). There was no use trying to deceive a God who "seeth not as man seeth; for man looketh on the outward appearance, but the Lord looketh on the heart" (1 Sam. 16:7).

The pure heart of the redeemed soul provided a standard against which Taylor repeatedly tests his willingness to offer himself as the sole sacrifice demanded under the New Dispensation. If the "Lightning Eye" of Christ enlightens his soul, "I shall be grac'd withall for glory fit. / My Heart then stufft with Grace, Light, Life, and Glee / I'le sacrifice in Flames of Love to thee" (1.16). Fired by holy love, he promises to "sacrifice to thee my Heart in praise, / When thy Rich Grace shall be my hearty Phrase" (2.6); "I now will climb / The stares up to thine Altar, and on't lay / Myselfe, and services, even for its shrine" (2.18); if he is perfumed with grace's odors, "then my life shall be a Sacrifice / Perfum'de with this sweet incense up arise" (2.121). The relentless interiority of verbal sacrifices performed "gospelly" explains why details from Taylor's daily life are conspicuously absent from the Meditations. For this conversation and this reader, such details simply didn't matter. Christ's presumed interest lay in his inward man, not his outward one, and when images from the natural world do appear, they confirm the perceptions of a soul who has pledged to count all things "but dung, that I may win Christ" (Phil. 3:8). "Were all the World a sparkling pearle," Taylor asserts, "'t would bee / Worse than a dot of Dung if weighd with thee" (2.34). The only real intrusion of the outside world occurs in the poems attacking Solomon Stoddard's innovations regarding admission to the Supper. But even then Taylor does not mention the Northampton preacher by name. Instead, he reiterates, though with a defensiveness that reveals the timeliness of the controversy, his view of the Supper as an eternal seal of the heavenly marriage of saint with Savior.[22]

Taylor's pursuit of a pure heart reflects his pious effort to assimilate, as fully as possible, the Christic perspective as his own and thereby to become a "text" that Christ would want to read. Everywhere he seeks to perceive the world, the flesh, and the devil from a redeemed point of view, bending his will to Christ's as a means of justifying a divine propensity to save him. The true motive of sincere prayer, Ames pointed out, was "to obtain by our prayer what we believe he wishes to grant."[23] It was theologically inevitable that Taylor's vehement self-castigations conform to the judgment of a Christic reader to whom sin was utterly foreign. The poet similarly adopts Christ's great Adversary as his own, as an external attacker who renders his soul "the very Soile / Where Satan reads his Charms, and sets his Spell" (1.40). And he piously emulates Christ's view of death as another external enemy whose defeat is a foregone conclusion. In Meditation 1.34 Taylor initially depicts death within a fallen perceptual framework, as a "King of Terrours" who casts "Ghostly Lookes which fling / Such Dread to see as raiseth Deadly groans." But he deliberately replaces the fearsome image with the view of death afforded by grace. To the saintly self death is transformed, "Made Usefull" as yet another agent of salvation. The grave, perceived through faculties restored by grace, becomes "a Down bed now made for your clay."

Taylor also adopts Christ's presumed view of his words, of the poetry itself. However harshly he criticizes his verse, we cannot assume that a poet who kept at it for over forty years really thought it so bad from a human point of view. Rather, when he describes his poetry as "Tattling" (1.21), "ragged Rhimes" (1.32), or a "Lisp of Non-sense" (1.17), he offers it as the flawed sacrifice that Christ expected and forgave, the verbal equivalent of the sin that Christ came to pardon. For Taylor the poems are always bad relative to their intended reader: "And all my Praise with which my heart runs ore / Unto thyself is but a poor dull note" (2.140); "An Ant bears more proportion to the World / Than doth my piping to thine eare thus hurld" (2.23). These opaque, leaden offerings dramatize in their very flaws the redemptive humility of Taylor's petitions. "I have no finer Stuff to use," he admits, "and I / Will use it now my Creed but to declare / And not thy Glorious Selfe to beautify" (2.43). Or as he confesses elsewhere, "My Rhymes do better suite / Mine own Dispraise than tune forth praise to thee" (1.22). By deprecating his poems as products, Taylor separates them, like the "Bubs" that torment him, from what he hopes is an essential self that would someday have no need for such verse in heaven. By judging his poetry from an eternal and celestial point of view, he merely confirmed that his literary taste accorded with Christ's—not such a bad thing, really, for a Puritan poet to have to admit.[24]

Within the framework of his verbal ritual, Taylor's artistic dilemma is no more serious—and no less—than any other reminder of human inadequacy. Divine praise was mandated in the command "that every tongue should confess that Jesus Christ is Lord, to the glory of God the father," that the believer was to "work out your own salvation with fear and trembling" (Phil. 2:11–12). Taylor knew full well that Paul posed a scriptural duty that he was foredoomed to bungle:

> Oh! Bright! Bright thing! I fain would something say:
>   Lest Silence should indict me. Yet I feare
> To say a Syllable lest at thy day
>   I be presented for my Tattling here.   (1.21)

In an echo of Bradstreet's "Contemplations," verbal inadequacy exposes a self trapped between depraved reality and saintly desire. Isolated by sin in a universe animated by divine praise, Taylor wonders why the "Bird" and "little Bee" can praise God, while he who can "see thy shining Glory fall / Before mine Eyes" stands "Blockish, Dull, and Dumb" (1.22). But like Bradstreet, Taylor knew that such conviction could, if taken to heart, stimulate salvific renewal. Taylor repeatedly enacts verbal "failure," as Charles W. Mignon maintains, in order to reconfirm his lack of merit. The rotten sacrifice of bad verse becomes yet another expression of a self laid low in the dust. In poem after poem Taylor's acknowledgment of artistic shoddiness reinforces his identity as a self who *must* rely on Christ not only for salvation but for help in singing its wonders.[25]

The bargains that Taylor extends to Christ at the end of many of the poems reiterate this need by celebrating what grace could do for him as believer and as poet. If he is saved, they confirm, Christ will accept his praise no matter how poorly he writes.[26] These exchanges repeatedly shift the performative burden of writing from Taylor to Christ-in-Taylor. Until that identity was fully realized, bad poetry would simply have to do. In the meantime, Taylor's persistence in doing his best despite these limits reflected the pure heart that would make his sacrifices acceptable: "I fain the Choicest Love my soule Can get, / Would to thy Gracious selfe a Gift present / But cannot now unscrew Loves Cabbinet" (1.25). The confession of flawed art, like the confession of any sin, prompted its own remedy. As the verbal mirror of depravity, bad poetry proved the honesty of his self-scrutiny by showing Christ that he *was* bringing "unto thine Altar th'best of all / My Flock affords. I have no better Story" (1.21). In his final Meditation Taylor once again invokes the language of a ritual botched not by intent but by infirmity. Here, as throughout the Meditations, he enacts redemptive self-splitting by chiding that part of himself in which his "sick Love" "hates confinement": "Hence Lord accept of this, reject the rest. / I grudg my heart if it send not thee th'best" (2.165). Taylor begs Christ to separate gracious wheat from sinful chaff in his song, a division corresponding to the duality that he seeks within himself:

> Had I but better thou shouldst better have.
>   I nought withold from thee through nigerdliness,
> But better than my best I cannot save
>   From any one, but bring my best to thee.
>   If thou acceptst my sick Loves gift I bring
> Thy it accepting makes my sick Love sing.   (2.165)

It is common to see Taylor as having placed himself, spiritually and artistically, in a no-win situation. "Whether I speake, or speechless stand," he concedes, "I spy, / I faile thy Glory: therefore pardon Cry" (1.22). But when his problems with art and sin are considered in terms of his spiritual aims and Christic audience, he could not lose. Failing Christ's glory was part and parcel of living, not just writing— and crying for pardon was the identifying mark of true belief. Repeatedly internalizing Paul's affirmation that "when I am weak, then am I strong" (2 Cor. 12:10), Taylor articulated the human weakness that proved divine strength. Earthly saints, Weemse explained, continued to sin in order that Christ's "grace may be perfitted by our weaknesse." That Taylor could supply the "Mite" by which Christ's "Almightiness" was fulfilled (2.48) supports Keller's assertion that the poet's "person-in-need . . . justifies the saving power of God." As Taylor confirmed in the *Christographia*, until the "application" of redemption took place within the elect, Christ had "a greate Vacancy, and an emptiness to be filld up."[27] "What mystery's here," he proclaims in Meditation 2.51, "Thou canst not wanty bee. / Yet wantest them, as sure as they want thee." Offering to make Christ less "wanty" by articulating a self whose weakness completed Christ's power, Taylor also pursued his hoped-for identity as an assured believer whose better half would join with the Savior and thereby be "complete in him, which is the head of all principality and power" (Col. 2:10). The consolation of writing is most evident when Taylor vividly feels the fractured identity that could be healed only through Christ. By voicing the humility requisite to true belief, he intensified his hope that Christ would consequently find "Something" (2.165) in him and his sacrifices worth saving. Persisting in addressing such a reader despite the vast, sin-caused gap that separated them, Taylor both demonstrated and strengthened his faith in the miracle "that Almighty should to mee / E're lend his Eare" (2.23).

Poetry eased Taylor's spiritual anxieties by providing a forum and a method for animating and maintaining salvific processes within himself. By enhancing his identification with the saintly metaself, he was able not only to monitor God's work in his soul but to help it along through pious verbal activity. Keller argued that because of the imperfect nature of assurance Taylor could not know his "ideal self." But if he could not know whether his experience of that self would be final and definitive, his theology certainly told him what such a self was like. Christ's presumed demands pushed him to try it on repeatedly in order to assess the fit.[28]

That these demands shaped the poet's voice so profoundly raises a fundamental but seldom-discussed question: who exactly *is* the Edward Taylor of the Meditations? As I have suggested, he is not a "persona" in the usual sense, a fictive construct that Taylor deliberately invented as a means of writing his way into heaven. He certainly did not think that the Christic reader could be duped by the poetic equivalent of wish fulfillment. On the contrary, his persistence in writing in the full recognition that poetry could not save him demonstrated that his hopeful self-readings had no taint of legality. As Ames confirmed, salvific "*Experience produces hope*." In the Meditations, Taylor wrote for himself the experience by which his pilgrim hope could be intensified. Like any good Puritan, he clung to this hope by acting out Shepard's affirmation that "to live by faith properly is to live upon the promise in the want of the thing, or to apprehend the thing in the promise."[29] Like Bradstreet, Taylor clarified his self-exegesis as saint not through legal or literary performance but through a relentless search for "the substance of things hoped for, the evidence of things not seen" but, for him, absolutely real (Heb. 11:1).

Taylor's poetic identity, however, assumes another dimension of which he was utterly unconscious. However "real" he felt his voice to be, there are dangers in sharing his view—in equating the voice of the Meditations simply with Taylor himself. Scheick and Keller, noting the presence of a "sacred" and "mythic" self in the Meditations, suggest the extrapersonal dimension of a voice shaped so profoundly by theological structures and assumptions that any expressions of the "private" Taylor are difficult to isolate. In projecting the self that gave his life meaning, Taylor was, in Patricia Meyer Spacks's phrase, "imagining a self," assuming a personality no less real to him for its indebtedness to what his theology taught him about Christ's demands. For him as for other Puritans, "self-fashioning," to use Stephen Greenblatt's term, was a matter not of artistic choice but of gracious hope. As Spacks argues in reference to eighteenth-century autobiography, "The author presents for public contemplation the self that he wants or needs or chooses to offer, rarely recognizing distinctly the imaginative components of that version." Change "public contemplation" to "divine judgment" and the statement stands equally for Edward Taylor.[30]

Taylor's honesty in the Meditations remains intact because he did not know that he was "acting." His was a sincerity not simply to be himself but to become what he thought Christ wanted him to be. The last thing that he wanted was to express a voice that we would label as strictly private, personal, or idiosyncratic. *That* self, which Puritans identified with the Old Creature, was to be suppressed with the full force of language even as language helped to expose and define it more clearly. What Christ wanted to "read" in Taylor was the New Creature toward which the poetry constantly strains. At one point the poet votes "For a new set of Words and thoughts hereon / And leap beyond the line such words to gain / In other Realms, to praise thee: but in vain" (2.106). The realm "beyond the line" where he could finally achieve definitive self-reading as a New Creature was not his everyday world but the eternal realm foretold in Scripture, a realm in which his humanity would be utterly transformed.

Because Taylor wanted to sing "seraphickwise" (1.20), not humanwise, the voice of the Meditations is answerable not so much to universal experience as to Puritan definitions of that experience based on traits that Christ presumably expected to find in all true believers. Taylor's success in forging cultural and theological patterns into a distinct poetic voice helps explain why he is both utterly conventional as a Puritan and profoundly original as an artist. Although the Meditations do not present a very clear picture of what we might wish to know about the Westfield pastor, they do offer a vivid portrait of what *he* considered to be his deepest and most important identity. The "real" Edward Taylor will, for this reason, continue to elude us in the Meditations: it was not the self that he put into them. Scripture told him, as it told Bradstreet and Wigglesworth, that "whosoever will save his life shall lose it: and whosoever will lose his life for my sake shall find it" (Matt. 16: 25). Because the "greatest enemy" of a Christian, as Hooker attested, "is his own Heart and Will," Taylor had to let Christ know not only that he wanted redemptive self-loss but that his faith allowed him to imagine it.

One of James Durham's justifications for singing, "studying edification our selves," thus assumes a nearly literal sense in the Meditations, whose speaker constantly tears down his carnal self in order to edify/build up that *other* self who could approach Christ and hope to be found acceptable in his sight. "A contrite heart," Hooker insisted, "is that which is powdered all to dust."[31] In the "Prologue" to the Meditations Taylor prayed that "th'attempts" to praise not "breake down my Dust." But in his search for blessed assurance, breaking down the self of mere dust was precisely what he wanted to do. He was convinced that his reader demanded nothing less.

CHAPTER TEN

"In Sacred Text I Write": The Taylorian

Self as the Word

In the "Prologue" to the *Preparatory Meditations* Taylor seeks to sharpen his "dull Phancy" on "Zions Pretious Stone," the revealed Word of Scripture as the sole source and arbiter of his ongoing meditative ritual.[1] His indebtedness to the Bible, as we have seen, extends far beyond the level of simple allusion to encompass his conception of writing as a neobiblical ceremony performed "gospelly" and validated not by the speaker but by the Spoken, the Christic reader who is Taylor's "Medium to God" (2.20). Repeatedly clarifying his grasp of biblical revelations of Christ's glory, Taylor pursues an exclusively Christocentric reading of Scripture as a means of reconfirming and intensifying the gracious identity that he seeks. What he sees of Christ when he reads the Word not only defines his single theme, it tells him who he *is* in relation to that theme.

From a modern perspective it is easy to see this pervasive biblicism as an artistic liability that restricted Taylor's voice and inflated his poetry with distracting allusions that barely cohere. But without the Bible he could not have written at all. It provided not just his subject matter but the very means by which he could think and write about it. As the great Poem that Puritans believed made all other poems possible, Scripture defined his self-experience as artist and believer. Determined to see whether its promises applied to him, he doggedly pursued his assurance by seeking glimpses of a neobiblical self whose traits were foretold in its pages. Constantly pursuing the resonance of biblical text with meditating self that marked the saved soul, Taylor internalized the gracious "Arguments" of Scripture as "Arrows" capable of penetrating his outer man and thereby widening the experiential gap between what he hoped was his essential self and a sinful self that still resisted biblical truth. Inspired reading, enabled by eyes and ears opened by faith, could "force" Taylor's "Will, and Reason" to conform with Christ's and thereby "stifle pleas made for the other part / That so my Soule, rid of their Sophistry / In rapid flames of Love to thee may fly" (2.36). Opposing his "other part" with poems of praise, Taylor repeatedly tested his ability to absorb biblical statement as felt experience. Each Meditation challenged his identity as a self animated by Scripture. Each verse in Zion's stone offered him a mirror as well as a message, an opportunity to see whether he was becoming not merely a reader of the Word but its prophetic subject.

As Taylor announced in a declaration acted out in each poem, "In Sacred Text I write" (2.58). On the simplest level, this declaration confirmed a Puritan rejection of extrabiblical revelation, of a Christ divorced from the Word. But the Meditations go further: in them Taylor rejects an extrabiblical self as well, repeatedly voicing the unity of self and Scripture that suggested a vital faith. Throughout the poetry, the "harmony and power of harmony betweene the spirit and the word" extolled by commentator Francis Rous shapes Taylor's view of the Bible as a divinely penned "Love Letter" addressed to him, provided he can respond warmly to its message: "Thy Love to mee spell out therein I will" (2.8). Entreating the Word *with* the Word, Taylor, like Bradstreet, explores the relation between private response and biblical paradigm, between the sinful self that he confesses and the saintly self that Scripture activates within him. He repeatedly underscores the distinct natures of these two selves by contrasting the words expressive of each. Although earthly—and frequently earthy—language is necessary for his self-conviction, biblical language constantly activates the better self that he pursues. Chief among the attributes of the "Selected Ones" are "Tongues tipt with Zions Languague" (2.109). Their speech, a perfect reflection of their pure hearts, would be brought into full harmony with the language of Scripture. Begging Christ to "Cloath" his tunes "with thy Shine" (2.12), Taylor seeks just such an echo of God's words in his own.[2]

To appropriate Zion's language as a saintly metaself was not merely to parrot the Word, but to absorb it so completely that the barrier between personal and biblical expression could begin to dissolve. The destruction of this barrier would occur at the saint's glorification, when all Scripture promises would be fulfilled. By anticipating with language what he hoped would take place in fact, Taylor framed each Meditation as an internalized Bible in miniature, a private speaking of the Word by a self whose story was embedded in the sacred narrative. After emerging at one point from a direct confrontation with his artistic dilemma, he embraces Scripture as a catalyst not just for being saved but for *speaking* saved:

> Lend mee thy Wings, my Lord, I'st fly apace.
>   My Soules Arms stud with thy strong Quills, true Faith,
> My Quills then Feather with thy Saving Grace,
>   My Wings will take the Winde thy Word displai'th.
>   Then I shall fly up to thy glorious Throne
> With my strong Wings whose Feathers are thine own. (1.20)

The "Winde" (*pneuma*, Spirit, breath) displayed/displaced by the Word (*Logos*, Christ, Bible) provides his sole medium of ascent. Asserting the "strong Quills" of faith that permit him both to write and to rise, Taylor gratefully accepts the loan of biblical language and the redemptive promise it contains. His share in the Resurrection, for instance, is made to seem more probable by his echo of Paul's repudiation of death in 1 Corinthians 15:55 ("O death, where is thy sting? O grave, where is thy victory?"): "And setting Foot upon its neck I sing / Grave, where's thy Victory? Death, Where's thy Sting?" (1.19). Here, as throughout the poetry, Taylor's nearly wholesale appropriation of biblical words embodies his meditative projection into the Bible as an assured saint capable of speaking its promises from the heart.

Taylor seeks an inner conformity with biblical discourse so complete that Scripture almost ceases to exist as a separate entity. When he begs Christ to "Slay my Rebellion, and make thy Law my Word" (2.16), the artist that he wants to become is enmeshed with the saved identity for which he prays:

> Lord dub my tongue with a new tier of Words
>   More comprehensive far than my dull Speech
> That I may dress thy Excellency Lord
>   In Languague welted with Emphatick reech.   (2.19)

"Emphatick" suggests not just vivid and engaged speech, but the saint's empathy with the Word as its subject as well as its reader. In Taylor's version of Herbert's reversed thunder, only divine language uttered by a divinely wrought self was suitable for "dressing" God. He repudiates self-conscious invention in favor of selflessness as God's musician and instrument: "Be thou my Song," he asks at one point, "and make Lord, mee thy Pipe" (1.22). Mere artistry could not produce such verbal transformation. Only saving faith could reshape Taylor's language into a pure conduit of the Word. If Christ accepts his gift of "but a Wooden toole," the divine hearer will "enrich" it "With Grace, thats better than Apollo's Stoole" (2.23).

However intimidating such a goal must have seemed, Taylor's artistic flaws only whet his desire to achieve it. "I fain would praise thee," he admits, "but want words to do't." What he needs is "a new set of Words and thoughts" that come from "beyond the line" separating earth from heaven (2.106). If he could cross that line and sing like a glorified saint, his words would harmonize with God's Word as completely as the songs of the redeemed in heaven. This constant deferral of successful praise manifests his ongoing concession that death alone would make him into the poet that he wanted to be: "I would do more but can't, Lord help me so / That I may pay in glory what I owe" (1.41); "Till then I cannot sing, my tongue is tide. / Accept this Lisp till I am glorifide" (1.43); "Accept I pray and what for this I borrow, / I'le pay thee more when rise on heavens morrow" (2.153).[3]

In the meantime, the partial fluency in biblical discourse that Taylor achieves brings comfort by reinforcing his duality as a self whose saintly reach still exceeds his sinful grasp. Meditating on Christ's "glorious body" (Phil. 3:21), for instance, he laments his lack of "a rich, fine Phansy" capable of laying "Curious pollishings" "on thy glorious Body bright / The more my lumpish-heart to animate" (2.74). He similarly concedes that generating an appropriate response to the promise that "I am come that they might have life" (John 10:10) "is a Taske too hard" for his "Goose Quill." The biblical theme "would thereby be marrd: / My inke would black it, though a gold Edition," and any "'Bellisht Definitions" of the poet's making could only darken the glory of the biblical metatext (2.87). But because it was desire and not attainment that defined the pilgrim soul, the persistence and energy with which Taylor engaged his biblical texts helped him maintain a warm assurance. Occasionally he achieves what he must have felt was an extraordinary empathy with the Word. After treating Christ's "Humane Frame," for example, "Well ting'd with Grace," he asserts the salvific rehabilitation of language that was his truest measure of artistic and spiritual success:

> That Golden Mint of Words, thy Mouth Divine,
>   Doth tip these Words, which by my Fall were spoild;
> And Dub with Gold dug out of Graces mine
>   That they thine Image might have in them foild.   (1.7)

Yet because he remains a self divided by the redemptive war within him, his request for further purification with the "Gold" of "Graces mine" — grace mined and Taylor's grace — dramatizes need as well as affirmation. Only tipped and not yet immersed in salvific language issuing from the divine mouth, his speech reveals, as it does in all of the Meditations, the profound spiritual challenge of narrowing the perceptual and expressive gap between self and Scripture.

The Bible itself both caused and eased this difficulty. Puritans believed that in its dual role of convicting and consoling the reader, Scripture at once concealed and revealed. As the Word made flesh made word again, the Bible exhibited something of Christ's glory to sensibilities partially restored by grace, but it also hid that full glory from an earthly self still plagued by sin. Simultaneously transparent and opaque, the biblical metatext constantly exposes a corresponding doubleness within Taylor as a self who seeks Christ's "Spectacles that I may see / To glorify aright thy glorious Selfe. / And see this Saving Faith grafted in mee" (2.155). The text that prompts this request is Paul's injunction to "Examine yourselves, whether ye be in the faith; prove your own selves" (2 Cor. 13:5). As the locus of Taylor's repeated self-examinations, the Bible clarifies his identity as a self who both sees and does not see. In his plea for Christ to "Open the Valving Doors" of faith "And give my Souls Cleare Eye of thee a Sight / As thou shinst its bright looking Glasses bright" (2.125), Scripture becomes a window that reveals a "little flash" of Christ's glory (2.99) as well as a mirror that reflects the degree to which Christ lives in the poet.

Despite his self-deprecation, Taylor usually passes the test of spiritual vision that the Bible offered him. He was convinced that Scripture revealed only what his faith allowed him to see: truths visible only to the "internall Eye Sight" of the saintly self developing within him (2.147). Yet his affirmations of a vision partially restored by "Christ's Eye Salve" are constantly tempered by a withholding of vision that exposes the "Sin blind Eye" of his outer man. When he is unable to absorb Scripture, it is his mortal element that makes the biblical mirror opaque: "Course Phancy, Ragged Faculties, alas! / And Blunted Tongue don't Suit: Sighs Soile the Glass" (1.21). But when he staggers at the glory of the Word, he reconfirms a perception of Scripture suggestive of true belief. By simultaneously proving his gracious ability to see and exposing his fallen tendency *not* to see, the Bible helped reinforce Taylor's dual experience as an earthly saint.⁴ In his ritualized vacillations between a flat response to the Word and an assured ability to read it with enflamed affections, the Bible sustained his ongoing position as a pilgrim hovering between sin and sanctity:

> Oh! that I had but halfe an eye to view
>   This excellence of thine, undazled: so
> Therewith to give my heart a touch anew
>   Untill I quickned am, and made to glow.   (2.1)

The Meditations repeatedly confirm this "halfe an eye," a partial vision that makes possible Taylor's tentative identification with the dual self foreshadowed in the biblical text. Is he a gracious plant rooted in Christ's garden? Has he been grafted onto the redeemed stock? Is he a client of Christ as advocate? Is he a bidden guest at Christ's banquet? Is he following the antitypical Exodus to the celestial Promised Land? Does he possess rights granted by the covenant of grace? Is he under Christ's banner? Are the healing wings of the Sun of Righteousness hovering over him? Is he Christ's Bride? The list could, of course, be expanded indefinitely: Taylor gauges his inner replication of every biblical text and image on which he meditates.

It is within this constant self-biblicizing that Taylor's alleged artistic flaws must be considered. Precisely when he succeeds most in achieving a neobiblical sense of self, he seems to fail *us* most as a poet. Modern readers might not care, for instance, to hear the dozen-odd ways in which Christ fulfills Joseph's role as personal type in Meditation 2.7. But more to the point, why would Taylor's Christic reader need to hear them? The Incarnate Word could certainly be expected to understand the mysteries of the types: Puritans believed, after all, that he had invented them—indeed, that he *was* them. But Taylor needed to show Christ that he had made full and proper use of these shadowy revelations of divine glory, that he could count the ways in which he could find Christ in Joseph and thus perform a gracious reading of Scripture. The poet needed to "sing with the spirit, and . . . with the understanding also" (1 Cor. 14:15) as he strove toward redeemed identity. Here, as throughout the poetry, he asserted a gracious ability to see Christ everywhere in Scripture—to confirm, as Henoch Clapham attested, that every book "in the whole Bible" teaches "Christ Jesus and him crucified."⁵

William Perkins insisted that "The Elect having the Spirit of God, doe first discern the voice of Christ speaking in the Scriptures."⁶ As tests of Taylor's capacity for finding Christ in the Word, the Meditations enact an extended game of hide-and-seek in which the poet is "It" and Christ peeks out like the Canticles Bridegroom from behind the scriptural lattice. In his pursuit Taylor engages every faculty, leaving scarcely a biblical stone unturned. Sometimes his relationship to Scripture is self-consciously exegetical, as he tries to penetrate the deepest mysteries of "Our text" (2.91) or "thy thoughts" (2.137). At the promise that "things present" and "things to come" are "yours" (1 Cor. 3:22), for instance, he professes faith in a divine love that he cannot yet understand:

> To find thee Lord, thus overflowing kinde,
> And t'finde mee thine, thus overflowing vile,
> A Riddle seems onrivetted I finde.
> This reason saith is hard to reconcile.   (1.36)

Each scriptural image similarly challenges Taylor's ability to extract hidden manna from the Word. In the typological poems his demonstrations of gracious reading are particularly exhaustive. Aaron's robes, for instance, "typify / Christ cloath'd in human flesh pure White, all fair, / And undefild" (2.23); his "Vessell" adumbrates the believer's heart as it catches the Redeemer's blood; his incense anticipates Christ's prayer and service; his cleansing of the tabernacle foreshadows Christ's propitiation for sin; the goat and bullock that he offers typify Christ's ultimate sacrifice. Pushing the type to its limits, Taylor draws out its full Christological significance as a revelation of how much of Christ he can see in the Word. Jonah offers a similar test of salvific reading. Jonah, whose name means "dove" in Hebrew, prefigures Christ "as a Turtle Dove" protecting the elect (2.30); like Christ, he is sacrificed for the safety of his companions; after he enters the gravelike belly of the "Mighty Whale," his rescue foreshadows the Resurrection; his preaching for forty days typifies Christ's preaching "to the Heathen." By lining out the full Christology of Jonah's story, Taylor assesses his capacity to absorb the mysteries of the Word. The more that he found there, the more likely it was that his own "Dreadfull Tempest" would be calmed by the protective power of the "Dovy wings" foreshadowed in Jonah's name.

Taylor frequently does not bother to spell out the biblical associations that he makes, resorting instead to an exegetical shorthand indicative of an assured familiarity with Christ. When he reveals too little about his hermeneutics he presents modern readers with difficulties equal to when he seems to tell too much. Meditation 2.59, for example, offers a seemingly random sequence of biblical images and allusions: the pillar of cloud and fire of the Exodus; the tabernacle; the darkness of unbelief and the heat of the law; Christ as the church's pilot; Christ's watchtower; Christ's chariot as the Incarnation; Christ's typical offices as priest, prophet, and king; and the Canticles Bridegroom, under whose shadow Taylor sings as the Bride. The logic governing how the imagery connects—and these are only the major images—is more evident from Puritan exegesis than from the poem itself. But as William Ames insisted, the Scriptures, when read with the eye of faith, "give light to themselves."[7] Taylor's radical conflation of diverse scriptural associations demonstrated his ability to perceive this light, to exercise a redeemed grasp of the fundamental unity of the Word.

Taylor does not develop biblical images with the self-evident logic found in metaphysical poetry. On the contrary, he asserts that their underlying "logic" is faith, not a linear rationality that is consistently "overflown" by the wonders of a Word that "Soares above her Sight" (1.41). Piling on one biblical image after another, he forces himself to move beyond interpretation toward pure response. "Reason," he chides himself at one point, "lie prison'd in this golden Chain. / Chain up thy tongue, and silent stand a while" (1.41). Repeatedly pushing his rationality to the point where its bond to the flesh reasserts itself, he sharpens his inner polarity of desire and limitation, of one self who penetrates biblical mysteries and another who cannot yet do so: "Reason stands for it, moving to persue't. / But Flesh and Blood, are Elementall things / That sink me down, dulling my Spirits fruit" (2.82). His only antidote to carnal opacity is a Puritan version of Augustine's *credo ut intelligam*, a confirmation that "Faith never blindeth reasons Eye but cleares / Its Sight to see things quite above its Sphere" (2.108).[8]

Hiding the Truth from the unclean but revealing it to those whom grace has made into partially sound interpreters, Scripture repeatedly challenged Taylor's inner man to get beyond reason's "Sphere." And because "Life Animall a Spirituall Sparke ne'er springs" (2.82), Taylor's enthusiasm for the Word verified the identity that the biblical metatext was forming within him. The Canticles description of the Bride becomes "these Metaphors we spirituallized" (2.151), dark language illuminated by the insights of grace. Solomon's allegory offers "Silver Metaphors and Tropes," a "Rhetorick of thine my Lord" (2.153) in which Taylor reads his own assurance. All of Scripture provides opportunities for similarly optimistic readings of the self. Isaiah's prophecy that the Lord shall reign "before his ancients, gloriously" (Isa. 24:23) offers "Glory as a Metaphor" (2.100) designed "to make thyselfe appeare" (2.101) to those who, like Taylor's speaker, had eyes to see. The central text of the Eucharist similarly separates the sheep from the goat within the poet's identity. The warning that "Except ye eat the flesh of the Son of man, and drink his blood, ye have no life in you" (John 6:53) prompts doubts arising from his carnal understanding: "What feed on Humane Flesh and Blood? Strang mess! / Nature exclaims. What Barbarousness is here?" (2.81). The self of "Nature," as Taylor demonstrates, is a hopeless literalist: "Christs Flesh and Blood how can they bee good Cheer? / If shread to atoms, would too few be known, / For ev'ry mouth to have a single one?" But such objections only reconfirm the priority within Taylor of "Some other Sense" than the merely rational:

> This Sense of this blesst Phrase is nonsense thus.
> Some other Sense makes this a metaphor.
> This feeding signifies, that Faith in us
> Feeds on this fare, Disht in this Pottinger.

Like Bradstreet's "Spirit," Taylor constantly exercises the "Spirituall Eye" (2.116) to which all seeming contradictions in the Word became clear. To eschew a merely literal meaning was to repudiate a carnal identity limited, like Bradstreet's "Flesh," to the literal because of faithlessness. The Bible offered little solace to such a self. Contemplating the Bridegroom's "lips like lilies" (Cant. 5:13), Taylor confirms that the myrrh of the Word cures only the "spirituall ailes" and "spirituall maladies" of the "spiritual man" (2.121).

Taylor repeatedly identifies with the "spiritual man" foretold in his biblical texts. Meditating on the myrrh and spice gathered by the Christic Bridegroom (Cant. 5:1), he wonders "doth thy Myrrh tree Flowrish in my Soule?" (2.84), or more directly, "Do thy Convictions bring mee to Condole / My Sinfulness with griefe, Hearts bitter fare?" Elsewhere the "sun of righteousness" with "healing in his wings" (Mal. 4:2) prompts him to seek a place for his own "megre Soule" within the text: "Art not a Chick of th'Sun of Righteousness? / Do not its healing Wings thy ailes redress?" (2.68[B]). The more secure his place within the Bible, the more clearly he can see Christ and himself as its twin subjects: "Lord, make me with thy likeness like to thee. / Upon my Soule thy Shining Image place. / And let thy glorious grace shine bright in mee" (2.99). When he responds as a Word-shaped self to biblical expressions of Christ's glory, he confirms that Christ dazzles "the Eye of such as have the Sight / Of anyone deckt with thy Sparklings rare."

To see Christ this clearly was to become like Christ. Like "Angells" and "Saints," Taylor repeatedly approaches his Christic reader with a gracious "hunger to bee filled with thy likeness."9

As the "golden Key" (2.115) that activates Taylor's possibilities as a saved soul, the "Holy Word" sometimes overwhelms him. Scripture becomes Christ's "Spirits Pensill," "And I do stut, commenting on the Same" (2.123[B]). Canticles texts consistently provoke special wonder: "what a word is this thy Lips Let fall" (2.136); "How precious are thy thoughts my Lord, to mee!" (2.137); "What, what a Say is this" (2.142); "Oh! what a Speech is this, thy lips do vent" (2.145). But all of Scripture can stimulate pious awe. Paul's promise that "if one died for all," then "all" are dead (2 Cor. 5:14) generates a joyous chant: "Oh, Good, Good, Good, my Lord. What more Love yet. / Thou dy for mee! What, am I dead in thee?" (2.112). At Matthew's description of the Last Supper Taylor exclaims "What Grace is here?" (2.102). The statement that "greater love hath no man than this, that a man lay down his life for his friends" (John 15:13) prompts him to ask "O! what a thing is Love? who can define / Or liniament it out?" (2.66). Gracious awe renders him incapable of grasping Christ's "power" (Matt. 28:18): "What Power is this? What all Authoritie / In Earth and Heaven too? What Lord is here?" (2.52).

Taylor connects such engaged responses with the conviction in sin that validates them. At the Bridegroom's invitation to "eat, O friends" (Cant. 5:1), he can scarcely believe his spiritual ears: "Callst thou me Friend? What Rhetorick is this? / It is a Piece of heavenly Blandishments," "lushious Complements" from Christ to the poet as Bride (2.156). That Christ would "prepare a place" for him (John 14:2) similarly becomes "A Clew of Wonders! Clusterd Miracles! / Angells, come whet your sight hereon. Here's ground" (1.41); the "Wealthy Theam" of Christ's fullness contrasts tellingly with the poet's "Feeble Phancy" (1.27); the promise that "all are yours" (1 Cor. 3:22) is a "Golden Word" (1.32) that Taylor scarcely believes can apply to him. At Paul's assurance that "ye are Christ's" (1 Cor. 3:23) he "quailes to thinke that I should bee / So high related" (1.37). How could "A Dirt ball" possibly be dressed in the "milk white Lawn" (1.46) of the elect soul's "white raiment" (Rev. 3:5)?

Such responses assured Taylor that his aesthetic sensibilities were being renovated along with every other trait. Because the miracle of election was inseparable from the holy language that set it forth, Christ's roles as Savior and as divine Poet of the Word were for Taylor one and the same. As Scheick points out, for the earthly poet "The Word is God's artist," serving "as those creative fingers from which all designs originate and from which all life flows."¹⁰ God's art—in the Word revealed and the Word made flesh—constantly stimulates Taylor's aesthetic and spiritual renewal. The "Charms" that are "bed" in Solomon's portrayal of the Canticles Bride, for instance, "spiritualize my dull affections mine / Until they up their heads in Loves flames reare" (2.121). Only an assured saint could so cherish the description of the Bride's teeth (Cant. 6:6) as "Golden words" dropped from Christ's "gracious lips," "Adorning of thy Speech with Holy paint" (2.138). Taylor's celebrations of the sheer beauty of the Word dramatize his relish of God's love letter to him. Although "Thou Courtst mine Eyes in Sparkling Colours bright, / Most bright indeed, and soul enamoring," he attests that "Embellisht knots of Love assault my minde / Which still is Dull, as if this Sun ne're shin'de" (2.12).

But for Taylor, the Sun/Son *does* shine even if he cannot always feel divine light and heat. What dulls his vision is not Christ's rejection but his inability to grasp the miracle that "Christs rich praises" of the Bride, "With Silver Metaphors and Tropes bedight" (2.153), apply to him. The "Dazzling Shining Flashes" (2.12) that the poet glimpses in the Bible were created by a divine Artist who gilded "ore with sparkling Metaphors / The Object thy Eternall Love fell on / Which makes her glory shine 'bove brightest stars" (2.152). Christ's "Object," of course, is the true Bride—the identity that Taylor pursues in the verse. Throughout the Meditations, the deepest scriptural beauty to which the poet remains only partially responsive is his own as a probable saint.

Taylor's desire to read and write himself into Scripture manifests itself in his identification with the supreme poets of the Bible, an identification suggested by his extensive verse paraphrases of nearly all the poetry of the Old Testament: the Psalms, Job, the Song of Moses (Deut. 32:15–43), the Song of Deborah and Barak (Judges 5:2–31), the Song of Hannah (1 Sam. 2:1–10), and David's lament for Saul and Jonathan (2 Sam. 1:19–27). As Davis observes, "By providing a means of fashioning his own experience in the framework of biblical *and* historical precedent, the paraphrases invite the poet to make poetry a central concern in his life." Although Taylor defends turning Job "into ver[se]" by citing Jerome's statement that the bulk of the text was written in hexameters, his deeper motives thus extend well beyond recovering Job's poetic form. Davis suggests that Job's story, with its focus on the trials of the individual saint, may have reinforced Taylor's shift from the public and communal concerns of *Gods Determinations* and the *Metrical History of Christianity* to the private devotion of the Meditations.¹¹

The Psalmist provided even more direct precedent for Taylor's identity as sacred poet. Trying to internalize the Psalmist's emotions was, as we have seen, warmly recommended as an antidote to a merely passive reading of Scripture. Offering what commentator Henry Hammond called a "great treasury and magazine" of the moods of "all sorts and states, Ages and Sexes" of believers, the Psalms provided a model for all who wished "to take care that our lives bear some conformity" with the spiritual "patterns" anticipated by David.[12] Consistent with the Psalmist's prophetic anticipation of the varieties of religious experience, Taylor's Psalm paraphrases echo inner moods recorded in the Meditations. Taylor's Psalmist, like Taylor himself, labors under a sharp conviction in sin—"My Soule is also vexed sore" (50)—and frequently makes confession his central task: "[For I]'l shew mine iniquity, / For my Sins, griev'd bee" (98). As in the Meditations, contrition divides the Psalmic speaker into one self who sins and another who repents: "I also strictly kept myselfe / From mine iniquity" (67). Taylor's David intensifies this split by repeatedly debasing the sinful element that impedes his perfect obedience:

> Then let the Foe [pur]sue my Soule
> & take it; [l]et him thrust
> My life down to the Earth, & lay
> Mine Honour in the dust. (51)

Such contrition effects a verbal dissolution of carnal identity parallel to that effected in the Meditations. The Psalmist is "poured out like water" and "My bones disjoynt all do / My heart's like wax, doth melting (stand) / Middst of my bowells (too)" (74). Frank confession generates the humility for which David, like his translator, wishes to be judged: "Judge mee, for I have walkt, o Lord / In mine integrity" (79). Utter reliance upon divine correction and support stimulates a salvific shift from iniquity to integrity and from affliction to assurance. Evildoers depart from Taylor's Psalmist "Because the Lord hath heard the tone / Th'Voice of my Weeping Eye" (51). In exchange for release from his "enemies," he vows to offer "thanksgiving" and "prayses [to] thy name" (69). Heartfelt repentance confirms the Psalmist's identity as a New Creature straining to see God's "face in righteousness" so clearly that he might become *like* God: "I'st satisfide be when I shall / Wake with thy likeness (fresh)" (65).

Given the biblical parameters of Taylor's poetry, it is no surprise that the Psalmist's spiritual and artistic aims match Taylor's perfectly. In the "Prologue" to the Meditations Taylor vows to "Prove thou art, and that thou art the best." Taylor's Psalmist similarly pledges to "give praises great, O Lord / With all my heart to thee" and to "shew forth all thy works / Full mervelous which be" (54). Like Taylor in the Meditations, the Psalmist offers song in exchange for the grace that permits him to sing: "Be thou, Lord . . . Exalted (evry hour) / We will tune out (melodiously) / And Psalms Sing of thy power" (73). In addition to articulating psychological states also recorded in Taylor's private poetry, the Psalm paraphrases point up Taylor's view of the Bible as the supreme verbal model for the believer who renders divine praise. As his Psalmist attests, "Jehovahs words" are as "pu[re] / As Si[lver] truly tride / Within an earthen Furnace (sure) / And Seven times purifide" (61). Pure as it was, however, the language of Scripture could not simply be aped. The Word was to be contemplated and cherished until it was sincerely and fully internalized by the gracious soul. If mere paraphrase were sufficient, meditative poetry would scarcely have been necessary. At about the time Taylor recopied his second version of the Psalms, he began what Rosemary Fithian has called "his own Book of Psalms," the *Preparatory Meditations*.[13]

While David mapped the pilgrimage through this life, Solomon provided a glimpse of what the pilgrim could expect in the next. Toward the end of the Meditations, as Taylor's concerns increasingly turn from earthly devotion to celestial joy, the Psalmic voice is overshadowed by an identification with the Canticles Bride as his final biblical vehicle of meditative projection beyond the self and the world. Taylor's identity as Bride culminates in the long sequence of poems on texts from the Song of Songs, begun in 1713 when he was around seventy, with which the Meditations end (Meds. 2.115–65). His selection of the Song as his final biblical goad to redeemed self-experience was consistent with the belief that the text was, as the compilers of the Westminster *Annotations* put it, "wholly Evangelicall." While other biblical books were "interwoven with goats hair, and skins, this is all gold and jewels." Freed from the historical restrictions of the types and the Gospels, Canticles was cherished, as Matthew Henry attested, "even above any other of the Scripture Songs, as having more of Christ in it." While the Incarnation was historical and fulfilled, the mystical Bridegroom enabled readers, as John Collinges maintained, to "see as much of Christ as can be seen of him, on this side Heaven." James Durham, whose commentary Taylor owned, compared the Song to "*John Baptist* among the Prophets" because while "other Scriptures speak of Christ as coming . . . and afar off: this speaks of Him, and to Him, as already come, and near hand." Theodore Beza insisted that Canticles offered readers a "contemplation of those heavenly blessings, as if they were already dwelling in, and inhabiting the heavens, or at the least did alreadie knocke at the gates thereof." "Who can read it with understanding," asked Joseph Hall, "& not bee transported from the world; from himselfe? and be any other where, save in heaven, before his time?" As Henry summarized the popular view, the Song presented nothing less than "the Gate of Heaven."[14]

Because of its enigmatic nature, Canticles had no equal in separating the quick readers of Scripture from the dead. "If any thing be able," wrote the Westminster commentators, "to warm and fire the soul, this will; if any thing can sweeten and conciliate the harder things of an holy life, this will." Read as an especially vivid representation of final union with Christ, the Song afforded understanding and pleasure only to those whom grace had prepared to hear it. Collinges, for example, argued that "no portion of Scripture will appear either more instructive to a spiritual understanding, or more sweet to a spiritual tast; nor consequently more pleasant to such as have their sense exercised to discern betwixt good and evil." For Durham an indispensable prerequisite for the Canticles reader was "some experimental knowledge of the way of God towards his own heart." Such "experience," Durham insisted, was "one of the best Commentaries upon this Text": without it, no believer could achieve a "lively frame for this."[15]

No other biblical text offered a better meditative escape from carnal identity. In a prefatory poem to a verse paraphrase of Canticles, John Reeve urged those approaching the Song to "Put off the Clog, your Body, if you can, / And melt your selves into a Mass of Love." Other writers agreed on the Song's power to instill redemptive selflessness. "When we apply our selves to the Study of this Book," Henry warned, "we must . . . with *Moses* and *Joshua, put off our Shoe from off our Foot, and even forget that we have Bodies, because the Place where we stand is Holy Ground.*" And Thomas Ager attested that "when we are in the lowest condition, by reason of Sin and the Cross, yet then the understanding of this Song will raise us up beyond our selves." Transcending the earthbound self was crucial to a proper reading of Canticles because of the dangers inherent in its erotic imagery. The Song's sensual surface thus became an infallible test of the reader's spiritual state. John Cotton insisted in his Canticles commentary that "as the light and heat of the Sunne extinguisheth a kitchin fire; so doth heavenly love to Christ extinguish base kitchin lusts."[16] Whoever perceived this greater love in the Song had already gone far in eschewing sinful self and fallen world.

Such a text was perfectly suited to Taylor's increasing desire to be brought "to thy Palace Glory" (2.117)—to enact the Bride's ascent on the "golden track unto Celestial Joy" (2.128) and to add his own "Angelick melody" of praise (2.144) "at that bright Doore" of the Bridegroom's "Hall" (2.142). His identification with the Bride strengthens his sense of an eschatological self destined to enter "Thy glorious City . . . whose Streets [are] pure gold" (2.118), the "Bride Chamber of Eternall joy" (2.122), and "glories Hall" (2.131). The rhetoric that he confronts in the Song also stimulates his anticipation of eschatological song, of the perfect praise he would achieve when his transformation from earthly poet to celestial Bride was complete. In the meantime Canticles inspires him to do the best he can with his "narrow pipe" (2.153): "Accept I pray and what for this I borrow, / I'le pay thee more when rise on heavens morrow." When "I Crownd in Glories Orb do stand," he proclaims, "I'le sing the golden glory of thy Hand" (2.122).

By strengthening an identity that would be completed only after death, the Song of Songs becomes Taylor's *ars moriendi*, a use of the text consistent with the widespread assumption that a full understanding of the Song was possible only when the marriage itself was at hand. Reeve, who wrote his metrical version of Canticles when he was sixty, confessed that he "never yet could find my heart in tune / For such a work as this; it plain appears, / Love's hard to be refined!" To cherish the Song was to heed the Bridegroom's call to "rise up . . . and come away" (Cant. 2:10) from the world. As commentator George Gyffard encouraged his readers, "We are here but pilgrimes & strangers for a time: why doo we then sit downe? why do we not, as we are here willed, arise and come away?" Sincere believers were to emulate the Bride's persistent search for the Beloved—to "Look, and long," as Thomas Vincent urged, "and prepare for Christ's second appearance, when the nuptials between you shall be solemnized, and you taken to live with him for ever in mansions of everlasting joyes."[17]

As it whetted Taylor's desire for heaven, the Song made his physical limitations even more apparent, further reinforcing the saintly doubleness voiced throughout the Meditations. To strive for an inner replication of the joys recorded in Canticles was to sharpen the contrast between an earthly present and a celestial future. The "hearts dim Eye" (2.121) and "lumpish Lookes" (2.123A) of the carnal self increase Taylor's irritation with his mortal element as a hindrance to his spiritual vision as Bride. Her joy inspires his own search for a renovated "Palates Constitution," "That what comes from thy heart in heart delight / Sweet to thy Palate may thus sweeten mine" (2.126). Later in the Canticles sequence Taylor links his pleas more explicitly to the Lord's Supper, "The sweetest dainties that were ever disht / On any Table by Best Cookery / In Heavens made" (2.157B). The Supper, the institutional equivalent of the Canticles "banqueting house" (Cant. 2:4), foreshadows the eschatological joys that he expects once he is freed from the body. Bible and Sacrament alike point toward the celestial communion of Christ with a self entirely of Christ's making. To exchange carnal selfhood for this identity as Bride, "though it bee / The meanest of all, a Toe, or Finger 'rayde" (2.143), is Taylor's chief goal in the later poetry. Meditating on the Bride's "pomegranate" temples (Cant. 6:7), he asks "My Lord my Temples pomegranate make thus / That I may ware this Holy Modesty / Upon my Face maskt with thy Graces blush" (2.140). Elsewhere he seeks the shoes (Cant. 7:1) that represent her progress toward the Bridegroom: "I then shall statly go and bravely Close / Even with thyselfe and keep the way most fair" (2.148). Taylor's awe of his gracious potential, especially in the poems based on the extended description of the Bride in Canticles 6:4–7:6 (Meds. 2.133–53), repeatedly generates the humility that gives him the right to imagine such a self:

> Wonders amazed! Am I espousd to thee?
> My Glorious Lord? What! shall my bit of Clay
> Be made more bright than brightest Angells bee,
> Looke forth like as the Morning every way? (2.143)

On occasion his identification with the Bride is nearly total. When he contemplates the Bridegroom's call for the Shulammite to return (Cant. 6:13), he inserts himself directly into the Canticles text: "So when thou hidst from me, I seek and sigh. / Thou saist return return Oh Shulamite" (2.146). Elsewhere he directly appropriates the Bride's words, warning the "Daughters of Jerusalem" to "think not / To steale from me my Souls beloved away. / I my Beloveds am, and he my lot" (2.133).[18] The Bride, no longer a mere biblical figure, becomes the overriding paradigm of Taylor's meditative self. Appropriating her identity constitutes his final repudiation of carnal selfhood, his final attempt to lose one self in order to gain another. And because the boundary between Word and self would collapse at the saint's death and glorification, Taylor's voice as Bride—his use, from a modern perspective, of an increasingly impersonal speaker—was for Puritans the most intensely personal form that biblical eschatology could assume.

While the Bride showed Taylor how to die, Solomon taught him how to grow old. Although some commentators argued that Solomon wrote the Song in his youth, before he fell into the sin that rivaled his wisdom in the popular imagination, most insisted that the Song was the product of his penitent old age, when he turned from "vaine lustes," as Clapham explained, "to contemplate loves passing betwene Messiah and his Church." Cotton Mather agreed that Solomon represented "The Wise man, in his old Age, bitterly Repenting of the Impure Loves which his younger years had been defil'd withall."[19] The figure of the old king renouncing the pleasures of this world for the joys of the next must have assumed a special significance for the aging Taylor. In a poem written a little over a year after he began his twelve-year treatment of Canticles texts, he drew an explicit parallel between his insufficient love as Bride and his advancing age:

> I also crave thy pardon still because
> My Muses Hermetage is grown so old
> Her Spirits shiver doe, her Phancy's Laws
> Are much trangresst. She sits so Crampt with cold.
> Old age indeed hath finde her, that she's grown
> Num'd, and her Musicks Daughters sing Ahone. (2.122)

Severe illness struck in 1720 when he was approaching eighty, and although he recovered he would not resume full pastoral duties except for a brief period in 1724. In "Upon my recovery out of a threatening Sickness," he immediately registers disappointment that "the golden Gate of Paradise" is "Lockt up 'gain that yet I may not enter" (218). Although he tries to "center" his heart "In thy Will" and to rejoice "heartily" at his recovery, he admits to the irony of resisting a deliverance: "Thy Will be done, I say, do ask me to do the same; / I'de rather dy than cast upon it blame." Taylor interprets his temporary exclusion from heaven's "Sweet house" as evidence of his need for further trial and purification. If he were "a Silken Plock & full of Seems," he concedes, " 'Twould be onely like to be a webbed Strainery" (218); even if he possessed "the Choicest wheate that ever grew" his best result would prove "Unfit for shew bread on thy golden Table" (219). Accepting the check on his pride, he settles for "Some bits" of Christ's glory "while I'm quartering" on earth: "Times Jurisdiction I here to thee bring / Entreating thy acceptance untill I / My Quarters moove into Eternity." "Entreating" is a far cry from the near-outburst with which the poem opens. While "Upon my recovery" ostensibly records a shift from illness to health, its deeper focus is Taylor's "recovery" from resisting to accepting God's plans for him.

Two self-elegies written during this period, "A Valediction to the Whole World" and "A Fig for thee Oh! Death," reconfirm Taylor's growing desire to be separated from his carnal element. Begun some two months after "Upon my recovery," the "Valediction" corrects the unreadiness for death discovered and confessed in the earlier poem through a full-scale farewell to the world and its charms. The final version, so sweeping and systematic in its renunciation of the world that it reads like a cosmological poem, is far too buoyant to be considered a *contemptus mundi*. The first three cantos bid farewell to "the Celestiall Bodies," "the Aire," and "the Terraqueous Globe"; the last five treat the problems of doubt and assurance. Because a sincere desire to transcend the merely physical had to precede the fruition of grace, the first three cantos make the last five possible. The initial cantos present a reversal of Genesis, an uncreating of the world by a pious soul who no longer needs it. For Taylor, as for Bradstreet in "As Weary Pilgrim," the natural world has already ended: the celestial bodies have already been "put out, you now no light can borrow" (233). Playfully anticipating God's final putting out of the light, Taylor links the private apocalypse of his own death with the dissolution of a realm that simply cannot compete with heaven. Hoping to dance "far above" the shine of stars whose "Sparkling glory shines too dim" (232) and to travel "Into a purer air by far" (234), he portrays the physical universe as a transitory "realm of Sense & Sensualities / Enveagling our Senses by shadow verities" (235), an illusory place that faith has allowed him to overcome.

Retracing the progression in Bradstreet's "Contemplations" from natural to revealed religion, Taylor concedes that the world's indiscriminate mix of good and evil cannot sustain the soul. The air serves as medium for "Sweet Melodies" and "nasty speech" alike (234): "The Worst of Words as well as best do ride / With top topy all out out upon thy tide." The "mocking Crew" of created things (237) offers no more salvific help than strong spirits: "I bid you all farewell both good & bad / You never elevated mee" (235). As glorious as the sun and moon may seem, their "golden Beams" and "Silver Tressell shall / In no wise be my ladders rounds to soare mee / To Christ's bright Mantion house" (233). "I never purposed," Taylor boasts, "on these Stares t' ascend / Up to Christs brightest Hall, deckt for his Friend." His worldly goods—"My House, & land, my Stock & State"—have served him no better: "You can't my Tooth ease, nor Head, nor Minde" (236). Not even earthly love can satisfy the graced self. "All could not keep me Sweet," he tells his family, "my vessell soon / Would Taint, tho' all your Love, & skill should bloom." Acknowledging the worldly self's ties to family and friends, Taylor defines his eschatological self solely in relation to Christ.

The impatience with carnal identity that marks the Meditations assumes especially vivid form in the "Valediction" as Taylor verbally dismantles his body and its parts. God has "lent mee them," he asserts, "to tend me to the banks, / Of thy all glorious Eternall Throne, / And here I leave them now altho' mine own" (237). Once he transfers all worth from a corporeal self as a "Sorry Crumb of dust" (239) to a Savior who offers "t' bleed for me & dy" (239), his body, a curiously wrought network of "Nerves" and "Vitall Spirits" (236), begins to unravel as swiftly and inexorably as the rest of creation. Death, he affirms in a borrowing from Ecclesiastes, will complete the salvific separation of saintly self from sinful self: "The Golden Bale is broken, & the silver Band, / Or Coard is loosed: all things do faile / And all attempts to help do not availe." As with Bradstreet, physical frailty stimulates a selflessness that transforms natural fear into gracious confidence: "Tush! I'm resolvde, my Faith shall never Crinkle / It on Christs Truth & Promises relies" (240). Taylor justifies his boldness by articulating his adherence to "Gospell Obedience" as the "Holy Way" and his vehement rejection of "Unbelief." This otherworldly perspective intensifies his "hope to take a trip" (234) to the far better place that he seeks, where his glorified identity will enjoy "higher tunes & melodie" (237).

Taylor's confidence invokes the balance of pious hope and holy fear that defined Puritan assurance: "All which I hope I in Some Sort possess. / For which I heartily thee thank & bless" (238). Such hope was sufficient unto the day for the pilgrim who overcame "these foggy Vailes" (240) to glimpse a neobiblical self in whom sanctification was nearly complete: "I am within Gods Paradise's View," Taylor declares, "Where my best life is; & no Physick there / Is ever needed" (236). As in the Meditations, he grounds his identity in holy desire. Between his assertion that his "best life" is in heaven and his wish to drink "Gods rich Aqua Vitae" forever lies the assured hope of the Puritan metaself. Proclaiming that God "decreedst & 'lect me to / Enjoy thy Gospell Grace which now I know" (238), he can thus celebrate his assurance of election "from Eternity" (237): "That lott thou then didst cast I now do See, / In Gospell times & places, Seated me" (238). The chantlike assertion that God has "graciously with grace thus graced mee" is balanced and legitimized by his inability to grasp what grace is making him into, by the persistence of "Churlish Clownish" thoughts that accuse him of "gross Presumptions" (239). Can he sing "Heavens songs," he chides himself, "While in thy skirts abides iniquity?" (239–40). Although he cautions himself not to sing "tryumphant joy before / Thou hast past thro' Christs blessed Palace doore" (240), the "Humble Selfe abasement" that he voices revives his confidence that "Faith never holds whats promisd in suspense":

> And as I enter do Christs Palace Hall
> He to the Angells Cry, help me to Sing
> Sweet praise to Christ my King that rules ore all.
> Who brought me hither to, & took me in.   (240)

Clarifying his selflessness as a soul who drinks "so deep of Sweet Felicity / I up am swallowed in heart ravishing joy" (239), Taylor asserts a final separation from the carnal dimension against which he has struggled all his life: "The house must be down puld to urge out Sin. / Our bodies that are Staind & blacked by it / Are wholy made our Souls house all unfit" (237). Only death and the final reunion of body and soul will complete the transformation of identity for which he yearns. Our bodies, he confirms, must "Be laid a mellowing within the grave. / And so be purged of these stains & disease, / And then be set together as God please."

Nowhere does Taylor's view of dying as a passage to "Christ's bright face" (264) emerge more clearly than in the second version of "A Fig for thee Oh! Death." Like Meditations 1.34 and 2.112, the poem contrasts the saint's acceptance of death with a carnal perspective in which death's head becomes a terrifying reminder of conviction and sin, a "King of Terrours with thy Gastly Eyes / With Butter teeth, bare bones Grim looks likewise. / And Grizzly Hide, & clawing Tallons" (263). Taylor's faith in Christ's victory over death, however, immediately undercuts the ferocity of the image: "Thou struckst thy teeth deep in my Lord's blest Side: / Who dasht it out, & all its venom 'Stroyde." Confirming that the skull is "not so dreadfull unto mee thro' Grace," Taylor articulates the experience of a believer for whom death *was* dead—a toothless skull attesting that the grave had no "victory" and death had no "sting" (1 Cor. 15:55). By destroying the sinful self that hinders the perfection of faith, death will liberate Taylor's saintly self from its "Cask," the corporeal "shell" in which his "Heavenly kernells box / Abides most safe" (263). Having released the soul "Out to bright glory of Gods blissful joyes," death will grind the body "to powder in thy Mill the grave," purifying "Each dust" "in death's Smoky furnace" until it is "well refinde." Like Satan in *Gods Determinations*, the "King of Terrours" becomes a comic foil who unknowingly brings about his antithesis, eternal life. As in the two Meditations on the emblem of the skull, Taylor's faith-based share in Christ's victory permits him to crow over death as a conqueror: "Altho' thy terrours rise to th' highest degree, / [I] still am where I was, a Fig for thee" (264).

The real focus of the poem is not physical death but the death of sin within the saved soul. By reducing the speaker's "Cask" to "powder," death recapitulates legal conviction as a grinding of the heart to dust. Moreover, Christ's destruction of death's "venom" links the skull with the serpent of Eden, while worldly sin becomes the most dangerous "grave" into which partakers of "evill joyes" fall (263). Even the final taunt echoes Christ's command to "Get thee hence, Satan" (Matt. 4:10).

Taylor's actual foe is not death itself but an unregenerate perspective on dying—not the death's head but the sinner's terror of it. Vowing to let death's "frozen grips" take his captured body to its "dungeon Cave," he instead attacks death's experiential counterpart, the "vile harlot" of a carnality that labors "to drown me into Sin's disguise / By Eating & by drinking such evill joyes." Defining himself in opposition to a dying body, Taylor, like Bradstreet in "As Weary Pilgrim," looks toward a final resolution of sin-grace turmoil when his soul would reunite with a purified body that was no longer an enemy. At that time the warring polarities of identity would be reconciled "as two true Lovers": "[E]ry night how do they hug & kiss each other. / [A]nd going hand in hand thus thro' the Skies / [U]p to Eternall glory glorious rise" (264).

Eschatology promises a healing of the split identity that has always defined Taylor's poetic and meditative voice. Like "Upon my recovery," the "Valediction," and the late Meditations on his possibilities as Bride, "A Fig for thee" anticipates the final cessation of redemptive turmoil in the next world, when the carnal self would be "raised up anew & made all bright / And Christalized" (264). Salvific hope empowers Taylor to claim such a future. "Grace preserv'd mee," he confirms, "that I nere have / Surprised been nor tumbled in Such grave" as worldly seductions presented (263). An especially full expression of assurance, "A Fig for thee" does not record a struggle to move from sinful to saintly self-experience so much as it witnesses a shift that has already occurred. Accordingly, while death undergoes a dramatic transformation in the poem, the speaker does not. As Taylor proclaims, "[I] still am where I was" (264). And where he "was" is where he had been for his entire artistic and spiritual life: squarely on the pilgrim's "Holy Way." Prompted by impending death to imagine a glorified identity in heaven, he speaks as if he were already there.

In his final group of Meditations (Meds. 2.160–65), Taylor treats an evocative Canticles passage describing the Bride's entry into the "banqueting house" of the Bridegroom: "I am the rose of Sharon, and the lily of the valleys. As the lily among thorns, so is my love among the daughters. As the apple tree among the trees of the wood, so is my beloved among the sons. I sat down under his shadow with great delight, and his fruit was sweet to my taste. He brought me to the banqueting house, and his banner over me was love. Stay me with flagons, comfort me with apples; for I am sick of love" (Cant. 2:1–5). This text was commonly read as an especially full expression of Christ's benefits. The "fruit" of the Bridegroom was interpreted variously—and often simultaneously—as Christ's acts of redemption, the ordinances provided for the sustenance of the soul, the "inward Influences of the spirit of Grace," or the "eternal Salvation, Life and Glory, which is the end to which Christ hath designed his death and appointed his Ordinances."[20] Despite the range of specific readings, the underlying significance of the passage was clear: the Bride's desire embodies the overpowering love of an eternal self for an eternal Savior.

Taylor bases his last Meditation on her urgent plea that the Bridegroom "Stay me with flagons, comfort me with apples; for I am sick of love" (Cant. 2:5). Conveying a sense of deliberate conclusion not only to the Canticles sequence but to the entire *Preparatory Meditations*, the poem summarizes a lifetime of poetic activity. Lamenting that his "heart hath little of this / Thee to assail therewith," Taylor trusts to the efficacy of "such a gift, that thou art pleast with": "Hence hope there's Something in't will please thee well. / Hence Lord accept of this, reject the rest. / I grudg my heart if it send not thee th'best" (2.165). Confirming that "Had I but better thou shouldst better have," he brings "my best" to Christ for the last time: "If thou acceptst my sick Loves gift I bring / Thy it accepting makes my sick Love sing." On the most immediate level, the poet's "sick" love reflects his increasingly frail health. But the lines assume a broader significance in light of common interpretations of the Bride's lovesickness. In one view, she is sick because she is separated from her Beloved and therefore cries out from "want of satisfaction." A second reading held that she swoons "from the weight and pressour of felt inconceivable love, damishing her (as it were) and weakning her, she cannot abide that sight and fulnesse which she injoyes." Taylor could certainly apply both interpretations—love withheld or love fulfilled—to his meditative self. Still trapped in the body and thus acutely aware of separation from his Lord, he felt with each passing day an increase in the holy love that made the true Bride grow faint. Had he continued the sequence he would have treated the next Canticles verse, which contains the embrace of Christ and the Bride: "His left hand is under my head, and his right hand doth embrace me" (Cant. 2:6). Aged and infirm, Taylor may simply have been too ill to go on. It seems likely, however, that he decided to end the Meditations here and simply wait for the time when earthly poems would no longer be necessary and he would experience the embrace firsthand.[21]

This final poem illustrates the most significant sense in which Taylor saw his Meditations as "preparatory." When the poetry ends he seems ready to be done with his earthly rehearsal and to sing the song of the Bride with an unfettered voice, face to face with his Beloved. Each Meditation had served as a spiritual workbook that existed not as an end in itself but as a stimulus to his self-reading as saint. Like the Bible, which also pointed to a time when all texts would be needless, and like the ordinances that God provided as guides through the wilderness, the poems were destined to be replaced with the celestial praise that united redeemed with Redeemer. By rehearsing a music that would be perfected only in heaven, Taylor could rehearse a self whose full glory would be realized there as well. Language, of course, could only partially animate such an identity. In the "Valediction" earthly air, hopelessly indifferent to the sounds it conveys, is a medium on which "The Worst of Words as well as best do ride" (234), a medium fit for a "Crumb of Dust" straining to penetrate its fogs and breathe the "purer air" of heaven. Living in a world "Of Sounds & Words both good & bad all Sorts" (233), Taylor forced himself to choose between standing "Blockish, Dull, and Dumb," as he wrote in Meditation 1.22, or using language with the same gratitude and perseverance with which he used other God-given tools. By choosing sound over silence, he dramatized the Puritan assertion of hope over despair and life over death. With this choice, too, he forged a spiritual empathy with Scripture that convinced him that he, like Paul, had "fought a good fight" and was "now ready to be offered" (2 Tim. 4:6–7). The most miraculous "Sacred Text" that God had written could be read within his own heart.

Three years before Taylor's death, Cotton Mather issued his warning against "harlot" muses as a frivolous distraction that could keep young ministers from more serious studies. Though hardly the kind of verse that Mather denounced, Roger Wolcott's *Poetical Meditations*, published the year before, reflected shifts in taste that marked the end of the Puritan experience of poetry. In its blend of biblical piety and classical allusion, Wolcott's poetry illustrates, as Scheick observes, "how the traditions and typological vocabulary of seventeenth-century Puritanism metamorphosed into the more worldly concerns and poetic conventions (especially the use of classical allusion) characteristic of eighteenth-century American writing." Just five years before Wolcott's collection appeared, Taylor affirmed that poem, self, and Scripture were all joined by faith, the "Golden Bosses of Gods Booke that do / Clasp it, the soule, to God and seals up fast" (2.154). Oblivious to the changing times, Taylor still cherished "Gods Booke" as the song of his best self. As he had proclaimed two decades before, "If I be in thy booke, my Life shall proove / My Love to thee, an Offering to thy Love" (2.33). Unlike Wolcott, who tempered biblical rhetoric with the lore of the Ancients, Taylor absorbed himself totally in psychological and aesthetic frameworks provided by "Zions Pretious Stone" ("Prologue"): God's Word had defined his work and voice for four decades.[22]

Taylor's way of experiencing poetry could not survive the profound decline in the prestige of Scripture during the eighteenth century. By 1744 Mather's nephew predicted at a Harvard commencement that the graduating ministers would derive pulpit eloquence not from the naked Word but from "the ravish'd nine" of the Muses. No longer the inspired Word of God but simply a great book, the Bible was increasingly subjected to historical and critical scrutiny that would have horrified Taylor. The fate of his favorite text, the Song of Songs, vividly illustrates this rapid demystification of Scripture. By the end of the century exegetes had historicized the Song as a collection of pastoral love lyrics whose inclusion in Scripture rested solely on their dubious attribution to Solomon. Read as God-made allegory the Song could define the very core of Taylor's art. But only sixty years after his death and fifty years after Jonathan Edwards attested that reading Canticles afforded him "an inward sweetness, that would carry me away, in my contemplations," the editor of Job Orton's Bible commentary bluntly noted that "There is neither exposition nor improvement of the chapters of this Book in Mr. Orton's manuscripts. Whatever might have been his opinion of the authenticity of that Book, or the propriety of admitting it into the sacred Canon, this I am well satisfied of, that he thought it improper to be read or expounded either in publick or in families."[23]

As Larzer Ziff has said of Puritan histories, Puritan poems repeatedly "illustrate that the religious pretext determined a rhetoric that regarded the book's audience as sharers of its ideology, as possessed of a spirit that validated the text." This pretext came, of course, from Scripture, and as we have seen, the Puritan poem asserted an insoluble bond with the Bible as a metatext informing its structure, its message, its voice, and even its very words. Poets did not merely cite or explain Scripture, but exploited its affective contexts as a means of generating the reader's desire for full participation in biblical promise. The selves articulated and addressed in Puritan poetry exhibited a similar relation to a metaself defined by redemptive psychology, the pilgrim soul whose turmoil as a worldly sinner helped confirm the faith of a hopeful saint. Although this identity represented a psychological and spiritual ideal, Puritans did not invoke it as inner fiction but as an embodiment of what they hoped was divinely ordained fact. Whether at special moments of assurance or during the severest trials that life had to offer, they clung to these patterns of self-experience as the truest identity imaginable. Convinced that such a self was created by faith, they insisted that whoever sensed something of its presence within could hope to live eternally in its form. This psychological paradigm governed rhetorical strategy as well as literary response. Not only did poetry force readers to judge their relation to saintly pattern, but their presumed relation to it—whether as headstrong reprobates, conscience-stricken sinners, or assured saints—determined how poets wrote for them. Commentator Durham praised the Song of Songs because it spoke so fully and eloquently to all kinds of believers undergoing the various spiritual conditions allegorized in the Bride's moods. There are "still some injoying Christ," Durham affirmed, but also "some deserted, some praying, some suffering."[24] Following Solomon's lead, the Puritan poet was expected not merely to anticipate these moods but to address them as directly as language allowed.

This was the Puritan experience of poetry—an experience of writing and reading that differed markedly from our own. In recovering this experience I have been less interested in reconfirming the truism that few Puritan poems continue to move us than in demonstrating the variety and complexity of artistic options available to poets working within a coherent aesthetic tradition. Only the bloodless, of course, can read texts from another time free from honest reactions inseparable from who we are, from the readers that our literary culture has made of us. Given the determining force of aesthetic assumptions, no historicizing of literary taste will make us genuinely enjoy poems such as *The Day of Doom*, the *Metrical History of Christianity*, or "As Weary Pilgrim." This is, finally, as it should be. Such poems were not, after all, written for us—nor were they written for their intended readers to "enjoy" in the modern sense of the word. It is naive, of course, to think that we can replace our own literary preferences with those promoted by a distant culture. But if we do not seek aesthetic empathy with readers from other times and places, we cannot exchange easy answers for richer if more problematic insights into the past experience of art. The difference between the Puritan experience of poetry and our own illustrates, once again, the radically historical parameters of art and of the self who engages with it, whether as poet, reader, or critic.

NOTES

PREFACE

1 This approach owes much to Stanley Fish's earlier work, which stressed how seventeenth-century British texts altered the self-perceptions of their intended readers, as well as to more recent reader-response criticism. My sense of Fish's later concept of the "interpretive community," however, is theological and cultural rather than demographic or political. Major statements of reader-centered criticism include Fish, *Surprised by Sin: The Reader in Paradise Lost* (1967; reprint, Berkeley: Univ. of California Press, 1971) and *Self-Consuming Artifacts: The Experience of Seventeenth-Century Literature* (Berkeley: Univ. of California Press, 1972); Wolfgang Iser, *The Implied Reader: Patterns of Communication in Prose Fiction from Bunyan to Beckett* (Baltimore: Johns Hopkins Univ. Press, 1974); Iser, *The Act of Reading: A Theory of Aesthetic Response* (Baltimore: Johns Hopkins Univ. Press, 1978); Hans Robert Jauss, *Aesthetic Experience and Literary Hermeneutics*, trans. Michael Shaw (Minneapolis: Univ. of Minnesota Press, 1982), and *Toward an Aesthetic of Reception*, trans. Timothy Bahti (Minneapolis: Univ. of Minnesota Press, 1982). The theories of Iser, Jauss, and other reception critics are conveniently surveyed in Robert C. Holub, *Reception Theory: A Critical Introduction* (London: Methuen, 1984). Two collections of reader-centered criticism are Jane Tompkins, ed., *Reader-Response Criticism: From Formalism to Post-Structuralism* (Baltimore: Johns Hopkins Univ. Press, 1980); and Susan R. Suleiman and Inge Crosman, eds., *The Reader in the Text: Essays on Audience and Interpretation* (Princeton: Princeton Univ. Press, 1980). Fish's concept of "interpretive community" is developed in *Is There a Text in This Class? The Authority of Interpretive Communities* (Cambridge: Harvard Univ. Press, 1980).

2 On the importance of texts in shaping Puritan spiritual and psychological structures, see David D. Hall, "The World of Print and Collective Mentality in

Seventeenth-Century New England," in *New Directions in American Intellectual History*, ed. John Higham and Paul K. Conklin (Baltimore: Johns Hopkins Univ. Press, 1979), 166–80; John Owen King, *The Iron of Melancholy: Structures of Spiritual Conversion in America from the Puritan Conscience to Victorian Neurosis* (Middletown: Wesleyan Univ. Press, 1983), 13–82; Patricia Caldwell, *The Puritan Conversion Narrative: The Beginnings of American Expression* (Cambridge: Cambridge Univ. Press, 1983); and David D. Hall, *Worlds of Wonder, Days of Judgment: Popular Religious Belief in Early New England* (New York: Knopf, 1989), 21–70. Arguments for the fundamental unity of Puritan collective mentality include David D. Hall, "Toward a History of Popular Religion in Early New England," *William and Mary Quarterly* 41 (1984): 49–55; George Selement, "The Meeting of Elite and Popular Minds at Cambridge, New England, 1638–1645," *William and Mary Quarterly* 41 (1984): 32–48; and David Grayson Allen, "Both Englands," in *Seventeenth Century New England*, ed. David D. Hall and David Grayson Allen (Boston: Colonial Society of Massachusetts, 1984), 55–82.

One. The Forgotten Pilgrim: Biblical Reading and the Puritan Experience of Poetry

1   Ann Stanford, "Anne Bradstreet," in *Major Writers of Early American Literature*, ed. Everett Emerson (Madison: Univ. of Wisconsin Press, 1972), 56. The text of "As Weary Pilgrim" cited here is from *The Works of Anne Bradstreet*, ed. Jeannine Hensley (Cambridge: Harvard Univ. Press, 1967), 294–95.
2   Stephen Gosson, *The School of Abuse* (1579), in *The Renaissance in England: Nondramatic Prose and Verse of the Sixteenth Century*, ed. Hyder E. Rollins and Herschel Baker (Boston: D. C. Heath, 1954), 601; *The Bay Psalm Book: A Facsimile Reprint of the First Edition of 1640*, ed. Zoltan Haraszti (Chicago: Univ. of Chicago Press, 1956), [**3v]; Michael Wigglesworth, "A Prayer unto Christ The Judge of the World," in *The Poems of Michael Wigglesworth*, ed. Ronald A. Bosco (Lanham, Md.: Univ. Press of America, 1989), 9; Urian Oakes, "An Elegie Upon . . . Thomas Shepard," in *American Poetry of the Seventeenth Century*, ed. Harrison T. Meserole (1968; reprint, University Park: Pennsylvania State Univ. Press, 1985), 210; Cotton Mather, *Manuductio ad Ministerium* (1726; reprint, New York: AMS Press, 1978), 42. Russell Fraser describes sixteenth- and seventeenth-century attacks on the stage and secular verse in *The War Against Poetry* (Princeton: Princeton Univ. Press, 1970).
3   John Milton, *The Complete Poetry of John Milton*, ed. John T. Shawcross (Garden City: Doubleday, 1971), 578. Ivy Schweitzer has recently argued that the male New Englanders' attitude toward Bradstreet went beyond pride to encompass her exploitation as an ideal of female selfhood, a model that Bradstreet both accepted and resisted (*The Work of Self-Representation: Lyric Poetry in Colonial New England* [Chapel Hill: Univ. of North Carolina Press, 1991], 127–80). On the popularity of *The Day of Doom* see Kenneth B. Murdock, "Introduction," *The Day of Doom; or, A Poetical Description of the Great and Last Judgment with other poems* (1929; reprint, New York: Russell and Russell, 1966), iii; and Bosco, *Poems*, x, 305–6. Taylor's comment on Westfield's "rusticity" is from a letter to Samuel Sewall dated September 29, 1676, quoted in Norman S. Grabo, *Edward Taylor: Revised Edition* (Boston: Twayne, 1988), 8.

4 Jonathan Mitchell, "On the following Work and Its Author," in Meserole, *American Poetry*, 412. Titles in Wigglesworth's library are listed in John Ward Dean, *Sketch of the Life of Rev. Michael Wigglesworth, A.M., Author of the Day of Doom* (Albany: J. Munsell, 1863), 16. On the Puritan familiarity with classical and English poets see Thomas Goddard Wright, *Literary Culture in Early New England, 1620–1730* (1920; reprint, New York: Russell and Russell, 1966), 25–61, 110–51; bookseller invoices, library holdings, and literary quotations are listed in Wright's "Appendix" (219–95). The underlying continuity of English and New English literary culture in the Colonial era is argued in William C. Spengemann, *A Mirror for Americanists: Reflections on the Idea of American Literature* (Hanover, N.H.: Univ. Press of New England, 1989). To be sure, some Puritans objected to the study of classical poets. In the early 1640s Thomas Shepard tried to allay Governor Winthrop's "apprehensions agaynst reading and learning heathen authors" by assuring that his doubts would "easily be answered" by noted classicist President Dunster of Harvard (Samuel Eliot Morison, *Harvard College in the Seventeenth Century* [Cambridge: Harvard Univ. Press, 1936], 176).

5 Ward's poem on Wilson is "Mr. Ward of Anagrams thus," in Meserole, *American Poetry*, 368; Mather's praise of Wigglesworth is from *A Faithful Man, Described and Rewarded* (Boston: 1705), 24; his elegy on Oakes is in *A Poem and an Elegy* (Boston: Club of Odd Volumes, 1896), 2; the Hinckley poem is in *The First Century of New England Verse*, ed. Harold S. Jantz (1944; reprint, New York: Russell and Russell, 1962), 43; Bradstreet's poems appear in the inventory of Taylor's library in *The Poetical Works of Edward Taylor*, ed. Thomas H. Johnson (1939; reprint, Princeton: Princeton Univ. Press, 1943), 212. On Elizabeth Taylor's acquaintance with *The Day of Doom* see Taylor, "A Funerall Poem," in *Edward Taylor's Minor Poetry*, ed. Thomas M. Davis and Virginia L. Davis (Boston: Twayne, 1981), 114. Mather's printing of Taylor's stanzas is described in Thomas H. Johnson, "A Seventeenth-Century Printing of Some Verses of Edward Taylor," *New England Quarterly* 14 (1941): 139–41.

6 Norman S. Grabo, "The Veiled Vision: The Role of Aesthetics in Early American Intellectual History" (1962; reprinted in *The American Puritan Imagination: Essays in Revaluation*, ed. Sacvan Bercovitch [London: Cambridge Univ. Press, 1974], 25). On the variance between Puritan literary theory and poetic practice, also see Robert Daly, *God's Altar: The World and the Flesh in Puritan Poetry* (Berkeley: Univ. of California Press, 1978), 40–81; Michael Clark, "The Honeyed Knot of Puritan Aesthetics," in *Puritan Poets and Poetics: Seventeenth-Century American Poetry in Theory and Practice*, ed. Peter White (University Park: Pennsylvania State Univ. Press, 1985), 68; and Mason I. Lowance, Jr., "Religion in Puritan Poetry: The Doctrine of Accommodation," in White, ed., *Puritan Poets*, 36.

7 Moses Coit Tyler, *A History of American Literature, 1607–1765* (1878; reprint, Ithaca: Cornell Univ. Press, 1949), 228. Perry Miller's monumental work on the intellectual underpinnings of the "New England mind" tended to support this view. Thomas H. Johnson, collaborating with Miller in the first anthology to reveal something of the richness and depth of Puritan writing, maintained that the Puritan poet "remained curiously indifferent to the quintessential breath and finer spirit of the poetic idiom." "The intrinsic value of Puritan poetry," Johnson argued, "is apparent only in snatches" (Miller and Johnson, eds., *The*

Puritans, 2 vols. [1938; reprint, New York: Harper and Row, 1963], 2:547, 552). Murdock also affirmed that Puritanism and poetry made for a bad mix: "When the Puritan aspired to poetry his flights were limited because elements in his beliefs on religion and art which were harmless or even useful to his prose were certainly unfriendly to his poetry" (*Literature and Theology in Colonial New England* [Cambridge: Harvard Univ. Press, 1949], 140). Daly surveys the critical reception to Puritan verse in *God's Altar*, 201–23.

8   Kathleen Blake, "Edward Taylor's Protestant Poetic: Nontransubstantiating Metaphor," *American Literature* 43 (1971): 2. Jantz was among the first to complain of anachronistic approaches to Puritan poetry when he noted "the misapplication of eighteenth-century smoothness and nineteenth-century romantic lyricism to seventeenth-century Baroque verse which had no interest in being either smooth or romantic" (*First Century*, 6–7). The modernist bias, of course, can be religious as well as aesthetic. Jantz commented, for example, that *The Day of Doom* had frequently been misread by "anachronistic critics who have deplored the fact that its fundamental premises were not those of the more comfortable nineteenth-century theology" (50).

Assessments of older literary texts rarely escape such privileging of current aesthetic and psychological norms. Although Hans Robert Jauss's "horizon of expectations" governing the past reception of texts acknowledges the historical dimension of taste, Jauss in fact universalizes the modern preference for innovation by calling texts that did not frustrate the expectations of their initial readers "culinary" or "entertainment" art (*Toward an Aesthetic of Reception*, 25). Wolfgang Iser, Jauss's colleague at Konstanz, has agreed that texts supporting the prevailing thought-systems of their time "tend to be of a more trivial nature, as they affirm specific norms with a view to training the reader according to the moral or social code of the day" (*The Act of Reading*, 77). Terry Eagleton voices an objection that must be raised in any discussion of the historical reception of older works, especially religious texts: "Has not a great deal of 'valid' literature precisely confirmed rather than troubled the received codes of its time?" (*Literary Theory* [Minneapolis: Univ. of Minnesota Press, 1983], 82). Roy Harvey Pearce implicitly answered this question in the negative with regard to the Puritan poem, commenting that "the power of American poetry from the beginning has derived from the poet's inability, or refusal, at some depth of consciousness wholly to accept his culture's system of values" (*The Continuity of American Poetry* [Princeton: Princeton Univ. Press, 1961], 5).

9   Daly has noted the critical tendency to isolate Taylor and Bradstreet "from the context provided by their fellow Puritan poets" and to see them as "exceptions to a general rule" (*God's Altar*, 201). David D. Hall attributes the isolation of these poets to an implicit search for aesthetic and nationalistic precedents in Colonial writing, to a "fusion of modernism and nativism" central to the traditional practice of American literary history ("On Native Ground: From the History of Printing to the History of the Book," *Proceedings of the American Antiquarian Society* 93 [1983]: 325). On this point also see Spengemann, *A Mirror for Americanists*, esp. 31–33.

10   Ann Stanford, "Anne Bradstreet: Dogmatist and Rebel," *New England Quarterly* 39 (1966): 373–89. While some of Bradstreet's poems, when read in light of subsequent literary and cultural history, indeed convey a feminist con-

sciousness and a proto-Romantic sensitivity to nature, the conclusion that she wrote in opposition to her culture and theology greatly understates the degree to which her poetry was shaped by both. Critics who read her work as an expression, to varying degrees, of seventeenth-century feminism include Adrienne Rich, "Anne Bradstreet and Her Poetry," in Bradstreet, *Works*, ix–xxi; Wendy Martin, "Anne Bradstreet's Poetry: A Study in Subversive Piety," in *Shakespeare's Sisters: Feminist Essays on Women Poets*, ed. Sandra M. Gilbert and Susan Gubar (Bloomington: Indiana Univ. Press, 1979), 19–31; Martin, *An American Triptych: Anne Bradstreet, Emily Dickinson, Adrienne Rich* (Chapel Hill: Univ. of North Carolina Press, 1984), 15–76; Rosamond R. Rosenmeier, *Anne Bradstreet Revisited* (Boston: Twayne, 1991); and Schweitzer, *The Work of Self-Representation*. Critics who have identified proto-Romantic features in her work include Richard Crowder, "Anne Bradstreet and Keats," *Notes and Queries* 3 (1956): 386–88; Josephine Miles, "The Poetry of Praise," *Kenyon Review* 23 (1961): 104–25; Josephine K. Piercy, *Anne Bradstreet* (New York: Twayne, 1965), 81–82; Alvin H. Rosenfeld, "Anne Bradstreet's 'Contemplations': Patterns of Form and Meaning," *New England Quarterly* 43 (1970): 79–96; and Ann Stanford, *Anne Bradstreet: The Worldly Puritan* (New York: Burt Franklin, 1974). Convenient surveys of Bradstreet scholarship include Pattie Cowell, "Introduction: Anne Bradstreet 'In Criticks Hands,'" in *Critical Essays on Anne Bradstreet*, ed. Pattie Cowell and Ann Stanford (Boston: G. K. Hall, 1983), ix–xxv; and Raymond F. Dolle, *Anne Bradstreet: A Reference Guide* (Boston: Twayne, 1991).

11 In its broad outline the story of Taylor scholarship records a gradual movement toward reading his work in terms of its own artistic aims and standards. In general, this has involved a shift from "non-Puritan" to "Puritan" literary and artistic contexts in which the more puzzling features of his work seem less like flaws than functional devices. Categories that have been applied to Taylor include "medieval" (Nathalia Wright, "The Morality Tradition in the Poetry of Edward Taylor," *American Literature* 18 [1946]: 1–17), "classical" (Willie T. Weathers, "Edward Taylor, Hellenistic Puritan," *American Literature* 18 [1946]: 18–26), "metaphysical" (Wallace C. Brown, "Edward Taylor: An American 'Metaphysical,'" *American Literature* 16 [1944]: 186–97), "baroque" (Austin Warren, "Edward Taylor's Poetry: Colonial Baroque," *Kenyon Review* 3 [1941]: 355–71), "meditative" (Louis L. Martz, "Foreword," *The Poems of Edward Taylor*, ed. Donald E. Stanford [New Haven: Yale Univ. Press, 1960], xiii–xxxvii), "mystical" (Norman S. Grabo, *Edward Taylor* [New York: Twayne, 1961]), "emblematic" (Alan B. Howard, "The World as Emblem: Language and Vision in the Poetry of Edward Taylor," *American Literature* 44 [1972]: 359–84), and, of course, "American" (Karl Keller, "'The World Slickt Up in Types': Edward Taylor as a Version of Emerson," *Early American Literature* 5 [1969]: 124–40).

Among the major studies that have pioneered a reading of Taylor's work in terms of Puritan or biblical spiritual and exegetical structures are Ursula Brumm, *American Thought and Religious Typology*, trans. John Hoaglund (New Brunswick: Rutgers Univ. Press, 1970), 56–85; William J. Scheick, *The Will and the Word: The Poetry of Edward Taylor* (Athens: Univ. of Georgia Press, 1974); Keller, *The Example of Edward Taylor* (Amherst: Univ. of Massachusetts Press, 1975); Barbara Kiefer Lewalski, *Protestant Poetics and the Seventeenth-Century*

Religious Lyric (Princeton: Princeton Univ. Press, 1979), 388–426; and Karen E. Rowe, *Saint and Singer: Edward Taylor's Typology and the Poetics of Meditation* (Cambridge: Cambridge Univ. Press, 1986). Two recent studies by Thomas M. Davis and William J. Scheick manage to escape a simplistic Puritan/un-Puritan dichotomy in reading Taylor, though in very different ways. Davis, warning against easy generalizations that ignore shifts in the poetry over time, discusses Taylor's changing artistic goals in the Meditations in the context of his life and ministry in Westfield (*A Reading of Edward Taylor* [Newark: Univ. of Delaware Press, 1992]), while Scheick treats Taylor's poems as reflections of a conscious artistry and intentional design usually ignored in discussions of Puritan writing (*Design in Puritan American Literature* [Lexington: Univ. Press of Kentucky, 1992]). Taylor scholarship is surveyed in Constance J. Gefvert, *Edward Taylor: An Annotated Bibliography* (Kent, Ohio: Kent State Univ. Press, 1971); William J. Scheick and JoElla Doggett, *Seventeenth-Century American Poetry: A Reference Guide* (Boston: G. K. Hall, 1977); Catherine Rainwater and William J. Scheick, "Seventeenth-Century American Poetry: A Reference Guide Updated," *Resources for American Literary Study* 10 (1980): 121–45; Norman S. Grabo and Jana Wainright, "Edward Taylor," in *Fifteen American Authors before 1900: Bibliographical Essays on Research and Criticism*, ed. Earl N. Harbert and Robert A. Rees (Madison: Univ. of Wisconsin Press, 1984), 439–67; and Jeffrey A. Hammond, *Edward Taylor: Fifty Years of Scholarship and Criticism* (Columbia, S.C.: Camden House, 1993).

12 Most assessments of Wigglesworth continue to echo Tyler's assertion that in his "intense pursuit of what he believed to be the good and the true, he forgot the very existence of the beautiful" (*A History*, 277). See, for example, Murdock, "Introduction," vii; and Daly, *God's Altar*, 132. Bosco summarizes Wigglesworth's critical reception in *Poems*, xi–xvii.

13 George Puttenham, *The Arte of English Poesie*, ed. Gladys Doidge Willcock and Alice Walker (Cambridge: Cambridge Univ. Press, 1936), 8; Richard Steere, "Earth Felicities, Heavens Allowances," in Meserole, *American Poetry*, 263. Commenting on the primacy of language in the Puritan imagination, Larzer Ziff observes that "Deep within the culture's overwhelming commitment to the certainty of words over commitment to ambiguous images, to the dominance of the pulpit over the altar, was a folk belief in the animism of language" (*Puritanism in America: New Culture in a New World* [New York: Viking, 1973], 199). William J. Scheick offers a full discussion of Puritan logocentrism in Taylor's Meditations (*The Will and the Word*, 93–149). On the sacramental core of Puritanism, see E. Brooks Holifield, *The Covenant Sealed: The Development of Puritan Sacramental Theology in Old and New England, 1570–1720* (New Haven: Yale Univ. Press, 1974).

14 Lynn Haims, "Puritan Iconography: The Art of Edward Taylor's *Gods Determinations*," in White, ed., *Puritan Poets*, 84, 96; Robert Daly, "The Danforths: Puritan Poets in the Woods of Arcadia," in White, ed., *Puritan Poets*, 148.

15 Puttenham, *The Arte of English Poesie*, 7; Luke Milbourne, *Psalmody Recommended in a Sermon* (London: 1713), 6; Matthew Henry, *An Exposition Of the Five Poetical Books of the Old Testament* (London: 1710), a2v; Nathaniel Holmes, *A Commentary Literal or Historical, and Mystical or Spiritual On the whole Book of Canticles*, in *The Works of Dr. Nathaniel Homes* [sic] (London: 1652), 463; Mather, *Manuductio*

ad Ministerium, 40; John Bunyan, "The Author's Apology for his Book," in *The Pilgrim's Progress* (New York: Dutton, 1978), 4; Robert Fleming, *The Mirrour of Divine Love Unvail'd, in a Poetical Paraphrase of the High and Mysterious Song of Solomon* (London: 1691), A3v.

16 William Tans'ur, *Heaven on Earth; or, The Beauty of Holiness* (London: 1738), 168; James Day, *A New Spring of Divine Poetrie* (London: 1637), 1; John Collinges, *The Intercourses of Divine Love Betwixt Christ and his Church; or, The Particular Believing Soul* (London: 1683), 36.

17 Jud[e] Smith, *A misticall devise of the spirituall and godly love betwene Christ the spouse, and the Church or Congregation* (London: 1575), [Aii]; Wigglesworth, *Poems*, 9; George Herbert, *The Works of George Herbert*, ed. F.E. Hutchinson (Oxford: Clarendon Press, 1941), 206; Michael Drayton, *The Harmonie of the Church* (London: 1691), in *The Works of Michael Drayton*, ed. J. William Hebel, 5 vols. (Oxford: Shakespeare Head Press, 1931), 1:b1.

18 William Baldwin, *The Canticles or Balades of Salomon* (London: 1549), Aiiiv; Joseph Stennett, *Hymns in Commemoration Of the Suffering of Our Blessed Saviour Jesus Christ, Compos'd For the Celebration of his Holy Supper* (London: 1713), xxxvii; Wigglesworth, "A Prayer unto Christ The Judge of the World," in *Poems*, 9; Mitchell, "On the following Work and Its Author," in *American Poetry*, 413.

19 Chauncy, "A Commencement Sermon," in Miller and Johnson, *The Puritans*, 2:707; Mather, "An Elegy on Ezekiel Cheever," in Miller and Johnson, *The Puritans*, 2:723; Henry Hammond, *A Paraphrase and Annotations Upon the Books of the Psalms* (London: 1659), A4v.

20 Arthur Jackson, *Annotations Upon The five Books immediately following the Historicall Part of the Old Testament, (Commonly called the five Doctrinall, or Poeticall Books)* (London: 1658), [iv]; James Durham, *Clavis Cantici; or, An Exposition of the Song of Solomon* (Edinburgh: 1668), 2, 45.

21 Hammond, *A Paraphrase*, 2; Westminster Assembly of Divines, *Annotations Upon all the Books of the Old and New Testament* (London: 1657), 7F4v; Henry, *An Exposition*, a2v. Anticipating Protestant aesthetic reformers, Jerome reacted to his terrifying dream of being judged not a Christian but a Ciceronean by pledging to reform his reading: "henceforth I read the books of God with a greater zeal than I had ever given before to the books of men" (*Select Letters of St. Jerome*, trans. F.A. Wright [London: William Heinemann, 1933], 129). An equally determined substitution of one canon for another reveals that such commentators as the Bay Psalm translators and Cotton Mather may have had, as Murdock remarked long ago, "more liking than they dared to confess, or their principles allowed them to indulge, for the literary flights which they professed to scorn" (*Literature and Theology*, 47). Pearce agrees that "The Puritan never hated literature—or, for that matter, the arts in general. Rather, he feared that he might like them too much and that he might therefore veer from the strait path he knew he must follow" (*Continuity*, 18).

22 Thomas Ager, *A Paraphrase of the Canticles; or, Song of Solomon* (London: 1680), 7; John Dove, *The Conversion of Salomon* (London: 1613), 7; Edward Leigh, *Annotations on Five Poetical Books of the Old Testament* (London: 1657), 25, [xi]; John Owen, *Meditations and Discourses Concerning the Glory of Christ* (London: 1691), 99; Francis Roberts, *Clavis Bibliorum. The Key of the Bible* (London: 1649), 385–86.

23 Samuel Clark, *The Holy Bible, Containing The Old Testament and The New: With Annotations and Parallel Scriptures* (London: 1690), Qqq; Mather, *Manuductio ad Ministerium*, 82.

24 Herbert, *Works*, 58, 132; Holmes, *Works*, 466; Durham, *Clavis Cantici*, 2; John Collinges, *The Spouse under the Apple-Tree; or, The state of the Elect by Nature* (London: 1649), A6v; George Wither, *A Collection of Emblemes, Ancient and Moderne: Quickened With Metricall Illustrations, both Morall and Divine* (London: 1635), A.

25 Ager, *A Paraphrase*, 10; Sir Philip Sidney, *Sir Philip Sidney's Defense of Poesy*, ed. Lewis Soens (Lincoln: Univ. of Nebraska Press, 1970), 11; Collinges, *The Intercourses of Divine Love* (1683), 36; Richard Sibbes, *Bowels Opened; or, A Discovery of the Neere and deere Love, Union and Communion betwixt Christ and the Church, and consequently betwixt Him and every beleeving soule* (London: 1639), 3.

26 Hammond, *A Paraphrase*, c2; John Reeve, *Spiritual Hymns upon Solomon's Song; or, Love in the Right Channel* (London: 1693), [1]; Thomas Draxe, *The Lambes Spouse* (London: 1608), B7v; Edward Pearse, *The Best Match; or, The Soul's Espousal to Christ* (Boston: 1708), 42.

27 Cotton Mather, *Psalterium Americanum* (Boston: 1718), xxiv; Mather, *The Nightingale. An Essay on Songs among Thorns* (Boston: 1724), 18.

28 Mather, *Psalterium Americanum*, vii, xiii; Harvard thesis listed in Morison, *Harvard College*, 584; Mather, *Manuductio ad Ministerium*, 34.

29 Stennett, *Hymns*, xxx. Edward H. Davidson proposes a similar connection between the Bible and the Puritan sermon: "A sermon and the sermon's form were like Scripture and history—part of a prior arrangement, all parts in a single design which held everything together. It was a design which had already been traced through Scripture: the Bible was a mosaic of citations, a resonance of meanings; thus one text led to another and to any number of corollary and supporting ideas" ("'God's Well-Trodden Foot-Paths': Puritan Preaching and Sermon Form," *Texas Studies in Literature and Language* 25 [1983]: 510–11). David D. Hall has argued that as a result of the pervasive influence of Scripture, "All other texts were copies of this one original": Puritan writers cited the Bible "always with the same objective, to reduce the distance between what they said and what was contained in the great original, the Word." Accordingly, the sanctity of the Bible affected "how other books were represented, and how they were read" as writers of godly texts "asked that readers respond to their books as though they were as sacred as the Bible" (*Worlds of Wonder*, 24, 28). On this point see also Schweitzer, *The Work of Self-Representation*, 69–70.

30 Puritan reading, Charles Hambrick-Stowe observes, invoked "stages that corresponded precisely to the order of the conversion experience and the redemptive drama" (*The Practice of Piety: Puritan Devotional Disciplines in Seventeenth-Century New England* [Chapel Hill: Univ. of North Carolina Press, 1982], 159). Hall, arguing that the slow, intense reading of devotional works was central to what he calls the "traditional" literacy of early New England, asserts that "The distance between books and life was very short"—a fact that applies especially to poetic texts designed to quicken the spiritual life of readers ("The Uses of Literacy in New England, 1600–1850," in *Printing and Society in Early America*, ed. William L. Joyce, David D. Hall, Richard D. Brown, and John B. Hench [Worcester, Mass.: American Antiquarian Society, 1983], 35). John Owen King goes further, arguing that the distance between pious texts and reading self was

virtually nonexistent. "Within the framework of the morphology of conversion that [Edmund] Morgan and others have described," King notes, "men and women in early New England did not simply record an immediately sensible experience or, conversely, have a structure of words forced upon their lives; they instead used past writings to build experience out of the innate confusion of sensation" (*The Iron of Melancholy*, 43).

Pious reading, as Hall has described it, was a process by which "books transformed the inner self or 'heart' in ways that carried over into everyday behavior" (*Worlds of Wonder*, 39). From *Paradise Lost* Stanley Fish infers a similar experience of texts by an audience capable of translating salvific message from page to heart. Milton's "imperative," Fish maintains, "is 'read!' and by not giving up, by not closing the book, by accepting the challenge of self-criticism and self-knowledge, one learns to read, and by extension how to live, and becomes finally the Christian hero who is, after all, the only fit reader." Fish anticipated his later decentering of the text by centering on Milton's reader, who functions "not as an observer who coolly notes the interaction of patterns . . . but as a participant whose mind is the *locus* of that interaction" (*Surprised by Sin*, 207, 11, 303). The American Puritan poem made similar heroes out of its readers by re-creating them as active participants in the great struggle against evil.

31 William Ames, *The Marrow of Theology*, trans. John Eusden (Boston: Pilgrim Press, 1968), 176, 256; Edward Taylor, *Edward Taylor's Christographia*, ed. Norman S. Grabo (New Haven: Yale Univ. Press, 1962), 229. Applying models of self/text interaction developed by Bakhtin, Foucault, and Lacan, King argues that "texts" narrating the story of the soul's salvation provided a coherent structure by which Puritan self-experience was shaped and understood. Individual believers, King maintains, attempted "to find spiritual peace through the narration of their own psychological experience, narrations that build experience according to formulas established in the Puritan generation of John Bunyan" (*Iron of Melancholy*, 7). On the apparent accord of private experience with models of that experience presented in sermons and soteriological treatises, see Charles Lloyd Cohen, *God's Caress: The Psychology of Puritan Religious Experience* (New York: Oxford Univ. Press, 1986), 162–200; and Schweitzer, *The Work of Self-Representation*, 1–39.

32 Shepard, *The Sound Believer*, in *The Works of Thomas Shepard*, 3 vols., ed. John A. Albro (Boston: Doctrinal Tract and Book Society, 1853), 1:256; Ames, *Marrow of Theology*, 170, 171; John Bunyan, *Grace Abounding and the Life and Death of Mr Badman* (New York: Dutton, 1928), 32; Thomas Shepard, *God's Plot: The Paradoxes of Puritan Piety*, ed. Michael McGiffert (Amherst: Univ. of Massachusetts Press, 1972), 135; Wigglesworth, *The Diary of Michael Wigglesworth, 1653–1657: The Conscience of a Puritan*, ed. Edmund S. Morgan (New York: Harper and Row, 1965), 3; Mather, *Paterna: The Autobiography of Cotton Mather*, ed. Ronald A. Bosco (Delmar, N.Y.: Scholars' Facsimiles and Reprints, 1976), 212; Taylor, "Personal Relation," in *Edward Taylor's "Church Records" and Related Sermons*, ed. Thomas M. Davis and Virginia L. Davis (Boston: Twayne, 1981), 101.

33 Mather, *Paterna*, 212; Taylor, "Personal Relation," 102; Shepard, *God's Plot*, 135; Wigglesworth, *Diary*, 3.

34 Wigglesworth, *Poems*, 165; Bunyan, *Pilgrim's Progress*, 39; John Weemse, *The Christian Synagogue* (London: 1623), 299; Milton, *Complete Poetry*, 319. Despite a wide variety of methods and assumptions, nearly all studies of Protestant

inner experience emphasize turmoil as its chief characteristic. See, for example, Edmund S. Morgan, *Visible Saints: The History of a Puritan Idea* (1963; reprint, Ithaca: Cornell Univ. Press, 1965); Norman Pettit, *The Heart Prepared: Grace and Conversion in Puritan Spiritual Life* (New Haven: Yale Univ. Press, 1966); Darrett Rutman, *American Puritanism: Faith and Practice* (New York: Lippincott, 1970); Michael McGiffert, "Introduction," *God's Plot: The Paradoxes of Puritan Piety*, ed. Michael McGiffert (Amherst: Univ. of Massachusetts Press, 1972), 3–32; Sacvan Bercovitch, *The Puritan Origins of the American Self* (New Haven: Yale Univ. Press, 1975); Philip Greven, *The Protestant Temperament: Patterns of Child-Rearing, Religious Experience, and the Self in Early America* (New York: Knopf, 1977); Sargent Bush, Jr., *The Writings of Thomas Hooker: Spiritual Adventure in Two Worlds* (Madison: Univ. of Wisconsin Press, 1980); David Leverenz, *The Language of Puritan Feeling* (New Brunswick: Rutgers Univ. Press, 1980); Caldwell, *The Puritan Conversion Narrative*; and Cohen, *God's Caress*.

35 Shepard, *God's Plot*, 198.

36 Hooker, *The Soul's Humiliation* (London: 1638), quoted in Miller and Johnson, *The Puritans*, 1:60; Cotton Mather, *Magnalia Christi Americana*, 2 vols., ed. Thomas Robbins (1852; reprint, New York: Russell and Russell, 1967), 1:38. Inferences regarding the personality of a Puritan author that ignore theological contexts always carry some risk, as early charges of Taylor's unorthodoxy suggest. Like Bunyan, who effected what Wolfgang Iser has called a "scaling down of characters to their exemplary values" in the poems interspersed throughout *The Pilgrim's Progress* (*The Implied Reader*, 11), Puritan poets both pursued and encouraged a rhetorical selflessness that they hoped would stimulate its inner correlary.

Grabo's early call for an "aesthetic" reading of early American texts included just such a rejection of the naive assumption "that a work of art is a symptom of the artist's predominant emotion at the time of creation" ("Veiled Vision," 23). Jauss identifies impersonality as a feature of pre-Romantic didactic texts generally, in which edification meant a "preparation for the imitation of Christ which was to be achieved by a depersonalization whereby the individual as part of a community becomes an 'edifice of belief' through a movement of his soul. What the term emphatically did not mean was a turning back to subjective inwardness" (*Aesthetic Experience and Literary Hermeneutics*, 99). The Puritan poem was similarly designed to move the reader from self to Savior, from a self-involved "I" to a self-effaced member of the Body of Christ. Scheick has described this process in the Puritan funeral elegy. By extolling the deceased as a saintly ideal to which readers could aspire, elegists made their readers see— and feel— that the communal and private dimensions of the Puritan mission were equally inseparable from a reading identity whose carnality was consumed in the deceased's example ("Tombless Virtue and Hidden Text: New England Puritan Funeral Elegies," in White, ed., *Puritan Poets*, 286–302). Fish remarks that self-effacement effected by the Anglican sermon curiously foreshadows poststructuralist views of text-reader interaction (*Is There a Text in This Class?*, 181).

37 The Puritan poem was, as Davidson has written of the sermon, an expression of "ritual in a serious sense that Puritans would not admit" ("'God's Well-Trodden Foot-Paths,'" 504). Critics who have suggested the importance of process and ritual in Puritan poetry include Charles W. Mignon, "Edward Tay-

lor's *Preparatory Meditations*: A Decorum of Imperfection," *PMLA* 83 (1968): 1423–28; Scheick, *The Will and the Word*, 161–68; Scheick, "Tombless Virtue and Hidden Text"; Keller, *The Example of Edward Taylor*, 88–97; Keller, "Edward Taylor, The Acting Poet," in White, ed., *Puritan Poets*, 185–97; Rosamond R. Rosenmeier, "The Wounds Upon Bathsheba: Anne Bradstreet's Prophetic Art," in White, ed., *Puritan Poets*, 129–46; and Jeffrey A. Hammond, "From Sinful Silence to Apostolic Voice: The Puritan Elegiac Ritual," *Studies in Puritan American Spirituality* 2 (1991): 77–106.

Fish's notion of the "self-consuming" text, developed in reference to English religious texts of the seventeenth century (*Self-Consuming Artifacts*), anticipated Scheick's view that the American Puritan elegy was "funerated" in the reader's assimilation of the redeemed perspective on the saint's life and death ("Tombless Virtue and Hidden Text," 298). Ivy Schweitzer agrees that elegies offered scripts designed to be assimilated by the living. Schweitzer argues that in his elegy on John Cotton, John Fiske established himself as heir to Cotton in a spiritualized patriarchy and thus reinforced his own "redeemed subjectivity" (*The Work of Self-Representation*, 41–74). For a different approach to the assimilation of the deceased's traits enabled by the Puritan elegy, one which stresses biblical rather than psychological models of grieving, see Hammond, "From Sinful Silence to Apostolic Voice."

38 Mitchell, in Meserole, *American Poetry*, 412, 413.
39 Bradstreet, *Works*, 244; Weemse, *The Christian Synagogue*, 295. The Puritan poem repeatedly fostered the "split reader" that Fish finds in *Paradise Lost*, a reader "who is continually responding to two distinct sets of stimuli—the experience of individual poetic moments and the ever present pressure of the Christian doctrine—and who attaches these responses to warring forces within him, and is thus simultaneously the location and the observer of their struggle" (*Surprised by Sin*, 42). This literary dynamic accounts for the popularity of the debate format among Puritan poets. Andrew Marvell penned a typical dialogue between the Body and "A Soul hung up, as 'twere, in Chains / Of Nerves, and Arteries, and Veins" (*The Complete Poetry of Andrew Marvell*, ed. Hugh Macdonald [Cambridge: Harvard Univ. Press, 1952], 15). Wigglesworth exploited the form in "Riddles Unriddled" through a series of debates within a consciousness divided into "Distressed Conscience" and "Rectified Judgment," into "Unbelief" and "Faith," and into "Flesh" and a "Spirit" who recognizes her twin as "a treacherous Thief, / That robs me of my Faith, and then / Condemns for Unbelief" (*Poems*, 161). Taylor's *Gods Determinations* features similar debates between a distressed "Soul" and a persistent Satan who accuses the nascent believer of mere "Lip Love" (*Poems*, 412). Bradstreet makes the duality of belief especially explicit in her debate between "Flesh" and a "Spirit" who finally commands her carnal twin to "Disturb no more my settled heart" (*Works*, 216).

In its encouragement of inner doubleness, Puritan reading may reflect a more thematically directed version of what happens in all reading. Iser theorizes that by temporarily adopting the writer's perspective, the reader undergoes a division into "the alien 'me' and the real, virtual 'me'—which are never completely cut off from each other" (*The Implied Reader*, 293). Iser elaborates this division into a background consisting of the reader's "own disposition" and a foreground consisting of "the prevailing thoughts of the author" (*The Act of Reading*, 155). Wayne Booth anticipated the split reader when he commented that "It is only as I read that I become the self whose beliefs must coincide with the author's. Regardless of my real beliefs and practices, I must subordinate my mind and heart to the book if I am to enjoy it to the full" (*The Rhetoric of Fiction* [Chicago: Univ. of Chicago Press, 1961], 138).

40 King affirms that for Puritans, "No sense of hypocrisy exists in speaking or in writing of oneself in terms of former scripts," nor is it a question "of choosing between words and experience, or between a language of conversion and conversion itself" (*The Iron of Melancholy*, 48, 49). King rightly observes that "Like Taylor, Anne Bradstreet could write in verse of cleansing a body of sin without conceiving that hers figured as a character abnormally described" (57). Rosenmeier has similarly called Bradstreet's speaker a "prophetic" self in whom biblical voice and spiritual purpose override particular selfhood ("The Wounds Upon Bathsheba," 133). She develops her argument for an artfully constructed voice that transcends personal expression in *Anne Bradstreet Revisited*.

41 Ames, *Marrow of Theology*, 191, 247, 248; William Perkins, *The Arte of Prophecying*, in *The Workes of . . . William Perkins*, 3 vols. (London: 1612), 2:671; John Davenport, *The Saint's Anchor-Hold*, in *Salvation in New England: Selections from the Sermons of the First Preachers*, ed. Phyllis M. Jones and Nicholas R. Jones (Austin: Univ. of Texas Press, 1977), 148. Cf. Romans 5:3–4: "we glory in tribulations also: knowing that tribulation worketh patience; / And patience experience; and experience, hope."

42 John Donne, "Hymne to God my God, in my sicknesse," in *The Complete Poetry of John Donne*, ed. John T. Shawcross (Garden City: Doubleday, 1967), 391; Milton, *Complete Poetry*, 577; Weemse, *The Christian Synagogue*, 297.

43 On the central role of the pilgrim motif in Bradstreet's spiritual life, see Hambrick-Stowe, *The Practice of Piety*, 13–19; and Piercy, *Anne Bradstreet*, 25–40.

44 Herbert, *A Priest to the Temple*, in *Works*, 228; Thomas Hall, *Centuria Sacra*, in *Vindiciae Literarum* (London: 1655), 72–73; Francis Rous, *The Mysticall Marriage* (London: 1631), 237.

45 Henoch Clapham, *Three Partes of Salomon his Song of Songs, expounded* (London: 1603), A4v; Henry, *An Exposition*, Yyy.

46 Henry, *An Exposition*, Yyyr.

47 Mitchell, in Meserole, *American Poetry*, 412.

48 Thomas Shepard, *The Sincere Convert* (London: 1655), quoted in Murdock, *Literature and Theology*, 62. Keller once suggested that "Poetry as a *liberating* art in Puritan culture may be an important, neglected idea. In Taylor's hands it became a way of extending the range of the myth that bound him. The ideology was perhaps livable without such a device, though perhaps not alive in *him* until he wrote" (*The Example of Edward Taylor*, 236). Elsewhere Keller argued that writing enabled Bradstreet to achieve "liberation via piety, via Puritan allegiance" (*The Only Kangaroo among the Beauty: Emily Dickinson and America* [Baltimore: Johns Hopkins Univ. Press, 1979], 16), a view corroborated in part by Rosenmeier's emphasis on Bradstreet's artistic imitation and blending of a variety of roles (*Anne Bradstreet Revisited*). John Gatta, Jr., similarly maintains that poetry helped Taylor animate within himself the "festival frame of spirit" of the assured soul (*Gracious Laughter: The Meditative Wit of Edward Taylor* [Columbia: Univ. of Missouri Press, 1989], 141–79). Cohen proposes a theological corrolary to the liberation and even joy that writing brought Puritans in the spiritual power that conversion brought to believers (*God's Caress*, 5, 210). These

comments are consistent with the Puritan belief that the best verbal art did not differ essentially from any heartfelt praise to God. With such guides as David and Solomon, any fully engaged celebrant of the Word became in this sense its antitypical singer, a role embodied in "Pilgrim" and even more dramatically in Taylor's *Preparatory Meditations*. As William Tans'ur articulated this role, "Can I cease, my *God*, from *Singing* daily grateful *Songs* to thee, / Whilst thy *Grace* is always bringing, all things richly unto me?" (*Heaven on Earth*, 169). In using the ordinance of pious song, congregation and the meditating soul alike were to sing with total conviction (1 Cor. 14:15: "I will sing with the spirit, and I will sing with the understanding also"), with concern for instructing others in the faith (Col. 3:16: "Let the word of Christ dwell in you richly in all wisdom; teaching and admonishing one another in psalms and hymns and spiritual songs, singing with grace in your hearts to the Lord"), and above all, with joy appropriate to a saint's gratitude toward a merciful God (Ps. 100:1–2: "Make a joyful noise unto the Lord, all ye lands. / Serve the Lord with gladness: come before his presence with singing"). To sing with delight and not fear, whether in an aroused congregation singing Psalms or in the privacy of meditation, was to be made God's poet through the eloquence of grace.

Two. "By Ladders of Your Own": Eschatology and the Selflessness of Reading

1 Edmund S. Morgan, "Introduction," *The Diary of Michael Wigglesworth, 1653–1657: The Conscience of a Puritan* (New York: Harper and Row, 1965), v. A more sympathetic portrait emerges in Richard Crowder, *No Featherbed to Heaven: A Biography of Michael Wigglesworth* (East Lansing: Michigan State Univ. Press, 1962), and in Richard M. Gummere, "Michael Wigglesworth: From Kill-joy to Comforter," in *Seven Wise Men of Colonial America* (Cambridge: Harvard Univ. Press, 1967), 25–40.

   As we have seen, Moses Coit Tyler established the prevailing view that Wigglesworth's pious aims subverted his art (*A History*, 277). Even such a sympathetic critic as Kenneth B. Murdock conceded that the poet "was handicapped on the one hand by his allegiance to the letter of the Bible as expounded by his school of theology, and on the other by his knowledge of his audience" ("Introduction," *The Day of Doom*, vii). Crowder agrees that "Only occasionally does the poet's burning sensitivity break through the wall of the theological treatise, and even then, the language and imagery are fenced in by Biblical phraseology" (*No Featherbed*, 108), while Daly attributes Wigglesworth's limitations to his "extreme dismissal of the natural world" and consequent "inability to perceive, and hence to use, metaphor" (*God's Altar*, 132). Similar assessments appear in F. O. Matthiessen, "Michael Wigglesworth, A Puritan Artist," *New England Quarterly* 1 (1928): 500; Pearce, *Continuity*, 220; and Hyatt H. Waggoner, *American Poets from the Puritans to the Present* (Boston: Houghton Mifflin, 1968), 120. Bosco provides an overview of nineteenth- and twentieth-century reception to Wigglesworth's verse ("Introduction," *Poems*, xi–xvii).

2 Mitchell, "On the following Work and Its Author," in Meserole, *American Poetry*, 413; Mather, *A Faithful Man, Described and Rewarded*, 24. On Wigglesworth's popularity see Murdock, "Introduction," iii; Matt B. Jones, "Notes for a Bibliography of Michael Wigglesworth's 'Day of Doom' and 'Meat Out of the

Eater,'" *Proceedings of the American Antiquarian Society*, New Series, 39 (1929): 77–84; Samuel Eliot Morison, *The Intellectual Life of Colonial New England* (1936; reprint, Ithaca: Cornell Univ. Press, 1960), 214; Meserole, *American Poetry*, 37; and Bosco, "Introduction," *Poems*, x, 305–6.

3   Wigglesworth, *Diary*, 51. For recent discussions that approach Wigglesworth's writings from the standpoint of psychological anxiety, see Eva Cherniavsky, "Night Pollution and the Floods of Confession in Michael Wigglesworth's Diary," *Arizona Quarterly* 45, no. 2 (1989): 15–33; and Walter Hughes, "'Meat Out of the Eater': Panic and Desire in American Puritan Poetry," in *Engendering Men: The Question of Male Feminist Criticism*, ed. Joseph A. Boone and Michael Cadden (New York: Routledge, 1990), 102–21.

4   Murdock, *Literature and Theology*, 145.

5   Tyler, *A History*, 277; Mitchell, in Meserole, *American Poetry*, 412. As Bosco notes, "From Wigglesworth's point of view and from that of several generations of colonials raised on his verse, the intentional didactic or sermonic aspect, orthodox content, and plain style of his poetry were its very strengths" ("Introduction," *Poems*, xix). The fullest discussions of *The Day of Doom*, all of which consider to varying degrees its homiletic aims, include Matthiessen, "Michael Wigglesworth," 497–500; Murdock, "Introduction," iii–xi; Crowder, *No Featherbed*, 101–13, 163–67; John F. Lynen, *The Design of the Present: Essays on Time and Form in American Literature* (New Haven: Yale Univ. Press, 1969), 61–62; Harsharan Singh Ahluwalia, "Salvation New England Style: A Study of Covenant Theology in Michael Wigglesworth's *The Day of Doom*," *Indian Journal of American Studies* 4 (1974): 1–12; Richard Crowder, "'The Day of Doom' as Chronomorph," *Journal of Popular Culture* 9 (1976): 948–59; Daly, *God's Altar*, 131–34; Jeffrey A. Hammond, "'Ladders of Your Own': *The Day of Doom* and the Repudiation of 'Carnal Reason,'" *Early American Literature* 19 (1984): 42–67; Douglas Robinson, *American Apocalypses: The Image of the End of the World in American Literature* (Baltimore: Johns Hopkins Univ. Press, 1985), 55–62; and Alan H. Pope, "Petrus Ramus and Michael Wigglesworth: The Logic of Poetic Structure," in White, ed., *Puritan Poets*, 217–20.

6   Thomas Hooker, *The Application of Redemption . . . The first eight Books* (1657; reprint, New York: Arno Press, 1972), 146; Shepard, *The Sincere Convert*, in *Works*, 1:82, 73. Murdock comments that "Wigglesworth had learned Francis Bacon's lesson: 'The prerogative of God extendeth as well to the reason as to the will of man; so that as we are to obey his law though we find a reluctation in our will, so we are to believe his word though we find a reluctation in our reason'" ("Introduction," x).

7   Wigglesworth, *Poems*, 5. All citations from Wigglesworth's poetry refer to page numbers of this edition.

8   Critics who stress Wigglesworth's otherworldly themes include Daly, *God's Altar*, 128–36; and Waggoner, *American Poets from the Puritans to the Present*, 11–12. On the sinners' reliance on the self and the world in *The Day of Doom*, see Crowder, *No Featherbed*, 163–67; and Ahluwalia, "Salvation New England Style," 6.

9   Hooker, *Application*, 196.

10 Tyler, *A History*, 287.

11 The infants' famous sentence to "the easiest room in Hell" (56) is less a concession to their relative innocence than a sarcastic mirroring of their futile

presumptions upon mercy. As Gerhard T. Alexis notes, their placement in the "easiest room" helped make Wigglesworth's depiction of the Judgment "sharper, not softer" ("Wigglesworth's 'Easiest Room,'" *New England Quarterly* 42 [1969]: 583).

12   Shepard, *The Sincere Convert*, in *Works*, 1:31; Hooker, *Application*, 211. Shepard here cites Psalms 50:16: "But unto the wicked, God saith, What hast thou to do, to declare my statutes, or that thou shouldest take my covenant in thy mouth?"

13   Hooker, *Application*, 211; Hooker, *The Application of Redemption . . . The Ninth Book*, in *Redemption: Three Sermons*, ed. Everett H. Emerson (Gainesville, Fla.: Scholars' Facsimiles and Reprints, 1956), 57; William Chappell, *The Preacher; or, The Art and Method of Preaching* (London: 1656), 130.

14   Thomas Hooker, *The Soules Preparation for Christ* (London: 1632), 26. Although Alan H. Pope ably identifies Ramean influences on the poem, most of Wigglesworth's readers would have been unaware of the syllogistic structures that he cites. While I agree that the debate "portrays the ways of God as logical and rational," the poem made it clear that the ultimate test of doctrine was not human logic but divine ("Petrus Ramus and Michael Wigglesworth," 220). On Wigglesworth and Ramus see also John C. Adams, "Alexander Richardson and the Ramist Poetics of Michael Wigglesworth," *Early American Literature* 25 (1990): 271–88.

15   Thomas Hooker, *The Soules Implantation* (London: 1637), 11; Hooker, *Application*, 206; Daly, *God's Altar*, 131.

16   Shepard, *The Sincere Convert*, in *Works*, 1:41. Crowder points out that the collapsing of the vast variety of sins into several broad categories of error creates "a concentration of action" that reinforced the urgency of repentance. As Crowder notes, the brisk pace and Wigglesworth's skillful use of verb tenses produce an effect of "horrific efficiency and devastating terror" ("Chronomorph," 955, 954). Lynen similarly maintains that "the preternatural smoothness of the poem as it spins on and on as equably as a cart on ball bearings must have impressed the Puritan reader with the sense of divine inevitability" (*The Design of the Present*, 61). The ballad meter, in addition to making the poem easier to memorize, could only have enhanced this effect, especially when the poem was read aloud. Lawrence A. Cremin points out that *The Day of Doom* was part of a body of popular literature which "was read and reread, often in groups and almost always aloud; much of it was memorized and thus passed into oral tradition, where it influenced many who could not themselves read" (*American Education: The Colonial Experience, 1606–1783* [New York: Harper and Row, 1970], 131). Lowance has commented that when *The Day of Doom* is "read aloud to a class of undergraduates, it is as effective an instrument for communicating the anxiety that lay beneath dogmatic Puritan assurances as any lecture by a sociologist or psychologist" ("Religion in Puritan Poetry," 43).

17   Richard Bernard, *The Faithfull Shepherd* (London: 1621), 312.

18   Shepard, *The Sound Believer*, in *Works*, 1:132–33; Hooker, *The Soules Implantation*, 11, 22. Bosco connects Wigglesworth's verse with the perceived declension of piety in late seventeenth-century New England ("Introduction," xix–xxi). For a discussion of the dual function of the jeremiad in simultaneously warning and consoling the saints, see Sacvan Bercovitch, *The American Jeremiad* (Madison: Univ. of Wisconsin Press, 1978), esp. 6–18. That *The Day of Doom* offered more hope than is commonly assumed was suggested by Murdock, who observed that

the harshness of the poem is "partly balanced" by the more gentle appeals of "To the Christian Reader" and the "Postscript" ("Introduction," x). Ahluwalia similarly notes that Wigglesworth avoids provoking despair in his readers by balancing predestination with "the need for human exertion" ("Salvation New England Style," 7).

19   Taylor, "A Funerall Poem upon . . . Mrs. Elizabeth Taylor," in *Minor Poetry*, 114; Hall, *Centuria Sacra*, 134.

20   On the perceived declension of the Puritan mission in the late seventeenth century and the jeremiad as an expression of communal grief and rededication, see Perry Miller, *The New England Mind: From Colony to Province* (Cambridge: Harvard Univ. Press, 1953), 1–39; Miller, *Errand into the Wilderness* (Cambridge: Harvard Univ. Press, 1956), 1–15; David Minter, "The Puritan Jeremiad as a Literary Form," in *The American Puritan Imagination: Essays in Revaluation*, ed. Sacvan Bercovitch (London: Cambridge Univ. Press, 1974), 45–55; Emory Elliott, *Power and the Pulpit in Puritan New England* (Princeton: Princeton Univ. Press, 1975); and Bercovitch, *The American Jeremiad*.

21   Perkins, *The Arte of Prophecying*, in *Workes*, 2:646. Bosco calls Wigglesworth's gentle narrator a "mediator" between Jehovah and the reader ("Introduction," xxvii). The epithet for the fiery role of Godly ministers derives from Mark 3:17, where Christ calls James and John, the sons of Zebedee. "Boanerges, which is, the sons of thunder." The preacher's role as a son of the dove recalls the many scriptural allusions to the Holy Spirit's descending like a dove (e.g., Matt. 3:16, Mark 1:10, Luke 3:22, and John 1:32). On the homiletic and psychological applications of the Law and the Gospel, see Babette May Levy, *Preaching in the First Half Century of New England History* (1945; reprint, New York: Russell and Russell, 1967), 25–27; Pettit, *The Heart Prepared*, 17–18; Owen C. Watkins, *The Puritan Experience* (London: Routledge and Kegan Paul, 1972), 8–9; David D. Hall, *The Faithful Shepherd: A History of the New England Ministry in the Seventeenth Century* (Chapel Hill: Univ. of North Carolina Press, 1972), 18–19, 63–66, 163–65; Jones and Jones, "Introduction," *Salvation in New England*, 3–13; John R. Knott, Jr., *The Sword of the Spirit: Puritan Responses to the Bible* (Chicago: Univ. of Chicago Press, 1980), 11, 133, 142–44; and Cohen, *God's Caress*, 47–74.

Other studies of Puritan homiletic theory and practice include W. F. Mitchell, *English Pulpit Oratory from Andrewes to Tillotson: A Study of Its Literary Aspects* (New York: Macmillan, 1932), 41–130, 255–75; Perry Miller, *The New England Mind: The Seventeenth Century* (1939; reprint, Cambridge: Harvard Univ. Press, 1954), 300–362; Josephine K. Piercy, *Studies in Literary Types in Seventeenth Century America* (1939; reprint, New York: Archon, 1969), 155–67; Phyllis M. Jones, "Biblical Rhetoric and the Pulpit Literature of Early New England," *Early American Literature* 11 (1977): 245–58; Jones, "Puritan's Progress: The Story of the Soul's Salvation in the Early New England Sermons," *Early American Literature* 15 (1980): 14–28; Hambrick-Stowe, *The Practice of Piety*. 116–23; Davidson, "'God's Well-Trodden Foot-Paths,'" 503–27; Harry S. Stout, *The New England Soul: Preaching and Religious Culture in Colonial New England* (New York: Oxford Univ. Press, 1986); and Teresa Toulouse, *The Art of Prophesying: New England Sermons and the Shaping of Belief* (Athens: Univ. of Georgia Press, 1987), 13–74.

22   Perkins, *Workes*, 2:671; Bernard, *The Faithfull Shepherd*, 75, 127, 75–76.
23   Perkins, *Workes*, 2:667.

24 Perkins, *Workes*, 2:668.
25 Hooker, *Application*, 156.

Three. "A Sinful Self ... Remaining in My Heart": Riddles of Comfort for the Saintly Self

1 Wigglesworth, *Poems*, ed. Bosco, 103. *Meat Out of the Eater* refers here to the entire volume, "Meat Out of the Eater" to the sequence of poems bearing that title. All quotations refer by page number to Bosco's text, which is based on the fourth edition (Boston: 1689), the last to appear in Wigglesworth's lifetime. Although the title page of a fifth edition (Boston: 1717) claims that the poems were "Corrected and Amended by the Author" two years before his death in 1705, Bosco finds no authority for its revisions ("Introduction," *Poems*, xlii).
Discussions of *Meat Out of the Eater* include Richard Crowder, "Meat Out of the Eater," *Boston Public Library Quarterly* 11 (1959): 179–92; Crowder, *No Featherbed to Heaven*, 132–46; Gummere, "Michael Wigglesworth: From Killjoy to Comforter," in *Seven Wise Men of Colonial America*, 38–39; Hambrick-Stowe, *The Practice of Piety*, 268–72; Ronald A. Bosco, "Michael Wigglesworth," in *American Colonial Writers, 1606–1734*, ed. Emory Elliott, vol. 24 of the *Dictionary of Literary Biography* (Detroit: Gale Research Company, 1984), 341–42; Pope, "Petrus Ramus and Michael Wigglesworth," 220–25; Ursula Brumm, "Meditative Poetry in New England," in White, ed., *Puritan Poets*, 326–30; and Bosco, "Introduction," xxvii–xxix, xxxiii.

2 Brumm, "Meditative Poetry in New England," 330. Crowder comments that "The poems in this work do not have the advantage of the physical movement and dramatic situation of *The Day of Doom*" ("Meat Out of the Eater," 181), while Brumm notes that flat "Descriptions of the miseries of the human condition are more prominent ... than the effort to understand and search the heart" (329). Brumm concedes, however, that *Meat Out of the Eater* is "a successful effort at pastoral counseling" (330), as does Hambrick-Stowe, who observes that the collection "was essentially a devotional manual, not a book of poetry in the modern sense, in that the poems were intended as models for the reader's own meditation and were arranged according to the order of redemption" (*The Practice of Piety*, 268).

3 As Alan H. Pope observes, the final emergence of this "gentler narrator" reflects a Ramean shift from "artificial" to "inartificial" arguments based on personal testimony ("Petrus Ramus and Michael Wigglesworth," 224–25), a shift that foreshadows the collection's larger movement to a more directly experiential mode in "Riddles Unriddled."

4 Cf. Ps. 89:31–32 ("If they break my statutes, and keep not my commandments; / Then I will visit their transgression with the rod, and their iniquity with stripes"), and Lev. 26:21 ("And if ye walk contrary unto me, and will not hearken unto me; I will bring seven times more plagues upon you according to your sins"). Wigglesworth's paraphrase is even closer in the posthumous edition, which substitutes "stripes" for "strokes" (*Meat Out of the Eater* [Boston: 1717], 33).

5 Bradstreet, *Works*, 272.
6 Brumm, "Meditative Poetry in New England," 329; Weemse, *The Christian Synagogue*, 296.

7. Although "Meat Out of the Eater" is, as Pope demonstrates, "organized in a Ramean pattern" with each Meditation "structured around a particular logical argument from 'Invention'" ("Petrus Ramus and Michael Wigglesworth," 220), Wigglesworth's chief goal, as in *The Day of Doom*, was to subvert the workings of natural or carnal reason. As Hambrick-Stowe observes, the meditation and prayer promoted by the sequence "resolved the opposites in a vision of heaven" (*The Practice of Piety*, 272).
8. Crowder, *No Featherbed*, 138.
9. Bradstreet, *Works*, 294. Bosco observes that "Wigglesworth was his own model for the enduring Christian, though the sense of Puritan modesty would never have allowed him to admit that he was his own source." Wigglesworth avoided arrogance through the Puritan convention of asserting what Bosco calls "the universality of his experience and the value of such advice as he might offer" ("Michael Wigglesworth," 431, and "Introduction," xxv).
10. Ames, *Marrow of Theology*, 170, 171.
11. Bradstreet, *Works*, 216.
12. Taylor, *Poems*, 414.
13. Mather, *A Faithful Man*, 25; Morison, *The Intellectual Life of Colonial New England*, 215.

Four. "Setting Up My Ebenezer": Anne Bradstreet and the Examined Self

1. Stanford, "Anne Bradstreet: Dogmatist and Rebel," 373–89. Elizabeth Wade White also cites "strong and conflicting forces in Anne Bradstreet's character which, if they had not been controlled by her innate sense of proportion and her faculty of objectivity, might have brought her into disastrous contention with her rigid environment" (*Anne Bradstreet: The Tenth Muse* [New York: Oxford Univ. Press, 1971], 172). Other critics have argued that "the currents within the poetry itself seem too often to run counter to a position of religious orthodoxy" (Rosenfeld, "Anne Bradstreet's 'Contemplations,'" 86), that Bradstreet finally "formed a belief in God whose presence she never experienced" (Emily Stipes Watts, *The Poetry of American Women* [Austin: Univ. of Texas Press, 1977], 19) and thereby "ultimately capitulated to her fathers—earthly and heavenly" (Martin, *An American Triptych*, 36). Similar views appear in Piercy, *Anne Bradstreet*, 26–29; Ann Stanford, "Anne Bradstreet," in *Major Writers of Early American Literature*, ed. Everett Emerson (Madison: Univ. of Wisconsin Press, 1972), 58; Stanford, *Anne Bradstreet*, 88–91; Martin, "Anne Bradstreet's Poetry," 19–31; and Schweitzer, *The Work of Self-Representation*, 127–80.
2. Tyler, *A History*, 253.
3. Bradstreet, *Works*, 241. Quotations from Bradstreet refer to page numbers of this edition. Daly suggests that Bradstreet's rising heart refers specifically to her profession of faith and subsequent entry into the church at Boston (*God's Altar*, 238, note 3). In this view, the confession either confirms the normal difficulty of a sincere conversion or reflects her objections to renewing a profession that she had already given in Old England. For a reading that stresses an unusually difficult adjustment to life in the New World, see Albert J. Von Frank, *The Sacred Game: Provincialism and Frontier Consciousness in American Literature, 1630–1860* (Cambridge: Cambridge Univ. Press, 1985), 11–26.

The extent to which Bradstreet adumbrated modern feminist values remains a central debate in the criticism. Martin, for example, maintains that Bradstreet's verse "reflects the tensions and conflicts of a person struggling for selfhood in a culture that was outraged by individual autonomy and that valued poetry to the extent that it praised God" ("Anne Bradstreet's Poetry," 31; see also *An American Triptych*, 54–57, 73–76). More recently Schweitzer has argued that Bradstreet was more a victim than a rebel, shaped by her family and her society into a cultural figure of the exemplary woman as an antidote to such threatening women as her sister Sarah Keayne and Anne Hutchinson (*The Work of Self-Representation*, 152–53). On the other side of the debate, Joseph R. McElrath, Jr., and Allan P. Robb argue that "the feminist focus" risks "narrowing and distorting the full cultural and autobiographical significance of the poetry and prose" ("Introduction," *The Complete Works of Anne Bradstreet* [Boston: Twayne, 1981], xii), while Karl Keller holds that Bradstreet was actually "elevated as a woman by her Puritan faith to a position of self-sufficient responsibility for her soul" (*The Only Kangaroo among the Beauty*, 9–10). What might be called a middle position, one that balances cultural and historical frameworks with insights derived from feminism and psychological theory, has been taken by Pattie Cowell and Rosamond Rosenmeier. Cowell argues that issues of voice and identity central to Bradstreet as a woman were analogous to problems that she faced as a "first-generation poet in the New World" ("Why Our First Poet Was a Woman: Bradstreet and the Birth of an American Poetic Voice," *Prospects* 13 [1988]: 2), while Rosenmeier stresses Bradstreet's artistic assimilation of varied roles as extensions of an overarching "feminine" identity derived from secular as well as biblical models (*Anne Bradstreet Revisited*).

General studies of women in Puritan culture reflect the same diversity of opinion that marks Bradstreet criticism. While Lyle Koehler argues that women were just as restricted in Puritan culture as they were in later periods (*A Search for Power: The "Weaker Sex" in Seventeenth-Century New England* [Urbana: Univ. of Illinois Press, 1980]), Laurel Thatcher Ulrich maintains that seventeenth-century New England was relatively supportive of women (*Good Wives: Image and Reality in the Lives of Women in Northern New England, 1650–1750* [New York: Knopf, 1982]). Despite the undeniably androcentric nature of Puritan society and the Puritan appropriation of Pauline assumptions regarding women (on this point see Margaret Olofson Thickstun, *Fictions of the Feminine: Puritan Doctrine and the Representation of Women* [Ithaca: Cornell Univ. Press, 1988], 1–36), the theology seems to have treated the genders equally. As Cohen points out, Puritan spiritual narratives reveal "the fundamental sameness of the conversion experience for each sex" (*God's Caress*, 222). Discussions of Puritanism as an enabling influence on seventeenth-century women in general and Bradstreet in particular include Jennifer R. Waller ("'My Hand a Needle Better Fits': Anne Bradstreet and Women Poets of the Renaissance," *Dalhousie Review* 54 [1974]: 445–46); Mary G. Mason ("The Other Voice: Autobiographies of Women Writers," in *Autobiography: Essays Theoretical and Critical*, ed. James Olney [Princeton: Princeton Univ. Press, 1980], 230); and Cheryl Walker (*The Nightingale's Burden: Women Poets and American Culture before 1900* [Bloomington: Indiana Univ. Press, 1982], 17; and "Anne Bradstreet: A Woman Poet," in *Critical Essays on Anne Bradstreet*, 257–58).

4   Robert D. Arner comments that by centering on Bradstreet's ambivalence

toward the faith, we "unwittingly" patronize her as "only another woman who cannot make up her mind" ("Anne Bradstreet," in *American Writers Before 1800: A Biographical and Critical Dictionary*, ed. James A. Levernier and Douglas R. Wilmes [Westport, Conn.: Greenwood Press, 1983], 192). On Bradstreet's popularity, see White, *Anne Bradstreet*, 271–73; Stanford, *Anne Bradstreet*, 121–24; and Pattie Cowell, "The Early Distribution of Anne Bradstreet's Poems," in *Critical Essays on Anne Bradstreet*, 276–77. Schweitzer sees this popularity as evidence of the poet's restricting appropriation, not only by her contemporaries but by such later male writers as John Berryman; for Schweitzer, Bradstreet underwent painful and diminishing subjective "constitution as a figure of gynesis at the hands of the New England patriarchy" (*The Work of Self-Representation*, 129).

5 John Harvard Ellis, "Introduction," *The Works of Anne Bradstreet in Prose and Verse* (1867; reprint, New York: Peter Smith, 1932), lviii. Rosenmeier (*Anne Bradstreet Revisited*) and Schweitzer (*The Work of Self-Representation*) both argue, correctly I think, for the "constructed" nature of Bradstreet's textual identity—an identity that transcends simple and literally autobiographical expression. Critics who suggest an extrapersonal dimension in Bradstreet's speaker by placing her struggles within Puritan and biblical meditative structures include Kenneth Ball, "Puritan Humility in Anne Bradstreet's Poetry," *Cithara* 13 (1973): 29–41; Robert Richardson, Jr., "The Puritan Poetry of Anne Bradstreet," in *The American Puritan Imagination: Essays in Revaluation*, ed. Sacvan Bercovitch (London: Cambridge Univ. Press, 1974), 108; Kenneth A. Requa, "Anne Bradstreet's Poetic Voices," *Early American Literature* 9 (1974): 3–18; Daly, *God's Altar*, 100; Keller, *The Only Kangaroo among the Beauty*, 14; Cheryl Walker, "Anne Bradstreet," in *American Writers: A Collection of Literary Biographies*, ed. Leonard Unger, Supplement I, Part 1 (New York: Scribner's, 1979), 100–109; Emily Stipes Watts, "'The posy UNITY': Anne Bradstreet's Search for Order," in *Puritan Influences in American Literature*, ed. Emory Elliott (Urbana: Univ. of Illinois Press, 1979), 35; McElrath and Robb, "Introduction," xii–xiv; Walker, *The Nightingale's Burden*, 14; Jeffrey A. Hammond, "'Make Use of What I Leave in Love': Anne Bradstreet's Didactic Self," *Religion and Literature* 17 (1985): 11–26; Dorothea Steiner, "Anne Bradstreet—Poet of Communication," *Arbeiten aus Anglistik und Amerikanistik* 10 (1985): 137–53; Rosamond Rosenmeier, "The Wounds Upon Bathsheba," 134–35; Karen E. Rowe, "Prophetic Visions: Typology and Colonial American Poetry," in White, ed., *Puritan Poets*, 63; Paula Kopacz, "'To Finish What's Begun': Anne Bradstreet's Last Words," *Early American Literature* 23 (1988): 175–87; and Beth M. Doriani, "'Then Have I . . . Said with David': Anne Bradstreet's Andover Manuscript Poems and the Influence of the Psalm Tradition," *Early American Literature* 24 (1989): 52–69.

6 Stanford, *Anne Bradstreet*, 104. The fullest discussions of Bradstreet as a meditative poet are Ann Stanford, "Anne Bradstreet as a Meditative Writer," in *Critical Essays on Anne Bradstreet*, 89–96; and Charles Hambrick-Stowe, "Introduction," *Early New England Meditative Poetry: Anne Bradstreet and Edward Taylor* (New York: Paulist Press, 1988), 22–38.

7 Wigglesworth, *Diary*, 93.

8 As Piercy notes, the poem extols "the ideal abstraction of a good woman," the "character" of the Puritan goodwife (*Anne Bradstreet*, 91) that derived, as

Rosenmeier points out, from Paul's celebration of the heavenly Jerusalem as the pious "mother of us all" (Gal. 4:26) ("The Wounds Upon Bathsheba," 139). See also Ann Stanford, "Images of Women in Early American Literature," in *What Manner of Women? Essays on English and American Life and Literature*, ed. Marlene Springer (New York: New York Univ. Press, 1977), 190.

9   Rosamond R. Rosenmeier, "'Divine Translation': A Contribution to the Study of Anne Bradstreet's Method in the Marriage Poems," *Early American Literature* 12 (1977): 130, 128; Durham, *Clavis Cantici*, 211. Stanford identifies the biblical source of these lines (*Anne Bradstreet*, 23–24). Richardson notes that the marriage poems enact a proper balance in which "this world and the next validate each other" ("The Puritan Poetry of Anne Bradstreet," 113). Daly agrees that Bradstreet's love for her husband is a crucial "part of the evidence of her election" (*God's Altar*, 104), while Steiner observes that Bradstreet places "the loving couple's relationship in the larger framework of the cosmos and nature with their innate laws and harmony" ("Anne Bradstreet—Poet of Communication," 146). Other discussions of the poems to Simon include Piercy, *Anne Bradstreet*, 84–88; Rosenmeier, *Anne Bradstreet Revisited*, 113–25; and Ellen B. Brandt, "Anne Bradstreet: The Erotic Component in Puritan Poetry," *Women's Studies* 7 (1980): 46–49.

10 Rosenmeier, whose focus on the biblical antecedents of Bradstreet's voice underscores the role of the poems in reenacting "the stages of the Christian journey," comments on the poet's projection of "a double self" indicative of a fully Puritan struggle between sin and grace ("The Wounds Upon Bathsheba," 134, 137). On the archetypal nature of Bradstreet's letter see Jeannine Hensley, "Anne Bradstreet's Wreath of Thyme," in Bradstreet, *Works*, xxvii; Daniel B. Shea, *Spiritual Autobiography in Early America* (Princeton: Princeton Univ. Press, 1968), 114; Ball, "Puritan Humility," 30; Stanford, *Anne Bradstreet*, 84; McElrath and Robb, "Introduction," xvi; and Mason, "The Other Voice," 213.

11 Rosenmeier, "'Divine Translation,'" 194. Recent studies confirming that Bradstreet's work is artistically shaped and thereby reflects purpose and design beyond mere personal expression include Rosenmeier, *Anne Bradstreet Revisited*; and Scheick, *Design in Puritan American Literature*, 35–45.

12 Rich, "Anne Bradstreet and Her Poetry," xviii.

13 Durham, *Clavis Cantici*, 52. As Rosenmeier observes, "Apparently she fully intended to interweave other poetic and biblical voices with her own" ("The Wounds Upon Bathsheba," 137). Bradstreet's indebtedness to the Psalms is also noted in Stanford, *Anne Bradstreet*, 81; Piercy, *Anne Bradstreet*, 79–81; Martin, "Anne Bradstreet's Poetry," 30; Doriani, "'Then Have I Said . . . With David'"; and Raymond A. Craig, "Singing with Grace: Allusive Strategies in Anne Bradstreet's 'New Psalms,'" *Studies in Puritan American Spirituality* 1 (1990): 148–63.

14 The emblematic quality of the scene becomes even more evident when the two openings are compared with the beginning of Wigglesworth's *Day of Doom*: "Still was the night, Serene and Bright, / When all Men sleeping lay; / Calm was the season, and carnal reason / Thought so 'twould last for ay" (*Poems*, 11). Steiner notes the similarity of these openings ("Anne Bradstreet—Poet of Communication," 148–49).

15 Mitchell, "On the following Work and Its Author," in Meserole, *American Poetry*, 412. Samuel Eliot Morison maintained that "unlike Wigglesworth she

wished not to instruct and warn, only to express her personal emotions" (*Builders of the Bay Colony* [1930; reprint, Boston: Northeastern Univ. Press, 1981], 219). Rich similarly calls her "the first non-didactic American poet" ("Anne Bradstreet and Her Poetry," xix), and Piercy argues that despite the "Puritan setting" of her work, "she does not impose either didacticism or religion upon her reader." Piercy concedes, however, that such occasional works as the "Meditations" were written "for her children only" (*Anne Bradstreet*, 115, 79), and Keller argues that throughout her work the poet tells "exemplary stories to her children" by affirming in her own life how God deals with all earthly pilgrims (*The Only Kangaroo among the Beauty*, 15, note 10). Rosenmeier observes that "her poetry is not primarily a retelling of the events of her life so much as it is a re-creation of afflictions so that her children may be changed by reliving them." The later poems in particular are designed, Rosenmeier argues, "to be a source of support to her posterity" ("The Wounds Upon Bathsheba," 140, 134). In these poems, too, Requa confirms the existence of "private lessons" appropriate to Bradstreet's intimate audience ("Anne Bradstreet's Poetic Voices," 10). Other discussions of Bradstreet's role as a teacher to family readers include McElrath and Robb, "Introduction," xxi, xxviii; Walker, "Anne Bradstreet: A Woman Poet," 257–58; Robert Hutchinson, "Introduction," *Poems of Anne Bradstreet* (New York: Dover, 1969), 25; Ross W. Beales, "Anne Bradstreet and her Children," in *Regulated Children/Liberated Children: Education in Psychohistorical Perspective*, ed. Barbara Finkelstein (New York: Psychohistory Press, 1979), 16–19; Hammond, "'Make Use of What I Leave in Love'"; and Steiner, "Anne Bradstreet—Poet of Communication," 143.

16   White, *Anne Bradstreet*, 126; Cotton Mather, *Ornaments for the Daughters of Zion*, intro. Pattie Cowell (1692; reprint, New York: Scholars' Facsimiles and Reprints, 1978), 105–7. On the unity of Bradstreet's poetic and parental vocations, see Walker, *The Nightingale's Burden*, 11. Schweitzer comments on Bradstreet's role as mother as a means of at least partial reassertion of a reintegrated feminine identity that her culture denied her (*The Work of Self-Representation*, 173), while Rosenmeier notes Bradstreet's role as a "prophetic mother who combines, yet transcends" her maternal representations both as a poet and as an actual mother in a recapitulation of the biblical Bathsheba, mother of Solomon (*Anne Bradstreet Revisited*, 142–44).

17   On this point see Eileen Margerum, "Anne Bradstreet's Public Poetry and the Tradition of Humility," *Early American Literature* 17 (1982): 157; and A. Owen Aldridge, *Early American Literature: A Comparatist Approach* (Princeton: Princeton Univ. Press, 1982), 29. Recent studies of Bradstreet's appropriation of Renaissance conventions include Timothy Sweet, "Gender, Genre, and Subjectivity in Anne Bradstreet's Early Elegies," *Early American Literature* 23 (1988): 152–74; and Ivy Schweitzer, "Anne Bradstreet Wrestles with the Renaissance," *Early American Literature* 23 (1988): 291–312.

18   Much of the debate regarding Bradstreet's feminism centers on whether "The Prologue" is seen as essentially serious or comic. Although Stanford notes that Bradstreet's "apology for lack of skill" was a popular convention, she also claims that Bradstreet's tone is unusual "as a defense of herself as a woman who dared to write" (*Anne Bradstreet*, 63, 64). White agrees that it is "a very serious poem" despite its "outward gaiety of expression," a reaction to "those whose tongues wagged viciously against the governor's daughter" (*Anne Brad-*

street, 240). Similar readings appear in Stanford, *Anne Bradstreet*, 63–64; and Martin, *An American Triptych*, 16–17. For recent discussions of the patronizing praise offered by the male poets whose work prefaced the *Tenth Muse* volume, see Kathryn Zabelle Derounian-Stodola, "'The Excellency of the inferior sex': The Commendatory Writings on Anne Bradstreet," *Studies in Puritan American Spirituality* 1 (1990): 129–47; and Schweitzer, *The Work of Self-Representation*, 145–65. As Jane Donahue Eberwein points out, however, no evidence exists that Bradstreet was ever criticized for writing ("'No Rhet'ric We Expect': Argumentation in Bradstreet's 'The Prologue,'" *Early American Literature* 16 [1981]: 21); Cheryl Walker similarly argues that the antifeminist satire of the dedicatory poems should not obscure the fact that these poets commended her work as lavishly as Renaissance convention allowed ("In the Margin: The Image of Women in Early Puritan Poetry," in White, ed., *Puritan Poets*, 121–22). Robert Arner observes that the battle between the sexes had long prompted such satirical attacks and counterattacks ("Wit, Humor, and Satire in Seventeenth-Century American Poetry," in *Puritan Poets*, 280), and McElrath and Robb similarly argue that "the author and her audience found such nonsense the stuff from which jokes are made" ("Introduction," xiii). Although "The Prologue" conveys serious lessons regarding literary pretense and the superiority of plain over fancy verse, its clear invocation of such a longstanding comic *topos* makes it difficult to support the claim that the poem expresses *only* anger.

19 Bradstreet's extensive learning is discussed in Stanford, *Anne Bradstreet*, 29–33, 66–68, 159–60; White, *Anne Bradstreet*, 57–70, 235–36, 269–71, 383–90; Piercy, *Anne Bradstreet*, 29–30, 58–65, 135–44; Ellis, "Introduction," xliv–lii; Aldridge, *Early American Literature*, 25–52; and Jane Donahue Eberwein, "Civil War and Bradstreet's 'Monarchies,'" *Early American Literature* 26 (1991): 119–44. The fullest discussions of the longer "public" poems include White, *Anne Bradstreet*, 182–92, 208–19, 228–38; Piercy, *Anne Bradstreet*, 42–55; Helen McMahon, "Anne Bradstreet, Jean Bertault, and Dr. Crooke," *Early American Literature* 3 (1968): 118–23; Anne Hildebrand, "Anne Bradstreet's Quaternions and 'Contemplations,'" *Early American Literature* 8 (1973): 117–25; Jane Donahue Eberwein, "'The Unrefined Ore' of Anne Bradstreet's Quaternions," *Early American Literature* 9 (1974): 19–26; Stanford, *Anne Bradstreet*, 29–51, 66–70; Robert D. Arner, "The Structure of Anne Bradstreet's *Tenth Muse*," in *Discoveries and Considerations: Essays on Early American Literature and Aesthetics Presented to Harold Jantz*, ed. Calvin Israel (Albany: State Univ. of New York Press, 1976), 46–66; Watts, "'The posy UNITY,'" 23–31; Helena Maragou, "The Portrait of Alexander the Great in Anne Bradstreet's 'The Third Monarchy,'" *Early American Literature* 23 (1988): 70–81; Eberwein, "Civil War and Bradstreet's 'Monarchies'"; and Rosenmeier, *Anne Bradstreet Revisited*, 46–54, 61–68.

20 On the millennialist framework of the "Dialogue," see White, *Anne Bradstreet*, 159–72; Stanford, *Anne Bradstreet*, 53–61; Watts, "'The posy UNITY,'" 36, note 14; and Arner, "The Structure of Anne Bradstreet's *Tenth Muse*," 59.

FIVE. "HIDDEN MANNA THAT THE WORLD KNOWS NOT": THE PILGRIM'S INNER LIFE

1 Bradstreet, *Works*, 243; Pearce, *Continuity*, 22. Quotations from Bradstreet's works refer to page numbers of the Hensley edition.

2   Stanford, *Anne Bradstreet*, 80. Robert Richardson argues that a world "represented only in abstractions" is fully consistent with the meditative goals of the text ("The Puritan Poetry of Anne Bradstreet," 110). Kenneth Ball similarly observes that the speaker of "Vanity" assumes "the role of the Puritan in search of salvation" ("Puritan Humility," 37), while Daly confirms Puritan and stoic traditions in Bradstreet's concession that this world and its pleasures are "transient" (*God's Altar*, 97–98).

3   White, *Anne Bradstreet*, 243; Rosenmeier, "The Wounds Upon Bathsheba," 137. Rosenmeier's views regarding Bradstreet's integration of diverse poetic voices and her artistic management of an ongoing "mutability" of roles are expanded in her excellent study, *Anne Bradstreet Revisited*.

4   As McElrath and Robb observe, the poem owes less to the cynicism of the Preacher than to the eschatological hope of John's vision of "a pure river of water of life, clear as crystal, proceeding out of the throne of God and of the Lamb" (Rev. 22:1) and Matthew's parable of the true believer "Who, when he had found one pearl of great price, went and sold all that he had, and bought it" (Matt. 13:46) (*Complete Works*, 517).

5   The source in Job is identified in McElrath and Robb, eds., *Complete Works*, 517.

6   For Rosenfeld the poem exhibits a conflict between Bradstreet's imagination and her religion; "as a poet," he argues, "she was more a worshipper of Phoebus than of Christ" ("Anne Bradstreet's 'Contemplations,'" 88). Piercy similarly maintains that the poet anticipates a Romantic sensibility in her use of "freer forms" and "her own personal experience" (*Anne Bradstreet*, 99). Stanford, finding a pre-Romantic strain in the fact that "the central character is the poet herself," argues that Bradstreet "preferred the visible to that which she could not see" (*Anne Bradstreet*, 101, 104). Martin agrees that the poem reflects the poet's unusual "struggle between her worldly inclinations and her longing for eternity" ("Anne Bradstreet's Poetry," 29).

An opposing view holds that "Contemplations" reflects a fulfillment rather than a denial of Puritan spiritual and aesthetic goals. Walker, for example, calls the poem Bradstreet's "pilgrim's progress" (*The Nightingale's Burden*, 15), while Rosenmeier defines the speaker's role as "the Christian everyman" ("The Wounds Upon Bathsheba," 135). Helen Saltman develops this view by arguing that the poet dramatizes the stages of an "ideal conversion," thereby effecting a full reconciliation of her "vocation as a poet and her spiritual state" ("'Contemplations': Anne Bradstreet's Spiritual Biography," in Cowell and Stanford, eds., *Critical Essays on Anne Bradstreet*, 236, 226). Other readings of "Contemplations" as a confirmation of Puritan spiritual patterns include Ball, "Puritan Humility," 37; William J. Irvin, "Allegory and Typology 'Imbrace and Greet': Anne Bradstreet's 'Contemplations,'" *Early American Literature* 10 (1975): 44; Daly, *God's Altar*, 117–26; Richardson, "The Puritan Poetry of Anne Bradstreet," 113–22; Stanford, *Anne Bradstreet*, 93–104; Lynen, *The Design of the Present*, 76–83; Watts, "'The posy UNITY,'" 31–33; William J. Scheick, "The Theme, Structure, and Symbolism of Anne Bradstreet's 'Contemplations,'" *Américana* 4 (1984): 147–56; Rosenmeier, *Anne Bradstreet Revisited*, 145–53; and Scheick, *Design in Puritan American Literature*, 35–45.

7   Steere, "Earth Felicities, Heavens Allowances. A Blank poem," in Meserole, *American Poetry*, 262; Shepard, *The Sound Believer*, in Jones and Jones, *Salva-*

tion in New England, 72; Hooker, *The Soules Effectual Calling* (London: 1637), quoted in Bush, *The Writings of Thomas Hooker*, 225; Scheick, "Theme, Structure, and Symbolism," 148–49. Scheick has recently incorporated his reading of "Contemplations" into an excellent study of artistic structures and intentional designs in Puritan writing (*Design in Puritan American Literature*). On the lesser insights afforded by a merely "notional" or "historical" faith, see Miller, *The New England Mind: The Seventeenth Century*, 31, 283.

8   *The Geneva Bible: A Facsimile of the 1560 Edition*, intro. Lloyd E. Berry (Madison: Univ. of Wisconsin Press, 1969), 238v. Cf. also Psalm 19:4–5: "In them hath he set a tabernacle for the sun; / Which is as a bridegroom coming out of his chamber, and rejoiceth as a strong man to run a race." Bradstreet's indebtedness to Psalm 19 is noted in Irvin, "Allegory and Typology," 35; Daly, *God's Altar*, 93; and Saltman, "'Contemplations': Anne Bradstreet's Spiritual Biography," 233. As Grabo points out, Bradstreet's use of "rapt" to describe her response to nature does not suggest tranquility but instead conveys sexual overtones indicating her perilous spiritual state ("The Veiled Vision," 32).

9   Phil. 2:10–11. On Taylor's use of this text to address a similar artistic dilemma, see James T. Callow, "Edward Taylor Obeys Saint Paul," *Early American Literature* 4 (1969): 89–96. Rosenmeier ("The Wounds Upon Bathsheba," 136) equates Bradstreet's mute "imbecility" with the condition voiced in Psalm 44: "My confusion is continually before me, and the shame of my face hath covered me" (Ps. 44:15); "If we have forgotten the name of our God, or stretched out our hands to a strange god; / Shall not God search this out? for he knoweth the secrets of the heart" (Ps. 44:20–21).

10 Lynen, *The Design of the Present*, 80. On the role of biblical history in convicting Bradstreet's speaker, see also Irvin, "Allegory and Typology," 38–39; Daly, *God's Altar*, 122; Saltman, "'Contemplations': Anne Bradstreet's Spiritual Biography," 231; Watts, "'The posy UNITY,'" 31–33; Rosenmeier, "The Wounds Upon Bathsheba," 136; Scheick, "Theme, Structure, and Symbolism," 149–50; and Rosenmeier, *Anne Bradstreet Revisited*, 146–47.

11 On this point see Saltman, "'Contemplations': Anne Bradstreet's Spiritual Biography," 231.

12 In his discussion of the artistry of "Contemplations," Scheick points out the emblematic nature of Bradstreet's imagery in creating a cruciform structure informing the entire poem. Scheick argues that the horizontality of the stream as an emblem of earthly experience and the verticality of the trees as emblems of a prelapsarian vision no longer available suggest the intersection of the two planes in pious meditation ("Theme, Structure, and Symbolism," 153–55; see also *Design in Puritan American Literature*, 35–45). Stanford observes that at this point in the poem Bradstreet's appreciation of nature is "bound to the structure of the emblem" ("Anne Bradstreet," 52).

13 As Daly observes, the poem articulates the Puritan mandate to live a "double life" in the temporal and the timeless realms (*God's Altar*, 122); Richardson similarly comments that the balance of heaven and earth effected by the poem was "best achieved by a life spent in searching rather than one spent in repose" ("The Puritan Poetry of Anne Bradstreet," 122). Anne Hildebrand relates the balance of opposing elements in "Contemplations" to the poet's search for cosmic harmony in the Quaternions ("Anne Bradstreet's Quaternions and 'Contemplations,'" 117–25).

14 On the otherworldly import of the white stone, see Richardson, "The Puritan Poetry of Anne Bradstreet," 121. Lynen comments that the ending "seems fitting just because it is conventional, because in a sense the whole purpose of the poem has been to arrive at this moment when orthodox opinion could be voiced appropriately" (*The Design of the Present*, 82), while Irvin observes that the "very conventionality" of the white stone "becomes part of the security of the promise it offers" ("Allegory and Typology," 43).
15 Critics noting the significance of Bradstreet's use of present tense in these stanzas include Richardson, "The Puritan Poetry of Anne Bradstreet," 116–17; and Walker, "Anne Bradstreet," 120.
16 Saltman identifies this Psalmic source ("'Contemplations': Anne Bradstreet's Spiritual Biography," 226). Bradstreet's structuring of time in the poem is discussed in Daly, *God's Altar*, 117–26; and Scheick, "Theme, Structure, and Symbolism."
17 Durham, *Clavis Cantici*, 151.
18 Rosenfeld, "Anne Bradstreet's 'Contemplations,'" 92; Lynen, *The Design of the Present*, 76; Rich, "Anne Bradstreet and Her Poetry," xviii.
19 Piercy, *Anne Bradstreet*, 69; Rosenmeier, "The Wounds Upon Bathsheba," 135; Walker, *The Nightingale's Burden*, 15.

Six. "Make Use of What I Leave in Love": The Saintly Self on Trial

1 Wigglesworth, *Poems*, 107; *The Geneva Bible*, 280v; Bradstreet, *Works*, 272. Subsequent quotations from Bradstreet refer to page numbers of this edition.
2 Piercy speculates that "The Flesh and the Spirit" reflects Bradstreet's "troubled conscience" for her "unabashed passion" for husband Simon (*Anne Bradstreet*, 88), while Elizabeth Wade White sees Flesh's arguments as evidence of the poet's particular struggle against the "sins of ambition and pride" (*Anne Bradstreet*, 340). Most recently, Martin finds an unusual inclination toward worldliness in the fact that Bradstreet's Spirit stresses "the *pleasures* of eternity" (*An American Triptych*, 52). As Rosenmeier points out, however, the Bible itself—in the book of Revelation—provides the precedent for the pleasure-centered description of heaven. "The infusion of scriptural overtones," she argues, "serves to augment the sensuousness of Bradstreet's imagery" ("The Wounds Upon Bathsheba," 132). By conceding the difficulty of resisting fleshly delights, Bradstreet's debate manifests what Richardson has called the "continual doubt of the sceptical mind" ("The Puritan Poetry of Anne Bradstreet," 111), a doubt inseparable, as Ball confirms, from "the morphology of conversion" ("Puritan Humility," 29–41).
3 Keller, *The Only Kangaroo among the Beauty*, 15.
4 Ball ("Puritan Humility," 33) and Mason ("The Other Voice," 211, 231) briefly relate Bradstreet's letter to the themes of the poetry.
5 "The Flesh and the Spirit" offered readers, as Richardson notes, a clear reminder that "a firm and doubt-free conviction of salvation was a probable sign of damnation" ("The Puritan Poetry of Anne Bradstreet," 111). Morison identifies Paul's treatise on inner struggle in Romans 8 as the chief source for the poem (*Builders of the Bay Colony*, 323).
6 See, for example, Stanford, "Anne Bradstreet: Dogmatist and Rebel," 387, and

Anne Bradstreet, 113–14; and Randall R. Mawer, "'Farewel Dear Babe': Bradstreet's Elegy for Elizabeth," *Early American Literature* 15 (1980): 33–35. By contrast, Daly (*God's Altar*, 109–17) and Hammond ("'Make Use of What I Leave in Love,'" 11–26) read this and the other family elegies as orthodox expressions of grief and of the spiritual challenge it posed. Ritamarie Sargent finds Bradstreet's elegies to be darker and more resigned than Edward Taylor's, which place greater emphasis on hope and resurrection ("Poetry and the Puritan Faith: The Elegies of Anne Bradstreet and Edward Taylor," in *A Salzburg Miscellany: English and American Studies, 1964–84*, ed. James Hogg [Salzburg: Universität Salzburg, 1984], 149–60).

7 Mawer, "'Farewel Dear Babe,'" 33, 30; Stanford, "Anne Bradstreet," 56. On the statement/question ambiguity of the inverted phrase, see Stanford, *Anne Bradstreet*, 113–14; and Michael Clark, "The Honeyed Knot of Puritan Aesthetics," in *Puritan Poets*, 78.

8 Mawer, "'Farewel Dear Babe,'" 33. The humility of Bradstreet's speaker is underscored by her biblical source for "humble hearts and mouths put in the dust," Lamentations 3:26–32: "It is good that a man should both hope and quietly wait for the salvation of the Lord. It is good for a man that he bear the yoke in his youth. He sitteth alone and keepeth silence, because he hath borne it upon him. He putteth his mouth in the dust; if so be there may be hope. . . . For the Lord will not cast off for ever: But though he cause grief, yet will he have compassion according to the multitude of his mercies." This source is identified in Cowell, "Why Our First Poet Was a Woman," 23.

9 Daly, *God's Altar*, 117; Mawer, "'Farewel Dear Babe,'" 32.

10 Mawer, "'Farewel Dear Babe,'" 36–37, 32; Martin, *An American Triptych*, 69–70; Weemse, *The Christian Synagogue*, 300; Daly, *God's Altar*, 111–12.

11 Perkins, *The Arte of Prophecying*, in *Workes*, 2:669; Bernard, *The Faithfull Shepherd*, 75.

12 Shepard, *God's Plot*, 198.

13 Critics who note the tension between pain and resignation in the house-fire poem include Martin, "Anne Bradstreet's Poetry," 30; Stanford, "Anne Bradstreet: Dogmatist and Rebel," 384, and *Anne Bradstreet*, 108–9; White, *Anne Bradstreet*, 349; Richardson, "The Puritan Poetry of Anne Bradstreet," 112; and Mawer, "'Farewel Dear Babe,'" 30–31.

14 On this point see Ball, "Puritan Humility," 31–33.

15 Rosenmeier, "'Divine Translation,'" 131–33. The role of eschatology in Bradstreet's work is discussed in Rosenmeier, "The Wounds Upon Bathsheba," 133–34; and Hambrick-Stowe, *The Practice of Piety*, 19–20, 59, 236–37.

16 Jane Donahue Eberwein, "Anne Bradstreet," in *Early American Poetry: Selections from Bradstreet, Taylor, Dwight, Freneau, and Bryant*, ed. Eberwein (Madison: Univ. of Wisconsin Press, 1978), 8.

17 On the "feminine" dimension of sainthood, see Margaret W. Masson, "The Typology of the Female as a Model for the Regenerate: Puritan Preaching, 1690–1730," *Signs: Journal of Women in Culture and Society* 2 (1976): 309–10; Amanda Porterfield, *Feminine Spirituality in America: From Sarah Edwards to Martha Graham* (Philadelphia: Temple Univ. Press, 1980), 19–50; and Schweitzer, *The Work of Self-Representation*, 1–39. Schweitzer concludes that because "redeemed subjectivity" in early New England was gendered as "female" and appropriated by male believers, actual women found themselves socially de-

valued and spiritually co-opted. For this reason, Bradstreet frequently adopted poetic roles that were forced upon her by her culture (165–80). Rosenmeier, by contrast, argues that Bradstreet was "comfortable" with the roles that she found, and that she artfully constructed a textual self from numerous manifestations of a biblical and spiritual "Wisdom" principle that was figured in "feminine" terms (*Anne Bradstreet Revisited*, esp. 80–101). Cowell also comments on Bradstreet's invocation of "a matrilineal 'family of sentiment' that included sanctified mothers like Hannah and St. Anne" ("Why Our First Poet Was a Woman," 19).

18 Rosenmeier, "The Wounds Upon Bathsheba," 139.
19 White, *Anne Bradstreet*, 380; Bernard, *The Faithfull Shepherd*, 385; Weemse, *The Christian Synagogue*, 301.

Seven. Apostle to a Naked Christ: *Gods Determinations* for Pilgrim Readers

1 Taylor, *Poems*, 1; Keller, "Edward Taylor, The Acting Poet," 188. For a summary of the early debate regarding Taylor's orthodoxy, see Grabo and Wainright, "Edward Taylor," 446–51; and Hammond, *Edward Taylor*, chapter 1. Full treatments of Taylor's conservative view of the Lord's Supper and his opposition to Solomon Stoddard's relaxed admission requirements can be found in Norman S. Grabo, "Introduction," *Edward Taylor's Treatise Concerning the Lord's Supper*, ed. Grabo (East Lansing: Michigan State Univ. Press, 1966), ix–li; and Thomas M. Davis, "Introduction," *Edward Taylor vs. Solomon Stoddard: The Nature of the Lord's Supper*, ed. Thomas M. Davis and Virginia L. Davis (Boston: Twayne, 1981), 1–57. Quotations from the *Preparatory Meditations* and *Gods Determinations* refer to page numbers of Stanford's edition; unless noted otherwise, all other poems are quoted from Taylor, *Minor Poetry*.
2 The fullest discussions of Taylor's early verse are Grabo, *Edward Taylor*, 108–15, and Dean G. Hall, "Edward Taylor: The Evolution of a Poet" (Ph.D. diss., Kent State University, 1977).
3 Taylor's poem was apparently inspired by "An Answer to a Popish Pamphlet," probably written by Robert Wild, which Taylor copied into his papers (see Taylor, *Minor Poetry*, 282–83; and David Sowd, "Edward Taylor's Answer to a 'Popish Pamphlet,'" *Early American Literature* 9 [1975]: 307–14).
4 Grabo, *Edward Taylor*, 110.
5 Edward Taylor, *A Transcript of Edward Taylor's Metrical History of Christianity*, ed. Donald E. Stanford (Cleveland: Micro Photo, 1962), 43, 229, 88; subsequent citations refer to page numbers of this edition. The fullest discussions of the *Metrical History* are Donald E. Stanford, "Edward Taylor's Metrical History of Christianity," *American Literature* 33 (1961): 279–95; and Keller, *The Example of Edward Taylor*, 141–59.
6 Keller, *The Example of Edward Taylor*, 149.
7 Keller, *The Example of Edward Taylor*, 157. Although he does not develop this dichotomy in terms of the poem's soteriological effects, Keller comments that "Taylor's uses of history in this poem show that before he can believe in the reality of salvation he must first have a perception of hell" (158). This passage in the *History* and the scornful reference in "An other answer" to "your Dad, Pope

Jone" anticipates Taylor's fascination late in life with the legend of the young Englishwoman who became Pope John VIII. The resulting "Verses on Pope Joan," which went through at least six versions, exemplifies the anti-Catholic core of Taylor's historiography. In his retelling, the gender ambiguity inherent in the legend—"be it Hick or Haec its dads delight"—becomes an allegory of a Papacy unmanned by corruption. "The Common Gender," he sneers, "necessarily / Doth with the popedom best of all comply" (Taylor, *Minor Poetry*, 259, 260). Joan's gender turns out to have been no impediment to her Papal duties: she "Holds out her Stinking toes to them to kiss / And Such as other popes did, so did this" (260). Claiming that "A Surer note is found lying in the taile" (261), he incorporates the "Porphory Chair" into a crude attack on Roman ceremony. At the confirmation of a new Pope's masculinity, "Habet, habet, is the trumpets sound." Like many Protestants of his era, Taylor clearly "delighted," as Davis observes, "in the discomfort—both personal and doctrinal—such a story caused" (249). Although it is difficult to judge whether Taylor accepted the legend as historical fact, he clearly wished to present the story, as Grabo points out, as "typical of Papal actions" (*Edward Taylor*, 114). Rome was, in the Puritan view, an institutional counterpart to the depravity hidden in each individual soul. A lukewarm struggle against such an enemy was worse than no struggle at all.

8   Donald E. Stanford, "Edward Taylor's Metrical History," 292.

9   The key study of *Gods Determinations* remains that of Michael Colacurcio, who was the first to define a specific rhetorical situation for the poem as a pastoral directive for Half-Way members of Taylor's congregation ("*Gods Determinations Touching Half-Way Membership*: Occasion and Audience in Edward Taylor," *American Literature* 39 [1967]: 298–314). Unlike treatments of Taylor's other verse, most discussions of *Gods Determinations* follow Colacurcio's lead by stressing the poem's effects on readers. See, for example, Grabo, *Edward Taylor*, 159–68; Lynen, *The Design of the Present*, 61–70; Keller, *The Example of Edward Taylor*, 129–38; Sargent Bush, Jr., "Paradox, Puritanism, and Taylor's *Gods Determinations*," *Early American Literature* 4 (1969–70): 48–66; Robert D. Arner, "Notes on the Structure of Edward Taylor's *Gods Determinations*," *Studies in the Humanities* 3 (1973): 27–29; John Gatta, Jr., "The Comic Design of *Gods Determinations touching his Elect*," *Early American Literature* 10 (1975): 121–43; David L. Parker, "Edward Taylor's Preparationism: A New Perspective on the Taylor-Stoddard Controversy," *Early American Literature* 11 (1976/77): 264–66; Dean G. Hall, "Edward Taylor: The Evolution of a Poet," 157–74; William J. Scheick, "The Jawbones Schema of Edward Taylor's *Gods Determinations*," in *Puritan Influences in American Literature*, ed. Emory Elliott (Urbana: Univ. of Illinois Press, 1979), 38–54; John Gatta, Jr., "Edward Taylor and Thomas Hooker: Two Physicians of the Poore Doubting Soul," *Notre Dame English Journal* 12 (1979): 1–13; Dennis H. Barbour, "*Gods Determinations* and the Hexameral Tradition," *Early American Literature* 16 (1981/82): 213–25; George Sebouhian, "Conversion Morphology and the Structure of *Gods Determinations*," *Early American Literature* 16 (1981/82): 226–40; J. Daniel Patterson, "*Gods Determinations*: The Occasion, The Audience, and Taylor's Hope for New England," *Early American Literature* 22 (1987): 63–81; Grabo, *Edward Taylor: Revised Edition*, 100–107; Gatta, *Gracious Laughter*, 107–40; Michael Schuldiner, *Gifts and Works: Spiritual Life and Political Controversy in Seventeenth-Century Massachu-*

setts (Macon, Ga.: Mercer Univ. Press, 1990), 111–22; Scheick, *Design in Puritan American Literature*, 23–29; and Thomas M. Davis, *A Reading of Edward Taylor*, 27–47.

10 Weemse, *The Christian Synagogue*, 284; Perkins, *The Arte of Prophecying*, in *Workes*, 2:668, 664, 666, 667.

11 Perkins, *Workes*, 2:664; Wigglesworth, *The Day of Doom*, in *Poems*, 17. Subsequent quotations from *The Day of Doom* refer to page numbers of this edition.

12 Barbour observes that by omitting Adam's name "Taylor seeks to force his readers to identify with 'man,' not to separate themselves from Adam and Eve, and to share the guilt for original sin" ("*Gods Determinations* and the Hexameral Tradition," 217). The role that conviction plays in the poem is also discussed by Colacurcio ("Occasion and Audience," 304–5), Sebouhian ("Conversion Morphology and the Structure of *Gods Determinations*," 227–28, 237–38), and Parker, who notes that Taylor stresses the efficacy of Soul's humiliation by linking it with mercy rather than justice ("Edward Taylor's Preparationism," 265).

13 Gatta calls the poem a "counterjeremiad" that combats "the evil of spiritual melancholia through the medicine of divine love" (*Gracious Laughter*, 103). On this point also see Colacurcio, "Occasion and Audience," 305–6. On the role of the second "Preface" in introducing pastoral consolation available within the church, see Arner, "Notes on the Structure," 28–29; and Gatta, *Gracious Laughter*, 129–33.

14 Shepard, *The Sound Believer*, in *Works*, 1:256; Hooker, *Application*, 381. Scheick underscores the contrast between dichotomous sin and unifying grace by pointing out that Taylor's Satan thrives on conflict and disputation, as opposed to the reconciliation forged by the divine dispensations ("Jawbones Schema," 47–49; *Design in Puritan American Literature*, 23–29). Elsewhere he discusses Taylor's attempts in the *Preparatory Meditations* to assert through metaphor a similarly gracious perception of the unity of heaven and earth (*The Will and the Word*, 8–22, 132–44). Scheick's comment on Taylor's ongoing attempt in the Meditations "to assert his self and to appraise that self's relation to the 'Sacred Self'" applies equally to the reader of *Gods Determinations*, especially in the second half of the poem (161). Gatta similarly notes that "one must regard Soul not simply as a personage acting within the narrative but also as that implied character who is 'outside the poem' looking in at his own sad reflection" (*Gracious Laughter*, 125).

15 Ames, *Marrow of Theology*, 214.

16 Thomas Hall, *Centuria Sacra*, 72–73. Studies of the imagery and language of *Gods Determinations* include Peter Nicolaisen, *Die Bildlichkeit in der Dichtung Edward Taylors* (Neumünster: Karl Wachholtz, 1966), 138–57; Dean G. Hall, "Edward Taylor: The Evolution of a Poet," 176–91; and Robert D. Arner, "Proverbs in Edward Taylor's *Gods Determinations*," *Southern Folklore Quarterly* 37 (1973): 1–13.

17 Shepard, *The Sound Believer*, in *Works*, 218. Herbert Blau long ago connected the lullaby with Taylor's "compassion" toward troubled readers ("Heaven's Sugar Cake: Theology and Imagery in the Poetry of Edward Taylor," *New England Quarterly* 26 [1953]: 341). An equally enticing Christ frequently appears in Taylor's sermons. At the foundation of the Westfield church, for instance, he turns the Canticles Bridegroom's call for the Bride into a direct challenge to his hearers' ability to "withstand such soul inravishing Rhetorick": "Methinks it

should be like unto Sweet wine, that Causeth the lips of him that is asleep to Speak & answer. O then attend on the Call & reply to the same saying I come Lord" (Taylor, *Edward Taylor's "Church Records" and Related Sermons*, 152–53).

18 Cf. the Canticles Bride's boast that "While the king sitteth at his table, my spikenard sendeth forth the smell thereof" (Cant. 1:12). Scheick ("Jawbones Schema"; *Design in Puritan American Literature*, 23–29) and Gatta ("Comic Design," 132–34, 137; *Gracious Laughter*, 120–27) offer the fullest discussions of Satan's role in the poem.

19 Keller (*The Example of Edward Taylor*, 136), Dean G. Hall ("Edward Taylor: The Evolution of a Poet," 145, 205–6), and Davis ("Introduction," *Edward Taylor's Minor Poetry*, xvi; *A Reading of Edward Taylor*, 42–46) note the correspondence in tone and diction between these lyrics and the Meditations, while Grabo sees the final lyrics as "a statement of moved affections" that completes the meditative structure of *Gods Determinations* as a whole (*Edward Taylor: Revised Edition*, 106).

20 Hooker, *Application*, 162.

21 Bernard, *The Faithfull Shepherd*, 75, 108. The "Profession" of faith that Taylor drew up at the founding of the Westfield church depicts hell in terms far more terrifying than anything in Wigglesworth. At one point Taylor affirms that if all the world were on fire and if all the winds on earth were fanning the flames directly on the hearer, "yet it would not be So much as a fleabiting compared unto the torments of Hell. Oh! the bodily tortures! as they reise upon it, which the body Sucks up as a spunge doth water. Oh! how are they drunke in at the Senses & every way." Although Wigglesworth holds the popular reputation for fire and brimstone, it is Taylor's hell that is filled with "roaring, yelling, frying, Crying, tering, rending, froathing, fo[a]ming under the wrath of the almighty, trembling. Oh! dreadfull sight, oh hidious screech!" (Taylor, *Edward Taylor's "Church Records" and Related Sermons*, 84).

22 Hooker, *The Soules Preparation*, 69; Shepard, *Works*, 1:161.

Eight. "Both Wayes Born": Edward Taylor as Weary Pilgrim

1 Taylor, *Minor Poetry*, 102; Davis, "Introduction," *Minor Poetry*, xi. The dating of these early poems supports Davis's view: most of them, recopied in the early 1680s in a manuscript alluding to "occurrants occasioning what follow" (297), seem to have been written at about the time of *Gods Determinations* and the earliest of the Meditations. Davis provides the most detailed discussions of Taylor's poetry in the context of his ministry in Westfield ("Introduction," *Edward Taylor's "Church Records" and Related Sermons*, xi–xl; and *A Reading of Edward Taylor*). Studies of Taylor's occasional and public poems, which have as yet received little scholarly attention, will likely be stimulated by the recent publication of Raymond A. Craig's *Concordance to the Minor Poetry of Edward Taylor (1642?–1729): American Colonial Poet*, 2 vols. (Lewiston, N.Y.: Edwin Mellen Press, 1992). Unless noted otherwise, all quotations from Taylor's verse in this chapter refer to page numbers of the *Minor Poetry*.

2 Thomas H. Johnson, "The Topical Verses of Edward Taylor," *Colonial Society of Massachusetts Publications* 34 (1943): 518; Grabo, *Edward Taylor: Revised Edition*, 62; Meditation 1.20, in Taylor, *Poems*, 35. On Taylor's familiarity with the classics, which comprised an important part of his studies at Harvard, see John C.

Shields, "Jerome in Colonial New England: Edward Taylor's Attitude toward Classical Paganism," *Studies in Philology* 81 (1984): 161–84.

3. For a reading of this poem that argues for Taylor's more secular interest in nature, see Lawrence Lan Sluder, "God in the Background: Edward Taylor as Naturalist," *Early American Literature* 7 (1973): 265–71. Catherine Rainwater discusses Taylor's relation to the science of his day in two excellent studies of the poet's creative accommodation to current astronomy and medicine ("Edward Taylor's Reluctant Revolution: The New Astronomy in the *Preparatory Meditations*," *American Poetry* 1, no. 2 [1984]: 4–17; and "'This Brazen Serpent is a Doctors Shop': Edward Taylor's Medical Vision," *Studies in Puritan American Spirituality* 2 [1991]: 51–75).

4. Bradstreet, *Works*, 207; Taylor, *Poems*, 37.

5. Taylor's account of the flood, which struck Westfield in the summer of 1683, can be found in *Edward Taylor's "Church Records" and Related Sermons*, 179.

6. The full title is illegible in the "Poetical Works" manuscript. The title supplied by Thomas H. Johnson was "An Address to the Soul Occasioned by a Rain" (*The Poetical Works of Edward Taylor*, 113); Davis and Davis read the title as ". . . a Let by rain" (*Minor Poetry*, 102). Donald E. Stanford's title, used here, is "[When] Let by Rain" (*Poems*, 463). John Gatta relates this poem to the salvific turmoil of Romans 8:22, in which "the whole creation groaneth and travaileth in pain together until now" (*Gracious Laughter*, 198). For a recent discussion of Herbert's influence on early American poetry, including Taylor's, see John T. Shawcross, "Some Colonial American Poetry and George Herbert," *Early American Literature* 23 (1988): 28–51.

7. Cotton Mather, *Right Thoughts in Sad Hours* (London: 1689), 56. Mather's publication of these stanzas was discovered by Thomas H. Johnson and described in "A Seventeenth-Century Printing of Some Verses of Edward Taylor," 139–41.

8. Bradstreet, *Works*, 237. As Grabo observes, "Taylor has learned Job's lesson: he is not to speak from the bitterness of his heart" (*Edward Taylor: Revised Edition*, 80).

9. Grabo, *Edward Taylor: Revised Edition*, 77.

10. Edward Pearse, *The Great Concern; or, A Serious Warning to a Timely and Thorough Preparation for Death* (Boston: 1711), 70–71. *The Great Concern* is item number 144 in Johnson's inventory of Taylor's library (*Poetical Works*, 216). As Roy Harvey Pearce observes, "the occasion of a death, the point just before final proof of election or damnation, gave the Puritan poet his greatest opportunity. Now a man, newly dead, would really *know*. And the poet would bear witness to that knowledge, if only he could work out the way of getting it" (*Continuity*, 25). On the importance of the *ars moriendi* tradition in Protestant culture see Louis L. Martz, *The Poetry of Meditation* (New Haven: Yale Univ. Press, 1962), 135–44; Nancy Lee Beaty, *The Craft of Dying: A Study in the Literary Tradition of the Ars Moriendi* (New Haven: Yale Univ. Press, 1970), 108–56; and David E. Stannard, *The Puritan Way of Death: A Study in Religion, Culture, and Social Change* (New York: Oxford Univ. Press, 1977).

Studies of the American Puritan elegy include John W. Draper, *The Funeral Elegy and the Rise of English Romanticism* (New York: New York Univ. Press, 1929), 155–77; Robert Henson, "Form and Content of the Puritan Funeral Elegy," *American Literature* 32 (1960): 11–27; Pearce, *Continuity*, 24–41; Kenneth Silverman, ed., *Colonial American Poetry* (New York: Hafner, 1968), 121–32;

Edwin T. Bowden, "Urian Oakes' Elegy: Colonial Literature and History," *Forum* 10 (1972): 2–8; T. G. Hahn, "Urian Oakes's *Elegie* on Thomas Shepard and Puritan Poetics," *American Literature* 45 (1973): 163–81; Dickran Tashjian and Ann Tashjian, *Memorials for Children of Change* (Middletown: Wesleyan Univ. Press, 1974), 39–44; William J. Scheick, "Standing in the Gap: Urian Oakes' Elegy on Thomas Shepard," *Early American Literature* 9 (1975): 301–6; Astrid Schmitt-v. Muhlenfels, "John Fiske's Funeral Elegy on John Cotton," *Early American Literature* 12 (1977): 49–62; Daly, *God's Altar*, 113–17, 147–51, 162–76; Emory Elliott, "The Development of the Puritan Funeral Sermon and Elegy: 1660–1750," *Early American Literature* 15 (1980): 151–64; Sargent, "Poetry and the Puritan Faith," 1:149–60; Scheick, "Tombless Virtue and Hidden Text," 286–302; Hammond, "From Sinful Silence to Apostolic Voice," 77–106; Schweitzer, *The Work of Self-Representation*, 41–74; and Scheick, *Design in Puritan American Literature*, 80–88. The only Taylor elegy not in *Minor Poetry* is the poem on David Dewey, which is quoted from Thomas M. Davis, "Edward Taylor's Elegy on Deacon David Dewey," *Proceedings of the American Antiquarian Society* 96, Part 1 (1986): 75–84.

11 Willard, *The High Esteem Which God hath of the Death of his Saints* (Boston: 1683), in *The Puritans*, ed. Miller and Johnson, 1:371, 373; Oakes, "An ELEGIE Upon . . . Thomas Shepard," in Meserole, *American Poetry*, 217; Ames, *Marrow of Theology*, 174. Silverman calls Puritan elegiac subjects "portraits of the Saved Soul" and the "idealized great man" (*Colonial American Poetry*, 123, 127), while Scheick argues that the elegist's portrayal of "the broad configuration of saintliness" enhanced the deceased's function as a communal self with whom each believer could identify ("Tombless Virtue and Hidden Text," 290–94, 296). Ronald A. Bosco discusses similarly generalized saintly portraits in funeral sermons, which were also designed to promote the deceased's pious example ("Introduction," *New England Funeral Sermons* [Delmar, N.Y.: Scholars' Facsimiles and Reprints, 1978], xxvi–xxviii).

12 Scheick ("Tombless Virtue and Hidden Text," 297), Hammond ("From Sinful Silence to Apostolic Voice," 87–90), and Schweitzer (*The Work of Self-Representation*, 69–71) comment on the deceased's role in the Puritan elegy as a text of piety, while Tashjian and Tashjian observe that "In a transcendent yet concrete bisecting dimension, the deceased *becomes* the poem, chanted by the elegist, reenacting the interpenetration of word and flesh" (*Memorials for Children of Change*, 44).

13 Ames, *Marrow of Theology*, 256; Willard, *The Puritans*, 1:373. In their discussion of the anagrams often affixed to Puritan elegies, Tashjian and Tashjian argue that Puritan language produces "a verbal correlative to the spiritual metamorphosis" of the saint: "In his discovery of the anagram the poet was simply recreating that which had already occurred spiritually, by demonstrating the iconic power perceived in words" (*Memorials for Children of Change*, 44).

14 Ruth Wallerstein, *Studies in Seventeenth-Century Poetic* (Madison: Univ. of Wisconsin Press, 1950), 110–11; Taylor, *Poems*, 283. On the Puritan belief that a saint's virtues subjected the elegist to the false charge of committing hyperbole, see Schmitt-v. Muhlenfels ("John Fiske's Funeral Elegy," 52–53), Silverman (*Colonial American Poetry*, 126), and Bowden, who comments that Urian Oakes's rejection of wit in his tribute to Thomas Shepard II reflects the "Augustinian assumption that true height in style springs not from rhetorical ornamentation

externally imposed, but from the height of the thought itself, the spontaneous and exalted contemplation of the truths being expressed. This is the 'high style' of the Bible" ("Urian Oakes' Elegy," 7). For a perceptive discussion of Puritan writing in terms of a tension between the Renaissance elevation of language as a sign of human specialness and the Reformation suspicion of language as yet another sign of postlapsarian corruption, see Scheick, *Design in Puritan American Literature*, 19–23.

15 Willard, *The Puritans*, 1:372.

16 To elegize, as Peter Sacks observes in reference to the English elegy, is to put into motion a necessary adaptation to change, to perform an act of concession in which "the mourner must prevent a congealing of his own impulses" (*The English Elegy: Studies in the Genre from Spenser to Yeats* [Baltimore: Johns Hopkins Univ. Press, 1985], 22). For Taylor, as for all Puritan elegists, this translated into a need *not* to remain silently convicted in the face of God's will, but to pull oneself and the reader out of sinful paralysis. At the death of John Hull, for example, John Saffin commands his muse to "Shake off the Shackles of thy Contemplation" and "Rouse up thy drooping Spirits, dull invention / That the most unconcern'd may give Attention" (*American Poetry*, 199).

17 On the relation of the "wedden garment" imagery of "Huswifery" to Taylor's views on the Lord's Supper, see Grabo, "Introduction," ix–li.

NINE. "THIS CRUMB OF DUST": PILGRIM VOICE AND CHRISTIC READER IN THE *PREPARATORY MEDITATIONS*

1 Earlier criticisms of Taylor's technique appear in Sidney E. Lind, "Edward Taylor: A Revaluation," *New England Quarterly* 21 (1948): 518–30; Blau, "Heaven's Sugar Cake," 337–60; and Donald E. Stanford, *Edward Taylor* (Minneapolis: Univ. of Minnesota Press, 1965), 44. More recently, Keller has argued that Taylor constructs his images randomly (*The Example of Edward Taylor*, 161–88); Lewalski asserts that his rigid adherence to typological and emblem traditions weakened his verse (*Protestant Poetics*, 144, 212); Rowe maintains that his indebtedness to typological frameworks reflects "a poet with limited skill, but glorious ambitions" (*Saint and Singer*, 270); and Grabo reconfirms Taylor's inconsistent development of themes and images (*Edward Taylor: Revised Edition*, 82).

Defenses of Taylor's poetic practice based on Puritan aesthetic and spiritual traditions include William J. Scheick, "'The Inward Tacles and the Outward Traces': Edward Taylor's Elusive Transitions," *Early American Literature* 12 (1977): 163–76; Michael Schuldiner, "Edward Taylor's 'Problematic' Imagery," *Early American Literature* 13 (1978): 92–101; Peter White, "An Analysis of Edward Taylor's *Preparatory Meditation 2.1*," *Concerning Poetry* 11 (1978): 19–23; Jeffrey A. Hammond, "Reading Taylor Exegetically: The *Preparatory Meditations* and the Commentary Tradition," *Texas Studies in Literature and Language* 24 (1982): 347–71; William J. Scheick, "Order and Disorder in Taylor's Poetry: Meditation 1.8," *American Poetry* 5 (1988): 2–11; Scheick, "Unfolding the Serpent in Taylor's 'Meditation 1.19,'" *Studies in Puritan American Spirituality* 1 (1990): 34–64; and Scheick, *Design in Puritan American Literature*, 24–29, 45–67.

2 Taylor, *Poems*, 1; Cohen, *God's Caress*, 101, 104. Quotations from the Medi-

tations, cited by Series and Meditation number, refer to Stanford's edition. The most detailed study of the spiritual processes informing the Meditations is Scheick, *The Will and the Word*; but also see Donald Junkins, "'Should Stars Wooe Lobster Claws?': A Study of Edward Taylor's Poetic Practice and Theory," *Early American Literature* 3 (1968): 88–117; Mignon, "Edward Taylor's *Preparatory Meditations*," 1423–28; Daly, *God's Altar*, 185–99; Rowe, *Saint and Singer*, 114–30; Grabo, *Edward Taylor: Revised Edition*, 20–51; Gatta, *Gracious Laughter*; Schweitzer, *The Work of Self-Representation*, 79–125; and Davis, *A Reading of Edward Taylor*.

3   Keller proposed that Taylor is best seen as an "acting poet" who made a "decision at some point to play a part before God, and now before us as rediscoverers." Taylor's role, Keller suggests, was that of a "Prepared Persona" shaped by Puritan notions regarding the psychology of the saved soul ("Edward Taylor, The Acting Poet," 190). Keller's proposition is useful so long as we recognize 1) that Taylor did not use a "persona" in the sense of deliberately manufacturing a fictive self, and 2) that his "prepared" speaker has nothing to do with preparation for salvation. Rather, the Meditations addressed his post-conversion search for what Louis Martz called an "assurance of an affectionate realization" of the faith that was the ongoing goal of all believers ("Foreword," *The Poems of Edward Taylor*, xxii). On this point also see Norman Pettit, "The Puritan Legacy," *New England Quarterly* 48 (1975): 283–94.

4   Durham, *Clavis Cantici*, 51. Durham appears in the inventory of Taylor's library in *The Poetical Works of Edward Taylor*, 206.

5   Keller, *The Example of Edward Taylor*, 74; Scheick, *The Will and the Word*, 161; King, *The Iron of Melancholy*, 7. Gatta similarly notes "the self's alchemical refashioning" as a function of Taylor's role as an "Everysaint" (*Gracious Laughter*, 155, 76), while Rowe comments that Taylor's "inward journey" is "paradigmatic of every Puritan saint's aspiration for spiritual transcendence" (*Saint and Singer*, 223). Other discussions of biblical and spiritual patterns informing Taylor's poetic voice include Karen E. Rowe, "Sacred or Profane? Edward Taylor's Meditations on Canticles," *Modern Philology* 72 (1974): 123–38; Lewalski, *Protestant Poetics*, 416–25; Jeffrey A. Hammond, "A Puritan *Ars Moriendi*: Edward Taylor's Late Meditations on the Song of Songs," *Early American Literature* 17 (1982/83): 191–214; Rosemary Fithian, "'Words of My Mouth, Meditations of My Heart': Edward Taylor's *Preparatory Meditations* and the Book of Psalms," *Early American Literature* 20 (1985): 89–119; Michael Schuldiner, "The Christian Hero and the Classical Journey in Edward Taylor's 'Preparatory Meditations. First Series,'" *Huntington Library Quarterly* 49 (1986): 113–32; Jeffrey A. Hammond, "Who Is Edward Taylor?: Voice and Reader in the *Preparatory Meditations*," *American Poetry* 7, no. 3 (1990): 2–19; and Schweitzer, *The Work of Self-Representation*, esp. 123–25.

6   Shepard, *The Sound Believer*, in *Works*, 1:256; Ames, *Marrow of Theology*, 171, 170, 176; Taylor, *Christographia*, 229.

7   Hooker, *The Soules Preparation*, 122; Shepard, *Sound Believer*, 146, 175; Perkins, *The Arte of Prophecying*, in *Workes*, 2:667; Shepard, *God's Plot*, 198; Taylor, *Christographia*, 61. Taylor's doubleness as one self who sins and another who looks on in disgust supports Gatta's observation that for all his self-recriminations, the poet attacks his sins and "not his own person" (*Gracious Laughter*, 20). Rowe agrees that Taylor "views his religion in dichotomous terms—as a

framework that disciplines the worldly and corrupt impulses of mankind and as a source of inspiration that promises man ineffable joys" (*Saint and Singer*, 276). For a contrasting reading that argues for Taylor's participation in "a poetics of panic" stemming from the homoerotic implications of the spiritual marriage, see Hughes, "Panic and Desire in American Puritan Poetry," 115–21.

8 Shepard, *God's Plot*, 198. On the Puritan need to preserve a clear sense of difference between the divine and human planes, a need that balanced ongoing attempts to bridge the gap between them, see Clark, "The Honeyed Knot of Puritan Aesthetics," 67–83.

9 Collinges, *The Intercourses of Divine Love* (London: 1676), 73. Several scholars comment on Taylor's ongoing suspension between such opposites as "certitude and doubt" (Charles W. Mignon, "A Principle of Order in Edward Taylor's *Preparatory Meditations*," *Early American Literature* 4 [1970]: 116), "pride and hypocrisy" (Michael Reed, "Edward Taylor's Poetry: Puritan Structure and Form," *American Literature* 46 [1974]: 311), "presumption and despair" (Scheick, "Order and Disorder," 8), "the temporal and the eternal realms" (Scheick, *The Will and the Word*, 131), and "rationality" and "heightened affections" (Rowe, *Saint and Singer*, 275–76). As Scheick points out, Taylor's refusal to resolve his suspension through total union with Christ illustrates why he should not be considered "mystical" in the usual sense of the word (*The Will and the Word*, 151–56; on this point also see Blake, "Edward Taylor's Protestant Poetic," 1–24; and Lewalski, *Protestant Poetics*, 417. In her provocative study, the first detailed discussion of the impact of gendered "subjectivity" on Puritan poetry, Schweitzer describes Taylor's appropriation of a "feminized" identity in relation to Christ as a means of representing and maintaining "the requisite difference" between the human and the divine "that the Augustinian strain in Puritanism, with its mystical tug toward unmediated vision, always threatens to dissolve" (*The Work of Self-Representation*, 97). The strongest argument for Taylor as a mystic was advanced by Grabo (*Edward Taylor*); in his revision Grabo modified his position, stating that the poet could follow "a mystical literary tradition without himself being a mystic" (*Edward Taylor: Revised Edition*, xi).

10 Weemse, *The Christian Synagogue*, 284; Keller, "Edward Taylor, The Acting Poet," 193.

11 Taylor, *Christographia*, 362; Scheick, *The Will and the Word*, 87.

12 Taylor, *Christographia*, 102, 305; Ames, *Marrow of Theology*, 131, 129; Weemse, *The Christian Synagogue*, 295. On Taylor's enactment of an *imitatio Christi* in the Meditations see Scheick, *The Will and the Word*, 159–61; Daly, *God's Altar*, 184; Rowe, *Saint and Singer*, 251–56; and Schweitzer, *The Work of Self-Representation*, 93, 98–99.

13 John Wilkins, *Ecclesiastes; or, A Discourse concerning the Gift of Preaching as it fals under the rules of Art* (London: 1646), 16; Perkins, *Workes*, 2:666.

14 Taylor, *Christographia*, 420.

15 Donald Stanford suggests that Taylor's desire to recover the intensity of the event recorded in the titled poems was a "prime motivation" for all of the Meditations ("Edward Taylor," in *Major Writers of Early American Literature*, 70); Gatta agrees that this "specific episode of mystical illumination" may have prompted his decision to begin his numbered poems (*Gracious Laughter*, 142). For an excellent study of Taylor's initial artistic and meditative ambitions and

his subsequent shift to a more limited view of his art, see Davis, *A Reading of Edward Taylor*.

16 Shepard, *The Sincere Convert*, in *Works*, 1:72; Perkins, *Workes*, 2:650. Scheick discusses Taylor's mandate to use reason to its fullest capabilities in *The Will and the Word*, 5–26.

17 Scheick argues that Taylor's optical images relate to the poet's desire for a renewed understanding, while images of hearing reflect most directly his desire for a renewed will (*The Will and the Word*, 83–84; "Edward Taylor's Optics," *American Literature* 55 [1983]: 234–40).

18 Smaller units in the Second Series include Meds. 31–33 (John 15:13); Meds. 36–40 (Col. 1:18); Meds. 58–61 (Exodus motifs); Meds. 62–65 (the Canticles Garden); Meds. 67[A]–68[B] (Mal. 4:2); Meds. 74–76 (Phil. 3:21); Meds. 77–78 (Zech. 9:11); Meds. 80–82 (John 6:53); Meds. 83–86 (Cant. 5:1); Meds. 87–89 [no. 88] (John 10:10); Meds. 91–92 (Matt. 24–27); Meds. 93–95 (John 14:2); Meds. 96–98 (Cant. 1:2); Meds. 99–101 (Isa. 24:23); and Meds. 113–14 (Rev. 22:16).

19 For an excellent discussion of the types in relation to Taylor's poetic ritual see Rowe, *Saint and Singer*, 114–30. Grabo also sees the Meditations as verbal sacrifices reflecting Taylor's spiritual and meditative duty (*Edward Taylor: Revised Edition*, 67–68). Studies of Taylor's use of typology include, in addition to Rowe, Peter Nicolaisen, *Die Bildlichkeit in der Dichtung Edward Taylors*, 110–31; Thomas M. Davis, "Edward Taylor and the Traditions of Puritan Typology," *Early American Literature* 4 (1969/70): 27–47; Robert Reiter, "Poetry and Typology: Edward Taylor's *Preparatory Meditations*, Second Series, Numbers 1–30," *Early American Literature* 5 (1970): 111–23; Brumm, *American Thought and Religious Typology*, 56–85; William J. Scheick, "Typology and Allegory: A Comparative Study of George Herbert and Edward Taylor," *Essays in Literature* 2 (1975): 76–86; Lewalski, *Protestant Poetics*, 405–9; Mason I. Lowance, Jr., *The Language of Canaan: Metaphor and Symbol in New England from the Puritans to the Transcendentalists* (Cambridge: Harvard Univ. Press, 1980), 96–111; Charles W. Mignon, "Introduction," *Upon the Types of the Old Testament* (Lincoln: Univ. of Nebraska Press, 1989), xix–lxxvii; and Davis, *A Reading of Edward Taylor*, 145–62.

20 Samuel Mather, *The Figures or Types of the Old Testament* (1705; reprint, New York: Johnson Reprint Corporation, 1969), 215, 209; Thomas Taylor, *Christ Revealed; or, The Old Testament Explained* (London: 1635), 271.

21 Mather, *Figures or Types*, 273.

22 Critics who identify the Bible and not the natural world as the predominant source of Taylor's imagery include Nicolaisen (*Die Bildlichkeit*, 38), Keller (*The Example of Edward Taylor*, 57–58), Daly (*God's Altar*, 176–79), Grabo (*Edward Taylor: Revised Edition*, 92–93), and Davis (*A Reading of Edward Taylor*, 17–18, 199–203).

23 Ames, *Marrow of Theology*, 260.

24 That Taylor deprecates his art from a divine and not human standpoint is noted by Scheick, *The Will and the Word*, 113; Daly, *God's Altar*, 186; Grabo, *Edward Taylor: Revised Edition*, 69; and Gatta, *Gracious Laughter*, 15, 64.

25 Mignon, "Edward Taylor's *Preparatory Meditations*." On Taylor's use of the Pauline injunction as a means of confronting his artistic dilemma, see Callow,

"Edward Taylor Obeys Saint Paul," 89–96. On Taylor's deliberate enacting of poetic failure, see also Lewalski (*Protestant Poetics*, 391) and Junkins (" 'Should Stars Wooe Lobster Claws?' ").

26 These bargains take two essential forms. In the first, Taylor petitions for stronger assurance and better song in the here and now: "If thou Conduct mee in thy Fathers Wayes, / I'le be the Golden Trumpet of thy Praise" (1.24); "Lord speak it home to me, say these are mine. / My Bells shall then thy Praises bravely chime" (1.32); "Be thou my head, and act my tongue whereby / Its tittle-tattle may thee glorify" (2.37); "When with this Paschall bread and Wine I'm brisk / I in sweet Tunes thy sweetest praise will twist" (2.71); "If thou my Lilly, I its Vally bee. / My Breath shall Lilly tunes sweet sing to thee" (2.132); "Lord feed mee with this promisd food of Life / And I will sing thy praise in songs most rife" (2.161A).

The second type of bargain projects better song into an eschatological future. As Taylor confirms in "The Experience," "I praise thee, Lord, and better praise thee would / If what I had, my heart might ever hold" – and the place where he anticipates genuinely sustained spiritual and artistic fulfillment is heaven: "And when my Clay ball's in thy White robes dresst / My tune perfume thy praise shall with the best" (1.46); "I'le read, and read it; and With Angells soon / My Mictams shall thy Hallelujahs tune" (2.8); "Then I shall weare thy Nazarite like Crown / In Glory bright with Songs of thy Renown" (2.15); "Still this on me untill I glory Gain. / And then Ile sing thy praise in better Strain" (2.25); "And though not now, I then shall sing thy praise. / In that thy love did tende me all my dayes" (2.96); "And leade mee on in Graces path along / To Glory, then I'l sing a brighter song" (2.105); "Then when my Crystall Cup grows full to the brim / Thy praise sweet to my tast my harp shall sing" (2.162).

27 Weemse, *The Christian Synagogue*, 301; Keller, "Edward Taylor, The Acting Poet," 191; Taylor, *Christographia*, 313.

28 Keller, "Edward Taylor, The Acting Poet," 194. Keller remarked that poetry "became a way of extending the range of the myth that bound him. The ideology was perhaps livable without such a device, though perhaps not yet alive in *him* until he wrote" (*The Example of Edward Taylor*, 236). A spiritual parallel to Keller's suggestion of a "liberating" role for Puritan poetry appears in Cohen's thesis that Puritans could be more certain of their salvation than is commonly thought: "God encourages the believer with hope of mercy, and hope, looking toward His 'unspeakable compassions,' makes it 'clear and certain' that the regenerate already possess His glory" (*God's Caress*, 101). Arguing that conversion gave the saint a power "to cooperate with grace in combating the flesh" (210), Cohen stresses the believer's transformation into a New Creature with a renewed will (95–98), a transformation that the Meditations repeatedly invoke. Other discussions of post-conversion spiritual experience in early New England include Hambrick-Stowe, *The Practice of Piety*, 198–203; and Schuldiner, *Gifts and Works*.

29 Ames, *Marrow of Theology*, 248; Shepard, *Works*, 1:218.

30 Scheick, *The Will and the Word*, 161; Keller, *The Example of Edward Taylor*, 74; Patricia Meyer Spacks, *Imagining a Self: Autobiography and Novel in Eighteenth-Century England* (Cambridge: Harvard Univ. Press, 1976), 19; Stephen Greenblatt, *Renaissance Self-Fashioning: From More to Shakespeare* (Chicago: Univ. of Chicago Press, 1980). Michael Clark, similarly rejecting a literally expressive or

autobiographical approach to Taylor's language, has called the poetry a "discursive gesture" by which the poet could "situate" himself "within a broad network of social relations and theological hierarchies" ("The Subject of the Text in Early American Literature," *Early American Literature* 20 [1985]: 125, 129).

The nature of Taylor's "self-fashioning" has been the focus of some debate. While Keller argues that the poet expanded himself into "the Taylor of his desires: a man actively engaged in a relationship with God" (*The Example of Edward Taylor*, 74), Scheick counters that "Taylor's cultural influences . . . resulted in a contraction of the poetic self in his work" ("Typology and Allegory," 85). Although Keller errs in terming Taylor's relation with the divine "forbidden by his theology" (if anything, his theology mandated such a relation), both critics are correct in suggesting that the voice of the Meditations is not simply Edward Taylor's: the poet contracts his "real" self—Taylor would call it his "carnal" self—by suppressing whatever was irrelevant to his search for assurance, but he also expands his voice by appropriating saintly patterns transcending that self.

31 Hooker, *Application*, 328; Durham, *Clavis Cantici*, 51; Hooker, *The Soul's Preparation*, 152.

TEN. "IN SACRED TEXT I WRITE": THE TAYLORIAN SELF AS THE WORD

1 Taylor, *Poems*, 1; quotations from the Meditations, cited by series and poem number, refer to this edition.
2 Rous, *The Mysticall Marriage*, 237. As Scheick observes, "Taylor looked to his own art for a sign of God's voice to him" (*The Will and the Word*, 122); Gatta similarly comments that for Taylor, writing released "the Word stored in Scripture" as a means of activating a warm sense of assurance (*Gracious Laughter*, 56).
3 On Taylor's anticipation of better song in heaven see Mignon, "Edward Taylor's *Preparatory Meditations*," 1424; Scheick, *The Will and the Word*, 113; Daly, *God's Altar*, 176; Lewalski, *Protestant Poetics*, 249, 423; and Rowe, *Saint and Singer*, 273.
4 For a discussion of reformed vision and will in the Meditations, see Scheick, *The Will and the Word*, and "Edward Taylor's Optics," 234–40.
5 Clapham, *Three Partes*, A4v.
6 Perkins, *The Art of Prophecying*, in *Workes*, 2:649.
7 Ames, *Marrow of Theology*, 188.
8 Taylor repeatedly concedes that while reason cannot grasp the Word, it is even less capable of responding to it properly because the understanding is still bonded to carnal identity. Christ's glory as the repository of "all the treasures of wisdom" (Col. 2:3) exposes Taylor's mind as "a nest of Brains dust" in which "Reason's wick" is hopelessly mingled with "Sensuall tallow" (2.45). Similarly, "Words though the finest twine of reason, are / Too Course a web for Deity to ware" (2.43). Faced with the eternal verities of Scripture, "Humane Wisdom's hatcht within the nest / Of addle brains which wisdom ne'er possesst" (2.95). The biblical promise of eternal life "snick snarls my Brains, thought on: / Its the Arithimaticians Wrack each way" (2.90); the union of God and man in Christ "Too deep's for reasons delving toole to finde" (2.105). On the role of reason in Taylor's meditative practice, see Scheick, *The Will and the Word*, 5–26.
9 On Taylor's view that the figurative language of Scripture validates his use

of metaphor as a bridge, however imperfect, between earth and heaven, see Scheick, *The Will and the Word*, 134–35; Keller, *The Example of Edward Taylor*, 122; Daly, *God's Altar*, 165; Michael North, "Edward Taylor's Metaphors of Promise," *American Literature* 51 (1979): 1–16; Alan Leander MacGregor, "Edward Taylor and the Impertinent Metaphor," *American Literature* 60 (1988): 337–58; and Grabo, *Edward Taylor: Revised Edition*, 66.

10 Scheick, *The Will and the Word*, 97.

11 Davis, "Introduction," *Minor Poetry*, xiv, xviii–xix. All quotations below from poems other than the Meditations refer to page numbers of *Minor Poetry*.

12 Hammond, *A Paraphrase*, b2, c2.

13 Fithian, "'Words of My Mouth, Meditations of My Heart,'" 110. On Taylor's indebtedness to the Psalms, see also Lewalski, *Protestant Poetics*, 249–50; Rowe, *Saint and Singer*, 271–72; and Davis, *A Reading of Edward Taylor*, 23–24, 71–73, 203.

14 Westminster Assembly, *Annotations*, 7G; Henry, *An Exposition*, Yyy; Collinges, *The Intercourses of Divine Love* (1676), A4; Durham, *Clavis Cantici*, 37; Theodore Beza, *Master Bezaes Sermons upon the Three First Chapters of the Canticle of Canticles*, trans. John Harmar (Oxford: 1587), 11; Joseph Hall, *An Open and plaine Paraphrase, upon the Song of Songs, Which is Salomons*, in *Salomons Divine Arts* (London: 1609), N2–N2v.

The fullest studies of Taylor's use of the Song of Songs in the later Meditations include Nicolaisen, *Die Bildlichkeit*, 131–37; Rowe, "Sacred or Profane?," 123–38; Lowance, *The Language of Canaan*, 91–96; Lewalski, *Protestant Poetics*, 416–25; Hammond, "A Puritan *Ars Moriendi*," 191–214; Rowe, *Saint and Singer*, 257–60; Gatta, *Gracious Laughter*, 188–92; Jeffrey A. Hammond, "Approaching the Garden: Edward Taylor's Progress Toward the Song of Songs," *Studies in Puritan American Spirituality* 1 (1990): 65–87; Schweitzer, *The Work of Self-Representation*, 108–25; and Davis, *A Reading of Edward Taylor*, 177–98.

15 Westminster Assembly, *Annotations*, 7Fv; Collinges, *The Intercourses of Divine Love* (1676), A2v; Durham, *Clavis Cantici*, 3.

16 Reeve, *Spiritual Hymns*, A2v; Henry, *An Exposition*, Yyy; Ager, *A Paraphrase*, 10; John Cotton, *A Brief Exposition Of the whole Book of Canticles, or, Song of Solomon* (London: 1642), 8.

17 Reeve, *Spiritual Hymns*, A2v; George Gyffard, *Fifteene Sermons, upon the Song of Salomon* (London: 1598), 78; Thomas Vincent, *Christ the Best Husband* (London: 1672), 28.

18 When the Daughters of Jerusalem ask where the Bridegroom may be found, the Bride replies that "My beloved is gone down into his garden, to the beds of spices, to feed in the gardens, and to gather lilies. / I am my beloved's, and my beloved is mine: he feedeth among the lilies" (Cant. 6:2–3). Most commentators interpreted the Bride's response as an offer to help others seek Christ (see, for example, Durham, *Clavis Cantici*, 337–41; Henry, *An Exposition*, Aaaa2v–Aaaa3; and Clark, *The Holy Bible*, Hhhh3). Taylor's paraphrase, which attributes a darker motive to the Daughters, is closer to Thomas Ager's: "By these words the Bride overcometh the Doctrine of the Daughters totally, who endeavour by their principles to strip her of the Title of Bride" (*A Paraphrase*, 285).

19 Clapham, *Three Partes*, 4; Cotton Mather, *A Companion for Communicants* (Boston: 1690), 136.

20 Collinges, *The Intercourses of Divine Love* (1676), 48.

21 Collinges, *The Intercourses of Divine Love* (1676), 95; Durham, *Clavis Cantici*, 124. Commentators adopting the first reading include Hall, *An Open and plaine Paraphrase*, 16–17; and Henry, *An Exposition*, Yyy. Collinges also acknowledges that saints may be "as unable to bear the manifestations of Divine Love, as the manifestations of Divine Wrath" (95); this second interpretation also appears in Jackson, *Annotations*, 7S4v. That Taylor deliberately conceived of Meditation 165 as his last numbered poem is supported by the fact that he apparently bound the "Poetical Works" manuscript shortly after the poem was written, some four years before his death (Thomas M. Davis, "Edward Taylor's 'Valedictory' Poems," *Early American Literature* 7 [1972]: 40, note 4).

22 Mather, *Manuductio ad Ministerium*, 42; William J. Scheick, "Roger Wolcott," in *American Colonial Writers, 1606–1734*, ed. Emory Elliott (Detroit: Gale Research Company, 1984), 372, 375. Silverman surveys the transition from Puritan to Neoclassical and Romantic modes in American verse (*Colonial American Poetry*, 202–9).

23 Mather Byles, "Commencement," in *Colonial American Poetry*, 242; Jonathan Edwards, "Personal Narrative," in *Jonathan Edwards: Representative Selections*, ed. Clarence Faust and Thomas H. Johnson (1935; reprint, New York: Hill and Wang, 1962), 60; Job Orton, *A Short and Plain Exposition of the Old Testament*, ed. Robert Gentleman, 6 vols. (Shrewsbury: 1791), 5:147.

24 Larzer Ziff, "Upon What Pretext?: The Book and Literary History," *Proceedings of the American Antiquarian Society* 95 (1985): 304; Durham, *Clavis Cantici*, 13.

Works Cited

Adams, John C. "Alexander Richardson and the Ramist Poetics of Michael Wigglesworth." *Early American Literature* 25 (1990): 271–88.
Ager, Thomas. *A Paraphrase of the Canticles; or, Song of Solomon*. London: 1680.
Ahluwalia, Harsharan Singh. "Salvation New England Style: A Study of Covenant Theology in Michael Wigglesworth's *The Day of Doom*." *Indian Journal of American Studies* 4 (1974): 1–12.
Aldridge, A. Owen. *Early American Literature: A Comparatist Approach*. Princeton: Princeton Univ. Press, 1982.
Alexis, Gerhard T. "Wigglesworth's 'Easiest Room.'" *New England Quarterly* 42 (1969): 573–83.
Allen, David Grayson. "Both Englands." In *Seventeenth Century New England*. Ed. David D. Hall and David Grayson Allen, 55–82. Boston: Colonial Society of Massachusetts, 1984.
Ames, William. *The Marrow of Theology*. Trans. John Eusden. Boston: Pilgrim Press, 1968.
Arner, Robert D. "Anne Bradstreet." In *American Writers Before 1800: A Biographical and Critical Dictionary*. Ed. James A. Levernier and Douglas R. Wilmes, 190–92. Westport, Conn.: Greenwood Press, 1983.
———. "Notes on the Structure of Edward Taylor's *Gods Determinations*." *Studies in the Humanities* 3 (1973): 27–29.
———. "Proverbs in Edward Taylor's *Gods Determinations*." *Southern Folklore Quarterly* 37 (1973): 1–13.
———. "The Structure of Anne Bradstreet's *Tenth Muse*." In *Discoveries and Considerations: Essays on Early American Literature and Aesthetics Presented to Harold Jantz*. Ed. Calvin Israel, 46–66. Albany: State Univ. of New York Press, 1976.
———. "Wit, Humor, and Satire in Seventeenth-Century American Poetry." In *Puritan Poets*, ed. White, 274–85.

Baldwin, William. *The Canticles or Balades of Salomon.* London: 1549.

Ball, Kenneth. "Puritan Humility in Anne Bradstreet's Poetry." *Cithara* 13 (1973): 29–41.

Barbour, Dennis H. "*Gods Determinations* and the Hexameral Tradition." *Early American Literature* 16 (1981/82): 213–25.

The Bay Psalm Book: A Facsimile Reprint of the First Edition of 1640. Ed. Zoltan Haraszti. Chicago: Univ. of Chicago Press, 1956.

Beales, Ross W. "Anne Bradstreet and her Children." In *Regulated Children/Liberated Children: Education in Psychohistorical Perspective*, ed. Barbara Finkelstein, 10–23. New York: Psychohistory Press, 1979.

Beaty, Nancy Lee. *The Craft of Dying: A Study in the Literary Tradition of the Ars Moriendi.* New Haven: Yale Univ. Press, 1970.

Bercovitch, Sacvan. *The American Jeremiad.* Madison: Univ. of Wisconsin Press, 1978.

———. *The Puritan Origins of the American Self.* New Haven: Yale Univ. Press, 1975.

———, ed. *The American Puritan Imagination: Essays in Revaluation.* London: Cambridge Univ. Press, 1974.

Bernard, Richard. *The Faithfull Shepherd.* London: 1621.

Beza, Theodore. *Master Bezaes Sermons upon the Three First Chapters of the Canticle of Canticles.* Trans. John Harmar. Oxford: 1587.

Blake, Kathleen. "Edward Taylor's Protestant Poetic: Nontransubstantiating Metaphor." *American Literature* 43 (1971): 1–24.

Blau, Herbert. "Heaven's Sugar Cake: Theology and Imagery in the Poetry of Edward Taylor." *New England Quarterly* 26 (1953): 337–60.

Booth, Wayne. *The Rhetoric of Fiction.* Chicago: Univ. of Chicago Press, 1961.

Bosco, Ronald A. "Introduction." *New England Funeral Sermons.* Ed. Ronald A. Bosco, xxvi–xxviii. Delmar, N.Y.: Scholars' Facsimiles and Reprints, 1978.

———. "Introduction." *The Poems of Michael Wigglesworth.* Ed. Ronald A. Bosco, ix–xliii. Lanham, Md.: Univ. Press of America, 1989.

———. "Michael Wigglesworth." In *American Colonial Writers, 1606–1734.* Ed. Emory Elliott, 337–42. Vol. 24 of the *Dictionary of Literary Biography.* Detroit: Gale Research Company, 1984.

Bowden, Edwin T. "Urian Oakes' Elegy: Colonial Literature and History." *Forum* 10 (1972): 2–8.

Bradstreet, Anne. *The Works of Anne Bradstreet.* Ed. Jeannine Hensley. Cambridge: Harvard Univ. Press, 1967.

Brandt, Ellen B. "Anne Bradstreet: The Erotic Component in Puritan Poetry." *Women's Studies* 7 (1980): 39–53.

Brown, Wallace C. "Edward Taylor: An American 'Metaphysical.'" *American Literature* 16 (1944): 186–97.

Brumm, Ursula. *American Thought and Religious Typology.* Trans. John Hoaglund. New Brunswick: Rutgers Univ. Press, 1970.

———. "Meditative Poetry in New England." In *Puritan Poets*, ed. White, 318–36.

Bunyan, John. *Grace Abounding and the Life and Death of Mr Badman.* New York: Dutton, 1928.

———. *The Pilgrim's Progress.* New York: Dutton, 1978.

Bush, Sargent, Jr. "Paradox, Puritanism, and Taylor's *Gods Determinations.*" *Early American Literature* 4 (1969/70): 48–66.

———. *The Writings of Thomas Hooker: Spiritual Adventure in Two Worlds*. Madison: Univ. of Wisconsin Press, 1980.
Caldwell, Patricia. *The Puritan Conversion Narrative: The Beginnings of American Expression*. Cambridge: Cambridge Univ. Press, 1983.
Callow, James T. "Edward Taylor Obeys Saint Paul." *Early American Literature* 4 (1969): 89–96.
Chappell, William. *The Preacher; or, The Art and Method of Preaching*. London: 1656.
Cherniavsky, Eva. "Night Pollution and the Floods of Confession in Michael Wigglesworth's Diary." *Arizona Quarterly* 45, no. 2 (1989): 15–33.
Clapham, Henoch. *Three Partes of Salomon his Song of Songs, expounded*. London: 1603.
Clark, Michael. "The Honeyed Knot of Puritan Aesthetics." In *Puritan Poets*, ed. White, 67–83.
———. "The Subject of the Text in Early American Literature." *Early American Literature* 20 (1985): 120–30.
Clark, Samuel. *The Holy Bible, Containing The Old Testament and The New: With Annotations and Parallel Scriptures*. London: 1690.
Cohen, Charles Lloyd. *God's Caress: The Psychology of Puritan Religious Experience*. New York: Oxford Univ. Press, 1986.
Colacurcio, Michael. "*Gods Determinations Touching Half-Way Membership*: Occasion and Audience in Edward Taylor." *American Literature* 39 (1967): 298–314.
Collinges, John. *The Intercourses of Divine Love Betwixt Christ and the Church; or, The Particular Believing-Soul; As Metaphorically expressed by Solomon in the Second Chapter of the Canticles*. London: 1676.
———. *The Intercourses of Divine Love Betwixt Christ and his Church; or, The Particular Believing Soul. Metaphorically expressed by Solomon in the first Chapter of the Canticles, or Song of Songs*. London: 1683.
———. *The Spouse under the Apple-Tree; or, The state of the Elect by Nature*. London: 1649.
Cotton, John. *A Brief Exposition Of the whole Book of Canticles, or, Song of Solomon*. London: 1642.
Cowell, Pattie. "The Early Distribution of Anne Bradstreet's Poems." In *Critical Essays on Anne Bradstreet*, ed. Cowell and Stanford, 270–79.
———. "Introduction: Anne Bradstreet 'In Criticks Hands.'" In *Critical Essays on Anne Bradstreet*, ed. Cowell and Stanford, ix–xxv.
———. "Why Our First Poet Was a Woman: Bradstreet and the Birth of an American Poetic Voice." *Prospects* 13 (1988): 1–35.
Cowell, Pattie, and Ann Stanford, eds. *Critical Essays on Anne Bradstreet*. Boston: G. K. Hall, 1983.
Craig, Raymond A. *A Concordance to the Minor Poetry of Edward Taylor (1642?–1729): American Colonial Poet*. 2 vols. Lewiston, N.Y.: Edwin Mellen Press, 1992.
———. "Singing with Grace: Allusive Strategies in Anne Bradstreet's 'New Psalms.'" *Studies in Puritan American Spirituality* 1 (1990): 148–63.
Cremin, Lawrence A. *American Education: The Colonial Experience, 1606–1783*. New York: Harper and Row, 1970.
Crowder, Richard. "Anne Bradstreet and Keats." *Notes and Queries* 3 (1956): 386–88.
———. "'The Day of Doom' as Chronomorph." *Journal of Popular Culture* 9 (1976): 948–59.
———. "Meat Out of the Eater." *Boston Public Library Quarterly* 11 (1959): 179–92.

———. *No Featherbed to Heaven: A Biography of Michael Wigglesworth*. East Lansing: Michigan State Univ. Press, 1962.

Daly, Robert. "The Danforths: Puritan Poets in the Woods of Arcadia." In *Puritan Poets*, ed. White, 147–57.

———. *God's Altar: The World and the Flesh in Puritan Poetry*. Berkeley: Univ. of California Press, 1978.

Davidson, Edward H. "'God's Well-Trodden Foot-Paths': Puritan Preaching and Sermon Form." *Texas Studies in Literature and Language* 25 (1983): 503–27.

Davis, Thomas M. "Edward Taylor and the Traditions of Puritan Typology." *Early American Literature* 4 (1969/70): 27–47.

———. "Edward Taylor's Elegy on Deacon David Dewey." *Proceedings of the American Antiquarian Society* 96, Part 1 (1986): 75–84.

———. "Edward Taylor's 'Valedictory' Poems." *Early American Literature* 7 (1972): 38–63.

———. "Introduction." *Edward Taylor's "Church Records" and Related Sermons*. Ed. Thomas M. Davis and Virginia L. Davis, xi–xl. Boston: Twayne, 1981.

———. "Introduction." *Edward Taylor's Minor Poetry*. Ed. Thomas M. Davis and Virginia L. Davis, xi–xxii. Boston: Twayne, 1981.

———. "Introduction." *Edward Taylor vs. Solomon Stoddard: The Nature of the Lord's Supper*. Ed. Thomas M. Davis and Virginia L. Davis, 1–57. Boston: Twayne, 1981.

———. *A Reading of Edward Taylor*. Newark: Univ. of Delaware Press, 1992.

Day, James. *A New Spring of Divine Poetrie*. London: 1637.

Dean, John Ward. *Sketch of the Life of Rev. Michael Wigglesworth, A.M., Author of the Day of Doom*. Albany: J. Munsell, 1863.

Derounian-Stodola, Kathryn Zabelle. "'The Excellency of the inferior sex': The Commendatory Writings on Anne Bradstreet." *Studies in Puritan American Spirituality* 1 (1990): 129–47.

Dolle, Raymond F. *Anne Bradstreet: A Reference Guide*. Boston: Twayne, 1991.

Donne, John. *The Complete Poetry of John Donne*. Ed. John T. Shawcross. Garden City: Doubleday, 1967.

Doriani, Beth M. "'Then Have I . . . Said with David': Anne Bradstreet's Andover Manuscript Poems and the Influence of the Psalm Tradition." *Early American Literature* 24 (1989): 52–69.

Dove, John. *The Conversion of Salomon*. London: 1613.

Draper, John W. *The Funeral Elegy and the Rise of English Romanticism*. New York: New York Univ. Press, 1929.

Draxe, Thomas. *The Lambes Spouse*. London: 1608.

Drayton, Michael. *The Works of Michael Drayton*. Ed. J. William Hebel. 5 vols. Oxford: Shakespeare Head Press, 1931.

Durham, James. *Clavis Cantici; or, An Exposition of the Song of Solomon*. Edinburgh: 1668.

Eagleton, Terry. *Literary Theory*. Minneapolis: Univ. of Minnesota Press, 1983.

Eberwein, Jane Donahue. "Anne Bradstreet." In *Early American Poetry: Selections from Bradstreet, Taylor, Dwight, Freneau, and Bryant*. Ed. Jane Donahue Eberwein, 3–13. Madison: Univ. of Wisconsin Press, 1978.

———. "Civil War and Bradstreet's 'Monarchies.'" *Early American Literature* 26 (1991): 119–44.

———. " 'No Rhet'ric We Expect': Argumentation in Bradstreet's 'The Prologue.' " *Early American Literature* 16 (1981): 19–26.

———. " 'The Unrefined Ore' of Anne Bradstreet's Quaternions." *Early American Literature* 9 (1974): 19–26.

Edwards, Jonathan. *Jonathan Edwards: Representative Selections*. Ed. Clarence Faust and Thomas H. Johnson. 1935. Reprint. New York: Hill and Wang, 1962.

Elliott, Emory. "The Development of the Puritan Funeral Sermon and Elegy: 1660–1750." *Early American Literature* 15 (1980): 151–64.

———. *Power and the Pulpit in Puritan New England*. Princeton: Princeton Univ. Press, 1975.

Ellis, John Harvard. "Introduction." *The Works of Anne Bradstreet in Prose and Verse*. Ed. John Harvard Ellis, v–lxxi. 1867. Reprint. New York: Peter Smith, 1932.

Emerson, Everett, ed. *Major Writers of Early American Literature*. Madison: Univ. of Wisconsin Press, 1972.

Fish, Stanley. *Is There a Text in This Class? The Authority of Interpretive Communities*. Cambridge: Harvard Univ. Press, 1980.

———. *Self-Consuming Artifacts: The Experience of Seventeenth-Century Literature*. Berkeley: Univ. of California Press, 1972.

———. *Surprised by Sin: The Reader in Paradise Lost*. 1967. Reprint. Berkeley: Univ. of California Press, 1971.

Fithian, Rosemary. " 'Words of My Mouth, Meditations of My Heart': Edward Taylor's *Preparatory Meditations* and the Book of Psalms." *Early American Literature* 20 (1985): 89–119.

Fleming, Robert. *The Mirrour of Divine Love Unvail'd, in a Poetical Paraphrase of the High and Mysterious Song of Solomon*. London: 1691.

Fraser, Russell. *The War Against Poetry*. Princeton: Princeton Univ. Press, 1970.

Gatta, John, Jr. "The Comic Design of *Gods Determinations touching his Elect*." *Early American Literature* 10 (1975): 121–43.

———. "Edward Taylor and Thomas Hooker: Two Physicians of the Poore Doubting Soul." *Notre Dame English Journal* 12 (1979): 1–13.

———. *Gracious Laughter: The Meditative Wit of Edward Taylor*. Columbia: Univ. of Missouri Press, 1989.

Gefvert, Constance J. *Edward Taylor: An Annotated Bibliography*. Kent, Ohio: Kent State Univ. Press, 1971.

The Geneva Bible: A Facsimile of the 1560 Edition. Intro. Lloyd E. Berry. Madison: Univ. of Wisconsin Press, 1969.

Grabo, Norman S. *Edward Taylor*. New York: Twayne, 1961.

———. *Edward Taylor: Revised Edition*. Boston: Twayne, 1988.

———. "Introduction." *Edward Taylor's Treatise Concerning the Lord's Supper*. Ed. Norman S. Grabo, ix–li. East Lansing: Michigan State Univ. Press, 1966.

———. "The Veiled Vision: The Role of Aesthetics in Early American Intellectual History." 1962. Reprinted in *The American Puritan Imagination*, ed. Bercovitch, 19–33.

Grabo, Norman S., and Jana Wainright. "Edward Taylor." In *Fifteen American Authors before 1900: Bibliographical Essays on Research and Criticism*. Ed. Earl N. Harbert and Robert A. Rees, 439–67. Madison: Univ. of Wisconsin Press, 1984.

Greenblatt, Stephen. *Renaissance Self-Fashioning: From More to Shakespeare*. Chicago: Univ. of Chicago Press, 1980.

Greven, Philip. *The Protestant Temperament: Patterns of Child-Rearing, Religious Experience, and the Self in Early America.* New York: Knopf, 1977.

Gummere, Richard M. *Seven Wise Men of Colonial America.* Cambridge: Harvard Univ. Press, 1967.

Gyffard, George. *Fifteene Sermons, upon the Song of Salomon.* London: 1598.

Hahn, T. G. "Urian Oakes's *Elegie* on Thomas Shepard and Puritan Poetics." *American Literature* 45 (1973): 163–81.

Haims, Lynn. "Puritan Iconography: The Art of Edward Taylor's *Gods Determinations.*" In *Puritan Poets,* ed. White, 84–98.

Hall, David D. *The Faithful Shepherd: A History of the New England Ministry in the Seventeenth Century.* Chapel Hill: Univ. of North Carolina Press, 1972.

———. "On Native Ground: From the History of Printing to the History of the Book." *Proceedings of the American Antiquarian Society* 93 (1983): 313–36.

———. "Toward a History of Popular Religion in Early New England." *William and Mary Quarterly* 41 (1984): 49–55.

———. "The Uses of Literacy in New England, 1600–1850." In *Printing and Society in Early America.* Ed. William L. Joyce, David D. Hall, Richard D. Brown, and John B. Hench, 1–47. Worcester, Mass.: American Antiquarian Society, 1983.

———. "The World of Print and Collective Mentality in Seventeenth-Century New England." In *New Directions in American Intellectual History.* Ed. John Higham and Paul K. Conklin, 166–80. Baltimore: Johns Hopkins Univ. Press, 1979.

———. *Worlds of Wonder, Days of Judgment: Popular Religious Belief in Early New England.* New York: Knopf, 1989.

Hall, Dean G. "Edward Taylor: The Evolution of a Poet." Ph.D. diss., Kent State University, 1977.

Hall, Joseph. *An Open and plaine Paraphrase, upon the Song of Songs, Which is Salomons.* In *Salomons Divine Arts.* London: 1609.

Hall, Thomas. *Centuria Sacra.* In *Vindiciae Literarum.* London: 1655.

Hambrick-Stowe, Charles E. "Introduction." *Early New England Meditative Poetry: Anne Bradstreet and Edward Taylor.* Ed. Charles E. Hambrick-Stowe, 7–62. New York: Paulist Press, 1988.

———. *The Practice of Piety: Puritan Devotional Disciplines in Seventeenth-Century New England.* Chapel Hill: Univ. of North Carolina Press, 1982.

Hammond, Henry. *A Paraphrase and Annotations Upon the Books of the Psalms.* London: 1659.

Hammond, Jeffrey A. "Approaching the Garden: Edward Taylor's Progress Toward the Song of Songs." *Studies in Puritan American Spirituality* 1 (1990): 65–87.

———. *Edward Taylor: Fifty Years of Scholarship and Criticism.* Columbia, S.C.: Camden House, 1993.

———. "From Sinful Silence to Apostolic Voice: The Puritan Elegiac Ritual." *Studies in Puritan American Spirituality* 2 (1991): 77–106.

———. "'Ladders of Your Own': *The Day of Doom* and the Repudiation of 'Carnal Reason.'" *Early American Literature* 19 (1984): 42–67.

———. "'Make Use of What I Leave in Love': Anne Bradstreet's Didactic Self." *Religion and Literature* 17 (1985): 11–26.

———. "A Puritan *Ars Moriendi:* Edward Taylor's Late Meditations on the Song of Songs." *Early American Literature* 17 (1982/83): 191–214.

———. "Reading Taylor Exegetically: The *Preparatory Meditations* and the Commentary Tradition." *Texas Studies in Literature and Language* 24 (1982): 347–71.

———. "Who Is Edward Taylor?: Voice and Reader in the *Preparatory Meditations*." *American Poetry* 7, no. 3 (1990): 2–19.

Henry, Matthew. *An Exposition Of the Five Poetical Books of the Old Testament*. London: 1710.

Hensley, Jeannine. "Anne Bradstreet's Wreath of Thyme." In *The Works of Anne Bradstreet*. Ed. Jeannine Hensley, xxiii–xxxvi.

Henson, Robert. "Form and Content of the Puritan Funeral Elegy." *American Literature* 32 (1960): 11–27.

Herbert, George. *The Works of George Herbert*. Ed. F. E. Hutchinson. Oxford: Clarendon Press, 1941.

Hildebrand, Anne. "Anne Bradstreet's Quaternions and 'Contemplations.'" *Early American Literature* 8 (1973): 117–25.

Holifield, E. Brooks. *The Covenant Sealed: The Development of Puritan Sacramental Theology in Old and New England, 1570–1720*. New Haven: Yale Univ. Press, 1974.

Holmes, Nathaniel. *A Commentary Literal or Historical, and Mystical or Spiritual On the whole Book of Canticles*. In *The Works of Dr. Nathaniel Homes* [sic]. London: 1652.

Holub, Robert C. *Reception Theory: A Critical Introduction*. London: Methuen, 1984.

Hooker, Thomas. *The Application of Redemption . . . The first eight Books*. 1657. Reprint. New York: Arno Press, 1972.

———. *The Application of Redemption . . . The Ninth Book*. In *Redemption: Three Sermons*. Ed. Everett H. Emerson, 51–64. Gainesville, Fla.: Scholars' Facsimiles and Reprints, 1956.

———. *The Soules Implantation*. London: 1637.

———. *The Soules Preparation for Christ*. London: 1632.

Howard, Alan B. "The World as Emblem: Language and Vision in the Poetry of Edward Taylor." *American Literature* 44 (1972): 359–84.

Hughes, Walter. "'Meat Out of the Eater': Panic and Desire in American Puritan Poetry." In *Engendering Men: The Question of Male Feminist Criticism*. Ed. Joseph A. Boone and Michael Cadden, 102–21. New York: Routledge, 1990.

Hutchinson, Robert. "Introduction." *Poems of Anne Bradstreet*. Ed. Robert Hutchinson, 1–33. New York: Dover, 1969.

Irvin, William J. "Allegory and Typology 'Imbrace and Greet': Anne Bradstreet's 'Contemplations.'" *Early American Literature* 10 (1975): 30–46.

Iser, Wolfgang. *The Act of Reading: A Theory of Aesthetic Response*. Baltimore: Johns Hopkins Univ. Press, 1978.

———. *The Implied Reader: Patterns of Communication in Prose Fiction from Bunyan to Beckett*. Baltimore: Johns Hopkins Univ. Press, 1974.

Jackson, Arthur. *Annotations Upon The five Books immediately following the Historicall Part of the Old Testament, (Commonly called the five Doctrinall, or Poeticall Books)*. London: 1658.

Jantz, Harold S., ed. *The First Century of New England Verse*. 1944. Reprint. New York: Russell and Russell, 1962.

Jauss, Hans Robert. *Aesthetic Experience and Literary Hermeneutics*. Trans. Michael Shaw. Minneapolis: Univ. of Minnesota Press, 1982.

———. *Toward an Aesthetic of Reception*. Trans. Timothy Bahti. Minneapolis: Univ. of Minnesota Press, 1982.

Jerome. *Select Letters of St. Jerome*. Trans. F. A. Wright. London: William Heinemann, 1933.

Johnson, Thomas H. "A Seventeenth-Century Printing of Some Verses of Edward Taylor." *New England Quarterly* 14 (1941): 139–41.
———. "The Topical Verses of Edward Taylor." *Colonial Society of Massachusetts Publications* 34 (1943): 513–54.
Jones, Matt B. "Notes for a Bibliography of Michael Wigglesworth's 'Day of Doom' and 'Meat Out of the Eater.'" *Proceedings of the American Antiquarian Society*, New Series, 39 (1929): 77–84.
Jones, Phyllis M. "Biblical Rhetoric and the Pulpit Literature of Early New England." *Early American Literature* 11 (1977): 245–58.
———. "Puritan's Progress: The Story of the Soul's Salvation in the Early New England Sermons." *Early American Literature* 15 (1980): 14–28.
Jones, Phyllis M., and Nicholas R. Jones, eds. *Salvation in New England: Selections from the Sermons of the First Preachers*. Austin: Univ. of Texas Press, 1977.
Junkins, Donald. "'Should Stars Wooe Lobster Claws?': A Study of Edward Taylor's Poetic Practice and Theory." *Early American Literature* 3 (1968): 88–117.
Keller, Karl. "Edward Taylor, The Acting Poet." In *Puritan Poets*, ed. White, 185–97.
———. *The Example of Edward Taylor*. Amherst: Univ. of Massachusetts Press, 1975.
———. *The Only Kangaroo among the Beauty: Emily Dickinson and America*. Baltimore: Johns Hopkins Univ. Press, 1979.
———. "'The World Slickt Up in Types': Edward Taylor as a Version of Emerson." *Early American Literature* 5 (1969): 124–40.
King, John Owen. *The Iron of Melancholy: Structures of Spiritual Conversion in America from the Puritan Conscience to Victorian Neurosis*. Middletown: Wesleyan Univ. Press, 1983.
Knott, John R., Jr. *The Sword of the Spirit: Puritan Responses to the Bible*. Chicago: Univ. of Chicago Press, 1980.
Koehler, Lyle. *A Search for Power: The "Weaker Sex" in Seventeenth-Century New England*. Urbana: Univ. of Illinois Press, 1980.
Kopacz, Paula. "'To Finish What's Begun': Anne Bradstreet's Last Words." *Early American Literature* 23 (1988): 175–87.
Leigh, Edward. *Annotations on Five Poetical Books of the Old Testament*. London: 1657.
Leverenz, David. *The Language of Puritan Feeling*. New Brunswick: Rutgers Univ. Press, 1980.
Levy, Babette May. *Preaching in the First Half Century of New England History*. 1945. Reprint. New York: Russell and Russell, 1967.
Lewalski, Barbara Kiefer. *Protestant Poetics and the Seventeenth-Century Religious Lyric*. Princeton: Princeton Univ. Press, 1979.
Lind, Sidney E. "Edward Taylor: A Revaluation." *New England Quarterly* 21 (1948): 518–30.
Lowance, Mason I., Jr. *The Language of Canaan: Metaphor and Symbol in New England from the Puritans to the Transcendentalists*. Cambridge: Harvard Univ. Press, 1980.
———. "Religion in Puritan Poetry: The Doctrine of Accommodation." In *Puritan Poets*, ed. White, 33–46.
Lynen, John F. *The Design of the Present: Essays on Time and Form in American Literature*. New Haven: Yale Univ. Press, 1969.
McElrath, Joseph R., Jr., and Allan P. Robb. "Introduction." *The Complete Works of Anne Bradstreet*. Ed. Joseph R. McElrath, Jr., and Allan P. Robb, xi–xlii. Boston: Twayne, 1981.

McGiffert, Michael. "Introduction." *God's Plot: The Paradoxes of Puritan Piety*. Ed. Michael McGiffert, 3–32. Amherst: Univ. of Massachusetts Press, 1972.

MacGregor, Alan Leander. "Edward Taylor and the Impertinent Metaphor." *American Literature* 60 (1988): 337–58.

McMahon, Helen. "Anne Bradstreet, Jean Bertault, and Dr. Cooke." *Early American Literature* 3 (1968): 118–23.

Maragou, Helena. "The Portrait of Alexander the Great in Anne Bradstreet's 'The Third Monarchy.'" *Early American Literature* 23 (1988): 70–81.

Margerum, Eileen. "Anne Bradstreet's Public Poetry and the Tradition of Humility." *Early American Literature* 17 (1982): 152–60.

Martin, Wendy. *An American Triptych: Anne Bradstreet, Emily Dickinson, Adrienne Rich*. Chapel Hill: Univ. of North Carolina Press, 1984.

———. "Anne Bradstreet's Poetry: A Study in Subversive Piety." In *Shakespeare's Sisters: Feminist Essays on Women Poets*. Ed. Sandra M. Gilbert and Susan Gubar, 19–31. Bloomington: Indiana Univ. Press, 1979.

Martz, Louis L. "Foreword." *The Poems of Edward Taylor*. Ed. Donald E. Stanford, xiii–xxxvii. New Haven: Yale Univ. Press, 1960.

———. *The Poetry of Meditation*. New Haven: Yale Univ. Press, 1962.

Marvell, Andrew. *The Complete Poetry of Andrew Marvell*. Ed. Hugh Macdonald. Cambridge: Harvard Univ. Press, 1952.

Mason, Mary G. "The Other Voice: Autobiographies of Women Writers." In *Autobiography: Essays Theoretical and Critical*. Ed. James Olney, 207–35. Princeton: Princeton Univ. Press, 1980.

Masson, Margaret W. "The Typology of the Female as a Model for the Regenerate: Puritan Preaching, 1690–1730." *Signs: Journal of Women in Culture and Society* 2 (1976): 304–15.

Mather, Cotton. *A Companion for Communicants*. Boston: 1690.

———. *A Faithful Man, Described and Rewarded*. Boston: 1705.

———. *Magnalia Christi Americana*. Ed. Thomas Robbins. 2 vols. 1852. Reprint. New York: Russell and Russell, 1967.

———. *Manuductio ad Ministerium*. 1726. Reprint. New York: AMS Press, 1978.

———. *The Nightingale. An Essay on Songs among Thorns*. Boston: 1724.

———. *Ornaments for the Daughters of Zion*. Intro. Pattie Cowell. 1692. Reprint. New York: Scholars' Facsimiles and Reprints, 1978.

———. *Paterna: The Autobiography of Cotton Mather*. Ed. Ronald A. Bosco. Delmar, N.Y.: Scholars' Facsimiles and Reprints, 1976.

———. *A Poem and an Elegy*. Boston: Club of Odd Volumes, 1896.

———. *Psalterium Americanum*. Boston: 1718.

———. *Right Thoughts in Sad Hours*. London: 1689.

Mather, Samuel. *The Figures or Types of the Old Testament*. 1705. Reprint. New York: Johnson Reprint Corporation, 1969.

Matthiessen, F. O. "Michael Wigglesworth, A Puritan Artist." *New England Quarterly* 1 (1928): 491–504.

Mawer, Randall R. "'Farewel Dear Babe': Bradstreet's Elegy for Elizabeth." *Early American Literature* 15 (1980): 29–41.

Meserole, Harrison T., ed. *American Poetry of the Seventeenth Century*. 1968. Reprint. University Park: Pennsylvania State Univ. Press, 1985.

Mignon, Charles W. "Edward Taylor's *Preparatory Meditations*: A Decorum of Imperfection." *PMLA* 83 (1968): 1423–28.

———. "Introduction." *Upon the Types of the Old Testament.* Ed. Charles W. Mignon, xix–lxxvii. 2 vols. Lincoln: Univ. of Nebraska Press, 1989.

———. "A Principle of Order in Edward Taylor's *Preparatory Meditations.*" *Early American Literature* 4 (1970): 110–16.

Milbourne, Luke. *Psalmody Recommended in a Sermon.* London: 1713.

Miles, Josephine. "The Poetry of Praise." *Kenyon Review* 23 (1961): 104–25.

Miller, Perry. *Errand into the Wilderness.* Cambridge: Harvard Univ. Press, 1956.

———. *The New England Mind: From Colony to Province.* Cambridge: Harvard Univ. Press, 1953.

———. *The New England Mind: The Seventeenth Century.* 1939. Reprint. Cambridge: Harvard Univ. Press, 1954.

Miller, Perry, and Thomas H. Johnson, eds. *The Puritans.* 1938. Revised Edition. 2 vols. New York: Harper and Row, 1963.

Milton, John. *The Complete Poetry of John Milton.* Ed. John T. Shawcross. Garden City: Doubleday, 1971.

Minter, David. "The Puritan Jeremiad as a Literary Form." In *The American Puritan Imagination,* ed. Bercovitch, 45–55.

Mitchell, W. F. *English Pulpit Oratory from Andrewes to Tillotson: A Study of Its Literary Aspects.* New York: Macmillan, 1932.

Morgan, Edmund S. "Introduction." *The Diary of Michael Wigglesworth, 1653–1657: The Conscience of a Puritan.* Ed. Edmund S. Morgan, v–xv. New York: Harper and Row, 1965.

———. *Visible Saints: The History of a Puritan Idea.* 1963. Reprint. Ithaca: Cornell Univ. Press, 1965.

Morison, Samuel Eliot. *Builders of the Bay Colony.* 1930. Reprint. Boston: Northeastern Univ. Press, 1981.

———. *Harvard College in the Seventeenth Century.* Cambridge: Harvard Univ. Press, 1936.

———. *The Intellectual Life of Colonial New England.* 1936. Reprint. Ithaca: Cornell Univ. Press, 1960.

Murdock, Kenneth B. "Introduction." *The Day of Doom; or, A Poetical Description of the Great and Last Judgment with other poems.* Ed. Kenneth B. Murdock, iii–xi. 1929. Reprint. New York: Russell and Russell, 1966.

———. *Literature and Theology in Colonial New England.* Cambridge: Harvard Univ. Press, 1949.

Nicolaisen, Peter. *Die Bildlichkeit in der Dichtung Edward Taylors.* Neumünster: Karl Wachholtz, 1966.

North, Michael. "Edward Taylor's Metaphors of Promise." *American Literature* 51 (1979): 1–16.

Orton, Job. *A Short and Plain Exposition of the Old Testament.* Ed. Robert Gentleman. 6 vols. Shrewsbury: 1791.

Owen, John. *Meditations and Discourses Concerning the Glory of Christ.* London: 1691.

Parker, David L. "Edward Taylor's Preparationism: A New Perspective on the Taylor-Stoddard Controversy." *Early American Literature* 11 (1976/77): 259–78.

Patterson, J. Daniel. "*Gods Determinations:* The Occasion, the Audience, and Taylor's Hope for New England." *Early American Literature* 22 (1987): 63–81.

Pearce, Roy Harvey. *The Continuity of American Poetry.* Princeton: Princeton Univ. Press, 1961.

Pearse, Edward. *The Best Match; or, The Soul's Espousal to Christ.* Boston: 1708.

———. *The Great Concern; or, A Serious Warning to a Timely and Thorough Preparation for Death.* Boston: 1711.

Perkins, William. *The Workes of . . . William Perkins* 3 vols. London: 1612.

Pettit, Norman. *The Heart Prepared: Grace and Conversion in Puritan Spiritual Life.* New Haven: Yale Univ. Press, 1966.

———. "The Puritan Legacy." *New England Quarterly* 48 (1975): 283–94.

Piercy, Josephine K. *Anne Bradstreet.* New York: Twayne, 1965.

———. *Studies in Literary Types in Seventeenth Century America.* 1939. Reprint. New York: Archon, 1969.

Pope, Alan H. "Petrus Ramus and Michael Wigglesworth: The Logic of Poetic Structure." In *Puritan Poets,* ed. White, 210–26.

Porterfield, Amanda. *Feminine Spirituality in America: From Sarah Edwards to Martha Graham.* Philadelphia: Temple Univ. Press, 1980.

Puttenham, George. *The Arte of English Poesie.* Ed. Gladys Doidge Willcock and Alice Walker. Cambridge: Cambridge Univ. Press, 1936.

Rainwater, Catherine. "Edward Taylor's Reluctant Revolution: The New Astronomy in the *Preparatory Meditations.*" *American Poetry* 1, no. 2 (1984): 4–17.

———. "'This Brazen Serpent is a Doctors Shop': Edward Taylor's Medical Vision." *Studies in Puritan American Spirituality* 2 (1991): 51–75.

Rainwater, Catherine, and William J. Scheick. "Seventeenth-Century American Poetry: A Reference Guide Updated." *Resources for American Literary Study* 10 (1980): 121–45.

Reed, Michael. "Edward Taylor's Poetry: Puritan Structure and Form." *American Literature* 46 (1974): 304–12.

Reeve, John. *Spiritual Hymns upon Solomon's Song; or, Love in the Right Channel.* London: 1693.

Reiter, Robert. "Poetry and Typology: Edward Taylor's *Preparatory Meditations,* Second Series, Numbers 1–30." *Early American Literature* 5 (1970): 111–23.

Requa, Kenneth A. "Anne Bradstreet's Poetic Voices." *Early American Literature* 9 (1974): 3–18.

Rich, Adrienne. "Anne Bradstreet and Her Poetry." In *The Works of Anne Bradstreet,* ed. Hensley, ix–xxi.

Richardson, Robert, Jr. "The Puritan Poetry of Anne Bradstreet." In *The American Puritan Imagination,* ed. Bercovitch, 107–22.

Roberts, Francis. *Clavis Bibliorum. The Key of the Bible.* London: 1649.

Robinson, Douglas. *American Apocalypses: The Image of the End of the World in American Literature.* Baltimore: Johns Hopkins Univ. Press, 1985.

Rollins, Hyder E., and Herschel Baker, eds. *The Renaissance in England: Non-dramatic Prose and Verse of the Sixteenth Century.* Boston: D. C. Heath, 1954.

Rosenfeld, Alvin H. "Anne Bradstreet's 'Contemplations': Patterns of Form and Meaning." *New England Quarterly* 43 (1970): 79–96.

Rosenmeier, Rosamond R. *Anne Bradstreet Revisited.* Boston: Twayne, 1991.

———. "'Divine Translation': A Contribution to the Study of Anne Bradstreet's Method in the Marriage Poems." *Early American Literature* 12 (1977): 121–35.

———. "The Wounds Upon Bathsheba: Anne Bradstreet's Prophetic Art." In *Puritan Poets,* ed. White, 129–46.

Rous, Francis. *The Mysticall Marriage.* London: 1631.

Rowe, Karen E. "Prophetic Visions: Typology and Colonial American Poetry." In *Puritan Poets*, ed. White, 47–66.

———. "Sacred or Profane? Edward Taylor's Meditations on Canticles." *Modern Philology* 72 (1974): 123–38.

———. *Saint and Singer: Edward Taylor's Typology and the Poetics of Meditation.* Cambridge: Cambridge Univ. Press, 1986.

Rutman, Darrett. *American Puritanism: Faith and Practice.* New York: Lippincott, 1970.

Sacks, Peter. *The English Elegy: Studies in the Genre from Spenser to Yeats.* Baltimore: Johns Hopkins Univ. Press, 1985.

Saltman, Helen. "'Contemplations': Anne Bradstreet's Spiritual Biography." In *Critical Essays on Anne Bradstreet*, ed. Cowell and Stanford, 226–37.

Sargent, Ritamarie. "Poetry and the Puritan Faith: The Elegies of Anne Bradstreet and Edward Taylor." In *A Salzburg Miscellany: English and American Studies, 1964–84.* Vol. 1, *Poetic Drama and Poetic Theory*, ed. James Hogg, 149–60. Salzburg: Universität Salzburg, 1984.

Scheick, William J. *Design in Puritan American Literature.* Lexington: Univ. Press of Kentucky, 1992.

———. "Edward Taylor's Optics." *American Literature* 55 (1983): 234–40.

———. "'The Inward Tacles and the Outward Traces': Edward Taylor's Elusive Transitions." *Early American Literature* 12 (1977): 163–76.

———. "The Jawbones Schema of Edward Taylor's *Gods Determinations*." In *Puritan Influences in American Literature.* Ed. Emory Elliott, 38–54. Urbana: Univ. of Illinois Press, 1979.

———. "Order and Disorder in Taylor's Poetry: Meditation 1.8." *American Poetry* 5 (1988): 2–11.

———. "Roger Wolcott." In *American Colonial Writers, 1606–1734.* Ed. Emory Elliott, 372–76. Vol. 24 of the *Dictionary of Literary Biography.* Detroit: Gale Research Company, 1984.

———. "Standing in the Gap: Urian Oakes' Elegy on Thomas Shepard." *Early American Literature* 9 (1975): 301–6.

———. "The Theme, Structure, and Symbolism of Anne Bradstreet's 'Contemplations.'" *Américana* 4 (1984): 147–56.

———. "Tombless Virtue and Hidden Text: New England Puritan Funeral Elegies." In *Puritan Poets*, ed. White, 286–302.

———. "Typology and Allegory: A Comparative Study of George Herbert and Edward Taylor." *Essays in Literature* 2 (1975): 76–86.

———. "Unfolding the Serpent in Taylor's 'Meditation 1.19.'" *Studies in Puritan American Spirituality* 1 (1990): 34–64.

———. *The Will and the Word: The Poetry of Edward Taylor.* Athens: Univ. of Georgia Press, 1974.

Scheick, William J., and JoElla Doggett. *Seventeenth-Century American Poetry: A Reference Guide.* Boston: G. K. Hall, 1977.

Schmitt-v. Muhlenfels, Astrid. "John Fiske's Funeral Elegy on John Cotton." *Early American Literature* 12 (1977): 49–62.

Schuldiner, Michael. "The Christian Hero and the Classical Journey in Edward Taylor's 'Preparatory Meditations. First Series.'" *Huntington Library Quarterly* 49 (1986): 113–32.

———. "Edward Taylor's 'Problematic' Imagery." *Early American Literature* 13 (1978): 92–101.
———. *Gifts and Works: Spiritual Life and Political Controversy in Seventeenth-Century Massachusetts*. Macon, Ga.: Mercer Univ. Press, 1990.
Schweitzer, Ivy. "Anne Bradstreet Wrestles with the Renaissance." *Early American Literature* 23 (1988): 291–312.
———. *The Work of Self-Representation: Lyric Poetry in Colonial New England*. Chapel Hill: Univ. of North Carolina Press, 1991.
Sebouhian, George. "Conversion Morphology and the Structure of *Gods Determinations*." *Early American Literature* 16 (1981/82): 226–40.
Selement, George. "The Meeting of Elite and Popular Minds at Cambridge, New England, 1638–1645." *William and Mary Quarterly* 41 (1984): 32–48.
Shawcross, John T. "Some Colonial American Poetry and George Herbert." *Early American Literature* 23 (1988): 28–51.
Shea, Daniel B. *Spiritual Autobiography in Early America*. Princeton: Princeton Univ. Press, 1968.
Shepard, Thomas. *God's Plot: The Paradoxes of Puritan Piety*. Ed. Michael McGiffert. Amherst: Univ. of Massachusetts Press, 1972.
———. *The Works of Thomas Shepard*. Ed. John A. Albro. 3 vols. Boston: Doctrinal Tract and Book Society, 1853.
Shields, John C. "Jerome in Colonial New England: Edward Taylor's Attitude Toward Classical Paganism." *Studies in Philology* 81 (1984): 161–84.
Sibbes, Richard. *Bowels Opened; or, A Discovery of the Neere and deere Love, Union and Communion betwixt Christ and the Church, and consequently betwixt Him and every beleeving soule*. London: 1639.
Sidney, Sir Philip. *Sir Philip Sidney's Defense of Poesy*. Ed. Lewis Soens. Lincoln: Univ. of Nebraska Press, 1970.
Silverman, Kenneth, ed. *Colonial American Poetry*. New York: Hafner, 1968.
Sluder, Lawrence Lan. "God in the Background: Edward Taylor as Naturalist." *Early American Literature* 7 (1973): 265–71.
Smith, Jud[e]. *A misticall devise of the spirituall and godly love betwene Christ the spouse, and the Church or Congregation*. London: 1575.
Sowd, David. "Edward Taylor's Answer to a 'Popish Pamphlet.'" *Early American Literature* 9 (1975): 307–14.
Spacks, Patricia Meyer. *Imagining a Self: Autobiography and Novel in Eighteenth-Century England*. Cambridge: Harvard Univ. Press, 1976.
Spengemann, William C. *A Mirror for Americanists: Reflections on the Idea of American Literature*. Hanover, N.H.: Univ. Press of New England, 1989.
Stanford, Ann. "Anne Bradstreet." In *Major Writers of Early American Literature*, ed. Emerson, 33–58.
———. "Anne Bradstreet as a Meditative Writer." In *Critical Essays on Anne Bradstreet*, ed. Cowell and Stanford, 89–96.
———. "Anne Bradstreet: Dogmatist and Rebel." *New England Quarterly* 39 (1966): 373–89.
———. *Anne Bradstreet: The Worldly Puritan*. New York: Burt Franklin, 1974.
———. "Images of Women in Early American Literature." In *What Manner of Women? Essays on English and American Life and Literature*. Ed. Marlene Springer, 185–210. New York: New York Univ. Press, 1977.

Stanford, Donald E. *Edward Taylor*. Minneapolis: Univ. of Minnesota Press, 1965.
——. "Edward Taylor." In *Major Writers of Early American Literature*, ed. Emerson, 59–91.
——. "Edward Taylor's Metrical History of Christianity." *American Literature* 33 (1961): 279–95.
Stannard, David E. *The Puritan Way of Death: A Study in Religion, Culture, and Social Change*. New York: Oxford Univ. Press, 1977.
Steiner, Dorothea. "Anne Bradstreet—Poet of Communication." *Arbeiten aus Anglistik und Amerikanistik* 10 (1985): 137–53.
Stennett, Joseph. *Hymns in Commemoration Of the Suffering of Our Blessed Saviour Jesus Christ, Compos'd For the Celebration of his Holy Supper*. London: 1713.
Stout, Harry S. *The New England Soul: Preaching and Religious Culture in Colonial New England*. New York: Oxford Univ. Press, 1986.
Suleiman, Susan R., and Inge Crosman, eds. *The Reader in the Text: Essays on Audience and Interpretation*. Princeton: Princeton Univ. Press, 1980.
Sweet, Timothy. "Gender, Genre, and Subjectivity in Anne Bradstreet's Early Elegies." *Early American Literature* 23 (1988): 152–74.
Tans'ur, William. *Heaven on Earth; or, The Beauty of Holiness*. London: 1738.
Tashjian, Dickran, and Ann Tashjian. *Memorials for Children of Change*. Middletown: Wesleyan Univ. Press, 1974.
Taylor, Edward. *Edward Taylor's Christographia*. Ed. Norman S. Grabo. New Haven: Yale Univ. Press, 1962.
——. *Edward Taylor's "Church Records" and Related Sermons*. Ed. Thomas M. Davis and Virginia L. Davis. Vol. 1 of *The Unpublished Writings of Edward Taylor*. Boston: Twayne, 1981.
——. *Edward Taylor's Minor Poetry*. Ed. Thomas M. Davis and Virginia L. Davis. Vol. 3 of *The Unpublished Writings of Edward Taylor*. Boston: Twayne, 1981.
——. *Edward Taylor's Treatise Concerning the Lord's Supper*. Ed. Norman S. Grabo. East Lansing: Michigan State Univ. Press, 1966.
——. *Edward Taylor vs. Solomon Stoddard: The Nature of the Lord's Supper*. Ed. Thomas M. Davis and Virginia L. Davis. Vol. 2 of *The Unpublished Writings of Edward Taylor*. Boston: Twayne, 1981.
——. *The Poems of Edward Taylor*. Ed. Donald E. Stanford. New Haven: Yale Univ. Press, 1960.
——. *The Poetical Works of Edward Taylor*. Ed. Thomas H. Johnson. 1939. Reprint. Princeton: Princeton Univ. Press, 1943.
——. *A Transcript of Edward Taylor's Metrical History of Christianity*. Ed. Donald E. Stanford. Cleveland: Micro Photo, 1962.
Taylor, Thomas. *Christ Revealed; or, The Old Testament Explained*. London: 1635.
Thickstun, Margaret Olofson. *Fictions of the Feminine: Puritan Doctrine and the Representation of Women*. Ithaca: Cornell Univ. Press, 1988.
Tompkins, Jane, ed. *Reader-Response Criticism: From Formalism to Post-Structuralism*. Baltimore: Johns Hopkins Univ. Press, 1980.
Toulouse, Teresa. *The Art of Prophesying: New England Sermons and the Shaping of Belief*. Athens: Univ. of Georgia Press, 1987.
Tyler, Moses Coit. *A History of American Literature, 1607–1765*. 1878. Reprint. Ithaca: Cornell Univ. Press, 1949.
Ulrich, Laurel Thatcher. *Good Wives: Image and Reality in the Lives of Women in Northern New England, 1650–1750*. New York: Knopf, 1982.

Vincent, Thomas. *Christ the Best Husband.* London: 1672.
Von Frank, Albert J. *The Sacred Game: Provincialism and Frontier Consciousness in American Literature, 1630–1860.* Cambridge: Cambridge Univ. Press, 1985.
Waggoner, Hyatt H. *American Poets from the Puritans to the Present.* Boston: Houghton Mifflin, 1968.
Walker, Cheryl. "Anne Bradstreet." In *American Writers: A Collection of Literary Biographies.* Ed. Leonard Unger. Supplement I, Part 1, 98–123. New York: Scribner's, 1979.
——. "Anne Bradstreet: A Woman Poet." In *Critical Essays on Anne Bradstreet,* ed. Cowell and Stanford, 254–61.
——. "In the Margin: The Image of Women in Early Puritan Poetry." In *Puritan Poets,* ed. White, 111–26.
——. *The Nightingale's Burden: Women Poets and American Culture before 1900.* Bloomington: Indiana Univ. Press, 1982.
Waller, Jennifer R. " 'My Hand a Needle Better Fits': Anne Bradstreet and Women Poets of the Renaissance." *Dalhousie Review* 54 (1974): 436–50.
Wallerstein, Ruth. *Studies in Seventeenth-Century Poetic.* Madison: Univ. of Wisconsin Press, 1950.
Warren, Austin. "Edward Taylor's Poetry: Colonial Baroque." *Kenyon Review* 3 (1941): 355–71.
Watkins, Owen C. *The Puritan Experience.* London: Routledge and Kegan Paul, 1972.
Watts, Emily Stipes. *The Poetry of American Women.* Austin: Univ. of Texas Press, 1977.
——. " 'The posy UNITY': Anne Bradstreet's Search for Order." In *Puritan Influences in American Literature.* Ed. Emory Elliott, 23–37. Urbana: Univ. of Illinois Press, 1979.
Weathers, Willie T. "Edward Taylor, Hellenistic Puritan." *American Literature* 18 (1946): 18–26.
Weemse, John. *The Christian Synagogue.* London: 1623.
Westminster Assembly of Divines. *Annotations Upon all the Books of the Old and New Testament.* London: 1657.
White, Elizabeth Wade. *Anne Bradstreet: The Tenth Muse.* New York: Oxford Univ. Press, 1971.
White, Peter. "An Analysis of Edward Taylor's *Preparatory Meditation 2.1.*" *Concerning Poetry* 11 (1978): 19–23.
——, ed. *Puritan Poets and Poetics: Seventeenth-Century American Poetry in Theory and Practice.* University Park: Pennsylvania State Univ. Press, 1985.
Wigglesworth, Michael. *The Diary of Michael Wigglesworth, 1653–1657: The Conscience of a Puritan.* Ed. Edmund S. Morgan. New York: Harper and Row, 1965.
——. *Meat Out of the Eater.* Boston: 1717.
——. *The Poems of Michael Wigglesworth.* Ed. Ronald A. Bosco. Lanham, Md.: Univ. Press of America, 1989.
Wilkins, John. *Ecclesiastes; or, A Discourse concerning the Gift of Preaching as it fals under the rules of Art.* London: 1646.
Wither, George. *A Collection of Emblemes, Ancient and Moderne: Quickened With Metricall Illustrations, both Morall and Divine.* London: 1635.
Wright, Nathalia. "The Morality Tradition in the Poetry of Edward Taylor." *American Literature* 18 (1946): 1–17.

Wright, Thomas Goddard. *Literary Culture in Early New England, 1620–1730*. 1920. Reprint. New York: Russell and Russell, 1966.

Ziff, Larzer. *Puritanism in America: New Culture in a New World*. New York: Viking, 1973.

——. "Upon What Pretext?: The Book and Literary History." *Proceedings of the American Antiquarian Society* 95 (1985): 297–315.

Index

Aaron, 219
Abel, 111, 118, 206
Abraham, 30, 89, 101, 199
Adam, 28, 44, 56, 111, 112, 114, 115, 117, 118, 128, 131, 158, 167, 268 (n. 12)
Ager, Thomas, 15, 16, 226, 278 (n. 18)
Ahluwalia, Harsharan Singh, 254 (n. 18)
Alexis, Gerhard T., 253 (n. 11)
Ames, William, 20, 21, 27, 28, 158, 178, 191, 196, 207, 210, 220
Arner, Robert D., 257–58 (n. 4), 261 (n. 18)
Augustine, 220

Bacon, Francis, 252 (n. 6)
Baldwin, William, 13
Ball, Kenneth, 262 (n. 2)
Barbour, Dennis H., 268 (n. 12)
Bathsheba, 15, 260 (n. 16)
Bay Psalm Book, 4, 245 (n. 21)
Bede, 152
Bernard, Richard, 50, 54, 135, 141, 162
Bible: Puritan poetry and exegesis of, 8, 9, 19, 31–32, 198–99, 219–20; as verbal model, 13–14, 106, 271–72 (n. 14), 277–78 (n. 9); as source of personal identity, 15–18, 25–26, 30, 104–5, 159, 179, 213–14, 215–18, 222, 223–25; as metatext for Puritan poem, 19–20, 138, 213, 246 (n. 29); and conviction, 111–13; decline in prestige of, 236
— BOOKS OF: Genesis, 89, 90, 166, 206; Exodus, 10, 30, 275 (n. 18); Leviticus, 255 (n. 4); Numbers, 204; Deuteronomy, 223; Judges, 62, 223; 1 Samuel, 47, 87, 206, 223; 2 Samuel, 173, 223; Job, 14, 27, 34, 72, 106, 137; Psalms, 8, 11, 13–18, 25, 46–48, 72, 93, 94, 110, 119, 125, 128, 129, 199, 205, 224, 225, 251 (n. 48), 253 (n. 12), 255 (n. 4), 259 (n. 13), 263 (nn. 8, 9) (*See also* David); Proverbs, 14, 15, 33, 44, 104, 206; Ecclesiastes, 14, 15, 104, 137, 138; Canticles (Song of Songs), 8, 11, 12, 13, 14–18, 31–34, 88, 93, 94, 103, 104, 120, 123, 159, 160, 170, 174, 188, 192, 194, 195, 199, 200, 220, 221, 222, 223, 225, 226, 227, 228, 229, 233, 234, 236, 268 (n. 17), 269 (n. 18), 275 (n. 18), 278 (n. 18) (*See also* Solomon); Isaiah, 32, 65, 105, 123, 194, 220, 275 (n. 18); Lamentations, 265 (n. 8); Hosea, 58; Zechariah, 195, 275 (n. 18); Malachi, 167, 195, 221, 275 (n. 18); Matthew, 27, 50, 52, 105, 129, 135, 169, 183, 202, 211, 222, 232, 254 (n. 21), 262 (n. 4); Mark, 254 (n. 21);

Bible (*continued*)
Luke, 28, 138, 254 (n. 21); John, 33, 130, 138, 152, 156, 195, 200, 216, 221, 222, 254 (n. 21), 275 (n. 18); Acts, x; Romans, 16, 18, 23, 26, 28, 29, 40, 44, 46, 54, 90, 124, 130, 140–41, 187, 190, 193, 195, 250 (n. 41), 264 (n. 5), 270 (n. 6); 1 Corinthians, 5, 33, 42, 50, 78, 91, 115, 126, 128, 195, 199, 202, 215, 218, 219, 222, 251 (n. 48); 2 Corinthians, 26, 28, 34, 46, 72, 75, 194, 209, 217, 222; Galatians, 199, 259 (n. 8); Ephesians, 89; Philippians, 27, 193, 194, 199, 202, 206, 208, 216, 263 (n. 9), 275 (n. 18); Colossians, 195, 209, 251 (n. 48), 275 (n. 18), 277 (n. 8); 2 Timothy, 105, 129, 235; Hebrews, 10, 30, 34, 155, 188, 195, 205, 210; James, 105; 1 Peter, 32, 34, 105, 129; 1 John, 194, 202; Revelation, 33, 103, 105, 108, 110, 120, 129, 137, 151, 159, 183, 192, 195, 199, 222, 262 (n. 4), 264 (n. 2), 275 (n. 18)
— POETRY OF: 8, 9, 11; best part of the Old Testament, 14; as antidote to secular verse, 14–15; as model for Puritan poem, 14–16; as spiritual test, 16, 226–27; and spiritual joy, 16–18

Booth, Wayne, 249–50 (n. 39)
Bosco, Ronald A., 244 (n. 12), 251 (n. 1), 252 (n. 5), 253 (n. 18), 254 (n. 21), 255 (n. 1), 256 (n. 9), 271 (n. 11)
Bowden, Edwin T., 271–72 (n. 14)
Bradstreet, Anne: modern critical reaction to, 3, 6, 7, 83–85, 103–4, 107, 108, 121, 124, 242 (n. 9), 242–43 (n. 10), 243–44 (n. 11), 256 (n. 1), 256–57 (n. 3), 262 (n. 6); as conflicted self, 3, 7, 25–26, 39, 83–85, 107, 138, 256 (n. 1), 256–57 (n. 3), 264 (n. 2); popularity in seventeenth century, 4, 84–85, 258 (n. 4); as model self, 23, 25–26, 28–31, 33, 102, 107, 124, 129, 137–38, 250 (n. 40), 258 (n. 5); and Puritan selfhood, 24, 26–34, 85–96, 91–92, 108, 115–16, 121–22, 125–30, 131–33, 135–41, 256 (n. 3), 259 (nn. 9, 10), 264 (n. 2); neobiblical selfhood in, 25, 31, 33, 91, 93–95, 104–7, 116, 118, 128–29, 259 (n. 13); uses of affliction in, 26–27, 92–93, 122, 123, 125–26, 130–38; and her readers, 27–31, 34, 85–86, 95–97, 106, 107, 116–20, 122, 124, 127, 129–30, 133, 135–36, 137–40, 260 (n. 15); as teacher, 27–31, 90, 95–102, 135, 140, 260 (n. 15); and consolation, 28–31, 34, 119–20, 124, 129–30, 137–38; depiction of world in, 32, 104–6, 108–16, 119, 120–21, 127, 129, 137–38, 262 (n. 2), 263 (nn. 12, 13); as reader of saintly lives, 32–33, 87–90; and eschatology, 32–34, 101, 116, 138, 261 (n. 20), 262 (n. 4), 265 (n. 15); and meditation, 34, 86, 108, 110–16, 128; compared with Michael Wigglesworth, 83, 84, 85–86, 96, 105, 106, 122, 126, 127, 131, 135, 137, 259 (n. 14), 259–60 (n. 15); and gender, 83–84, 90, 97–98, 101, 139–40, 240 (n. 3), 243 (n. 10), 257 (n. 3), 260–61 (n. 18), 265–66 (n. 17); on New England, 84, 101; and self-examination, 86–87, 95; and Renaissance, 88, 97–99, 260 (n. 17), 261 (n. 18); earthly and divine love in, 88–91, 259 (n. 9), 264 (n. 2); as Canticles Bride, 88–92, 93–94; and paternal God, 91; and Psalms, 94; as idealized mother, 96, 140, 260 (n. 16); as family historian, 96–97; as sacred historian, 99–102, 112, 118; and eschatology, 101–2, 116, 120, 137; and conviction, 104, 111–12, 117–18, 125, 135–37; compared with Edward Taylor, 107, 126, 131, 139, 140; role of reason in, 109–10; uses of confession in, 110, 135–37, 139, 140–41; depiction of time in, 118–21; on death, 131–36
— WORKS: "As Weary Pilgrim," 3, 6, 7, 8, 9, 20, 23, 25–36, 45, 49, 54, 56, 57, 58, 61, 62, 70, 72, 83, 85, 88, 92, 95, 103, 104, 116, 117, 123, 128, 129, 131, 138, 139, 145, 146, 230, 233, 237; "The Author to Her Book," 98–100; "Before the Birth of One of Her Children," 126, 130–31; "By Night when Others Soundly Slept," 94–95; "Contemplations," 7, 32, 99, 107–22, 123, 129, 138, 139, 153, 156, 166, 167, 171, 208, 230, 262–63 (n. 6); "David's Lamentation," 87; "A Dialogue between Old England and New," 100, 101–2, 146, 149; "An Elegy upon Sir Philip Sidney," 97, 100; "An Epitaph on . . . Mrs. Dorothy Dudley," 88, 91, 131; "The Flesh and

the Spirit," 7, 69, 74, 75, 84, 121, 124, 126–30, 131, 133, 138, 146, 197, 221, 249 (n. 39), 264 (n. 2); "For Deliverance from a Fever," 124, 130; "For the Restoration of My Dear Husband from a Burning Ague," 97, 125; "The Four Monarchies," 97, 99–100, 150; "In Honour of Du Bartas," 97, 100; "In Honour of Queen Elizabeth," 97, 100–101; "In Memory of Anne Bradstreet," 133–34; "In Memory of Elizabeth Bradstreet," 134–35; "In Memory of Mrs. Mercy Bradstreet," 90, 134; "In My Solitary Hours," 91–92; "In Reference to Her Children," 96, 114; "In Thankful Remembrance for My Dear Husband's Safe Arrival," 96–97; "A Letter to Her Husband," 89; "Meditations Divine and Moral," 86, 91, 92, 93, 123, 125; "Meditations when my Soul hath been Refreshed," 93–94, 115–16, 125; "Occasional Meditations," 126; "On My Son's Return," 96; "On Simon Bradstreet," 7, 132–33, 135; "Phoebus Make Haste," 89–90; "The Prologue," 7, 83, 97–98, 99, 100, 260–61 (n. 18); "The Quaternions," 91, 97, 99, 263 (n. 13); "To Her Father with Some Verses," 91; "To My Dear and Loving Husband," 88–89, 92, 114; "To My Dear Children," 84, 86, 90, 91, 92, 95, 103, 108–9, 117–18, 120, 125–26, 131, 136, 140, 256 (n. 3), 259 (n. 10), 264 (n. 4); "To the Memory of . . . Thomas Dudley Esq.," 87–88, 131; "Upon a Fit of Sickness," 126, 130, 131; "Upon my Daughter Hannah Wiggin Her Recovery from a Dangerous Fever," 96; "Upon the Burning of Our House," 83, 84, 95, 126, 128, 136–38; "The Vanity of All Worldly Things," 7, 92, 103–7, 117, 120, 121, 122, 123, 127, 138, 139, 262 (n. 2)

Brumm, Ursula, 63, 68
Bunyan, John, 11, 21, 22, 136, 190, 248 (n. 36)
Byles, Mather, 236

Cain, 111, 115, 118, 156, 206
Cambridge University, 5
Chappell, William, 48
Characters, 63, 64, 74

Chaucer, Geoffrey, 12
Chauncy, Charles, 13
Christ: as divine metaphor, 9–10, 222–23; transforming power of, 26, 29, 123; dual nature of, 33, 51; as Bridegroom, 33, 89, 90, 116, 159–60, 200, 201, 219, 220, 221, 222, 233–34, 268–69 (n. 17), 278 (n. 18); and the Law, 41, 44–45, 51; and the Gospel, 52, 76–77; as Advocate, 52, 194. See also *Logos*
Cicero, 12
Clapham, Henoch, 218, 228
Clark, Michael, 276–77 (n. 30)
Clark, Samuel, 15–16, 278 (n. 18)
Cohen, Charles Lloyd, 187, 250 (n. 48), 257 (n. 3), 276 (n. 28)
Colacurcio, Michael, 267 (n. 9), 268 (nn. 12, 13)
Collinges, John, 12, 16, 17, 192, 225, 279 (n. 21)
Cotton, John, 226, 249 (n. 37)
Cowell, Pattie, 257 (n. 3), 266 (n. 17)
Cremin, Lawrence A., 253 (n. 16)
Criticism of Puritan verse, x–xi, 6–8, 39, 40, 83–85, 103–4, 121, 145, 186, 241–42 (n. 7), 242 (nn. 8, 9), 242–43 (n. 10), 243–44 (n. 11), 244 (n. 12), 248 (n. 36), 251 (n. 1), 272 (n. 1)
Crowder, Richard, 69, 251 (n. 1), 253 (n. 16), 255 (n. 2)

Daly, Robert, 10, 49, 133, 135, 242 (n. 9), 251 (n. 1), 256 (n. 3), 259 (n. 9), 262 (n. 6), 263 (n. 13), 265 (n. 6)
Daniel, 66
Dante, 121
Davenport, John, 28
David, 8, 11, 13–14, 15, 17, 18, 19, 25, 87, 94, 110, 125, 128, 173, 176, 194, 199, 224, 225, 251 (n. 48)
Davidson, Edward H., 246 (n. 29)
Davis, Thomas M., 165, 223, 244 (n. 11), 267 (n. 7), 269 (n. 1), 270 (n. 6)
Davis, Virginia L., 270 (n. 6)
Day, James, 12
Death: redemptive significance of, 33, 130–31, 175–76, 180, 181, 230–33, 270 (n. 10), 272 (n. 16)
Demosthenes, 98
Dispensations, Legal and Evangelical, 14, 32, 41, 46, 49, 51, 52, 53, 57, 58,

Dispensations (*continued*)
    77, 105, 118, 120, 155–56, 162, 177,
    179, 192–93, 205, 206, 254 (n. 21)
Donne, John, 5, 28
Dove, John, 15
Drayton, Michael, 12–13
Du Bartas, Guillaume, 5, 98, 100
Dunster, Henry, 241 (n. 4)
Durham, James, 14, 16, 89, 94, 120,
    188, 212, 225, 237, 273 (n. 4)

Eagleton, Terry, 242 (n. 8)
Eberwein, Jane Donahue, 139, 261
    (n. 18)
Eden, 56, 75, 117, 118, 158, 171, 232
Edwards, Jonathan, 236
Elegies, 87–88, 131–35, 170–82, 248–49
    (n. 37), 270–71 (n. 10), 271 (nn.
    11–13), 271–72 (n. 14), 272 (n. 16)
Eliot, T. S., 104
Eliphaz, 106
Ellis, John Harvard, 85
Eschatology, 33, 34, 68–69, 101, 105,
    120–21, 138, 161, 162, 225–28, 233
Euripides, 5
Eve, 56, 110, 111, 118, 268 (n. 12)

Fish, Stanley, 239 (n. 1), 247 (n. 30), 248
    (n. 36), 249 (nn. 37, 39)
Fiske, John, 249 (n. 37)
Fithian, Rosemary, 225
Fleming, Robert, 11
Fraser, Russell, 240 (n. 2)

Gatta, John, Jr., 250 (n. 48), 268 (nn.
    13, 14), 270 (n. 6), 273 (nn. 5, 7), 274
    (n. 15), 277 (n. 2)
Geneva Bible, 110, 123
Gosson, Stephen, 4, 6
Grabo, Norman S., 6, 148, 165, 248
    (n. 36), 263 (n. 8), 267 (n. 7), 270
    (n. 8), 272 (n. 1), 274 (n. 9), 275
    (n. 19)
Greenblatt, Stephen, 211
Gyffard, George, 227

Hall, David D., 239–40 (n. 2), 242
    (n. 9), 246 (n. 29), 246–47 (n. 30)
Hall, Joseph, 226
Hall, Thomas, 30, 51, 159
Hambrick-Stowe, Charles E., 246
    (n. 30), 255 (n. 2), 256 (n. 7)
Hammond, Henry, 13, 14, 17, 224

Harvard College, 5, 18, 77, 165, 269
    (n. 2)
Heman, 75
Henry II, 150
Henry, Matthew, 11, 14–15, 34, 225, 226
Herbert, George, 5, 12, 16, 30, 168, 216,
    270 (n. 6)
Hildebrand, Anne, 263 (n. 13)
Hinckley, Thomas, 5
Holmes, Nathaniel, 11, 16
Homer, 11
Hooker, Thomas, 24, 42, 43, 47, 48, 49,
    51, 58, 109, 157–58, 161, 162, 191, 211,
    212
Horace, 5
Hull, John, 177, 272 (n. 16)
Hutchinson, Anne, 257 (n. 3)

Imitatio Christi, 62, 68, 196, 248 (n. 36),
    274 (n. 12)
Irvin, William J., 264 (n. 14)
Isaiah, 220
Iser, Wolfgang, 239 (n. 1), 242 (n. 8),
    248 (n. 36), 249 (n. 39)

Jackson, Arthur, 14
Jacob, 66, 75
Jantz, Harold S., 242 (n. 8)
Jauss, Hans Robert, 239 (n. 1), 242
    (n. 8), 248 (n. 36)
Jeremiad, 51, 52, 149, 253 (n. 18), 254
    (n. 20)
Jerome, 14, 223, 245 (n. 21)
Job, 27, 34, 72, 75, 106, 107, 136, 223,
    270 (n. 8)
John Chrysostom, 152
Johnson, Edward, 4
Johnson, Thomas H., 165, 241 (n. 7),
    270 (n. 7)
John the Baptist, 225
Jonah, 219
Jonathan, 173, 223
Joseph, 66, 75, 218
Joshua, 226

Keayne, Sarah, 257 (n. 3)
Keller, Karl, 124, 145, 150, 188, 190,
    193, 209, 210, 250 (n. 48), 257 (n. 3),
    260 (n. 15), 266 (n. 7), 272 (n. 1), 273
    (n. 3), 276 (n. 28), 277 (n. 30)
Kenosis, 27, 210–12
Kerygma, 181

King, John Owen, 190, 246–47 (n. 30), 247 (n. 31), 250 (n. 40)
Koehler, Lyle, 257 (n. 3)

Lazarus, 130, 181
Leigh, Edward, 15
Lewalski, Barbara Kiefer, 272 (n. 1)
Logos, 10, 215. *See also* Christ
Lord's Supper, 9, 10, 145, 180, 188, 197, 201–2, 204, 205–7, 221, 228, 244 (n. 13), 272 (n. 17)
Lowance, Mason I., Jr., 253 (n. 16)
Lynen, John F., 112, 121, 253 (n. 16), 264 (n. 14)

McElrath, Joseph, 257 (n. 3), 261 (n. 18), 262 (n. 4)
Martin, Wendy, 135, 256 (n. 1), 257 (n. 3), 262 (n. 6), 264 (n. 2)
Martz, Louis L., 273 (n. 3)
Marvell, Andrew, 249 (n. 39)
Mather, Cotton, 4, 5, 6, 10, 11, 13, 16, 17–18, 21, 24, 40, 77, 96, 170, 228–29, 235, 241 (n. 5), 245 (n. 21), 270 (n. 7)
Mather, Samuel, 10, 204, 205
Mawer, Randall R., 132, 133, 134, 135
Methuselah, 112
Michael, 112
Mignon, Charles W., 208
Milbourne, Luke, 11
Miller, Perry, 241 (n. 7)
Milton, John, 4, 5, 13, 22, 28, 110, 112, 121, 128, 247 (n. 30), 249 (n. 39)
Mitchell, Jonathan, 5, 13, 25, 35, 40, 42, 96
Morgan, Edmund S., 39, 247 (n. 30)
Morison, Samuel Eliot, 77, 259–60 (n. 15), 264 (n. 5)
Murdock, Kenneth B., 41, 242 (n. 7), 245 (n. 21), 251 (n. 1), 252 (n. 6), 253–54 (n. 18)
Moses, 30, 58, 66, 75, 226

Nathaniel, 73
Neptune, 113
Nicodemus, 73

Oakes, Urian, 4, 5, 177, 271 (n. 14)
Orton, Job, 236
Ovid, 5, 147
Owen, John, 15

Parker, David L., 268 (n. 12)

Paul, 5, 10, 16, 23, 26, 28, 29, 30, 42, 66, 72, 89, 91, 111, 115, 126, 130, 190, 193, 195, 199, 209, 215, 217, 222, 257 (n. 3), 259 (n. 8), 275 (n. 25)
Pearce, Roy Harvey, 103, 242 (n. 8), 245 (n. 21), 270 (n. 10)
Pearse, Edward, 17, 175
Perkins, William, 27, 52, 54, 55, 57, 135, 155, 156, 191, 199, 219
Peter, 34
Philip, 73
Philomel, 114, 119
Phoebus, 108, 121, 262 (n. 6)
Piercy, Josephine K., 121, 258 (n. 8), 260 (n. 15), 262 (n. 6), 264 (n. 2)
Pilgrim motif and selfhood, 29–31, 34, 90, 165, 185, 198, 206, 233
Poetry: popularity of in early New England, 4–6; and redemptive experience, 8, 18, 24, 103, 105, 107–8, 138–39, 183–88, 193–94, 206, 210, 234–37; affective power of, 9; and other genres, 9; as original religious discourse, 11; corruption of, 11–13; and biblical rhetoric, 18; Bible as metatext for, 19–20; autobiographical expression, 23–24, 139, 146, 190, 210–11, 250 (n. 40), 276–77 (n. 30); as test of spiritual standing, 24, 27, 33–35, 181, 214, 250–51 (n. 48); ritual dimension of, 24, 185, 194, 195, 198, 203–10, 248–49 (n. 37); and reader's needs, 162
Pope, Alan H., 253 (n. 14), 255 (n. 3), 256 (n. 7)
Puritan Reading: and spiritual experience, x-xi, 8, 16–18, 19, 20, 23–24, 25, 34–36, 42, 44, 46, 107, 118, 161, 236–37, 239–40 (n. 2), 246–47 (n. 30), 247 (n. 31), 248–49 (n. 37), 249–50 (n. 39); as test of spiritual status, 16–18, 25, 29–31, 35, 43, 46, 127, 133; and community, 35, 72–73, 76, 79, 175, 178; pleasure of, 35–36
Puritans: cohesive culture of, x; and battle against secular verse, 3–4, 11–13, 16, 245 (n. 21); attitudes toward poetry, 4–6, 11–13, 245 (n. 21); familiarity with classical and Renaissance poetry, 5, 88, 241 (n. 4), 272 (n. 14); aesthetic pronouncements of, 6; unified religious and aesthetic response of, 8; symbolic

Puritans (*continued*)
  thought of, 9–10, 236, 244 (n. 12);
  and Second Commandment, 10
Puritan Selfhood: and reading, x–xii,
  16–18, 20, 27, 236–37; as psychomachia, 20–24, 25, 26, 28, 124, 126,
  154, 179, 190–91, 192, 193, 196–97,
  216–17, 247–48 (n. 34); generalized
  patterns of, 27–30, 87, 90, 93, 121–22,
  173–74, 178–79, 186, 250 (n. 40)
Puttenham, George, 9, 11

Quarles, Francis, 5

Rainwater, Catherine, 270 (n. 3)
Raleigh, Sir Walter, 100
Ramus, Petrus, 253 (n. 14), 255 (n. 3),
  256 (n. 7)
Reader-response criticism, 239 (n. 1),
  242 (n. 8), 249 (n. 39)
Redemption: and inner struggle, 20–22,
  108, 133–34; stages of, 20–23, 31, 28–
  29, 34; role of confession in, 23, 73,
  134–36, 140–41, 153, 191, 193, 197,
  208; role of weakness in, 26–29, 72,
  125–26, 130, 209, 234
Reeve, John, 17, 226
Renaissance, 9, 88, 98, 272 (n. 14)
Requa, Kenneth A., 260 (n. 15)
Rich, Adrienne, 121, 260 (n. 15)
Richardson, Robert, Jr., 259 (n. 9), 262
  (n. 2), 263 (n. 13), 264 (nn. 2, 5)
Robb, Allan P., 257 (n. 3), 261 (n. 18),
  262 (n. 4)
Roberts, Francis, 15
Rosenfeld, Alvin H., 256 (n. 1), 262
  (n. 6)
Rosenmeier, Rosamond R., 89, 90, 104,
  121, 137, 140, 250 (nn. 40, 48), 257
  (n. 3), 258 (n. 5), 259 (nn. 8, 10, 11,
  13), 260 (nn. 15, 16), 262 (nn. 3, 6),
  264 (n. 2)
Rous, Francis, 30, 214
Rowe, Karen E., 272 (n. 1), 273 (n. 5),
  273–74 (n. 7)

Sacks, Peter, 272 (n. 16)
Saffin, John, 272 (n. 16)
Saltman, Helen, 262 (n. 6), 264 (n. 16)
Samson, 28, 62, 67, 86
Samuel, 206
Sargent, Ritamarie, 265 (n. 6)
Satan, 22, 47, 55, 75, 76, 148, 152, 157,
  158, 159, 160, 167, 179, 207, 232, 249
  (n. 39), 268 (n. 14), 269 (n. 18)
Saul, 173, 206, 223
Scheick, William J., 109, 190, 196, 210,
  222–23, 235, 244 (nn. 11, 13), 248
  (n. 36), 262 (n. 6), 263 (nn. 7, 12), 268
  (n. 14), 271 (nn. 11, 12), 274 (n. 9),
  275 (nn. 16, 17, 24), 277 (nn. 30, 2)
Schweitzer, Ivy, 240 (n. 3), 249 (n. 37),
  257 (n. 3), 258 (nn. 4, 5), 260 (n. 16),
  265–66 (n. 17)
Sermons, 9, 18, 27, 41, 50, 53, 57, 155–
  56, 192–93, 196, 246 (n. 29), 248 (nn.
  36, 37), 254 (n. 21)
Sewall, Samuel, 240 (n. 3)
Shepard, Thomas, 20, 21, 23, 35, 42, 47,
  49, 50, 109, 136, 157, 162, 191, 198,
  210, 241 (n. 4)
Shepard, Thomas II, 4, 177, 271 (n. 14)
Sibbes, Richard, 17
Sidney, Sir Philip, 5, 16, 100
Silverman, Kenneth, 271 (n. 11), 279
  (n. 22)
Smith, Jude, 12
Solomon, 8, 11, 12, 13, 14–19, 100, 104–
  5, 107, 223, 225, 229, 236, 237, 251
  (n. 48)
Spacks, Patricia Meyer, 211
Speakers of poems: and biblical models,
  17–18; as redemptive paradigms, 23–
  24, 34, 147, 150; as models for
  readers, 27–28, 34–35, 52–55, 102,
  124, 129, 138
Spenser, Edmund, 5
Stanford, Ann, 3, 7, 83, 86, 259 (n. 9),
  262 (n. 6), 263 (n. 12)
Stanford, Donald E., 153, 274 (n. 15)
Steere, Richard, 10, 109
Steiner, Dorothea, 259 (nn. 9, 14)
Stennett, Joseph, 13, 19
Stoddard, Solomon, 202, 206, 266 (n. 1)
Sylvester, Joshua, 100

Tans'ur, William, 11–12, 251 (n. 48)
Tashjian, Ann, 271 (nn. 12, 13)
Tashjian, Dickran, 271 (nn. 12, 13)
Taylor, Edward: modern critical
  reaction to, 6, 7, 8, 39, 145–46, 186,
  190, 242 (n. 9), 243 (n. 11), 248
  (n. 36), 266 (n. 1), 272 (n. 1); on
  redemptive process, 20, 191; and
  Puritan selfhood, 21, 24, 146, 147,
  150, 154, 164–65, 168–69, 183–85,

187–89, 190, 191, 192, 194, 198, 201, 208–12, 216–17, 243–44 (n. 11), 273 (n. 5), 273–74 (n. 7), 274 (n. 9), 276 (n. 30); and his readers, 64, 146–47, 154–58, 161–63, 267 (n. 9); compared with Michael Wigglesworth, 145–46, 147–48, 149, 150, 151–153, 154–63, 164, 166, 168, 186, 189, 193, 197, 208, 211, 214, 221, 230, 233, 269 (n. 21); compared with Anne Bradstreet, 145–46, 149, 150, 153, 164–74 passim, 181, 184, 186, 189, 193, 197, 208, 211, 214, 221, 230, 233; relation of private to public verse, 146–47, 151, 153, 161, 164, 187, 189, 193, 223, 268 (n. 14), 269 (n. 19); as social commentator, 147–50; anti-Catholicism of, 148, 152–53, 266–67 (n. 7); and assurance, 150, 168–69, 180, 182, 184, 192–95, 201–2, 209, 216–17, 221–23, 231, 233, 235, 273 (n. 3); as sacred historian, 150–54; depiction of time in, 151, 158, 161; as neobiblical prophet, 151–52, 181–82; and conviction, 153, 157, 158, 171, 173, 178, 183, 194, 222, 268 (n. 12); and consolation, 153–54, 157, 158, 159–61, 171, 175, 181–82, 209–10, 234–35, 276 (n. 28); homiletic strategy in, 155–57, 179, 192–93, 196–97; role of reason in, 157, 198–99, 220, 275 (nn. 16, 17), 277 (n. 8); depiction of Christ in, 159–60, 268–69 (n. 17); depiction of sin in, 160, 191, 193; depiction of world in, 165, 166–68, 229–32; on earthly and heavenly love, 169–70, 174; and family grief, 170–75; as elegist, 170–82; on redemptive significance of death, 170–82, 207, 227–33; as reader of saintly lives, 172–78; on New England, 178, 182; and eschatology, 179, 216, 225–28, 230, 233, 234–35; and metaphysical verse, 182, 220; and ritual dimension of poetry, 185, 194, 195–96, 198, 202, 203–10, 275 (n. 19); Christ as reader of, 187–89, 195, 196, 197, 210, 211, 218, 222; and typology, 189, 195, 203–6, 219–20, 275 (n. 19); and self-examination, 190, 191–92, 200, 203, 204–7, 217, 219–21; neobiblical selfhood in, 194–95, 198–200, 213–35; Christ as model for identity in, 196, 207; his view of his poetry, 205–9, 275 (nn. 24, 25); his bargains with Christ, 208, 276 (n. 26); and selflessness, 210–12; and the Psalms, 224–25; as Canticles Bride, 225–28, 233–34

— WORKS: "An other Answer," 148, 266 (n. 7); *Christographia*, 20, 191, 195–96, 209; "A Dialogue between the writer and a Maypole Dresser," 147–48; "The Ebb & Flow," 183–85, 188, 197; "An Elegy on Richard Mather," 176, 179, 181; "An Elegie upon . . . Francis Willoughby," 176, 178; "An Elegy upon . . . John Allen," 178, 182; "An Elegie upon . . . Mr. Sims," 177, 178; "An Elegy upon . . . Samuel Hooker," 176, 177–78, 179–80, 181, 182, 187; "An Elogy upon . . . Charles Chauncey," 176, 178, 181; "An Elogy upon . . . Mehetabel Woodbridge," 177, 182; "A Fig for Thee Oh! Death," 131, 229, 232–33; "Foundation Day Sermon," 268–69 (n. 17); "A Funerall Poem . . . upon Mrs. Elizabeth Taylor," 172–75, 176, 177, 180, 186, 241 (n. 5); "A funerall Teare dropt upon the Coffin of that holy [man of] God, Dr. Increase Mather," 176, 180, 182; *Gods Determinations*, 6, 28, 33, 57, 63, 69, 70, 73, 74, 75, 76, 126, 146, 152, 153, 154–63, 164, 168, 183, 187, 192, 193, 223, 232, 249 (n. 39); "The Great Bones Dug Up at Clavarack," 166; "Huswifery," 182–83, 272 (n. 17); Job paraphrases, 223; "The Lay-mans Lamentation," 148–50, 154, 177; *Metrical History of Christianity*, 150–54, 164, 165, 166, 183, 186, 223, 237; "My last Declamation in the Colledge Hall," 165–66; Old Testament Songs, paraphrases of, 223; "A Poem, upon the Death of Deacon David Dewey," 178, 179, 271 (n. 10); *Preparatory Meditations*, 5, 6, 7, 9, 41, 70, 107, 140, 145, 146, 147, 152, 153, 161, 164, 165, 167, 180, 182, 184, 185, 186–212, 213–28, 229, 230, 232, 233–35, 242 (n. 11), 273 (nn. 3, 5), 274–75 (n. 15), 275 (n. 18), 277–78 (n. 9), 278 (n. 14), 279 (n. 21); "Profession of Faith," 21, 269 (n. 21); Psalm paraphrases, 224–25; "This

Taylor, Edward (*continued*)
Dove & Olive Branch," 169–170; "To his Brother Joseph Taylor & his wife," 147; "To My schoolfellow. W.M.," 147; "Upon a Spider Catching a Fly," 167–68; "Upon a Wasp Child with Cold," 166–67; "Upon my Recovery out of a threatening Sickness," 229, 233; "Upon the Sweeping Flood," 168; "Upon Wedlock, & Death of Children," 170–72, 183; "A Valediction to the Whole World," 229–32, 233, 235; "Verses on Pope Joan," 266–67 (n. 7); "Were but my Muse an Huswife Good," 170; "When Let by Rain," 164–65, 168–69, 183, 184
Taylor, Thomas, 204
Thetis, 113
Time, depiction of, 32–33, 116, 118–20, 151, 158, 161
Tyler, Moses Coit, 6, 41, 44, 244 (n. 12), 251 (n. 1)
Typology, 30, 32, 189, 195, 203, 275 (n. 19)

Ulrich, Laurel Thatcher, 257 (n. 3)

Vincent, Thomas, 227

Walker, Cheryl, 121–22, 261 (n. 18), 262 (n. 6)
Wallerstein, Ruth, 180
Ward, Nathaniel, 5, 98
Watts, Emily Stipes, 256 (n. 1), 262 (n. 6)
Weemse, John, 22, 26, 28, 68, 135, 141, 155, 192–93, 209
Westminster Assembly of Divines, 14, 225, 226
White, Elizabeth Wade, 96, 104, 140, 256 (n. 1), 260 (n. 18), 264 (n. 2)
Wigglesworth, Michael: popularity in seventeenth century, 4, 5, 39–40, 251–52 (n. 2); and aesthetic reformation, 4, 12, 13; modern critical reaction to, 8, 39, 41, 242 (n. 8), 244 (n. 12), 251 (n. 1), 252 (n. 3); and conviction, 22, 42–46, 48, 49, 51–52, 55–56, 60; as model self, 25, 52–55, 58, 64, 71–72, 76, 256 (n. 9); and his readers, 35, 40–43, 48, 49–50, 51, 54–55, 56–59, 60–61, 63– 64, 65, 67–79, 85–86, 96, 154–56, 162; compared with Anne Bradstreet, 39, 40, 41, 45, 49, 54, 58, 61, 62, 67, 69, 70, 72, 74, 75, 78, 79, 83, 85–86, 96, 105; compared with Edward Taylor, 39, 41, 57, 63–64, 69, 70, 73, 74, 75, 76, 78, 79; reading and redemptive experience in, 39–40, 58–59, 60, 67, 68–70, 72–77, 77–79, 256 (n. 7); depiction of Christ in, 41, 44–45, 47, 51–52, 76–77; homiletic strategies in, 43, 48, 49, 50, 53, 54–55, 57, 155–56; depiction of world in, 43, 61, 70; depiction of sinners in, 43–44, 46–49, 66, 71; depiction of saints in, 45–46, 50–51, 61, 64–65, 66, 74, 76–77; views of language, 46–47, 49; and Bible, 47–48, 51–53, 55, 65, 66, 78, 79; role of reason in, 48–49, 63, 253 (n. 14), 256 (n. 7); depiction of time in, 49, 56, 161; and consolation, 49–51, 54–59, 60–64, 68–77, 78, 253–54 (n. 18), 255 (n. 2); on New England, 52–59, 63, 79; depiction of God in, 53, 55–56; communal and private redemption in, 53–54, 57, 65–66, 79; on uses of affliction, 61–62, 71–73, 123; as teacher, 63–66, 67, 78–79; and paradoxes of belief, 67–69, 73; and eschatology, 68–69, 73, 161–62
— WORKS: *The Day of Doom*, 4, 5, 33, 35, 39, 40, 41–52, 53, 60, 61, 63, 64, 68, 70, 73, 76, 77, 78, 127, 137, 146, 147, 154–63, 175, 237, 241 (n. 5), 242 (n. 8), 259 (n. 14); *Diary*, 21, 40, 87; "God's Controversy with New-England," 52–59, 60, 61, 64, 68, 69, 70, 71, 78, 122, 146, 147, 150, 152, 168; *Meat Out of the Eater* (book), 4, 9, 40, 60, 68, 156, 157, 198, 255 (nn. 1, 2); "Meat Out of the Eater" (sequence), 61–66, 67, 68, 156, 157, 198, 255 (n. 1); "A Postscript unto the Reader," 42, 50, 78; "Riddles Unriddled, or Christian Paradoxes," 22, 28, 61, 63, 64, 67–77, 125, 126, 131, 146, 193, 249 (n. 39), 255 (n. 3); "A Short Discourse on Eternity," 43, 47, 51, 160; "To the Christian Reader," 42, 50, 254 (n. 18); "Vanity of Vanities" ("A Song of Emptiness, to fill up the Empty Pages following"), 43, 105, 127
Wild, Robert, 266 (n. 3)

Wilkins, John, 196
Willard, Samuel, 177, 180, 181
Wilson, John, 5
Winthrop, John, 241 (n. 4)
Wither, George, 16
Wolcott, Roger, 235

Women in Puritan culture, 139–40, 257 (n. 3), 265–66 (n. 17)
World, depiction of, 30, 32, 43, 104–6, 109, 113, 120, 127, 166–68, 229–30

Ziff, Larzer, 236, 244 (n. 13)